AQA A-level History

The Tudors
England 1485–1603

David Ferriby
Angela Anderson
Tony Imperato

Approval message from AQA

This textbook has been approved by AQA for use with our qualification. This means that we have checked that it broadly covers the specification and we are satisfied with the overall quality. Full details of our approval process can be found on our website.

We approve textbooks because we know how important it is for teachers and students to have the right resources to support their teaching and learning. However, the publisher is ultimately responsible for the editorial control and quality of this book.

Please note that when teaching the *AQA A-level History* course, you must refer to AQA's specification as your definitive source of information. While this book has been written to match the specification, it cannot provide complete coverage of every aspect of the course. Please also note that the practice questions in this title are written to reflect the question styles of the AS and A-level papers. They are designed to help students become familiar with question types and practise exam skills. AQA has published specimen papers and mark schemes online and these should be consulted for definitive examples.

A wide range of other useful resources can be found on the relevant subject pages of our website: www.aqa.org.uk.

 DYNAMIC LEARNING

 HODDER EDUCATION
AN HACHETTE UK COMPANY

The Publishers would like to thank the following for permission to reproduce copyright material in this book:

Photo credits: p.v *l* © World History Archive/Topfoto; *r* © Georgios Kollidas/Fotolia; **p.vi** King Edward VI (1537–53) and the Pope, c.1570 (oil on panel), English School (16th century)/National Portrait Gallery, London, UK/Bridgeman Images; **p.vii** © Stephen Conlin/Crown copyright: Historic Royal Palaces; **p.viii** © The Granger Collection. TopFoto; **p.1** © Apic/Hulton Fine Art Collection/ Getty Images; **p.34** © Angelo Hornak/Corbis; **p.40** © Photos.com/Thinkstock; **p.43** © 2006 TopFoto; **p.47** Portrait of Cardinal Thomas Wolsey (c.1475–1530) (oil on panel), English School, (16th century)/National Portrait Gallery, London, UK/Bridgeman Images; **p.67** © Photos.com/Thinkstock; **p.69** *l* © Corbis, *r* © Photos.com/Thinkstock; **p.72** © GL Archive/Alamy; **p.73** © Universal History Archive/Getty Images; **p.100**: © GL Archive/Alamy; **p.126** © Georgios Kollidas/Fotolia; **p.129** King Edward VI (1537–53) and the Pope, c.1570 (oil on panel), English School, (16th century)/National Portrait Gallery, London, UK/Bridgeman Images; **p.141** © The Art Archive/Alamy; **p.143** Philip II and Mary I, 1558, Eworth or Ewoutsz, Hans (fl.1520–74)/Trustees of the Bedford Estate, Woburn Abbey, UK/Bridgeman Images; **p.150** © GL Archive/Alamy; **p.155** © World History Archive/Topfoto; **p.172** © A beggar is tied and whipped through the streets, c.1567 (woodcut) (b/w photo), English School, (16th century)/Private Collection/ Bridgeman Images; **p.178** © Fine Art Images/Heritage Images/Getty Images; **p.181** © Archivart/Alamy; **p.182** © Stephen Conlin/ Crown copyright: Historic Royal Palaces; **p.183** © Fine Art Images/Heritage Images/Getty Images; **p.189** © The Print Collector/ Print Collector/Getty Images; **p.201** © Mary Evans Picture Library/Alamy; **p.214** © World History Archive/TopFoto; **p.221** © The Granger Collection/TopFoto; **p.225** © World History Archive/TopFoto; **p.229** ©TopFoto; **p.235** © DeAgostini/Getty Images.

Acknowledgements: p.7: Christopher Haigh: from *The English Reformation Revised* (Cambridge University Press, 1987); **p.16**: Roger Lockyer: from Polydore Vergil's 'Books of English History (Anglicae Historicae Libri), as quoted in from *Henry VII (Seminar Studies in History)* (Longman, 1983); **p.32**: Caroline Rogers and Roger Turvey: from *Henry VII* (Hodder Education, 2005); From *The Reign of Henry VII*, ed. Benjamin Thompson (Oxbow Books, 1995); **p.34**: Jocelyn Hunt and Carolyn Towle: from *History in Depth: Henry VII* (Longman, 1998); **p.45**: Jez Ross: from 'Henry VIII's Early Foreign Policy, 1509–29' from *History Review* (*History Today*, December 2001); **p.51**: Peter Marshall: from 'Cardinal Wolsey and the English Church' from *History Review* (*History Today*, March 2008); **p.56**: T. A. Morris: from *Europe and England in the Sixteenth Century* (Routledge, 1998); **p.60**: A. F. Pollard: from *Wolsey (Fontana Library)* (Collins, 1965); **p.61**: John Guy: from 'Henry VIII and his Ministers' from *History Review* (*History Today*, December 1995); **p.61**: J. J. Scarisbrick: from *Henry VIII (Yale English Monarchs series)* (Yale University Press, 1997); **p. 61**: from *Cardinal Wolsey: Church, State and Art*, eds. S.J. Gunn and P. G. Lindley (Cambridge University Press, 1991); **p.66**: J. D. Mackie: from *The Earlier Tudors* (Oxford University Press, 1987); **p.66**: C. S. L. Davies: from *Peace, Print and Protestantism 1450–1558* (Paladin, 1977); **p.82**: A. Fletcher and D. MacCulloch: from *Tudor Rebellions* (Pearson, 1997); **p.97**: Christopher Haigh: from *English Reformations: Religion, Politics and Society under the Tudors* (Clarendon Press, 1993); **p.97**: Eamon Duffy: from *The Stripping of the Alters: Traditional Religion in England, 1400–1580* (Yale University Press, 1992); **p.99**: Claire Cross: from *Church and People, England 1450–1660* (HarperCollins, 1976); **p.102**: Gervase Phillips: from 'Henry VIII and Scotland' from *History Review* (*History Today*, September 2006); **p.107**: E. Ives: from *The Reign of Henry VIII: Politics, Policy and Piety*, ed. D. MacCulloch (Macmillan, 1995); **p.108**: Derek Wilson: from 'Thomas Cromwell: Brewer's Boy Made Good' from *History Review* (*History Today*, December 2012); **p.116**: Keith Randell: from *Access to History: Henry VIII and the Government of England* (Hodder Education, 2001); **p.116**: Denys Cook: from *Sixteenth Century England 1450–1600 (Documents and Debates Series)* (Palgrave Macmillan, 1980); **p.116**: J. J. Scarisbrick: from *Henry VIII* (Eyre & Spottiswoode, 1968); **p.145**: G. R. Elton: from *Reform and Reformation, England 1509–1558* (Harvard University Press, 1977); **p.149**: D. Rogerson *et al.* from *The Early Tudors: England 1485–1558* (Hodder Education, 2001); **p.149**: Nigel Heard: from *Edward VI and Mary: A Mid-Tudor Crisis?* (Hodder Education, 2000); **p.149**: Warren: from *Elizabeth I: Meeting the Challenge, England 1541–1603* (Hodder Education, 2008); **p.154**: Neville Williams: from *Elizabeth I, Queen of England* (Sphere Books, 1971); **p.166**: G. Regan: from *Elizabeth I (Cambridge Topics in History)* (Cambridge University Press, 1988); **p.186**: Susan Brigden: from *New Worlds, Lost Worlds: The Rule of the Tudors, 1485–1603 (Penguin History of Britain)* (Viking Books, 2000); **p.198**: A. G. R. Smith: from *The Emergence of a Nation State: the Commonwealth of England 1529–1660* (Longman, 1984); **p.213**: S. T. Bindoff: from *Tudor England* (Penguin, 1950); **p.213**: John Guy: from *Tudor England* (Oxford University Press, 1988); **p.213**: Neville Williams: from *Elizabeth I, Queen of England* (Weidenfeld & Nicholson, 1967); **p.216**: S.T. Bindoff: from *Pelican History of England, No. 5: Tudor England* (Penguin Books, 1952); **p.217**: L. B. Smith: from *Elizabethan Epic (Panther History)* (Panther, 1969); **p.227**: R.B. Wernham: from 'Elizabethan War Aims and Strategy' from *Elizabethan Government and Society*, eds. S. T. Bindoff, J. Hurstfield and C. H. Williams (Athlone Press, 1961); **p.230**: Map adapted from *Britain, Europe and the World 1485–1713* by Dennis Witcombe, (Heinemann, 1974); **p.231** Map adapted from *Elizabethan England – Schools Council History 13–16 Project*, (HarperCollins, 1977).

AQA material is reproduced by permission of AQA.

Every effort has been made to trace or contact all copyright holders, but if any have been inadvertently overlooked the Publishers will be pleased to make the necessary arrangements at the first opportunity.

Although every effort has been made to ensure that website addresses are correct at time of going to press, Hodder Education cannot be held responsible for the content of any website mentioned in this book. It is sometimes possible to find a relocated web page by typing in the address of the home page for a website in the URL window of your browser.

Hachette UK's policy is to use papers that are natural, renewable and recyclable products and made from wood grown in sustainable forests. The logging and manufacturing processes are expected to conform to the environmental regulations of the country of origin.

Orders: please contact Bookpoint Ltd, 130 Milton Park, Abingdon, Oxon OX14 4SB. Telephone: +44 (0)1235 827720. Fax: +44(01235) 400454. Lines are open 9.00a.m.–5.00p.m., Monday to Saturday, with a 24-hour message answering service. Visit our website at www.hoddereducation.co.uk

© David Ferriby, Angela Anderson and Tony Imperato
First published in 2015 by
Hodder Education,
An Hachette UK Company,
50 Victoria Embankment,
London EC4Y 0DZ

Impression number   10 9 8 7 6 5 4 3 2

Year   2019 2018 2017 2016 2015

Cover photo: © duncan1890/iStockphoto

Illustrations by Integra Software Services

Typeset in 10.5/12.5pt ITC Berkeley Oldstyle Std Book by Integra Software Services Pvt. Ltd., Pondicherry, India

Printed in Italy

A catalogue record for this title is available from the British Library

ISBN 978 1 471 837586

Contents

Part Two: England: Turmoil and Triumph, 1547–1603

Section 1: Instability and consolidation: 'the mid-Tudor Crisis', 1547–1563

Section 2: The triumph of Elizabeth, 1563–1603

Introduction

This book on the Tudor period is written to support the Tudor option of AQA's A-level History Breadth Study specification. It is an exciting period, full of characters who seem larger than life – partly because elements of the story have so often been transferred to stage, television and film. It is a story that includes love, jealousy, hatred and violence. It is a century that includes some fascinating characters whose exact motives can still be debated 500 or so years later. Recent research has unearthed new details which have led to reinterpretations of some decisions and events.

▲ Portrait of Elizabeth at her coronation.

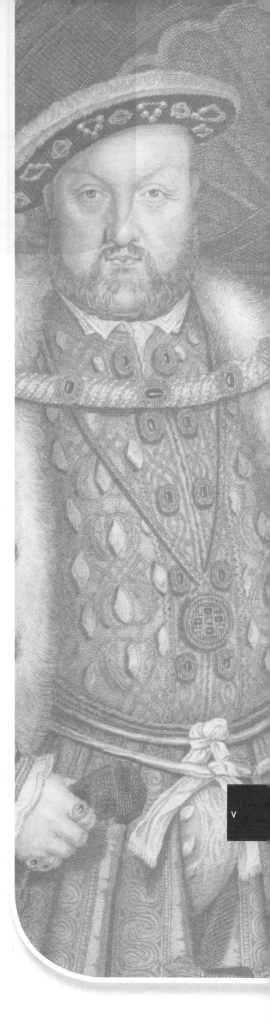

The key content

'The Tudors: England, 1485–1603' is one of the breadth studies offered by AQA, and as such covers over 100 years. The content is divided into two parts:

Part One (1485–1547) is studied by those taking the AS examination.

Parts One and Two (1485–1603) are studied by those taking the full A-level examination.

Each part is subdivided into two sections.

> ### PART ONE: CONSOLIDATION OF THE TUDOR DYNASTY: ENGLAND, 1485–1547
>
> This covers the reigns of Henry VII and Henry VIII – not just the personalities, but also aspects of historical study such as economic, social, ideological and cultural.
>
> #### Henry VII, 1485–1509
>
> This reign can mistakenly be seen as the prologue to the exciting events and personalities in his son, Henry VIII's, reign. In fact, Henry VII's seizure of the crown and the way in which he consolidated power are epic stories in themselves. He still had doubts about his success in creating a dynasty – especially after the death of his eldest son, Arthur, in 1502. Fortunately Henry VII lived long enough for his second son, Henry, to be able to become king when he was just about old enough to rule at the age of seventeen.
>
> #### Henry VIII, 1509–47
>
> The first twenty years, when for most of the time Cardinal Wolsey was the chief minister, was a period during which the foundations laid by Henry VII were consolidated.
> Henry VIII's main preoccupation from the later 1520s onwards was securing the succession to ensure that the Tudor dynasty continued. To guarantee this, he needed a son (only a daughter had survived childbirth and infancy). Famously Henry VIII was declared Supreme Head of the Church of England after breaking with the Pope in Rome, to obtain a divorce and marry Anne Boleyn.
> Henry eventually gained a male heir (through his third wife, Jane Seymour).

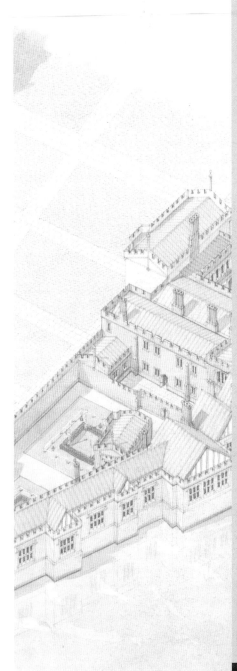

PART TWO: ENGLAND: TURMOIL AND TRIUMPH, 1547–1603

This covers the reigns of Henry VIII's three children who ruled in turn: Edward VI (1547–53), Mary (1553–58) and Elizabeth (1558–1603). Again, the focus is not just on the personalities but also on issues of breadth as highlighted in the key questions.

Instability and consolidation: 'the mid-Tudor Crisis', 1547–1563

Edward VI was king for six years, during which time the government was first of all led by the Duke of Somerset and later the Duke of Northumberland. There were many problems during these years – not entirely caused by the lack of an adult monarch. England faced inflation, bad harvests, trade problems and a population rise. Changes in religious belief were introduced.

Edward died when he was fifteen and Mary was proclaimed queen. The Catholic faith was reintroduced in England – with the agreement of Parliament. Mary married Philip of Spain, but failed to produce a child who would have inherited the throne.

When the crown passed to Elizabeth her coronation was celebrated – partly because of her Protestant religion but also because of the unpopularity of Mary's Spanish marriage. Elizabeth showed, within the first few years of her reign, that a woman could rule successfully.

The triumph of Elizabeth, 1563–1603

Elizabeth's achievements are legendary – ruling for over 44 years, defeating the Spanish, presiding over a country that flourished in the arts, literature and music. Yet she constantly faced problems: what to do with the threat of Mary Queen of Scots, uprisings against her rule, social problems over poverty and disagreements with Parliament over many issues – including her failure to find a husband and provide an heir. Thus when she died in 1603 there was much on both sides of the balance sheet. It has often been the glitter that has predominated in interpretations of her reign.

Key concepts

But the study of history does not just include narrative – interesting though the stories often are! There are four concepts which steer our thinking and our understanding of the past. These are important in your study and questions are likely to be centred on one or more of these.

- Change and continuity: To what extent did things change? What are the similarities and differences over time?
- Cause and consequence: What were the factors that led to change? How did the changes affect individuals and groups within society, as well as the country as a whole?

You will find that all the essay questions that you face involve one or more of these concepts. They will be asking you to assess, for example:

- the extent you agree with a statement
- the validity of a statement
- the importance of a particular factor relating to a key question
- how much something changed or to what extent something was achieved.

In addition, you will be learning about different interpretations: how and why events have been portrayed in different ways over time by historians. In the first section of both the AS and A-level examination you will be tested on this skill with a selection of contrasting extracts.

The key questions

The specification lists six key questions around which the study is based. These are wide-ranging in scope and can be considered across the whole period. They reflect the broadly based questions (usually covering 20–30 years) that will be set in the examination.

1 How effectively did the Tudors restore and develop the powers of the monarchy?

You will learn how Henry VII established the Tudor dynasty; how it was consolidated by Henry VIII, and how under Edward VI and Mary the Tudor monarchy appeared to be under threat before being rescued during the reign of Elizabeth.

2 In what ways and how effectively was England governed during this period?

You will examine how the government of England remained the same, but with important changes within a system which left the ruling elite with the political power. In the shires of England the nobility were in control, aided by the gentry. Parliament gained in status through the process of the Reformation.

3 How did relations with foreign powers change and how was the succession secured?

You will discover that throughout the period England had at various times to face threats from France (often allied with the Scots) and Spain. There were frequent changes of alliances, with Spain becoming the enemy for the last 20 years of Elizabeth's reign.

4 How did English society and economy change and with what effects?

English society had never been static, but you will learn that it changed at a faster pace in the sixteenth century for a variety of reasons. The economy developed too, with more people, rising prices, increased trade, and the consequences of discoveries of new lands around the world.

5 How far did intellectual and religious ideas change and develop and with what effects?

You will discover that the Renaissance brought different ways of thinking, including rediscovering the writings of ancient Greece and Rome. The Reformation meant that there was no longer a consensus in religious ideas – and the differences could be spread easily with the expansion of printing. Although many people still could not read, England was becoming a more literate society.

6 How important was the role of key individuals and groups and how were they affected by developments?

You will already probably know that the Tudor period is famous for its kings and queens, for Wolsey, Thomas More, Thomas Cromwell, the Earl of Leicester and many others. They all played a key role in policy and were in turn affected by the situations they faced – in some cases leading to their execution. Groups, such as sections of society or religious groups or courtiers, also had a key role in developments.

How this book is designed to help your studies

1 With the facts, concepts and key questions of the specification

At the beginning of each chapter the book flags up the elements of the specification and the key questions that are being covered.

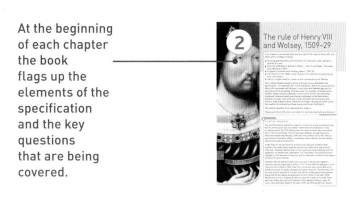

Activities are provided, helping you to create notes, and enabling you to consider the main areas of interpretation throughout the period.

The Look again feature encourages you to look back and compare your learning with previous periods in the book, to make comparisons across time.

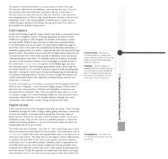

Key words and phrases are defined at the first relevant point in the text, and there is a full glossary on pages 251–52.

Chapter summaries and diagrams are provided to help consolidate your learning.

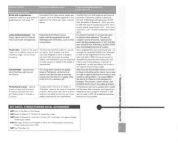

Key dates are listed throughout.

2 With the skills needed to answer examination questions

The book provides guidance in answering different types of examination questions in the form of a separate 'skills' section at the end of each chapter.

3 With the skills in reading, understanding and making notes from the book

Note-making

Good note-making is really important. Your notes are an essential revision resource. What is more, the process of making notes will help you understand and remember what you are reading. Some of you will make notes using a laptop, tablet or other device. Others will use a more traditional approach. No matter what approach you use, however, the same general principles apply to note-making.

How to make notes

Most note-making styles reflect the distinction between key points and supporting evidence. Below is advice on a variety of different note-making styles. Throughout each section in the book are note-making activities for you to carry out.

The important thing is that you understand your notes. Therefore, you don't have to write *everything* down and you don't have to write in full sentences.

While making notes you can use abbreviations:

Full text	Abbreviation
Parliament	Parlt
England	Eng
Development	Devt
Henry VIII	HVIII

You can develop your own abbreviations. Usually it is only yourself who has to understand them!

You can use arrows instead of words:

Full text	Arrow
Increased	↑
Decreased	↓

You can use mathematical notation:

Equals	=
Plus, and	+
Because	∵
Therefore	∴

Note-making styles

There are a large number of note-making styles. You can find examples of four popular styles below. All of them have their strengths and it is a good idea to try them all and work out which style suits you.

Style 1: Bullet points

Bullet points can be a useful method of making notes because:

- they encourage you to write in note form, rather than in full sentences
- they help you to organise your ideas in a systematic fashion
- they are easy to skim read later
- you can show relative importance visually by indenting less important, or supporting points.

Usually it is easier to write notes with bullet points after you have skim-read a section or a paragraph first in order to get the overall sense in your head.

Style 2: The 1–2 method

The 1–2 method is a variation on bullet points. The method is based on dividing your page into two columns: the first for the main point, the second for supporting detail. This allows you to see the structure of the information clearly. To do this, you can create a chart to complete, as follows:

Main point	Supporting detail

Style 3: Spider diagrams

Spider diagrams or mind maps can be a useful method of making notes because:

- they will help you to categorise factors: each of the main branches coming from the centre should be a new category
- they can help you see what is most important: often the most important factors will be close to the centre of the diagram
- they can help you see connections between different aspects of what you are studying. It is useful to draw lines between different parts of your diagram to show links
- they can help you with essay planning: you can use them to get down the main points quickly and develop a clear structure in response to an essay question
- you can set out the spider diagram in any way that seems appropriate for the task, but usually, as with a spider's web, you start with the title or central issue in the middle with connecting lines radiating outwards.

The establishment of the Tudors: Henry VII

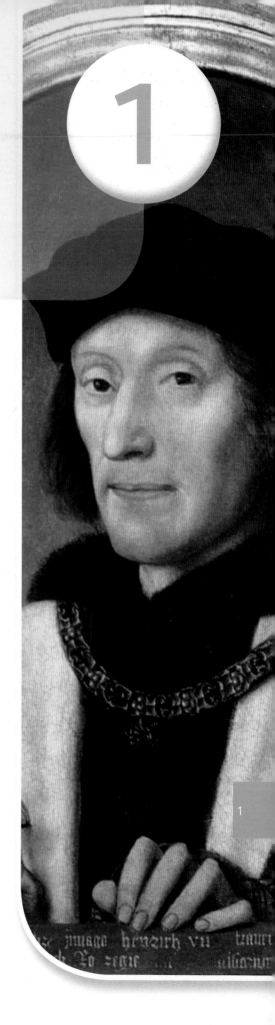

In August 1485, at the Battle of Bosworth Field, Richard III was killed. Allegedly, his crown was found in a thorn bush and placed by Lord Stanley on the head of Henry Tudor, who became Henry VII and ruled England for nearly a quarter of a century. This chapter is concerned with key events and policies during Henry VII's reign and deals with a number of areas:

- The England that Henry VII inherited when he became King in August 1485 – the country, society, religion, learning, the arts.
- How he consolidated his power on the throne, and his style of government.
- How he removed threats to his power.
- How he made England stronger through his foreign policy, including relations with Scotland, and encouraging overseas trade and exploration.

These areas relate directly to the key questions in the specification on monarchy, government and foreign policy. The background provided in the first part of the chapter relates to society, the economy and intellectual and religious ideas.

The question to be asking at this stage is:

To what extent was Henry VII personally responsible for his success in establishing Tudor rule?

CHAPTER OVERVIEW

Henry VII is seen as the founder of the Tudor dynasty who laid down secure foundations for his son and grandchildren. Sporadic fighting between rival noble factions in the fifteenth century had become worse in the 1450s. This led to what we know as the Wars of the Roses – the Red Lancastrians and the White Yorkists – yet these terms were in fact invented in Henry VII's reign in order to emphasise how he, as a Lancastrian king who married a Yorkist princess, had united the rival families and brought the fighting to an end. This, like all propaganda, is a huge over-simplification.

This chapter, after an initial survey of England in 1485, explains how Henry VII dealt with the many problems that he faced:

- from rivals and rebels
- from financial pressures and the need to build up royal income and encourage trade
- from foreign threats at a time when wars were commonplace in Europe
- from the need to ensure that there was a peaceful succession after his death.

It assesses how successful Henry VII was in his aims and the reasons for his achievements, including the seemingly harsh and unsentimental way in which he consolidated his power in the last decade of his reign.

Arable farming – Labour-intensive farming which produced crops using basic tools including ploughs.

Enclosure – The fencing off of land from open fields with the ending of all common rights over it.

1 England in 1485

Before you begin to study the Tudors, you need to have a clear picture in your mind of what life was like in England in 1485. What did the countryside look like? How did people live and earn their living? What did they believe? Were ideas fixed or open to change? In politics, what had adults lived through which would affect their views about events under the new king, Henry VII?

The countryside, the economy and English society

What was England like in 1485?

So what was this country of England like in 1485? Its landscape would, in the hilly and mountainous areas, be familiar to the England of today. But in every other respect life was unrecognisable. The total population was about three million, 90 per cent of whom lived in very rural communities. Towns were small: a very large town, such as Norwich, had a population of 12,000 – more than enough to be considered a city. London was the largest by far, but this had only about 60,000 residents, living in very cramped and overcrowded conditions. Other urban settlements such as Salisbury had about 5,000 inhabitants. These larger urban settlements were not evenly distributed across the country, with the result that some very small settlements assumed considerable importance as centres for local government as well as for the sale of goods at markets and fairs. These occurred mostly in the more sparsely populated areas of the country. For example, there were no large towns in Sussex, and Lewes, with a population of under 1,000, was important as a commercial centre as well as for local government.

Farming

Rural communities varied enormously across the country, depending largely on the terrain and the landscape. In parts of southern England and the Midlands open field arable farming with a variety of crops was common. Elsewhere, fens, marshes, forests and uplands all had their own identities. In the more hilly areas, for example, livestock farming (cattle, sheep and pigs) was common. Woodland and forests were important for timber as well as grazing animals. Fishing was important in the rivers, lakes and marshes. People, especially the poor, had to be resourceful in order to survive, and the geography and climate of England provided plenty of opportunities for specialisation.

The large open fields were common in many areas of arable farming. The land was divided into strips and given by the local landowner to tenants. Most villages also had common land – land where all villagers had the right to graze their animals. However, this description is over-simplified. Even in the late fifteenth century there was some concern about enclosure. Enclosure involved putting a fence around a field so that either one crop could be produced on a larger scale or the field could be used for livestock. This was especially popular in parts of the Midlands where some farmers were moving from arable to pasture farming because sheep farming was more profitable. Tenant farmers could lose their strips of land when landowners wanted to change farming methods. Sometimes the common land was enclosed, and this was likely to provoke fierce opposition, as villagers claimed customary rights of access to common land. Fencing off these areas deprived villagers of land for their animals, cutting timber, or for fishing and hunting. There was an early attempt in 1489 to deal with the perceived problem when an anti-enclosure law was passed, but it had little practical effect.

The amount of enclosed land did not increase much in Henry VII's reign. The area most affected was the Midlands, and even here less than 3 per cent was enclosed. Much more had been enclosed in the years of the Wars of the Roses when law and order was less effective. However, it was seen as an increasing grievance in Henry's reign, partly because it became confused with engrossing – that is, the joining together of several farms to make one unit, usually through a process of one farmer buying up the land of the others, as this usually led to families being evicted.

Cloth industry

Linked with farming, England's major industry was cloth, accounting for nearly 80 per cent of England's exports. Although agriculture provided the main livelihood for people in Tudor England, the woollen cloth industry created the most wealth. Different types and sizes of cloths were exported mainly to the Netherlands, but also to Spain, the Holy Roman Empire (see page 28) and Venice. Most of this trade was controlled by the Merchant Adventurers, a powerful company based in London. It exported the cloth and imported foreign goods in return. The quality of wool produced by English sheep made both the raw material and cloth woven from it greatly in demand at home and abroad. Tudor governments from Henry VII onwards would all be keen to encourage this sector of the economy because its success brought in valuable income to the Crown from customs duties on exports. In the Middle Ages, raw wool was a primary export, but increasingly governments tried to discourage this as it meant that the finishing work to produce a piece of cloth was being done elsewhere, costing the Crown export income and hampering the development of a domestic finishing industry. All this, of course, brought the industry into conflict with arable farmers who objected to farmland being converted into sheep-runs, or enclosed.

Woollen cloth production was widely scattered, but the best quality cloth came from the west of England – from towns and villages along the Welsh borders and down into Gloucestershire, Wiltshire and Hampshire. Production was specialised but not intensive. Most cloth was made by hand, either in a room in a peasant cottage or in a small workshop within the cloth merchant's house. Few people worked full-time in the woollen industry, although there were 'journeymen' who travelled to make a living, hiring out their skills.

English society

It was expected that everyone recognised their place in society – from the King, downwards through the ranks of clergy, nobles, gentry, merchants, commoners, servants and paupers. It was generally accepted that 'The Great Chain of Being' had been ordered by God with a strict hierarchy of ranks. Social status dominated society. This put the Church in a powerful position to control the people by preaching obedience to the will of God and it made the Church an indispensable ally of the government.

The nobles were few in number – just over 50 – who owned large areas of land which provided power and influence in the localities. Strict inheritance rules of primogeniture meant that estates were passed down intact to the eldest son or the nearest male relative. The King relied on the support of these noble families to maintain law and order in their areas of the country, otherwise rebellions could easily occur. A successful monarch, therefore, ruled co-operatively with the nobles and it was one of his duties to make sure that was possible. Some monarchs in the fifteenth century had tried to 'buy' support by granting many new titles. Henry VII did the opposite; he created only three Earls in his reign, thus making the honour very special and ensuring that those who wanted the

Customs duties – Money paid on goods entering or leaving the country. Money came from tunnage (taxes on exports) and poundage (taxes on imports).

Finishing – The final stages of woollen production when spun yarn is converted into cloth by weaving, which includes fulling (cleansing the wool to eliminate oil, dirt and other impurities) and dyeing it.

Primogeniture – The eldest son or nearest male relative inherited everything.

title were loyal and supportive of him. Important nobles maintained extensive households, consisting of all family members, friends and servants. For example, Richard, Duke of Northumberland, had 187 household members in 1503–04.

Below the nobles were the gentry, the merchants, the commoners (ranging from those who farmed on small areas of land down to those who were landless and worked for others) and the beggars. In the Tudor period the commoners often suffered badly because of changes in agriculture, such as enclosure, and because of the rise in prices that was a major feature of the period (see Chapter 6, pages 170-71).

At the pinnacle of the social hierarchy was the monarch. He ruled under God, though the later theory of **Divine Right of Kings** had not been fully set out. These theoretical powers did not mean that the monarch could be a dictator. He needed the support of leading nobles to provide law and order and an army in times of war. Indeed, he was expected to consult with his advisers who would largely be drawn from the nobility. Henry VII was fortunate to have loyal noble advisers whom he could trust. Henry also needed to summon Parliament from time to time to get support and to pass laws.

> **Divine Right of Kings** – The belief that monarchs were ruling on behalf of God. They were therefore answerable to God, and the monarch's subjects were expected to obey the monarch, otherwise they were disobeying God.

The country of England was more unified than countries in Europe such as France. In England there was a common law; there was an accepted language (except in the peripheries such as Cornwall). Wales was regarded as a part of England, in spite of the Welsh language that predominated in some parts. In theory the monarch controlled the whole country, but in practice some areas were semi-independent, either under the control of leading nobles or ruled by the Church from Durham or York.

The Catholic Church

Why was the Catholic Church so powerful? And why had it been criticised?

In this section you will examine how powerful the Church was in late fifteenth century society – and why it was being criticised. However, it is important not to view the situation through the eyes of a twenty-first century student living in a society where religion is often not so central. Try to understand how it was five hundred years ago.

The Catholic Church was immensely powerful in the late fifteenth century. It owned about one-third of the land and had considerable wealth. Mirroring the structure of **secular** society, the Church had a hierarchy from Archbishops to Bishops, all the way down the chain to poor parish priests who earned less than £15 a year. There were about 35,000 ordained clergy and about 10,000 monks and nuns. The Church had its own legal system, and clergy were tried in Church courts. In theory, the Pope in Rome decided on all matters both religious and political. There was a constant flow of paperwork between England and Italy, dealing with legal cases and administrative issues. As such, England was a fully integrated part of the international Catholic Church. However, often the Pope's primary political focus was on the Papal States which were frequently in conflict with neighbouring states.

> **Secular** – The opposite of 'sacred', i.e. worldly things, not spiritual.

The power of the Catholic Church stemmed from people's beliefs and fears. Life was often short, disease was common and medicines were few. People needed certainties and the Church provided for this. Many church walls had contrasting and lurid pictures of heaven and hell. Others, such as the wall paintings at Pickering in Yorkshire, showed scenes of the life of Christ, with special emphasis on his suffering and crucifixion. Illiterate peasants could easily understand where they wanted to go after death, but their religious beliefs were of necessity rather simple and sometimes close to what we would term 'folk religion'. Their lives were dominated by the seasons of the year and the contrasts of the weather. Priests tried hard, by using paintings and statues, to explain Christian beliefs, but it is hardly surprising if beliefs focused more on the god of nature and the fear of going to hell than on the subtleties of Christian belief centring on the death of Jesus on a cross 1,500 years earlier.

Therefore at the beginning of the sixteenth century, English people, with few exceptions, followed the teachings (or doctrines) of the Catholic Church. This meant that they accepted the following:

- The Pope, in Rome, was head of the Church and had supreme authority over all spiritual matters. The Papacy was also recognised as a Court of Law. The *Papal Curia* under the Pope also acted as a Court of Appeal.
- There was an elaborately organised hierarchy of churchmen, many of whom worked in the community tending to the spiritual needs of ordinary people. These included clergy attached to parishes and also friars and nuns. Some, including monks, closed themselves off to concentrate on prayer. Even those were often active in the local community and owned large estates, which they managed.

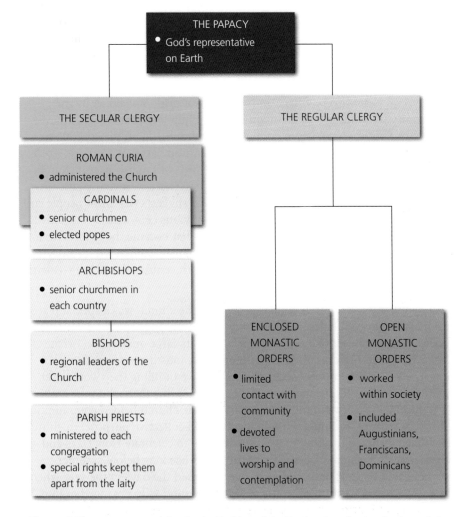

▲ Figure 1 The structure of the Catholic Church in England at the beginning of the sixteenth century.

- The clergy held a special and powerful place within the community. Only formally ordained appointed priests could conduct services in church. Access to the Bible, written in Latin, was limited to priests and others who could read the language. Priests interpreted what it said for the benefit of their parishioners. The unique role of the priesthood was confirmed by their appearance at church services (they wore particular clothes – vestments – to conduct services) and their status set them apart (they were not allowed to marry or have sex).
- People should submit to the authority of the Church in their lives. According to the teachings of the Catholic Church there were seven essential sacraments which the Church performed. These were:
  - the eucharist (the commemoration of the Last Supper of Jesus with his disciples)
  - baptism
  - holy orders (the granting of the status of priest to someone who had completed their religious training)
  - confirmation (the recipient confirming the acceptance of God's spirit in their hearts)
  - marriage
  - confession, leading to penance (doing tasks to show repentance)
  - unction (otherwise known as the anointing of the sick, part of the Last Rites).
- For their souls to be saved, people should attend church regularly, believe in the sacraments and show their faith in God.

Churches within the community

The church was also part of the social fabric of the community. It was the most common building to be found across the country, an easily identifiable landmark in nearly every village and town. Great pride was taken by the community in building and maintaining their church as a sign of their devotion to God. In Louth, Lincolnshire, for example, fundraising produced £305 to build the parish church and more money was raised between 1501 and 1515 to construct a magnificent spire. Nearly two-thirds of English parish churches were built or rebuilt during the fifteenth century. There were many gifts to churches of vestments, plate and jewels. All this suggests that most people still supported the Church in the same way as in previous centuries. It was only when Henry VIII wanted a divorce, leading to what became the Reformation, that the focus was on criticisms of the Church. This has often led historians to paint a picture of church life in the early sixteenth century that was excessively focused on the failings of some church officials.

Most people went to church regularly, because the church was a special place and most of the population believed in its basic teaching. Think for a moment about how the interior of a parish church, with its large open space, ornate windows, images, statues and many decorations, must have seemed to its congregation. It was probably the most impressive building they would ever enter. From constructing and maintaining the building through to the emphasis on communal rather than individual worship, the church helped communities, especially villages, to find a sense of identity and collective purpose. In church, the village gathered together to worship but also to celebrate Holy Days and other festivals with dancing and drinking. In an age long before summer vacations and Bank Holidays, the church organised the days in the year when the daily routine was broken. In these ways, it bound villagers together into one community. There were in fact quite a few such days during the year, some local and some common throughout the country. Two examples of the latter were 23 April, St George's Day, which had been declared a saints' day in 1222, and May Day, with dancing round the maypole and much merry-making.

The Church was powerful, but it also suffered from faults. Indeed, its very power encouraged corruption. Some clergy were absent from their parishes (yet claiming the stipend); some clergy were pluralists (that is, claiming the stipends from several parishes); some clergy were immoral (they had mistresses) and some clergy were ignorant and could not even recite the Lord's Prayer.

Historians have held different views about the state of the pre-Reformation Church. Some, such as Professor A.G. Dickens, looking at the evidence from a Protestant perspective, found plenty to suggest that the Catholic Church in England faced much criticism because of the faults and shortcomings that undoubtedly existed in some parishes. These historians saw the Reformation process and England becoming a Protestant nation as a logical consequence. Other more recent historians have argued that shortcomings in the Church were nothing new; the Catholic Church had strength and vitality and much active support, both in worship and in outward signs such as church building projects. These historians argue that the Reformation's origins were primarily political – that is, Henry VIII's wish for a divorce – and this political reformation by coincidence happened at the same time as the European Reformation had started under Martin Luther.

The Church's political sphere

In these different ways the Church had become an accepted and intrinsic part of the lives of ordinary people. However, it was also a force in national and international politics. Since the Norman Conquest the Church had operated its own law courts to try crimes involving priests or breaches of doctrine. These were still active in the fifteenth century, although medieval kings had done their best to weaken the Church courts' independent power. Bishops and abbots had a political role; they sat in the House of Lords. Churchmen were often the best educated, most literate people in the country, so their skills as administrators were valued. In the early Tudor period it was not uncommon to find that government advisers and ministers were also members of the clergy. Henry VII promoted Bishop Morton to Archbishop of Canterbury and then Lord Chancellor, where he had an important role in advising the King. Henry was keen to work closely with the Church because it could be used as a powerful ally if his claim to the throne were to be challenged. The Church also offered an additional service to monarchs. Its power over people's minds through its teachings created a channel through which obedience to the will of the King could also be taught.

The beginnings of change

Why were changes in thinking occurring in the early sixteenth century, and with what consequences?

It would be wrong to suggest that in terms of beliefs and attitudes everything was totally static and unchangeable. There were some signs of impatience with the failings of the Church and influences from Europe were encouraging educated people to think in less restricted ways.

Humanism

During the fifteenth and early sixteenth centuries the cultural movement known as the Renaissance spread from its home in Italy to England. An important part of Renaissance thinking was the emphasis on the power and potential of mankind. Henry VII commissioned new buildings, including a new palace at Richmond and the Henry VII chapel in Westminster Abbey. He and his wife are buried in the chapel, whose magnificence links the greatness of kings with belief in the power

Stipend – The term used for the payment received by a priest for his appointment to a parish.

Norman Conquest – The events in which William came from Normandy and defeated the English King, Harold, in 1066. William and his successors imposed their own laws and system of government.

Source A How our view of the Catholic Church c.1500 has been changed by events that followed. From *The English Reformation Revised* by C. Haigh, (Cambridge University Press), 1987, p.58.

Relations between priests and parishioners were usually harmonious, and the laity complained astonishingly infrequently against their priests. There were local tensions, certainly, but they were individual rather than institutionalized, occasional rather than endemic. In a frantic search for the causes of reformation, we must not wrench isolated cases of discord from their local context, and pile them together to show a growing chorus of dissatisfaction.

Why do you think there are differing views on the state of the Church in c.1500 (Source A)?

of God. Renaissance scholars believed that it was possible to improve human knowledge and behaviour through education. They were also keen to study classical literature and architecture, and to discuss ideas and beliefs. Humanism was a positive movement, borne out of optimism about the present and future. It was only much later, in the nineteenth century, they were dubbed 'humanists'.

What we call 'humanist' ideas were not entirely new. Scholars in the fifteenth century had been studying classical and medieval authors, including Plato, Aristotle, Cicero and Plutarch. Some travelled to Italy, attended lectures at universities there, and returned with copies of classical and medieval manuscripts. Some Italian scholars came to England and taught at Oxford and Cambridge. As a result of increasing interest in learning, over 100 endowed schools were set up in England in the fifteenth century, and many became influenced by humanism. Greek began to be taught at Oxford, and a generation of scholars benefited from this.

Henry VII himself was a patron of the arts. He encouraged writers, poets, musicians and artists, including those from Europe. Polydore Vergil was commissioned to write a history of England which told the story of England leading up to Tudor rule. Poets such as John Skelton were employed to write enthusiastically about England's happy situation under the wise rule of Henry VII. John Colet, Dean of St Paul's Cathedral, founded St Paul's School. Another scholar, William Grocyn, taught Greek at Oxford University, and stimulated much interest in the study of Plato and other Classical writers. Henry VII's own children received an education that reflected the Renaissance, with an emphasis on foreign languages, classics, music and religion, as well as learning the arts of being a courtier, which included dancing and hunting.

Humanists became involved in the religious debate in England because they were disturbed by the poor quality of the parish clergy and wanted to improve standards of education among both the clergy and the laity. They attacked the Church's exploitation of practices, such as the veneration of saints and the selling of indulgences in order to raise money. They were concerned that this exploitation not only led souls away from God, but also raised money that was spent on luxurious living for the higher clergy, rather than the promotion of education or charitable works. One such writer was William Melton, a Cambridge scholar and Chancellor of York Minster from 1496 to 1528. His studies led him to believe that many of the parish clergy were lacking in training and discipline – a theme echoed by his friend John Colet (see page 9).

Source B From William Melton's *Exhortation*, published at the beginning of Henry VIII's reign. It is translated from a Latin sermon addressed to a group of trainee priests in York by Melton, the Chancellor of York Minster.

... Everywhere throughout town and countryside there exists a crop of oafish and boorish priests, some of whom are engaged on ignoble and servile tasks, while others abandon themselves to tavernhaunting, swilling and drunkenness. Some cannot get along without their wenches; others pursue their amusement in dice and gambling and other such trifling all day long. There are some who waste their time in hunting and hawking ... This is inevitable, for since they are all completely ignorant of good literature, how can they obtain improvement or enjoyment in reading and study?

We must avoid and keep far from ourselves that grasping, deadly plague of avarice for which practically every priest is accused and held in disrepute before the people, when it is said that we are greedy for rich promotions ... and spend little or nothing on works of piety...

Laity/Laymen – A general term referring to people who had not been trained and accepted as priests.

Indulgences – The indulgence was a document, issued with the Pope's authority, setting out the cancellation of punishment in purgatory – a place where it was believed souls of the dead went to while waiting to be sent to heaven.

8

Based on what you have read in this chapter so far, do you think that Melton is portraying an accurate picture of the clergy in the early sixteenth century (Source B)?

Erasmus' teachings

In 1499 Erasmus, a celebrated Dutch humanist scholar, visited England for the first time. He found a few scholars with whom he was in great sympathy. One was John Skelton, a poet and linguist, who became one of the tutors to the future Henry VIII. Skelton's flamboyant attitude and wit widened Henry's horizons. Another person Erasmus admired was John Colet, Dean of St Paul's Cathedral and founder of St Paul's School. He had travelled in Italy and been greatly influenced by his revulsion at the misuse of wealth and extravagance in the Church that he came to detest. Back in England he delivered a famous set of lectures about St Paul, which included forthright denunciations of the abuses of the Church and the corruption of the clergy. Another humanist was Thomas More, who became Chancellor to Henry VIII in 1530 (see Chapter 3, page 68).

Erasmus spent several years in England, briefly in 1499 and then at Oxford between 1504 and 1506. He was then based at Queens' College, Cambridge in the first few years of Henry VIII's reign. He had enormous influence at the time across Europe and to some extent in England because of his wide circle of influential writers. Many works were published, encouraging learning and reform within the Catholic Church. For example, in 1500 he published *The Adages*, in which he took ancient Roman proverbs and made them relevant to his time, urging all to live a wise and good life. In 1511 he published *In Praise of Folly* which is a biting satire on all forms of human folly. Among his targets were those monks who did not live godly lives. In his *Handbook of the Christian Knight (Enchiridion Militis Christiani)*, written in 1501 but not published in England until 1533, he set out what he saw as the guidelines for a Christian life. He advocated an inward and personal faith, centred on prayer and reflection, with a focus on the example of Jesus.

Source C From *The Adages* of Erasmus (1500)
Dulce bellum inexpertis (War is sweet to those who have not tried it)

There is nothing more wicked than war, more disastrous, more widely destructive, more deeply tenacious, more loathsome, in a word, more unworthy of man, not to say of a Christian. Yet strange to say, everywhere at the present time war is being entered upon lightly, for any kind of reason, and waged with cruelty and barbarousness, not only by the heathen but by Christians, not only by lay people but by priests and bishops, not only by the young and inexperienced but by the old who know it well, not so much by the common people and the naturally fickle mob, but rather by princes whose functions should be to restrain with wisdom and reason the rash impulses of the foolish rabble.

Source D From *In Praise of Folly* (1511), a satire by Erasmus (written in 1509).

As for the Supreme Pontiffs [Popes], if they would recall that they take the place of Christ and would attempt to imitate his poverty, tasks, doctrines, crosses and disregard of safety; if they were even to contemplate the meaning of the name Pope – that is, Father – or of the title of Most Holy, then they would become the most humble and mortified of men. How many men would then be willing to spend all their wealth and efforts in order to procure the position [of Pope]?

Under the present system what work that needs to be done is handed over to Peter or Paul to do, while pomp and pleasure are personally taken care of by the Popes ... The Popes, neglecting all their other functions, make war their only duty ... a thing befitting of beasts, not men.

1 In Sources C and D, what can you learn about the beliefs of Erasmus?
2 Why would these be seen as important at the time?

It is important, however, to put the impact of humanist thought and religion in perspective. Only some educated people were under its influence. What we can term 'medieval attitudes' to piety and study predominated. Traditional forms of worship remained unquestioned. Pilgrimages, saints, miracles and the veneration of images remained central to religious devotion. The writings of mystics such as Julian of Norwich, who lived in the fourteenth century, remained popular two centuries later.

The invention of printing

The printing press was brought to England from Germany in 1476. Edward IV (1461–83) encouraged this, and books in English were printed after being translated from French and Latin. Previously it had been mainly the clergy who could read using handwritten manuscripts. Now there was the opportunity to read printed material in English. It also helped the standardisation of English across the country. There were five main regional dialects at the time, with many local variations.

Printing encouraged the spread of new ideas including those of humanist writers. People who could read could then study humanist ideas. However, many of the early books printed in English were mythical tales or popular stories, such as Chaucer's *Canterbury Tales* or Thomas Malory's *King Arthur*. This situation was reflected at court. Henry VII supported the development of printing. In 1504 he created the post of King's Printer. However, both Henry VII and Henry VIII showed little interest in the new thinking that was being publicised by humanist writers, and preferred stories of chivalry.

In fact, it was printing, partly encouraged by the royal family, rather than new ideas, that led to change. Printing led to more of the gentry and noble classes learning to read and assimilate a wider culture than had been traditional in England. More and more books were published. The market became much larger from the 1520s onwards, partly because of the Reformation. Print runs were small by modern standards, but books were expensive items and so were shared, and then ideas passed on orally. Due to printing, England became a more literate nation, leading to the cultural Renaissance of Elizabeth's reign.

Widening horizons

It was not just the printed word that was widening horizons in educated people's thinking. From Portugal and Spain intrepid sailors were setting out on dangerous missions to explore the unknown and to find new routes to the lucrative Spice Islands in the East. A new, reliable route was needed as the Turks, who were Muslim in religion, controlled the overland route from the Mediterranean to the Indian Ocean. The Portuguese were the first to reach the southern tip of the African continent in 1487, just after Henry VII had become King of England. Ten years later Vasco da Gama sailed from Portugal, round the southern tip of Africa and reached Calicut in India. In between these two voyages, Columbus sailed west from Spain in 1492 and discovered what was later named as **America** in a bid to find an alternative route to Asia. He thought that the world was much smaller than it actually is, and Europeans did not know of the existence of the continent of America. Tales of non-Christian civilisations beyond Europe, both in America and Asia, later had an impact on European thinking in a society dominated by the Catholic Church. In the new age of the printing press, accounts of other civilisations could be published, drawings showing the different appearances of humans in other continents could be circulated, and detailed maps could be drawn up. Explorers also brought back new plants – potatoes, tomatoes, tea and coffee – which affected people's way of life as well as their attitude to the wider world.

America – America was named in 1500 on an early sketch map of the newly-discovered continent after the explorer Amerigo Vespucci.

2 Henry VII and the consolidation of power

The monarchy had been unstable for substantial parts of the previous century. There was no obvious reason why Henry VII would be as successful as he actually was. In many ways, the odds were against him. Therefore, you need to consider this when studying what actually happened. His success was certainly not inevitable.

Henry becomes King

How was Henry able to move rapidly from a 'claim' to being crowned King of England?

Background of Henry Tudor

Henry did not have a strong claim to the throne of England. His claim lay through his mother, Margaret Beaufort, who was a direct descendant of Edward III by the marriage of his third son, John of Gaunt, Margaret's great grandfather. However, this claim was weakened by the fact that John of Gaunt and Catherine Swynford were not married when John Beaufort, Margaret's grandfather, had been born. Henry was also linked to royalty on his father's side. His grandmother, Catherine, had been married to the King of England, Henry V, before she married Owen Tudor, his grandfather. Because of this marriage, Henry's father and brother, Edmund and Jasper, were half-brothers to Henry VI and had been created Earls.

Henry was born in 1457, the son of Edmund Tudor, Earl of Richmond, who had died a few months before his son's birth. As a young boy, Henry grew up with his mother and uncle, Jasper Tudor. After various deaths (both natural and in battles) during the Wars of the Roses, Henry unexpectedly became the main Lancastrian claimant to the throne. His uncle, Jasper, took Henry to safety in France. Most of the next fourteen years was spent in Brittany, which at that

NOTE-MAKING

Using pages 11–14, make notes on the ways Henry established his *right* to rule (see page x for advice on note making).

What were the Wars of the Roses about?

In the earlier fifteenth century groups of nobles had wrestled for power under a monarchy that sometimes appeared to be weak, especially that of Henry VI (1422–61). It was towards the end of his reign that two groups of families under the banners of 'Lancaster' and 'York' fought to control the Crown. Although there were a few quite large battles, many of the conflicts were no more than skirmishes; there was little physical destruction and the fighting was not continuous. But the open hostility encouraged violence, instability and weakness within society. Many nobles used this period of weak rule to take more control of their local areas.

The term 'Wars of the Roses' comes from the supposed heraldic badges worn by Lancastrians and Yorkists. It came into popular use only after the publication of a novel by Sir Walter Scott in 1829. He based one part of his novel on a scene from Shakespeare's *Henry VI, Part 1*, where a group of noblemen pick red or white roses to show their loyalty to the Lancastrians or Yorkists.

time was still independent from the government of France. King Edward IV felt threatened by a potential claimant living abroad and possibly gaining support. Edward attempted negotiations to secure his return, but these failed. It is also true that there is no evidence that Henry attempted to challenge Edward's right to be King.

In 1483 the situation changed suddenly. Edward IV died. His brother, Richard, Duke of Gloucester, was supposed to become Regent, ruling on behalf of Edward's sons. But then he proclaimed himself King, thus denying the succession of his nephew, the young Edward V. The young princes, Edward and Richard, were put in the Tower of London and disappeared. It is not surprising that Richard has been widely held responsible for their deaths. Richard's seizure of the throne led to more disunity in the country, and his ruthless methods provoked more opposition. An unsuccessful rebellion by the Duke of Buckingham further weakened Richard's authority. It was at this point that Henry Tudor, until then a distant claimant living in exile in France, decided to invade – initially in support of Buckingham. However, after the defeat of that rebellion, he decided to seek to become king himself. Whereas Henry had been a distant claimant living in exile in France against the strong rule of Edward IV, now he had become a potential rival to the unpopular Richard III.

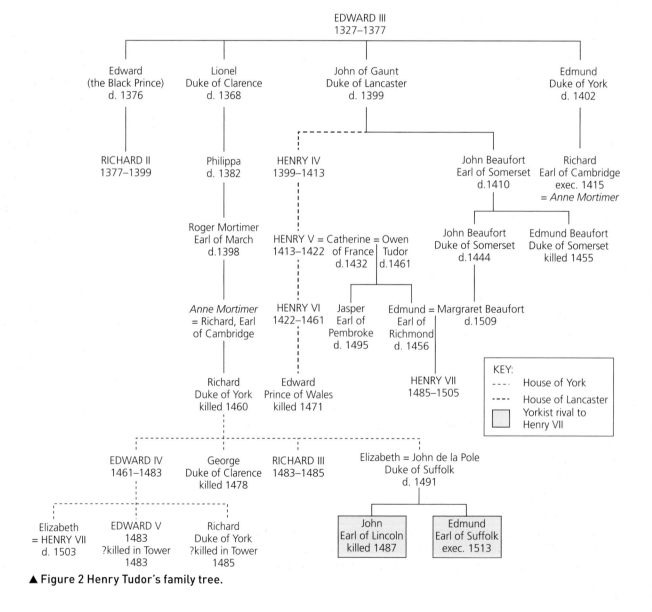

▲ Figure 2 Henry Tudor's family tree.

Henry had been living in Paris and quickly built up a following there with support from those who disliked Richard's rule, especially after Richard's son died, leaving no direct heir. Richard's wife had also died, and there were rumours that he intended to marry his niece, Elizabeth of York. By 1485 Henry had attracted several influential and experienced men to his cause. The Earl of Oxford, a loyal Lancastrian, and Jasper Tudor, his uncle, were both experienced soldiers. Others had experience of government. Henry was persuaded that it was the right time to attempt to seize the Crown.

Henry VII received financial support from the French King, Charles VIII. By providing this, he hoped to distract Richard III from offering assistance to the Duke of Brittany, thus allowing Charles to assimilate the territory as part of France.

Battle of Bosworth, August 1485

Henry set sail from France on 1 August 1485 with a small army of English supporters and French soldiers. They landed near Pembroke in Wales and marched north and then east towards the English border. He gained the support of Rhys ap Thomas, one of the most powerful landowners in Wales, by promising to make him the Lieutenant of Wales and thereby gained more soldiers. He gained more supporters still as he marched towards Shrewsbury and then further into the Midlands. Even then his forces could not match those of Richard III who was based at Nottingham Castle.

On the morning of 22 August 1485 the five thousand-strong army collected together by Henry Tudor, Earl of Richmond, met the royal army commanded by King Richard III in battle at Bosworth Field, near Leicester. The battle was fought in the area on and around a hill near the village of Bosworth. Richard III's forces had arrived first and had gained the better position. The King had put most of his archers, protected by foot soldiers, on the hillside from where they could fire down on Henry's advancing men. Richard himself led the cavalry. However, he had not been able to count on the loyalty of all of his commanders.

Crucially, Lord Thomas Stanley (Henry's stepfather) and his brother Sir William Stanley were positioned at the north of the battle site with 4,000 men. Both men were reluctant to support Richard, who had taken Thomas Stanley's son hostage to ensure their loyalty, but they were also afraid to support Henry openly in case he lost the battle and they were ruined along with him. For the time being, they stood off to one side, weighing up what was happening. The Earl of Northumberland was also at the battle, but he too had refused to take part until the outcome was clearer.

When the battle began, Henry's foot soldiers ran towards the hill while the royal forces fired arrows at them and Richard's cavalry cut into them from the sides. Henry's forces grouped together to defend themselves and in the midst of the confusion the Duke of Norfolk, one of Richard's commanders, was killed. At this point the two sides disengaged and Henry assessed the situation. He knew that it was only a matter of time before Richard's superior forces wore his men down, so he decided to approach the Stanleys to ask them to join him.

Richard saw what was happening and led his personal guard to attack Henry as he rode out to the Stanleys. Richard came very close to success: his men killed Henry's standard bearer and nearly reached Henry himself. However, at that moment Sir William Stanley decided to take action. He ordered his cavalry to attack Richard, who was caught completely by surprise. The King was thrown

What do we really know about the Battle of Bosworth Field?

Although it is one of the most famous battles fought on English soil, few accounts survive to tell historians for certain what happened. All are secondhand, written after the battle from stories heard at court or by foreign observers who collected information for other rulers. Unsurprisingly, then, the details of the battle vary significantly between accounts. The number of troops at Richard's disposal, for example, was put as high as 120,000 and as low as 10,000. Writers disagree about which **magnates** were present at the battle and about what they did. They even disagree about exactly where the battle was fought – at Bosworth, or closer to the market town of Dadlington, a mile and a half away. If you are interested in looking more closely at the evidence about the battle, the Richard III Society (a group dedicated to preserving his memory and setting the misleading Tudor propaganda about him to rights) has posted the documentary evidence on its website: www.richardiii.net.

Magnate – A term describing a member of the greater nobility – the barons – who owned large estates. The greater families had consolidated their holdings through marriage and family links, building up a significant territorial base where they effectively governed in the king's name.

ACTIVITY

1 What does the story of the Battle of Bosworth tell you about the fragile basis of Henry Tudor's authority?

2 Study Figure 2 (the Tudor family tree) on page 12. Find those who had a claim to the throne.

Richard III's body

The skeleton of Richard III was found in September 2012 underneath a car park in the centre of Leicester. The search had used old maps to locate the site of Grey Friars Church where Richard had been hastily buried in 1485.

By February 2013 there was conclusive proof that the skeleton was that of Richard III. The physical appearance reconstructed from the skeleton was similar to contemporary descriptions. The remains showed extensive injuries received in battle. The conclusive proof, however, was provided by DNA testing using a seventeenth-generation descendant living in Canada.

The city of Leicester had assumed that re-burial would take place there. However, there was a powerful lobby for this to happen in York as Richard III lived most of his life in York and in Yorkshire. A court decision in May 2014 agreed that the skeleton should stay in Leicester, and the re-interment ceremony took place in March 2015.

from his horse, but he ordered that another should be brought to him. Meanwhile, the Earl of Northumberland still remained off to the side of the battlefield, choosing not to protect his King.

Richard rejoined the fight, but was cut down and killed, the last English king to die in battle. Once their leader was dead, the royal forces broke up in confusion and fled.

According to the legend surrounding the battle, a soldier found Richard III's golden crown in a thorn bush near where the King had fallen. He brought it to Thomas Stanley who placed it on Henry's head, crowning him 'Henry VII, King of England' amid the fallen bodies and blood. Now that the 28-year-old Earl of Richmond had seized the crown, the Tudor family replaced the House of York as the ruling dynasty in England and Wales.

Accession of Henry VII

Taking the crown from Richard did not end the difficulties facing Henry VII. Keeping it on his own head was likely to prove extremely challenging, and the omens were not good. As the story of Henry's early life shows, English politics in the later fifteenth century had been dominated by the struggle between the rival families of Lancaster and York for the throne. In the midst of their battles, which had been fought on and off since 1455, the status and authority of the monarchy had suffered.

Henry's seizure of the crown in 1485 could be seen by contemporaries as just another example of the instability of the times, similar to the actions of Edward IV in 1461 or Richard III in 1483, rather than the point at which the monarchy became more stable. Henry's own claim to the throne was weak. Although he had won the crown by right of conquest this was not sufficient to guarantee him loyalty across the kingdom unless he could enforce it further.

Although Richard and his nephews in the Tower were dead, the House of York lived on through the de la Pole brothers. Edward IV's sister, Elizabeth, had married John de la Pole, Duke of Suffolk. Their two sons, John (Earl of Lincoln) and Edmund (Earl of Suffolk) had a claim to the crown at least as valid as Henry's own.

Another threat to Henry VII was from Margaret of Burgundy. She was Edward IV's mother, and had married the Duke of Burgundy. Burgundy was a powerful dukedom in what is now part of the Netherlands and France, and an important trading partner with England. Margaret, with the help of her husband, the Duke, quickly showed support for the Yorkists against Henry at various times during his reign.

Nonetheless, Henry possessed some advantages. Although the disputes between the Lancastrians and Yorkists had encouraged lawlessness and crime, their wars also meant that members of the greater nobility were engaged in mutual destruction. The death of many noble heirs had allowed their lands to be returned to the Crown, while the misfortune of being on the losing side had allowed others to be punished and disinherited as traitors. Those beneath the warring great houses – the gentry, merchants and landowning farmers – were tired of the disruption that a generation of sudden changes in political power had brought and were ready to support the recovery of royal power as the best means of restoring order and prosperity.

Henry also had some personal advantages. He was an adult and had recently proven himself both as a leader and as a successful soldier (even if his victory in 1485 was not entirely due to him!). These were admirable qualities and were likely to lessen opposition to his claim to the Crown. He was an only child, with no fear of the family rivalry that had shaped events when Edward IV had died. His obscure Welsh origins and years of exile in France also helped because they meant that he had few personal enemies in high places.

While none of these factors was sufficient on its own to guarantee success, they provided Henry with the opportunity to build on the power that he had won, if he had the political skill to take it. His objectives were therefore clear:

- To establish and secure his right to the throne.
- To strengthen royal government by better control of the nobility.
- To strengthen the monarchy and the kingdom for the future by ensuring a strong financial foundation.

The following sections consider how Henry pursued these objectives and examine how successfully he did so. And once he had consolidated his power, Henry needed to ensure that threats to his power were decisively removed.

Henry VII establishes his right to the throne

After the Battle of Bosworth Field, Henry moved quickly to legitimise his claims by being officially crowned as king and by marrying Elizabeth of York. The coronation of a monarch was more than simply a public ceremony to confirm his or her power; it signified the approval of the Church and, through this, of God himself. In feudal law the coronation required the nobility to swear an oath of loyalty to the king, which could not be broken, and since Anglo-Saxon times the ceremony had conferred a divine status that defined rebellion as a sin against God as well as a crime against the State. The speed of Henry's coronation was therefore a safety measure as well as a symbol that he claimed the crown as a legitimate heir, not just through battle. He made sure that the ceremony took place a week before Parliament met, so that no one could say later that Parliament had helped to make him King.

He was also careful to ensure that his coronation in October 1485 came before his marriage in January 1486, so that no one could say that he had gained the throne through his wife. The marriage, however, was an essential part of his strategy to win support. Elizabeth was the daughter of Edward IV so the union symbolised the reconciliation between the families of Lancaster and York. Elizabeth soon gave birth to a son, Prince Arthur, in September 1486. This helped to establish a future for the new Tudor dynasty, creating a greater sense of permanence about the change that had taken place in 1485.

To cement his power further, Henry summoned Parliament (the traditional act of a new king) in November 1485 and embarked on a royal progress to the north in April 1486. The progress was essentially a tour of the kingdom by the monarch and his court. During the progress it was traditional for the king to hear petitions and cases and to grant justice and favours. In this way, he could demonstrate his royal power and presence to his subjects.

Henry displayed the same kind of tactical and political awareness in his handling of the nobility after his victory. His supporters were well rewarded. John de Vere, who had joined him in France, became Earl of Oxford. Lord Stanley was honoured for deserting Richard at Bosworth with the title Earl of Derby, and the hand of Henry's mother in marriage. This gave Henry two loyal supporters in the east Midlands and the north-west. His uncle, Jasper Tudor (now Duke of Bedford) represented royal authority in Wales. Other supporters were rewarded with high office. Sir William Stanley became Lord Chamberlain. John Morton (see page 16) became Lord Chancellor from 1486 to 1500 and later Archbishop of Canterbury and a cardinal. Henry's ability to attract and

LOOK AGAIN

Look at the six key questions on page viii. Note how Henry VII's objectives are directly linked to aspects of key questions 1 and 2, with clear implications for the others.

Cardinal – One of the senior officials of the Catholic Church, having the right to vote in the election of a Pope. Cardinals were appointed by the Pope, usually with the approval of the monarch. In return for wealth, status and the protection of its privileges, the Church provided monarchs with an educated force of trained administrators and a cheap way of rewarding those who served them well.

maintain the loyalty of talented men such as these, and his willingness to reward them with recognition and power, were key elements in the stability of his government.

Henry's handling of his opponents was also carefully balanced. He dated his reign from 21 August, the day before the battle at Bosworth, which allowed him to treat Richard's supporters as traitors. He imprisoned Yorkists with a better claim to the throne than his own, such as the young Earl of Warwick, in the Tower of London and left them there. Nobles whose loyalty was suspect were stripped of their lands and titles, but Henry was shrewd enough to realise that by showing leniency he would win at least the gratitude, and possibly the loyalty, of key families.

John Morton (1420–1500)

Morton was born in 1420 and supported the Lancastrians until disaster befell Henry VI at the Battle of Tewkesbury in 1471. He then shrewdly switched sides and became a strong ally of Edward IV. He joined the Royal Council in 1473 and was appointed Bishop of Ely in 1479. However, when Richard III seized the throne Morton was one of the men who resisted him. His activities during Richard's reign marked him out as a true friend of Henry Tudor. He warned Henry of Richard's attempt to arrest and remove him from Brittany in 1485, giving the future king time to escape to the French court. He also voiced his criticism of Richard's government and solicited support for Henry from discontented Yorkist nobles.

Morton was 65 when Henry took the throne – nearly 40 years older than the King. Despite the age difference, Henry regarded him as a close friend and ally. He appointed Morton as Lord Chancellor (the closest post to being Chief Minister at the time) and in 1486 he became Archbishop of Canterbury, the most senior religious office in England and Wales. In 1493 the Pope made him a cardinal.

Morton was an effective servant of the Crown, showing his strengths, particularly in financial matters. He was active in encouraging the nobility to offer 'loans' to the Crown and gained a reputation for not taking 'no' for an answer. One story about him concerns the tactic he used to force everyone to hand over money – nicknamed 'Morton's Fork'. The 'fork' was a dilemma that he exploited – if a nobleman appeared rich because he was dressed expensively, Morton argued that he was well-off enough to make a loan to his master. If he appeared to be poorer and struggling, Morton argued that this was because he was hoarding his money like a miser, so he could still afford to make a loan. Either way, the nobleman could not escape.

Henry VII's character

Henry VII's character was moulded by his upbringing. He was astute and clear-thinking, but not sentimental. He was respected, but not popular. Read what Sources E and F say about him.

Source E From the *Books of English History (Anglicae Historicae Libri)* by Polydore Vergil (1534). Vergil was an Italian diplomat who came to England in 1502 and was commissioned by Henry to write a history of England. His account of Henry's character is believed to be among the most reliable because Vergil knew Henry personally; quoted in *Henry VII* by R. Lockyer (1983).

Henry reigned 23 years and 7 months. He lived 52 years. By his wife Elizabeth he had 8 children. He was distinguished, wise and prudent in character; and his spirit was so brave and resolute that never, even in moments of greatest danger, did it desert him. In government, he was shrewd and far-seeing, so that none dared to get the better of him by deceit or sharp practice. To those of his subjects who did not do him due honour, he was hard and harsh. He knew well how to maintain his royal dignity and everything belonging to it. He was successful in war, although by nature he preferred peace to war. Above all else, he cherished justice.

Source F *History of the Reign of King Henry VII* by Francis Bacon, written in 1622.

He was of a high mind and loved his own way. Had he been a private man he would have been termed 'proud'; but in a wise prince it was but keeping of distance, which he did towards all, not admitting any near or full approach, neither to his power nor to his secrets. For he was governed by none.

In Bacon's character sketch of Henry VII, Source F, written well over a century after his death, the writer creates the impression of a strong king who projected an aura of majesty. According to Bacon, Henry seems to set himself apart from other men and to keep power jealously to himself. Like most writers of the time, Bacon was presenting Henry according to the 'Tudor myth', a rewriting of history by Tudor monarchs to strengthen their authority and undermine challengers. In fact, Bacon had just been dismissed from King James I's service on allegations of fraud and wrote his history of the reign of Henry VII in the hope of currying favour with his royal master.

The reality of Henry VII's reign was less glamorous. He came to the throne, as we have seen, by killing his rival and snatching the crown, and he went on to rule efficiently, but with a constant fear that the same thing might one day happen to him. Historians have taken different views of his character and the scale of his achievements. You can revisit this at the end of the chapter when looking back over all the different aspects of his reign.

> What are the points of agreement between the two accounts of Henry's style of kingship in Source E and Source F?

Strengthening royal government

How did Henry VII build up his control over the country?

If Henry and his family were to achieve genuine security he would need to defeat rivals and pretenders (see pages 24–26). It was also essential to strengthen the power and effectiveness of the monarchy as an institution so that he could build the support and resources needed to ward off any further shocks. Once again, this would not be an easy task.

Problems facing Henry VII in England

Government by 1485 was well organised, but had come perilously close to collapse on a number of occasions during the fifteenth century. Because of this, the actual authority that it had over the people of England – and, more importantly, the nobility – was questionable. The particular problems facing Henry were:

1 Nobles whose wealth and territorial power made them potential rivals to the Crown.
2 The uneven control that the Crown had over the kingdom: stronger in the more populated areas of the south and east, but looser in the borderlands, especially with the lack of a developed system of local administration.
3 The poor finances of the Crown, which had been depleted by wars at home and abroad.

Henry had no master plan to tackle these problems. His solutions, which are examined below, were often reactions to situations as they arose. However, Henry was determined to manage government by himself (look back at Francis Bacon's comment about his style of kingship above) rather than to delegate too much power to advisers. His natural suspicion and anxieties about rivals forced him to act firmly, and, on occasion, to take harsh measures. This gave Henry a poor reputation. A visitor to England from Florence summed this up well when he said that Henry was 'more feared than loved'.

> **NOTE-MAKING**
>
> Using pages 11–26 make notes on how Henry VII attempted to strengthen his position on the throne in relation to the nobles and the government of the country. Try dividing your page into two columns and put the methods used in the left-hand column and some brief details in support on the right.

The nobility

Henry's biggest challenge was to win the support of the nobles, while at the same time making sure that their power and arrogance were controlled. There were two obvious lines that he could take with them: either to buy their support by rewarding them with lands and titles, or to force them to support him by showing them the unwelcome consequences of opposition. Although Henry used the first approach on occasion, he was more inclined to the second.

Henry's relationship with his leading nobles was critical to his survival as King. He depended on them to maintain law and order in the areas where they held land and estates. However, the nobility had grown powerful during the fifteenth century, gaining more lands at the expense of the Crown. Their large estates generated income from rents and leases, which some had used to build impressive strongholds and to recruit and retain private armies. Henry was fortunate in 1485 that his victory had been so decisive and that a series of deaths in the 1480s meant that key families, such as the houses of Warwick, Northumberland and Buckingham, were now headed by children.

Henry VII used a number of different policies to reduce his reliance on the nobility and to limit their power, as described below. The nobility depended upon three factors – land, wealth and support – to maintain their independence from the King. Henry reduced all three during his reign, while being careful not to push them into open rebellion.

a) Attainders

From the start of his reign Henry used attainders to seize the titles and possessions of nobles he suspected of disloyalty. Attainders were special laws passed by Parliament which allowed someone to be declared guilty of treason without going through the process of a trial. Henry asked his first Parliament to issue attainders against men who had opposed him at the Battle of Bosworth, and resorted to using them periodically during his reign. As with other policies, Henry was often prepared to reverse an attainder and restore lands and titles if he thought that would secure the gratitude and future loyalty of the victim. During his reign 138 attainders were passed, of which 46 were reversed. However, a more detailed breakdown shows an increasing severity as the reign progressed, suggesting insecurity and paranoia right to the end of his reign. 51 of the attainders were passed in the years 1504–09. Severity was also a feature on many occasions when an attainder was reversed, especially from those below noble rank, with payment demanded as the price. Sir Thomas Tyrell had to pay £1,738 for the reversal of his and his father's attainders.

b) Patronage

Patronage – The monarch granting special favours, such as land or positions at court, to groups of people in order to retain their support. The term can also be used for the actions of local nobles who showed favours to people in their locality.

Henry largely abandoned Edward IV's policy of distributing lands to loyal followers. There were some grants at the beginning of the reign, but Henry was concerned not to create a new group of nobles who could rise to become a potential threat. The result of his caution was that the number of people who could be described as nobles fell by about one-quarter during his reign through deaths and attainders. Vacant lands were absorbed into Henry's personal domains, making him by far the largest landowner in the country. Often, when Henry needed royal agents in local communities, he looked to men lower down the social scale who did not have extensive lands in the area. These men were therefore dependent on him for the position and status they held and were not distracted by competing loyalties.

c) Attacks on retaining

Retaining was the practice by which a nobleman kept a large number of men as his personal staff, in theory to be used as household servants, but in practice as gangs of enforcers. Retainers could be used to put pressure on tenants who were slow in paying their rent, or on juries to return the verdict their master wanted. Henry, like Edward IV before him, rightly regarded them as a lawless element. New laws were passed in 1485 and 1504 against illegal retaining. In the 1485 Parliament, Lords and Commons had to swear that they would not retain illegally. The 1504 Act required nobles to obtain a special licence from the King before they could retain large numbers of men, and imposed severe fines if they did not. The penalty was £5 per month per illegal retainer. The ideas behind the law were sound, but the problem had gone on for too long to be settled so easily. Nobles found ways to avoid getting a licence, for example by covering up records of the wages they paid to servants, so that no one knew exactly how many men were being retained.

d) Financial controls

Another of Henry's devices was to demand a financial bond from individual nobles or their families. This would place the noble in debt to the Crown, so that he would remain loyal in future. In effect, Henry forced nobles to agree to behave themselves or face a ruinous fine. It was a widely used policy – in Henry's last decade as King about two-thirds of the nobility were held under bonds.

The most extreme example was Lord Burgavenny. He was convicted in 1507 of illegally retaining 471 men and fined £70,000. Henry knew that paying this amount would bankrupt the lord, so he generously agreed to place him under a bond to repay £5,000 over ten years. The conditions attached to this included an instruction that Burgavenny should not set foot on his family lands in the south-east until the debt was settled. In this way, Henry both raised money from someone he did not trust and obliged him to keep in the King's favour or risk ruin. To enforce these rights, Henry established the Council Learned in Law to act as a royal debt collector.

> **The Council Learned in Law** – An offshoot from the main Royal Council which dealt initially with managing and pursuing the King's feudal rights, but soon assumed control of all financial matters relating to Crown lands. All the members of the Council had legal training (hence the name) and acted both as investigators and judges in cases where there was suspicion that a nobleman was not paying his proper dues to the King. As a result, the Council and its leading figures – Sir Reginald Bray to 1503, then Edmund Dudley and Richard Empson – were universally hated and feared.

Local and regional government

Effective government depended on having a reliable network of officials throughout the country to carry out the King's laws. Particular parts of the country, especially those most distant from London, were notoriously difficult to control except by relying on the presence of the local nobility. Elsewhere, in the more settled regions, earlier kings had built up the numbers and powers of Justices of the Peace (JPs). These JPs were appointed annually from among the local landowners, several per county. They were responsible for public order, making sure that laws were implemented and dispensing justice to criminals brought before them. Four times a year they met at the Quarter Sessions so that they could try those accused of more serious crimes – all except treason, which was left to the Crown.

Since royal control over the kingdom was so uneven from place to place, Henry did not attempt to create one system of local government but relied instead on the most appropriate solution for each region, as Figure 3 on page 20 illustrates.

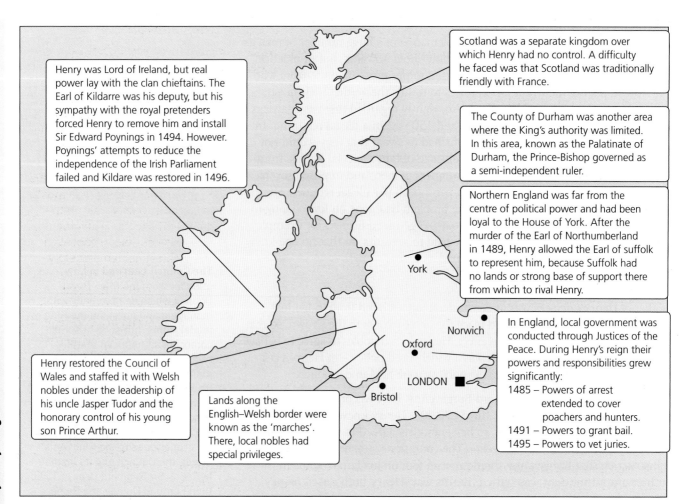

Henry was Lord of Ireland, but real power lay with the clan chieftains. The Earl of Kildarre was his deputy, but his sympathy with the royal pretenders forced Henry to remove him and install Sir Edward Poynings in 1494. However. Poynings' attempts to reduce the independence of the Irish Parliament failed and Kildare was restored in 1496.

Scotland was a separate kingdom over which Henry had no control. A difficulty he faced was that Scotland was traditionally friendly with France.

The County of Durham was another area where the King's authority was limited. In this area, known as the Palatinate of Durham, the Prince-Bishop governed as a semi-independent ruler.

Northern England was far from the centre of political power and had been loyal to the House of York. After the murder of the Earl of Northumberland in 1489, Henry allowed the Earl of suffolk to represent him, because Suffolk had no lands or strong base of support there from which to rival Henry.

In England, local government was conducted through Justices of the Peace. During Henry's reign their powers and responsibilities grew significantly:
1485 – Powers of arrest extended to cover poachers and hunters.
1491 – Powers to grant bail.
1495 – Powers to vet juries.

Henry restored the Council of Wales and staffed it with Welsh nobles under the leadership of his uncle Jasper Tudor and the honorary control of his young son Prince Arthur.

Lands along the English–Welsh border were known as the 'marches'. There, local nobles had special privileges.

York

Norwich

Oxford

LONDON ■

Bristol

▲ Figure 3 Local and regional government in England and Wales under Henry VII.

Figure 4 Parliamentary meetings under Henry VII.

Year(s)	Approximate length of session
1485–86	3 months
1487	1 month
1489	1.5 months
1491	0.5 month
1495	2 months
1497	2 months
1504	2.5 months

1 Look at Figure 4. In what proportion of Henry VII's reign was Parliament actually meeting?

2 How does this support the information in the section on National government?

National government

Fifteenth-century government was, in effect, personal government by the King and his advisers at court. Parliament existed but had a minor role in political life – mainly to pass laws that the King wanted and to vote him additional taxes. Parliament met infrequently and usually not for more than a few weeks or months at a time. For most of the time, the King ruled directly through decrees and proclamations. Henry kept things this way. He used Parliament sparingly, usually during his first decade as King to support him in controversial policies such as limitations on the traditional privileges of the nobility or new financial demands on his subjects, but he usually ignored it.

Henry had a clear purpose in the way in which he used Parliament once he had been crowned. His assumption – not challenged by Parliament – was that all power derived from the monarch. Parliaments were called to serve the interests of the monarch and keep his subjects under control, often by Acts of Attainder. Therefore there was no chance of Parliaments ceasing to exist, but they met on the monarch's terms.

Of more importance to Henry were the committees and law courts within his government. Chief among these was the Royal Council. It was the place where Henry gathered together his most trusted supporters to give him advice and to take on some of the tasks of day-to-day management of the kingdom. Although records from Henry's reign list 227 men as members of the council, in practice regular membership was much smaller and included John Morton and Reginald Bray.

How did Henry improve the administration of his finances?

The Royal Council met when the King needed it and there were no written rules governing its procedure. During Henry's reign the key development was the emergence of committees of the council to deal with specific matters of policy. As we have already seen, the Council Learned in Law and the Star Chamber were two such committees.

Henry VII has gained a reputation for having a keen financial mind, so historians have tended to look at his policies in this area with special interest. By the end of his reign he had ensured that the Crown had built up enough annual income to meet its commitments, and that money was carefully accounted for. In part, Henry achieved this by taking a more direct personal interest in the state of national finances. At the beginning of his reign when Henry was inexperienced, he allowed departments of state such as the Treasury and the Exchequer to take control, but they were clumsy and inefficient. From 1487 onwards Henry quickly followed Edward IV's example by dealing with the administration of finance from his private rooms in the palace – the Chamber and Privy Chamber. This Chamber system became, as it had been in Edward IV's reign, the most important institution of financial administration. He also established a new post of Surveyor of the King's Wards to investigate cases of money owed to him from wardships (see Figure 5, page 22) and a Court of Audit to monitor government spending. As well as these institutional reforms, Henry also improved and developed the sources of his income.

Henry's financial policies were cautious and realistic. He understood that foreign wars had been the single biggest reason for the poverty of earlier kings, so he largely avoided conducting an aggressive foreign policy. He exploited his legal rights to claim special payments from his nobles, both to swell his treasury and to remind them of his control over them, but he was also prepared to overlook or to reverse his claims when it was necessary to win support.

To some writers, Henry was a miser, obsessed with hoarding more and more money from every source he could find. There is some truth in this, especially in the final decade of his reign. However, Henry always spent money extravagantly when it was necessary to enhance the image of his kingship. Henry's reputation for being greedy was begun by the contemporary writer, Polydore Vergil, who wrote that people:

'considered they were suffering not on account of their own sins but on account of the greed of their monarch'.

Star Chamber

Historians have debated the importance of this court of law in Henry's methods of controlling his leading subjects. It was created by the Star Chamber Act in 1487 and was responsible for prosecuting anyone who behaved in a rebellious or lawless manner. Members of the Royal Council – the King's most favoured advisers – sat on the court to make these judgments, so it was possible to haul even the greatest nobleman before it. It also came to be used as a Court of Appeal. Its exact importance in Henry VII's reign is unclear owing to a shortage of relevant records. Some writers argue that Henry made little use of Star Chamber during his reign, preferring instead to control unruly subjects by financial and other means. What is certain is that it became much more developed in its organisation and use under Wolsey.

In fact, for most of his reign, Henry's methods of accumulating wealth were quite normal – just very efficiently carried out. It was in the last few years, after the deaths of his son Arthur (in 1502) and his wife Elizabeth (in 1503), that he appears to have become obsessed with accumulating money. How far was this because he feared that the succession was not yet secure, and he wanted to end his reign with a lavish display of affluence at Court in order to make the Tudors appear even more powerful? His income was nearly 20 times greater than that of his wealthiest noble. However, Professor J. R. Lander who has researched the subject suggests that Henry's income in real terms was probably only roughly what the monarch's income had been a century before. What Henry VII gained each year (about £113,000) was certainly a lot less than the £800,000 the King of France had at his disposal.

Figure 5 Sources of royal income under Henry VII.

Source of income	Organisation/administration	Improvements/developments under Henry VII
Ordinary revenue		
Crown lands – Henry inherited all the lands held by the Houses of York and Lancaster, the Earldoms of Richmond and Warwick, the Duchy of Lancaster and the Principality of Wales. These were further increased by attainders (51 in one Parliament alone) and *escheats* – the reversion of land to the King if a tenant died without an heir.	Edward IV had improved the administration of Crown lands by introducing techniques of estate management. Sir Reginald Bray developed these further and applied them to other lands. Henry was less inclined to grant lands to friends and family than Edward. He preferred to hold on to them to maximise both his influence and his income from leases and rents.	In 1486 Henry used the Act of Resumption to reclaim all Crown lands that had been granted away since the start of the Wars of the Roses, but he did not always act on these claims. The potential threat to a noble family could be more useful to control them than actually pressing the demand for return of the land to the King.
Feudal dues – traditional rights held by the Crown to demand money, deriving from the principle that the King was the sole owner of all the kingdom's land and that others held it as his tenants.	The main types of payments that the King could demand from the nobility were: **Relief** – paid by an heir when he received his inheritance. **Marriage** – the King's right to arrange marriages of the daughters of tenants at a profit. **Wardship** – control of the estates of heirs under adult age, which allowed the King to manage these lands for his own profit. **Livery** – payment made by a ward on reaching adulthood and taking control of his lands.	Henry exploited feudal payments for both financial and political purposes. He used them to ensure good behaviour, but also benefited from wardships in certain powerful families, for example when the Earl of Northumberland was killed in 1489, leaving a ten-year-old son. Henry also improved the management of these revenues. For example, he appointed a Master of the King's Wards (Sir John Hussey) in 1503 to administer wardships. In 1487 his income from wardship and marriages was £350; by 1507 it had risen to £6,000 per year.
Customs duties – paid on goods entering or leaving the country. By the fifteenth century it was traditional practice for Parliament to grant these revenues to a monarch for life.	Money came mainly from tunnage (taxes on exports) and poundage (taxes on imports), particularly on the sale of wool, wine and leather. Both Edward and Henry tried to promote trade to maximise this type of income, and to close loopholes.	Henry largely continued the work and methods of Edward. He introduced certificates for coastal trade and twice updated the Book of Rates, which set out the charges on imports and exports of a wide range of items. Customs duties rose from about £33,000 per year at the beginning of his reign to about £40,000 at the end.
Legal dues – money from fines and other payments made by people appearing before the King's courts.	Payments came from both common law courts and the special courts operated by the Royal Council.	Henry increased the use of fines and attainders. These could be very lucrative sources of income – the attainder of Sir William Stanley in 1495 brought an immediate payment of £9,000 and £1,000 per year thereafter.

Source of income	Organisation/administration	Improvements/developments under Henry VII
Extraordinary revenue		
Bonds and recognisances – payments made as a guarantee of good behaviour (see page 19).	Demanded from those whose loyalty was suspect, such as Yorkist supporters. Also applied to merchants who owed customs duties.	Used by Henry for both political and financial purposes. Payments could be substantial – the Earl of Westmorland had to pay £10,000 after the Battle of Bosworth – but it was also an effective way of maintaining control. Henry used a special government court – the Council Learned in Law – to enforce payment of these debts.
Loans and benevolences – the King's right to ask for financial help in particular emergencies.	Organised by the Royal Council, loans could be requested from both individuals and institutions, such as town corporations.	The Council Learned in Law was also used to enforce these payments. This was an irregular source of income, raised as and when the King needed funds. In 1491, £48,000 was raised for war in Brittany, of which £9000 was contributed by the City of London.
Feudal dues – based on the same claims as in ordinary revenue, but related to single, extraordinary occasions.	The King was entitled to gifts for special occasions, such as when one of his sons was knighted or when a daughter married. Gifts were paid by leading nobles, but Parliament was also expected to make a grant on behalf of the people it represented.	Henry exploited this source of income fully – for example, he received £30,000 from Parliament in 1504 for the knighthood of Prince Arthur (who had died in 1502). He also increased his demands for payments from nobles who had tried to save money by being 'in distraint of knighthood', i.e. who had chosen not to take on the expense of becoming a knight.
Clerical taxes – special taxes which the King could levy on the Church.	The clergy were exempt from paying taxes to Parliament, so this form of taxation was the only way of securing money from the Church. It usually came in the form of a voluntary 'gift'.	Gifts from the Church were similar in amount to those received by earlier rulers. Henry used his right to appoint leading churchmen to raise money by selling offices – he raised £300 for the post of Archdeacon of Buckingham for example. This practice, called 'simony', was forbidden by the Church but widely practised.
Parliamentary taxes – special grants of taxes by Parliament to finance royal policies such as military action in Europe or Scotland.	Usually voted in the form of 'tenths' or 'fifteenths', taxes on the value of moveable property. Henry also tried a form of direct taxation, not unlike income tax, but it was widely resented and soon abandoned.	Parliamentary taxes were available when needed, but they were often unpopular, and triggered two rebellions in Henry's reign (in Yorkshire in 1489 and Cornwall in 1497). He avoided parliamentary taxes as much as possible.

KEY DATES: STRENGTHENING ROYAL GOVERNMENT

1455 Start of the Wars of the Roses

1483 Death of Edward IV; Richard III seized the crown

1485 Battle of Bosworth; accession of Henry VII; coronation; Act against illegal retaining by nobles

1486 Marriage of Henry to Elizabeth of York; Act of Resumption (reclaiming Crown lands lost since 1455)

1487 Star Chamber Act

3 Removing threats to Henry's power

Henry VII was always aware of the circumstances by which he had gained the throne. Therefore, rebellions and potential rebellions were treated very seriously.

Rebellions against Henry VII

What threats to his right to rule did Henry face between 1485 and 1500, and how did he deal with them?

The events of this section run parallel with the previous section on how Henry consolidated his power. The threats were most serious in the first few years, but he could never be fully secure even in the last few years of his reign, when he was more concerned about the succession.

It is very easy to believe that, because Henry survived as King, the threats to him were more imaginary than real. This section seeks to assess how real the threats were from a variety of directions.

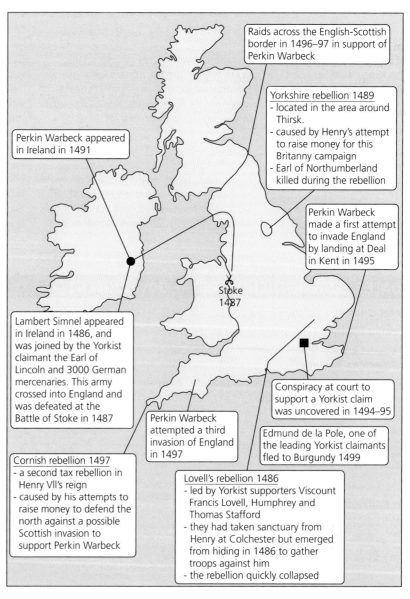

Raids across the English-Scottish border in 1496–97 in support of Perkin Warbeck

Yorkshire rebellion 1489
- located in the area around Thirsk.
- caused by Henry's attempt to raise money for this Britanny campaign
- Earl of Northumberland killed during the rebellion

Perkin Warbeck appeared in Ireland in 1491

Perkin Warbeck made a first attempt to invade England by landing at Deal in Kent in 1495

Stoke 1487

Lambert Simnel appeared in Ireland in 1486, and was joined by the Yorkist claimant the Earl of Lincoln and 3000 German mercenaries. This army crossed into England and was defeated at the Battle of Stoke in 1487

Perkin Warbeck attempted a third invasion of England in 1497

Conspiracy at court to support a Yorkist claim was uncovered in 1494–95

Cornish rebellion 1497
- a second tax rebellion in Henry VII's reign
- caused by his attempts to raise money to defend the north against a possible Scottish invasion to support Perkin Warbeck

Edmund de la Pole, one of the leading Yorkist claimants fled to Burgundy 1499

Lovell's rebellion 1486
- led by Yorkist supporters Viscount Francis Lovell, Humphrey and Thomas Stafford
- they had taken sanctuary from Henry at Colchester but emerged from hiding in 1486 to gather troops against him
- the rebellion quickly collapsed

▶ Figure 6 England and Ireland, showing the location and events of the rebellions of 1486–99.

Henry had grown up in uncertain times and had been isolated from the people he now depended on to help him govern the country. He was king only by virtue of conquest; others lived with a better right to be monarch than he. There was no doubt that he had enemies and that they were waiting to strike.

Although Henry worked hard during his first years as King to establish his claim to rule, he still faced opposition from the remnants of the House of York and its supporters. Figure 6 on page 24 shows the different threats to Henry's Crown before 1500. Between 1486 and 1499 his political enemies at home (the Yorkist de la Pole family) and abroad (Edward IV's sister, Margaret of Burgundy) remained a serious danger to Henry. There was also discontent within some regions of the country at the financial demands the King was making, provoking rebellions at inconvenient times.

The main threat that his enemies posed came from their support for 'pretenders' to the Crown – boys who were set up either as one of Edward IV's sons (who had been murdered in 1483, but whose bodies had never been revealed to the public) or as the imprisoned Earl of Warwick. These pretenders challenged Henry's claim to the throne and attracted dissatisfied nobles and foreign rulers wanting to undermine or be rid of him altogether.

Although neither Lambert Simnel (see below) nor Perkin Warbeck (see page 26) was a genuine contender for the throne, they posed a real threat because they were used by the Yorkists to question Henry's right to rule and to draw loyalty away from him at a time when he was still new to kingship. The weakness of his claim to the throne and the recent history of sudden changes of monarch made Henry vulnerable to attack; a victorious rival would soon have been able to justify seizing the throne from someone who had, himself, come to it through battle. Henry's marriage to Elizabeth of York and the birth of an heir had divided Yorkist loyalties, but widows could be remarried and baby princes controlled by their guardians.

On balance, the only effective obstacles to Yorkist success in the early years of Henry's reign were a certain war-weariness that favoured the occupant of the throne, and the skills and abilities exercised by Henry himself. Fortunately for Henry, his skills were up to the task. He placed key Yorkists under arrest and used spies and informers to keep track of what his more distant enemies, like

Lambert Simnel (1475?–1525)

Lambert Simnel was born in Oxford, where at the age of ten or eleven his marked resemblance to the younger son of Edward IV was spotted by his teacher, a priest named Richard Symonds. Symonds taught Simnel to claim that he was Richard, Duke of York, and took him to Ireland, which had become a centre of Yorkist support. There, Symonds seems to have decided that it would be more effective to pass Simnel off as the young Earl of Warwick (who was in the Tower of London at the time), and with the help of Yorkist lords like the Earl of Kildare, Simnel was proclaimed King Edward VI.

This plot was amateurish at best, because Henry immediately produced the real Earl of Warwick to demonstrate the falseness of Simnel's claims. What made it more dangerous was the support offered by Margaret of Burgundy in the form of 2,000 soldiers, and the flight of John de la Pole, the Earl of Lincoln, to join the rebels. Lincoln must have known that Simnel was an impostor and may have intended to use him to further his own claims.

Simnel's arrival in Ireland in the company of the soldiers was the signal for the start of an invasion of England in May 1487. They landed at Furness in Lancashire and marched across the Pennines before turning south, but raised little support in the north, which had only recently seen the fighting of the Wars of the Roses. Henry met them with his army at East Stoke, just outside Newark, and the rebels were defeated in what historians have termed the last battle of the Wars of the Roses. Lincoln and several Yorkist leaders were killed, and Henry showed his ability to judge the nature of his enemies by sparing Simnel and offering him work in the royal kitchens. Symonds was also arrested, but escaped death because of his status as a priest. Henry's real enemies – Kildare, Margaret and the other Yorkists – lived to fight another day.

KEY DATES: REBELLIONS AGAINST HENRY VII

1486 Lovell rebellion, by supporters of the House of York

1487 Simnel rebellion and the Battle of Stoke; tax rises

1489 Yorkshire rebellion against tax rises

1491 First appearance of Perkin Warbeck

1495 Warbeck landed at Deal in Kent

1496–97 Warbeck raided northern England from Scotland

1497 Cornish rebellion against high taxes

1498 Warbeck imprisoned in the Tower

1499 Warbeck and the Earl of Warwick executed

1502 Edmund de la Pole (Earl of Suffolk) fled to the Netherlands, but was returned

1513 Earl of Suffolk executed by Henry VIII

the Earl of Kildare, were doing. Once the Simnel rebellion had been defeated at Stoke in June 1487 he made an important gesture towards the Yorkists by having Elizabeth crowned Queen in November. It is noticeable that when Warbeck appeared, his support was principally from outside England and his two attempts to invade both failed miserably. By isolating Warbeck through agreements with his fellow European rulers, Henry gradually cut off the support he was receiving. At the same time, he was prepared to be generous to Warbeck himself until the young man betrayed his trust. A more cynical view is that Henry was in sufficient control of the situation to use the Warbeck crisis both to root out potential enemies at court in the purge of 1495 and to provide the excuse finally to get rid of the Earl of Warwick in 1499.

The other major source of a threat to Henry after the death of Warwick was Edmund de la Pole, Earl of Suffolk. After a short period of Suffolk appearing to accept Henry's rule, he fled to the court of the Holy Roman Emperor (see page 28), Maximilian, in 1501. It was not surprising that Henry perceived him as a major Yorkist threat, especially when, from 1502 onwards, the future Henry VIII was Henry's own male heir. Some of Suffolk's relatives were imprisoned and when Parliament met in 1504 some were attainted. There were rumours of Suffolk plotting either to overthrow Henry or to alter the succession. Fortunately for Henry, diplomatic manoeuvres allowed him to gain possession of Suffolk on condition that he would not be killed. He was put in the Tower – where he remained until he was executed in Henry VIII's reign in 1513. Thus Henry could not have felt really secure from Yorkist threats until the last two years of his reign – and even then a peaceful succession depended largely on the teenage Henry.

Perkin Warbeck (1474?–99)

Perkin Warbeck first appeared as a threat to Henry in Ireland in 1491. Aged seventeen at the time, he was employed as a servant but claimed that he was Richard of York, the youngest son of Edward IV. Warbeck later admitted that his real name was John Osbeck and that he was born in Tournai and educated in Antwerp. His Burgundian origins and his appearance in Ireland suggest that the instigators of Simnel's rebellion, particularly Margaret of Burgundy and the Earl of Kildare, were involved at an early stage, but it was Charles VIII of France who first recognised his claims and welcomed him at Court in Paris. Charles was probably using Warbeck to embarrass Henry and to divert him while he attempted to annex Brittany (see pages 28–29).

In 1492, Charles made peace with Henry so Warbeck was forced to move on to Burgundy, where he was welcomed by Margaret and her son-in-law, the Holy Roman Emperor Maximilian I. However, Maximilian was too busy with affairs in Italy to offer much immediate support. This gave Henry breathing space to deal with the English end of the conspiracy. A number of leading figures, including Sir William Stanley, were accused and executed for treason in

1495. So, when Warbeck landed in Kent in July 1495, he failed to rouse support and had to sail north to Scotland. There, he was befriended by King James IV, who may have been convinced that Warbeck was genuine, since he granted him an income of £1,200 per year and his own cousin in marriage.

However, James's attempt to invade England on Warbeck's behalf in 1497 was a disaster. Warbeck was horrified by the brutish behaviour of the Scottish troops in raiding the northern borderlands of England and refused to travel further south with them. When Henry offered James a truce, Warbeck fled to Ireland. By now he was running out of support and gave himself up in August 1497, making a full confession of who he really was. Since this achieved what Henry wanted, the King exercised calculated mercy and allowed Warbeck to remain at Court, but in 1498 Warbeck ran away and was imprisoned in the Tower upon recapture. There, he was involved in plotting to escape with the young Earl of Warwick and both were executed in 1499. Whether this plot was genuine or encouraged by the King's agents, it allowed Henry finally to dispose of two troublesome individuals.

4 Relations with other countries, 1485–1509

Henry VII faced a difficult international situation from the moment he became King. England's relationships with foreign powers were closely tied to developments in England, especially concerning marriage alliances, and the picture in Europe was complex:

- France was a much smaller country than it is now, with several areas such as Brittany virtually independent of the French King. Calais was controlled by England, the only remnant of the conquests by England of French territories during the Hundred Years' War (1338–1453).
- Spain was becoming united under Ferdinand of Aragon and Isabella of Castile – though both provinces were mostly ruled separately.

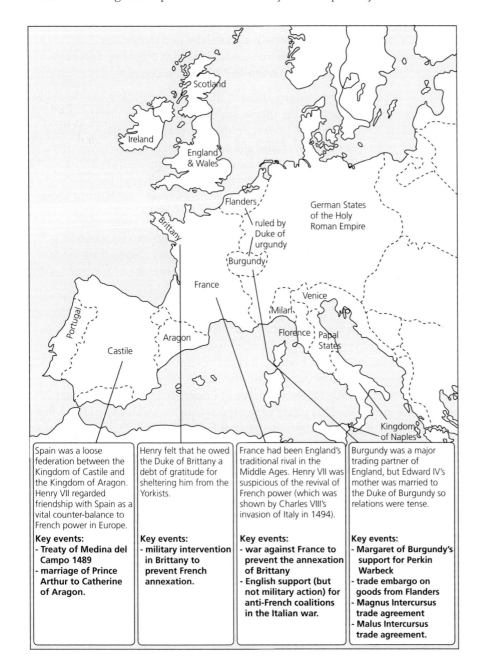

Spain was a loose federation between the Kingdom of Castile and the Kingdom of Aragon. Henry VII regarded friendship with Spain as a vital counter-balance to French power in Europe.

Key events:
- **Treaty of Medina del Campo 1489**
- **marriage of Prince Arthur to Catherine of Aragon.**

Henry felt that he owed the Duke of Brittany a debt of gratitude for sheltering him from the Yorkists.

Key events:
- **military intervention in Brittany to prevent French annexation.**

France had been England's traditional rival in the Middle Ages. Henry VII was suspicious of the revival of French power (which was shown by Charles VIII's invasion of Italy in 1494).

Key events:
- **war against France to prevent the annexation of Brittany**
- **English support (but not military action) for anti-French coalitions in the Italian war.**

Burgundy was a major trading partner of England, but Edward IV's mother was married to the Duke of Burgundy so relations were tense.

Key events:
- **Margaret of Burgundy's support for Perkin Warbeck**
- **trade embargo on goods from Flanders**
- **Magnus Intercursus trade agreement**
- **Malus Intercursus trade agreement.**

◀ Figure 7 Europe in the reign of Henry VII.

- A huge area of central Europe was known as the Holy Roman Empire, a conglomeration of states and territories under the nominal control of the Holy Roman Emperor. It included modern-day Germany and much land beyond. One large part was Burgundy and the Duke of Burgundy also ruled Flanders, which included what we now call the Netherlands. Their ports, especially Antwerp, were important for English trade. Antwerp was the most important centre for the cloth trade in Europe and wool was England's chief export (see Figure 7 on page 27).
- Italy was divided into city states that competed with each other for power, and European powers were constantly being tempted to intervene for their own benefit. This situation led to the so-called Italian Wars that started with the invasion of Italy by the French King, Charles VIII, in 1494.

NOTE-MAKING

As you work through pages 28–32 on Henry VII's foreign policy, list:
- what appear to have been his aims
- the successes he had
- the reasons why his successes were limited.

Henry VII's aims in foreign policy

What considerations shaped Henry's relations with foreign powers and how successful was he?

Henry VII's foreign policy was initially dictated by two things: the circumstances surrounding his succession and his lack of money. Later his focus was on trade, dynastic expansion and his own succession.

Henry had become King by killing Richard III, but his legal status was insecure. There were other claimants to the throne and England's recent history had been punctuated by struggles for the Crown. In the first years of his reign, Henry's priority was to gain acceptance of his right to rule from other monarchs. This was important not only because rivals for his crown might seek shelter or assistance from other countries (as Henry had done in Brittany), but also because favourable words from a foreign ruler might give him more credibility at home.

Between 1485 and 1492 Henry built a series of truces with potentially dangerous neighbours: France in 1485, Scotland in 1486 and the Habsburg Empire (which included the Netherlands) in 1487. Henry also saw advantages in building a longer-term alliance with Spain as an insurance policy against any future problems with France.

In 1489, as part of the Treaty of Medina del Campo, England and Spain decided to work together to defend their lands and promised not to make agreements with France without consulting each other first. The treaty set up equal trading rights for merchants from both countries and fixed customs duties which actually tended to favour English merchants. To deepen the alliance, arrangements were made for the marriage of Prince Arthur to the daughter of the Spanish monarchs. This treaty cemented an Anglo-Spanish friendship that lasted for much of the time until the reign of Elizabeth.

Relations with France were initially friendly because Henry's fight for the throne had been encouraged by the French court. However, he had also depended on Brittany (which was semi-independent from French rule) for sanctuary during his fourteen-year exile. This put Henry in a difficult position when France moved to absorb Brittany between 1488 and 1492. He faced a serious problem because an accepted view of national security included the belief that the coastline across the Channel should not be held by just one power. If France gained control of Brittany the south coast of England would be in a militarily weaker position; Calais (the last surviving outpost of England's medieval empire in France) would be more vulnerable; and trade could be disrupted. These considerations made the 'Breton Crisis' of 1488–92 the major foreign policy problem of Henry's reign, and the only time he committed troops outside the British Isles.

Breton Crisis

The way in which the crisis unfolded tells us much about Henry's aims and methods in foreign policy. He did not rush towards war because it would be dangerous to annoy France when pretenders to the throne were active, and also because he lacked funds. Instead, Henry opened negotiations with France while at the same time secretly allowing English troops to cross to Brittany to help the Bretons repel the French army. When these manoeuvres failed, he tried to win support at home and abroad for a short campaign. The Treaty of Medina del Campo bought off Spain and Henry also approached the rulers of the Netherlands, some north German states and even the Pope for either assistance or at least their neutrality. Parliament was summoned to make a grant of £100,000 to finance a small force (estimates suggest between 3,000 and 6,000 men).

When this army crossed the Channel in April 1489 Henry made it clear to the French that he was only acting in defence of Brittany; there was no intention to go further and re-open the longstanding English claims to French lands that had been the issue in the Hundred Years' War. These reassurances did not satisfy the French, who showed their displeasure by receiving the pretender Perkin Warbeck at court and by pouring more of their own troops into Brittany. In the final stages of the war, Henry took a great risk. He led a larger force of 12,000 troops into Brittany, gambling that France did not want a long conflict. He was right: France was beginning to take an interest in the divisions within the Italian peninsula and wanted to be free of commitments elsewhere. Under the terms of the Treaty of Etaples (1492), Henry's army left France in return for a payment of 745,000 crowns (payable at the rate of 50,000 crowns per year, about five per cent of the King's annual income) to cover the costs of the expedition, and an agreement by the French King not to support Henry's enemies. This was very important in Henry's dealings with Perkin Warbeck (see page 26).

At face value, the Breton Crisis had been a successful baptism of fire for Henry VII. Early in his reign, while still insecure at home, he had pursued a difficult diplomatic path with skill. England's basic friendship with France had remained intact; military intervention had been brief and had not damaged England's reputation. Moreover, France had been persuaded to stop supporting pretenders to the throne and had made payments that offset the cost of the conflict. However, it must be remembered that England's armies did not win any of the main engagements in Brittany and at the end of the crisis the fact remained that Brittany was little more than a satellite of France (it was finally absorbed into the French state in 1532). All of the southern shore of the English Channel except for Calais was in French hands. Henry had failed to restore English glories in Europe.

Expanding trade and exploration

As part of Henry's policy of building up the country's strength and wealth, he was keen to encourage trade. This was particularly important in the years immediately after 1485 when his position was precarious, and he knew that building up trade would help with creating wealth. Yet an analysis of his actions shows no coherent pattern. Henry was an opportunist – hence his actions often seem fragmentary and inconsistent.

Henry VII and Scotland

In the Tudor period Scotland was a distinct country, with its own Parliament and monarch. Relations between Scotland and England were usually strained. To preserve their independence, the Scots had looked to France for support, which created the uncomfortable situation for England of having potential enemies to both the north and the south. Henry VII was concerned that if James III of Scotland refused to accept him as King of England there could be problems in the north, where the Yorkists still had support. He quickly arranged a truce in 1486, but his efforts were ruined by James's death two years later, and with the accession of fifteen-year-old James IV. As you will see in later chapters, Scottish history in this period was to be punctuated by the sudden deaths of monarchs and the instability caused by long regencies.

The nobles who governed on behalf of James IV were hostile to England and James himself showed a willingness to upset his southern neighbour by harbouring Perkin Warbeck between 1495 and 1497. Relations were improved by the Truce of Ayton in 1497 which matured into a formal peace treaty in 1502. In a significant move for the future, Henry's eldest daughter, Margaret, was married to James IV in 1503, apparently settling the ill-feeling between the two monarchs.

Hanseatic League – A league of German towns which dominated trade in the Baltic. They aimed to maintain a monopoly of trade there.

New World – This was the term being used to describe the continent of America that was discovered by Spanish sailors during the reign of Henry VII.

In particular, he sought to break up the stranglehold of the Hanseatic League. Navigation Acts were passed (1485–86) which encouraged the use of English ships to carry goods rather than foreign ships. In particular wines from France could only be imported in English ships. All this assisted the activities of the London-based Merchant Adventurers.

An Act was passed in 1489 which limited the export of English wool and made it illegal for foreigners to buy wool for making into cloth on the continent. This reflected the needs of the important cloth industry in England, and Henry was keen to show his support. At the end of his reign the export of raw wool was 30 per cent lower than it had been in 1485.

Henry also tried to encourage the English cloth trade by trading agreements with the rulers of Burgundy who controlled the port of Antwerp. The most important agreement was the *Intercursus Magnus* of 1496 which allowed English merchants to trade freely with all parts of Burgundy except Flanders. There were occasional disagreements and interruptions to this trade agreement, but by 1509 English merchants were shipping more than half the cloth exported to Europe. Overall, 60 per cent more cloth was being exported to Europe in 1509 than had been at the beginning of the reign. Henry hoped, through England's alliance with Spain, to encourage trade in southern Europe and the developing New World.

Henry also hoped to develop trade in the Mediterranean, especially with Florence. Venice was the Italian city state that dominated trade there and therefore the Venetians were seen as a rival. Indeed, as soon as Henry had persuaded some merchants to trade in the region, Venice retaliated by imposing heavy tariffs on all English goods imported into Venice. In 1490 a treaty was signed that allowed English wool to be imported into Pisa, the main port of Florence. Henry also restricted the sale of wool to the Venetians. Fearing that Florence would gain trade at their expense, the Venetian government lifted the import duties on English goods. Therefore Henry had gained the right for English merchants to trade with the wealthiest state in the west Mediterranean.

Henry also started to build up an English navy which Henry VIII was able to expand. Although it was small – he left his son only nine ships – the ships were of good quality. They were bigger and better equipped than those of his predecessors. The *Regent* carried large guns and anticipated the development of warships under Henry VIII and Elizabeth. Portsmouth was established as the country's first fortified naval base.

Henry showed interest in the geographical discoveries of the age by supporting the voyages of John and Sebastian Cabot. John Cabot reached Newfoundland in 1497 and claimed it for England. Unfortunately Cabot died on the way home. His son, Sebastian, sailed with Henry's blessing in 1509, to find a route to China round the north of America. This was, of course, impossible, but he did reach what we now call Hudson Bay. When he returned, convinced that he was on the way to finding a route to the Far East, Henry VII had died and the new king was not interested in maritime exploration.

Henry's overseas policy on trade therefore achieved some success, but in a limited way. Customs duties rose at the beginning of the reign, but compared with the Hanseatic League, Spain and Venice, England's merchants were only trading small amounts. The main importance lies in the foundations laid and with the way in which the encouragement of overseas trade helped Henry to sit on his throne more securely.

Foreign policy in the last years of Henry VII's reign

Henry found it difficult to maintain his early achievements in the last years of his reign because of changing situations. In England the death of Prince Arthur (1502) and his wife Elizabeth (1503) caused renewed worries about the succession. Henry began to consider whether he should marry again, but a possible Spanish match became less of a possibility when Queen Isabella died in 1504. There was no guarantee that Spain would stay united, and Ferdinand's first priority was to ensure that this happened by becoming Regent. He did so on behalf of Isabella's daughter Joanna, married to Philip, Duke of Burgundy, who had ambitions himself to succeed.

Henry was thus forced to reappraise England's foreign policy. He needed to maintain good relations with Spain (for dynastic and trading reasons) but also with Burgundy (because of England's trade with Europe and also as a possible ally against France should this be needed). Henry's actions were therefore frequently short term, reacting to the latest European situations.

In 1505 Henry was moving towards more friendly relations with Philip of Burgundy in case of possible aggression from France. He opened discussions about a possible Burgundian bride for his son, Henry. This automatically made relations with Ferdinand of Spain worse. Ferdinand turned to France. Louis XII had felt surrounded by Spain, Burgundy and the Netherlands, and was also ready for friendship. This was cemented in late 1505 when Ferdinand married Louis XII's niece, Germaine de Foix.

However, all this diplomacy was turned on its head when Philip of Burgundy suddenly died in October 1506. This weakened Burgundy. Joanna was said to be mad with grief and deemed unfit to rule. Ferdinand took the opportunity to declare himself King of Castile, in succession to his deceased wife, Isabella. The heir in the Netherlands was the six-year-old Archduke Charles (son of Joanna and Philip), with Margaret of Savoy acting as Regent for her nephew. Bearing in mind the importance of the Netherlands for English trade, Henry was afraid that France might take the opportunity to take some of the Netherlands. It was Ferdinand who was now well-placed in international diplomacy and he was seen as a threat to the other rulers.

Henry thought that his best hope now was friendship between England, the Netherlands and France. It allowed Henry to end the temporary disagreements over trade that had developed. There were several plans for marriage alliances involving these countries, with the intention of isolating Ferdinand.

This all changed when in 1508 the League of Cambrai came into existence. Louis XII and Ferdinand came together, with the Archduke Charles and the Pope, in an alliance against Venice, the powerful city state that controlled an important part of the Italian coastline. It looked as if England had been left isolated, but in fact the alliance moved the focus of attention away from England towards Italy for what turned out to be the last few months of Henry's life. None of the other countries saw England as the enemy.

How successful was Henry VII's foreign policy?

Henry wanted security from invasion and recognition of the succession after his death; he wanted England to be a major player on the European stage, and he wanted to secure England's trade. Overall, he succeeded – though not with a carefully thought-out plan that was maintained during his reign. Especially at the beginning and in the last few years he had to be pragmatic. His limited financial budget curbed his aspirations towards expanding English territory.

KEY DATES: FOREIGN RELATIONS IN HENRY VII'S REIGN

1486 Truces signed with Scotland and France; commercial treaty with Brittany

1488 Succession of 15-year-old James IV as King of Scotland; French attack on Brittany

1489 Henry intervened to help Brittany remain independent from France; Treaty of Medina del Campo with Spain

1491 Perkin Warbeck made his claim to the throne

1492 Resolution of the Breton Crisis in the Treaty of Etaples

1497 Scottish invasion of northern England; Truce of Ayton

1501 Marriage of Prince Arthur to Catherine of Aragon

1503 Marriage of Henry VII's eldest daughter, Margaret, to James IV of Scotland

1504 Death of Queen Isabella of Spain

1506 Death of Philip of Burgundy – led to succession crisis there and in Castile

1508 League of Cambrai set up

Source G A verdict on Henry's foreign policy. From *Henry VII* by C. Rogers and R. Turvey, (Hodder Education), 2005, p.153.

In 1509 Henry could be well pleased with the results of his diplomacy. England was on good terms with most of Europe, his dynasty was secure and was recognised by other rulers, and, most importantly, all this had been achieved without draining his treasury of its hard-won treasures.

Source H Another verdict on Henry VII's foreign policy. From *The Reign of Henry VII* by B. Thompson (ed.), (Oxbow Books), 1995, p.8.

The avoidance of war was no panacea for a new monarchy, since war was more popular than not, and was therefore backed by money and manpower, especially when successful. Even Henry's foreign policy, though astute, was more problematic than it needs to have been as a result of his own need for dynastic security ... In his quarter-century of instability and uncertainty, Henry never secured the loyalty of the realm through stable and representative rule, and therefore never escaped from the consequences of being a usurper.

Using your knowledge, how far do you agree with Sources G and H?

The last decade of Henry VII's reign

What major problems did Henry VII face in the last few years of his reign, and how successful was he in dealing with them?

By 1502 Henry seemed to have achieved most of his aims. He had established his dynasty with the marriage of Arthur to Catherine of Aragon in 1501, defeated key rivals, strengthened the institutions of government, put finances back on a sound footing and reduced his dependence on the nobility for support. Overall, England was better governed, more prosperous and more peaceful than at any time in the past fifty years. Nevertheless, when Henry died he was not popular. His death in 1509 was greeted with relief. His ministers, Empson and Dudley, were so unpopular that the young King Henry could gain instant popularity by acting against them. They were arrested two days after Henry VII's death (before the death had even been made public) and executed the following year.

The explanation for this change in Henry's fortunes can be found in two factors: first, a series of deaths that suddenly made his dynasty seem insecure; and, resulting from this, the increasingly harsh application of the financial and political measures that Henry used to maintain control.

Renewed instability

By 1500, Henry had four children, including three sons (Arthur, Henry and Edmund). The prospect of a smooth succession to his eldest child Arthur, who was fourteen at the time, seemed certain. However, a series of shocking events changed all that. In 1500 his youngest son, Edmund, died. This was followed in 1502 by the death of Arthur, and in early 1503 by the death of Henry's wife, Elizabeth of York, shortly after she had given birth to a daughter. This sequence of events clearly devastated Henry personally and politically. The loss of two sons left the future of the Tudor dynasty dependent on the life of Prince Henry, and Elizabeth's death robbed him of some Yorkist loyalty as well as the possibility of more children born from a union of Lancastrians and Yorkists. The renewed danger was highlighted by the departure of Edmund de la Pole, the Earl of Suffolk, to take refuge in Burgundy in 1503.

A further complication was the damage that the death of Arthur might do to relations with Spain. Henry was keen to remain on good terms with the Spanish monarchs, Ferdinand and Isabella, as they shared a common distrust

The problem of the royal marriage in 1509

The issue of Catherine's marriages was to cause enormous problems in English politics in the reign of Henry VIII. The official position of the Catholic Church was complicated, but in general terms marriage between a man and his brother's widow was forbidden. However, if there had been no sexual relations between the couple, then it was not a proper marriage so the restriction did not apply. According to Catherine, their youth (Arthur was fifteen and she was thirteen when they married), Arthur's poor health and the fact that they had only been married for five months before he died, all meant that she had remained a virgin, so was free to marry Prince Henry. This marriage took place in the first year of Henry VIII's reign.

of France. To secure this friendship, he had negotiated the marriage in 1501 of Prince Arthur to Catherine of Aragon, daughter of the Spanish monarchs. Arthur's death threatened to disrupt the close relationship that Henry had worked hard to achieve, but he was able to secure a new royal marriage between Catherine and Prince Henry. Because Catherine was marrying her husband's brother, Henry had to get special permission from the Pope, but he felt that this was a small price to pay to protect the Anglo-Spanish alliance and to keep the money and gifts that she had brought with her to her first marriage.

Harsh policies

The sudden deaths of Henry's wife and two sons had exposed a weakness in the Tudor dynasty that its enemies might exploit. To prevent this, Henry seems to have spent his final years using the powers at his disposal to make certain that the nobility was not in a position to threaten him or his only surviving son. Earlier in his reign, Henry had exercised his powers flexibly. He had used punishments such as placing nobles under a bond or recognisance sparingly, often showing leniency or reversing a fine after a few years to win gratitude and loyalty. This skill of manipulating the powers at his disposal lay in using them just enough to maintain the threat of penalties for disloyalty or rewards for service, while not over-using them to the point where they created resentment and open opposition. In the last years of Henry's reign there is evidence that he got that balance wrong.

The most obvious source of resentment was the activity of the Council Learned in Law. This council was used by Henry, in conjunction with his other special courts such as Star Chamber, to maintain his feudal rights over his leading subjects. In 1493 bonds from the nobility brought in £3,000 in cash, although much more had been demanded and promised. In 1505 the equivalent sum was £35,000. To some extent this might have reflected a change of personnel – the death of Sir Reginald Bray led to the appointment of Sir Richard Empson as the Chancellor of the Duchy of Lancaster in 1504. He and Edmund Dudley created a system of spies and informers who looked for signs of misdeeds among wealthy people. In Henry's reign 46 out of 62 noble families suffered financially for one reason or another, and the level of activity increased rapidly in the last years of the reign. Royal demands were increased and enforced far more rigorously than in earlier years. For example, someone might be fined for an alleged offence, but then forced to sign a bond in which there was a promise to pay a sum of money to the Crown each year as a guarantee of their future good behaviour. Edmund Dudley confessed in 1509 that in at least 84 cases he had extracted money illegally. Since this information was revealed after he had been arrested by Henry VIII, it is difficult to know how accurate it is, because he might have been pressured into exaggerating the scale of his crimes. Allowing for this, it remains the case that the Council Learned in Law was conducting its activities in a way likely to cause resentment, and it is difficult to avoid the conclusion that Henry VII was aware of this.

Death of Henry VII

Henry VII died in April 1509, aged 52. He had been visibly ailing for the previous few months and had hardly been seen in public since February. He had continued working, planning ahead and especially securing the future of the Tudor dynasty.

Henry had achieved stability, defeated rivals, controlled the nobles, improved finances, and was able to pass all this on to his eldest surviving son who became Henry VIII. His secure foundations made possible the achievements of the later Tudors. However, as explained above, he died more respected than loved. The extent of his achievements has also been questioned.

Study Source I. On a piece of paper, draw a line down the middle. In one column list all the reasons you can find to agree with the source. In the other column list all the reasons that suggest partial or total disagreement.

Source I One verdict on Henry VII's reign. From *History in Depth: Henry VII* by C. Towle and J. Hunt, (Longman), 1998.

How well did Henry govern? If you compare the situation before and after his reign you have to say that he had done well. Law and order was established; the budget was in surplus; trade was flourishing, and with it the merchant classes; nobles were no longer a danger to national order; the Church was less corrupt than it had been. Though still far from perfect; ordinary people could be confident that their lives would not be disrupted by the kind of disorder which their forefathers had suffered.

Some other historians have been much more limited in their praise for Henry VII. For example, Colin Pendrill's view that:

'Henry's reign was unstable because he had no real claim to the throne, and he over-reacted to the threats'.

In your study of his reign you must analyse and reach your own judgement based on the evidence you have accumulated.

▲ The tomb of Henry VII and his wife Elizabeth in the Henry VII Chapel in Westminster Abbey. The gilt-bronze effigies of the king and queen were made by the Italian, Pietro Torrigiano, and added by Henry VIII. Both the Chapel and the effigies show how much Henry VII and his successors were prepared to spend money on lavish displays to build up the appearance of grandeur of the Tudor monarchy.

Chapter summary

- England in 1485 was a relatively unimportant country on the edge of Europe, with a weak monarchy and over-powerful nobles.
- Henry VII established Tudor rule, ending the Wars of the Roses.
- He used propaganda skilfully to justify becoming King, including symbolically uniting the Red and White Roses by marrying Elizabeth of York.
- He kept the nobles in check through good government, patronage and limiting noble retainers.
- He improved the Crown's finances.
- He defeated rebellions, for example, Lovell and Stafford.
- He dealt successfully with pretenders (Lambert Simnel and Perkin Warbeck).
- He worked hard to build up diplomatic and trading relations in Europe.
- After the death of Arthur in 1502, he worked hard to re-build his achievements so that his legacy would be secure.
- His reputation was one of fairness but harshness; he was respected rather than loved.

Chapter summary diagram

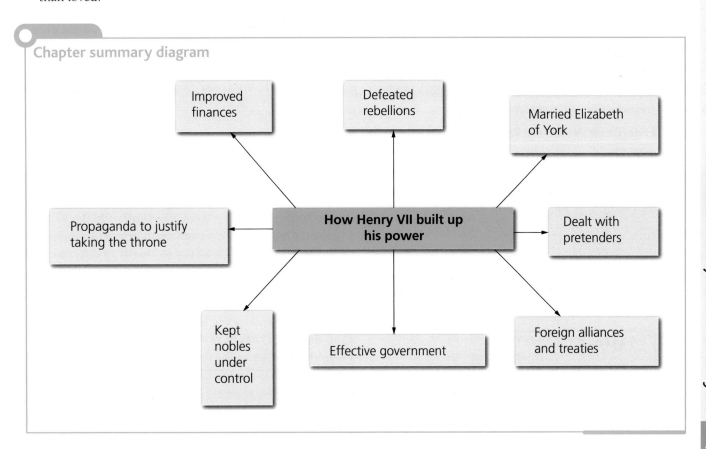

Working on essay technique: focus, structure and deploying detail

As well as learning the facts and understanding the history of the period you are studying, it is very important to develop skills in answering the types of question that will be set.

Essay focus

Whether you are taking the AS exam or the full A-level exam, Section B presents you with essay titles. Each question is marked out of 25.

AS examination	Full A-level examination
Section B – Answer ONE essay (from a choice of two)	Section B – Answer TWO essays (from a choice of three).

Several question stems are possible as alternatives, but they all have the same basic requirement. They all require you to analyse and reach a conclusion, based on the evidence you provide.

For example, 'Assess the validity (of a quotation)', 'To what extent …', 'How successful …', 'How far …' etc.

The AS titles always give a quotation and then: 'Explain why you agree or disagree with this view'. Almost inevitably, your answer will be a mixture of both. In essence, it is the same task as for the full A-level – just more basic wording.

Each question will reflect, directly or indirectly, one of the breadth issues in your study. The questions will have a fairly broad focus.

EXAMPLE

Look at the following AS-level practice question:

'Rebellions can be seen as the greatest challenge facing Henry VII's rule, 1485–1509'. Explain why you agree or disagree with this view.

(25 marks)

This type of question requires you to identify the challenges that faced Henry VII. You must discuss rebellions as one of those challenges. So there are two parts to the question:

● The challenges facing Henry VII (your primary focus).
● The challenge that was posed specifically by rebellions (your secondary focus).

Structuring your answer

A clear structure makes for a much more effective essay. In order to structure this question effectively you need approximately three or four paragraphs. In each paragraph you will deal with one factor. One of these must be the factor in the question.

It is a good idea to cover the factor in the question first, so that you don't run out of time and forget to do it. After you have covered that factor, then cover the others in what you think is their order of importance.

Remember that you also need a short but clear introduction that briefly explains your argument in relation to the question and a conclusion that provides a summary. This is a useful structure to apply to many questions.

Writing a focused introduction

It is vital that you maintain focus on the question from the beginning of your essay. One way to do this is to use the wording of the question to help write your argument. The first sentence in answer to the practice question above, for example, could look like this:

> Rebellions were an important threat to the reign of Henry VII, but they were not the only challenge that he faced in his reign in the years 1485–1509.

That opening sentence provides a clear focus on the demands of the question, recognising that the task is to balance 'rebellions' against other challenges. It provides a spring-board for a clearly planned essay. Remember, you must learn how to apply this approach to other questions you may encounter. You are not just learning how to respond to this question.

Focus throughout the essay

Structuring your essay well will help with focus throughout the essay, but you also need to remember to maintain this throughout the piece. Here are some ideas that will help you to focus your answer.

- Use the wording of the question to help write your answer.

> For example, in answer to the practice question on page 36, you could begin your first main paragraph with 'rebellions'.
>
> *Rebellions were a major factor in the challenges faced by Henry VII.*
>
> This sentence begins with a clear point that refers to the primary focus of the question (the challenges faced by Henry VII) while linking it to a factor (the challenge posed specifically by rebellions).

- Have a paragraph for each of your other factors. You may wish to number your factors. This helps to make your structure clear and helps you to maintain focus. Later we will look at prioritising factors in order of importance.

Summary

- Work out the main focus of the question.
- Plan your essay with a series of factors focusing on the question, starting with the 'named' factor.
- Use the words in the question to formulate your answer.
- Return to the primary focus of the question at the beginning of every paragraph.
- Make sure that your structure is clear to the reader.

ACTIVITY

Having now read the advice on how to write a structured and focused essay, plan and write the first sentence to the following AS-level practice question:

'Securing the Tudor succession was the most important aim of Henry VII's foreign policy.' Explain why you agree or disagree with this view.

(25 marks)

Deploying detail

As well as focus and structure your essay will be judged on the extent to which it includes accurate detail. Detailed essays are more likely to do well than essays which are vague or generalised.

There are several different kinds of evidence you could use that might be described as detail. This includes correct dates, names of relevant people, statistics and events. You can also make your essays more detailed by using the correct technical vocabulary. Here you could use words and phrases such as 'parliamentary session' and 'tonnage and poundage' that you have learnt while studying this subject.

ACTIVITY

Consider the following A-level practice question:

'Henry VII's financial policies were the most important reason for the success of his rule.' Assess the validity of this view.

(25 marks)

- Create your own brief essay plan for this question, making a list of points you will include.
- Using your notes from this chapter, find at least three pieces of detail to support each of these points. It is best to use different types of detailed evidence, for instance, not just statistics or technical vocabulary, but also dates and specific people.

As well as studying the facts of an event in history, historians also use these facts in order to reach conclusions on, for example, why something happened. In other words, they have to interpret the facts in order to reach their conclusions. Often the evidence does not just point in one direction. There is scope for historians reaching different conclusions and producing different interpretations.

Section A of the examination requires you to read and evaluate different interpretations – that is, looking at how historians do not always agree in the judgements they reach. In Chapters 2, 3, 5 and 6 there are contrasting interpretations for you to study and activities for you to practise your skills – that is, your skills in using evidence to see how far you agree with each interpretation.

In this chapter, as well as Chapters 4, 7, and 8, there is one, longer interpretation to read, followed by some questions that are designed to help you build up your skills as well as helping you to consolidate your knowledge of each chapter.

Working on interpretation skills: extended reading

How great a monarch was Henry VII?

Historian Dr David Grummitt considers why Henry VII has claims to be a great monarch as the founder of the Tudor dynasty.

Few English monarchs can have come to the throne with as little preparation or experience as Henry VII. He had previously been in exile in Brittany and France for some fourteen years. His promise to marry Elizabeth of York, the daughter of the recently deceased Edward IV, before a gathering of die-hard Lancastrians and disaffected former Yorkists in Rennes cathedral on Christmas Day 1484 transformed him into a credible claimant to the throne and a serious threat to the usurper, Richard III. Yet here was a would-be king who had no practical experience of English politics or government, and whose formative years had been spent in the very different political world of continental princely courts. 5 ... 10

In those circumstances the simple fact that Henry survived a reign that lasted twenty-three and a half years and was able to pass the throne uncontested to his eldest son might be seen to qualify him for greatness. Historians have struggled to agree whether Henry should be judged as the last medieval king of England or the founder of a 'New Monarchy'. Scholars writing in the nineteenth and early twentieth centuries identified him as the champion of the 'Middle Classes', keen to consolidate the crown's power and crush the barons who had caused the civil wars of the fifteenth century. More recently historians have identified continuities between early Tudor government and rule of his Plantagenet predecessors, or even argued that Henry was a poor king who fundamentally misunderstood the nature of the kingdom he ruled. Henry VII, however, does have a claim to greatness and for laying the foundations of a distinctive Tudor polity. 15 ... 20

In two keys areas of government Henry transformed the nature of the English realm. First, he prepared the foundations for a fundamental shift in the nature of the king's relationship with his greatest subjects, the parliamentary peerage. Unlike the Yorkist kings, Henry did not inflate the ranks of the nobility. Instead he weakened their local power by using the royal estates, spread widely throughout the realm as a result of forfeiture 25

ACTIVITY

Having read the essay, answer the following questions.

Comprehension

1 What does the author mean by the following phrases?
   a) 'New Monarchy' (paragraph 2) [line 15]
   b) 'king's household' (paragraph 3) [line 33]
   c) 'his feudal rights' (end of paragraph 3) [line 40]

Evidence

2 Using paragraphs 3 and 4, list the ways in which the author states that Henry VII deserves the title of greatness.

Interpretation

3 Using your knowledge from your study of Henry VII's reign, list evidence to suggest that Henry VII was not necessarily as great as the author suggests.

Evaluation

4 Write an essay in answer to the following question:

'Henry VII does not deserve to be considered a great King. Above all, he was lucky.'

To what extent do you agree with this?

and accidents of inheritance during the fifteenth century, to project his authority at a local level. Similarly, he drew members of the nobility to his court, informally by making it a cultural and political centre, but also formally by expanding the membership of the king's household and through a system of bonds that enforced the nobles' attendance at court. Second, Henry oversaw a radical shift in the nature of royal finance. The poverty of the crown had been one of the most pressing concerns of much of the later Middle Ages, but under the Yorkist kings the much-expanded royal estates had provided the basis for a recovery. Henry took this one step further, exerting his personal control over all aspects of royal finance and pressing hard to collect taxes, customs and, especially, his feudal rights. This resulted in a huge treasure which gave him the freedom to pursue radical policies at home and realise his diplomatic ambitions on the continent.

In other ways Henry presided over a revolutionary change in English political culture. His government was staffed by 'new men', often men trained in the common law or in the new humanist learning that was sweeping the continent. These individuals fostered a culture in which the authority of the crown was strengthened against challenges from the church, the nobility and town corporations. Initiatives such as the *Quo Warranto* ('By what authority') proceedings in the 1490s sought to abolish separate legal franchises and bring every aspect of English law under royal control. This paved the way for the challenge to Papal authority in the 1530s and the English Reformation. Changes in education and in the ways that people thought about politics and government during his reign were a result both of the impact of the Renaissance, but also of Henry's own exposure to the continental practice of government. As the Spanish ambassador observed in 1498, Henry 'would like to govern England in the French fashion'. There developed between 1485 and 1509 a court-based politics, based on intrigue and plots as much as on violence or debate in parliament, that would characterise the rule of the Tudors.

Henry VII thus deserves to be considered a great king. He saw off challenges both domestic and foreign to pass the throne to his son. He ensured the financial stability of the crown and consolidated royal authority in almost every aspect of English life. More importantly, his rule prepared the way for the monumental changes that took place in the sixteenth century.

Dr David Grummitt, Senior Lecturer in History, University of Kent

2

The rule of Henry VIII and Wolsey, 1509–29

This chapter is concerned with the first half of the reign of Henry VIII, and deals with a number of areas:

- The England that Henry VIII inherited; his character, skills and aims; and life at court.
- The role of Wolsey in domestic affairs – Church and State – his power and influence in both.
- England's relations with foreign powers, 1509–29.
- The Church in the 1520s; early influence of Lutheranism and growing anti-clericalism.
- Henry's urgent need for a divorce and consequences for Wolsey.

This content relates closely to some of the key issues identified in the specification – for example, the role of individuals, where the young dashing Henry VIII contrasted with Wolsey's meticulous and detailed approach to everything the King wanted. This was seen, for example, in foreign policy. Another theme concerns Wolsey's control of the Church at a time when traditional religious beliefs were being challenged as the Reformation started in Europe. Henry VIII was concerned about the succession and came to want a divorce from Catherine of Aragon. Arising out of this came the need for the monarchy to have more control over the Church.

The central question to be asking at this stage is:

Wolsey and Henry VIII: who controlled who and how important was Wolsey?

CHAPTER OVERVIEW

The youthful Henry wanted to make his mark as a young successful king, but his enthusiasm was not always matched by his dedication to day-to-day business. By 1515 Wolsey was the chief minister who dominated life in Church and State. There have been debates among historians about the extent that Wolsey controlled the youthful Henry VIII. Wolsey was active in domestic affairs, instituting some reforms, as the leading churchman and as Chancellor.

In the Church, he was keen to promote learning and establish new schools; he made moves against monasteries that were said to be of little use. However, Wolsey did not set a good personal example with his emphasis on wealth and ostentation. As Chancellor, he instituted minor changes in the law and in finances, but his attempts to build on the legacy of Henry VII were limited.

However, Wolsey did work with some success in advancing England's interests abroad, especially initially in 1513–14 and with the splendour of the Field of Cloth of Gold in 1520. After this, successes were more difficult to achieve because of rapidly changing European alliances. He and Henry VIII focused almost entirely on Europe, and almost totally ignored possibilities being offered by trading developments further afield. In the later 1520s Wolsey had to try to respond to Henry's need for a divorce from the Pope who was under the control of Charles V, the nephew of Henry's wife. As such, initial attempts failed in the later 1520s and Wolsey fell from power.

1 Henry VIII: the start of a new era

The early years of Henry's reign

How strong was Henry VIII's position in the first few years of his reign?

The contrasts between Henry VIII and his father could not have been more marked. Henry VIII succeeded to the throne when he was nearly eighteen, a young, athletic and charismatic figure who, if not born to be king, had known that this was his destiny since his brother's death in 1502. Where Henry VII had endured years of poverty and exile, succeeding to the throne only through luck and military success, Henry VIII had known only wealth and expectation, if tinged with insecurity. His accession was popular. He represented the union of the Houses of York and Lancaster, a symbol of domestic peace and harmony, and the dawn of a new era after the years of mistrust and financial oppression that had overshadowed his father's relationship with his nobility. In the words of Sir Thomas More:

This day is the end of our slavery, the fount of our liberty; the end of our sadness and the beginning of joy.

Early life of Prince Henry

Prince Henry's upbringing had not initially been, of course, as heir to the throne. That only changed in 1502 when his elder brother, Arthur, died when Henry was nearly eleven. Already Henry had been well-educated, taught by a group of tutors who included the poet John Skelton. Henry studied languages, history, astronomy and arithmetic. He learnt several musical instruments, including the lute, and could sing well. Outdoors he learnt horse riding and archery, and later played tennis and became skilled in jousting. He was being well-prepared for the role of a Renaissance prince.

In particular, his education reflected the belief that a monarch should follow the code of chivalry which had been developed in the Burgundian court in the Netherlands in the fifteenth century. One essential part of the chivalric code was the need to perform valiant deeds. This could be in jousting (often staged as elaborate court spectacles) or in warfare. This code of chivalry not only greatly influenced life at court but also Henry's attitude to foreign policy.

After Arthur's death in 1502 and his mother's death in 1503, Henry lived at court at Richmond with his father with his own suite of rooms and 100 servants. However, he does not seem to have been particularly well-prepared by his father for the day-to-day duties of kingship. Despite this, he showed himself (even allowing for the flattering accounts by courtiers and ambassadors) to have been intellectually gifted. He had a brilliant memory for factual details and could analyse information and argue on subjects such as religion. His education had reinforced the notion of the monarch ruling in the interests of the country and of the Tudor line.

First decisions of Henry VIII

Henry VIII inherited from his father a group of experienced and trusted councillors. They included:

- Sir Thomas Lovell, who was reappointed Chancellor of the Exchequer.
- Bishop Fox, who was Lord Privy Seal and a trusted important adviser until the rise of Wolsey.
- Archbishop Warham, who was also Lord Chancellor.

NOTE-MAKING

In this opening section covering the first few years of Henry VIII's reign, make notes on the ways in which the start of Henry's reign indicated change from the reign of his father.

- Thomas Howard, Earl of Surrey, who as Earl Marshall had a prominent role in the coronation of Henry VIII.

The difference between Henry VIII's approach and his father's was, however, immediately apparent when he became king in April 1509. Within days of his accession he ordered the arrest of his father's chief financial enforcers, Empson and Dudley of the Council Learned in Law, and abolished this hated court. His second announcement was that he would honour his promise to marry Catherine of Aragon. Since the death of her husband, Arthur, in 1502, Catherine had been kept at court by Henry VII while he conducted the apparently complicated negotiations needed to secure approval from both her parents and the Pope for the remarriage. In reality, Henry had deliberately delayed permitting the marriage until he could be certain that it would bring diplomatic advantage to England. Henry VIII's decision to enact the marriage was a typically honourable and chivalrous thing to do. The early years of his reign provide abundant evidence that he took the concepts of knightly valour and honour seriously. Catherine, however, would live to see an entirely different side to his character as Henry passed from youth to middle age.

Henry's character and skills

There is, of course, much debate about Henry's character, especially as events unfolded during his long 37-year reign. Contemporary propaganda showed him in glowing terms, but written descriptions and portraits can be misleading if, as often happened, they reflected a particular purpose. However, the information we have about Henry VIII in the first fifteen years or so of his reign all agrees on his attractive appearance, his flamboyant manner, his learning and his skills.

In addition to being chivalrous and a warrior-king, Henry also wanted to be an imperial king. The idea of imperial kingship came from the Roman Empire whose government was being studied by Renaissance men of letters. He was keen to promote his monarchy as one that recreated the glories of Henry V's victory at Agincourt in 1415, and to establish the belief in everyone's mind that he was ruling on behalf of God. The language of imperial kingship became important in the 1530s when the English Church separated from Rome and England was referred to as 'an Empire governed by one supreme head and king'.

There is, however, less agreement about his character. Was Henry fundamentally a strong king or essentially weak? Most historians now accept that the former was the dominant trait, but that he had periods of chronic uncertainty and indecision, and this showed up as a crippling weakness in his role as monarch at crucial moments of his reign. This will be investigated in particular when considering the roles of Thomas Wolsey and Thomas Cromwell, and the extent to which he allowed his ministers to make their own decisions.

Source A From a letter written by the Venetian ambassador, Guistiniani, in 1521.

His Majesty is twenty-nine years old and extremely handsome. Nature could not have done more for him. He is much handsomer than any other sovereign in Christendom; a great deal handsomer than the King of France; very fair and his whole frame admirably proportioned. He is very accomplished, a good musician, composes well, is a most capital horseman, a fine jouster, speaks good French, Latin and Spanish, is very religious, hears masses three times a day when he hunts, and sometimes five on other days. He is very fond of hunting, and never takes his diversion without tiring eight or ten horses. He is extremely fond of tennis, at which game it is the prettiest thing in the world to see him play, his fair skin glowing through a shirt of the finest texture.

Imperial king

Henry wanted to revive the notion of England conquering large areas of France. This had been the intention during the Hundred Years' War (1338–1453), but with only limited success. One of the main highpoints was the battle of Agincourt in 1415, later made famous in Shakespeare's play, *Henry V*.

What qualities do you think made Henry a popular monarch, and different from his father?

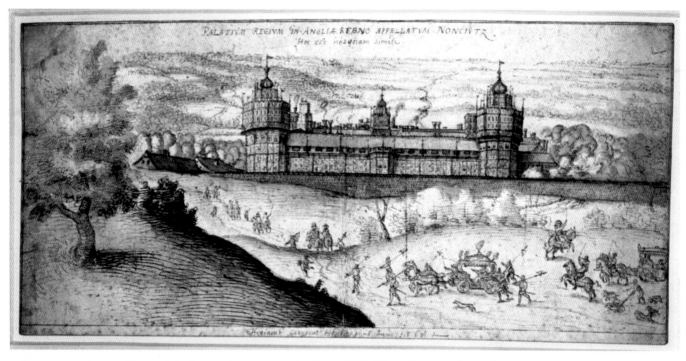

▲ The royal palace at Nonsuch in Surrey, in an engraving from 1582. The palace was intended to show the glory and power of Henry VIII through its impressive size and architectural style.

Henry's court

The image and reality of the new king was also reflected in the court that he created around himself. The royal court was not only the centre of politics and government, it was also a projection of the King's personality and the aura of majesty that he sought to create. Henry VII had maintained a lavish court, with generous hospitality and patronage of scholars and explorers. The court of Henry VIII was dedicated to pleasure and refinement. While the King's favourite activities were hunting, tennis and jousting, at which he excelled, he was also intelligent enough to enjoy the company of scholars steeped in the new learning of the Renaissance. Henry also enjoyed music and composed some creditable pieces of his own (albeit with some expert help which he kept quiet about). He also increased the number and quality of royal residences.

Treatment of the nobility

Henry VII had controlled the ambitions of the nobility more by threatening their status and wealth than by making concessions to them. Some historians have even gone as far as to wonder whether he intended to undermine the power of the nobility to the point where he could replace them in government with talented administrators. Henry VIII's attitude towards them seemed different from the outset. Early gestures of goodwill included disbanding the Council Learned in Law and cancelling 175 bonds and recognisances that were still owing. There is no doubt that the young king regarded the nobility as his friends and associates, with whom he could share his sporting and artistic pleasures. By gathering important men around him, Henry also enhanced the prestige of his court.

However, Henry shared his father's suspicion of possible rivals among the ranks of the nobility. Although the Yorkist threat was substantially weaker by 1509, there were still members of the greater nobility who carried royal blood in their veins, and who might be tempted to challenge the claims of the Tudors. The main candidate of the 'White Rose' party, as the Yorkists had come to be known, was Edmund de la Pole, the Earl of Suffolk. When Henry came to the throne, Suffolk was already imprisoned in the Tower of London. In 1513, Henry had him executed for treason, but his younger brother, Richard, remained free and in French service until his death at the Battle of Pavia in 1525. Although the French exploited his claims during negotiations with Henry, and even recognised him as 'King Richard IV', there was no serious attempt to replace Henry from abroad.

Style of government

Henry VII's style of government had been personal and extremely conscientious. He took major decisions himself, without the aid of a powerful chief minister. He moved the administration of finances into his private rooms at court, out of the Treasury and Exchequer. He largely ignored Parliament and showed time and again that he was not prepared to trust members of the nobility until he was certain that they could be forced to obey him.

Henry VIII adopted some of his father's tactics. He continued to use Justices of the Peace to carry out his wishes in local government rather than rely on the nobility. He also followed his father's practice of encouraging talented advisers and administrators from outside the nobility.

During Henry VIII's reign the Privy Chamber became even more important. It was part of the King's household, but had its own separate existence. When Henry dined in his Privy Chamber, only the most intimate advisers and courtiers were allowed to attend him there – a sure sign of who was in favour and who was out of favour in the politics of court life. The Gentlemen of the Privy Chamber had access to the King and were, by definition, members of the Court who travelled around when Henry moved from house to house. Henry had over 30 residences of his own in and near London, but he also travelled further afield, especially in July and August. The Privy Council consisted of about 20 of the men at Court and they gave advice on matters of state. In the earlier part of the reign Wolsey and then Sir Thomas More (as Lord Chancellor) took charge at meetings. In the last years of the reign the Comptroller of the King's Household (Sir William Paget) took charge of the meetings and sought advice or approval from the King on matters being discussed. In between, from 1532 to 1540, Thomas Cromwell gained the leading role.

However, there were crucial differences between Henry VIII's attitude towards day-to-day government and the attitudes of his father. In the first place, Henry VIII never gave the affairs of government the personal attention that his father had exercised, tending instead to delegate far greater power to his chief advisers. The adult years of Henry VIII's reign were dominated by two men – Cardinal Thomas Wolsey, between 1515 and 1529, and Thomas Cromwell, between 1532 and 1540. This was a new development in government. Henry VII's close personal control of the day-to-day running of the country did not suit his younger and more secure son. Although Henry VIII kept overall control, especially in the 1530s, he preferred to act out a combination of medieval and Renaissance images of kingship – the medieval 'good lord', who exhibited courage and honour, and the Renaissance 'universal man', as skilled in courtly etiquette and the arts as in warfare. He did not share his father's dedication to the unglamorous side of ruling, so left much of this to his chief ministers. However, as the careers of both Wolsey and Cromwell show, they depended heavily on maintaining the King's favour to survive. By allowing ministers to assume more power, Henry also encouraged what his father had largely avoided – factionalism at court.

Foreign policy at the beginning of the reign

The accession of Henry VIII in 1509 opened a new phase in foreign policy. Henry VII's foreign policy had been that of an insecure adult; Henry VIII's began as the actions of a confident teenager. Unlike his father, Henry VIII came to the throne peacefully and with money in the royal treasury. His priorities were therefore different: he was keen to establish his presence in international affairs and to demonstrate his strengths to his subjects. He wanted to win glorious victories on the field of battle to establish his image as a Renaissance warrior.

Relations with France

The easiest way to accomplish these aims was to revive hostilities with France. As part of an international alliance against France in 1512 he led an army there, but achieved very little. With rapidly increasing expenditure and little real gain, the demoralised soldiers, many ill or suffering from disease, returned to England. Having persuaded his advisers that a foreign campaign would be good for England's reputation, the result was an embarrassment.

Later in 1512 he turned to Thomas Wolsey, one of the young officials at court who had impressed Henry with his efficiency and enthusiasm to serve in any role. Wolsey organised a second expedition which went to France in 1513. The whole campaign was seen as a huge success. The English drove off the French in a cavalry encounter dubbed 'the Battle of the Spurs', and went on to capture the fortress of Therouanne and the town of Tournai. In 1514 the achievement was sealed in the Treaty of Saint Germaine-en-Laye, negotiated by Wolsey, which left England in possession of Tournai and Therouanne and Henry with a handsome annual payment for agreeing to give up his claims to the French throne. Henry had gained the reputation that he had sought as a young warrior king.

Relations with Scotland

Henry also had to face the Scots who allied against the French in 1512. James IV of Scotland led an army to invade the north-east of England with the intention of diverting English troops from going to France. Cannons from Edinburgh Castle were dragged by oxen on to English soil. With Henry in France, Catherine, his wife, was acting as Regent. The Earl of Surrey was given the title of Lieutenant-General of the North with instructions to take an army north to repel the invasion. The Battle of Flodden (September 1513) has been referred to as the last large-scale medieval-style battle in England. Artillery played an important part as well as hand-to-hand fighting. The English lost 1,500 men, but the Scots are said to have lost about 10,000. These included nine Earls, thirteen barons, three bishops and, most crucially, King James IV. This tremendous blow served to enhance the reputation of the English army.

Scotland was immeasurably weaker as a result of the defeat. A committee was set up to rule in the name of the wife of James IV, Margaret Tudor, and of her one-and-a-half-year-old son, James V. Scotland was not going to be an active threat to Henry VIII for some years to come.

Factionalism – The royal court, not Parliament, was the centre of political power and influence during the Tudor period. Courtiers advanced by attracting the King's attention, often with the help of someone who was one of his friends or supporters. In this way, groups of ambitious courtiers clustered around powerful nobles and ministers. Rivalry developed between these groups – or factions – as all were keen to win what limited royal patronage there was.

Source B From 'Henry VIII's early foreign policy, 1509–29' by Jez Ross, published in *History Today*, Issue 41, December 2001.

Henry VIII was indeed, unlike his father, a warlike monarch, seeking gloire [glory] and prestige and pursuing his dynastic rights, just like any other Renaissance prince. However, it would be wrong to argue that Henry was obsessed with warfare for its own sake, even though the cult of chivalry continued to make war appealing to contemporary monarchs. For example, as important as Henry VIII's claim to France was in justifying his cherished objective of occupying French territory, it also served a more practical purpose as a lever to extract concessions from the French.

What do you understand from Source B about Henry's aims in foreign policy?

KEY DATES: HENRY VIII: THE START OF A NEW ERA

1509 Accession of Henry VIII, aged seventeen; arrest of Empson and Dudley

1511–12 Henry led expedition to France

1513 Second expedition to France; victory at Battle of the Spurs; Battle of Flodden against Scots; execution of Edmund de la Pole, Earl of Suffolk

1514 Peace treaty with France

2 Wolsey as chief minister – Church and State

Wolsey dominated the government of England from the mid-1510s until 1529, as well as being the country's most influential churchman. These two aspects are investigated in turn, and his important role in foreign policy is featured in the following section.

The rise of Thomas Wolsey

Why was Wolsey able to gain so much influence and power by the mid-1510s?

Thomas Wolsey was born in 1472 or 1473, the son of a butcher in Ipswich. He won a scholarship to Oxford, where he began to study towards the priesthood. Wolsey was outstandingly able, receiving a degree at Oxford at the age of fifteen. While at Oxford he became the bursar (treasurer) of his college, a position which allowed him to develop his talent for organisation until a disagreement about whether he had obtained proper permission to authorise a large building project forced him to leave. He then tried, with little success, to find a powerful patron who would introduce him at court. Finally, in the last years of Henry VII's reign he gained patronage at court under Bishop Fox, one of the King's most trusted councillors.

The new atmosphere at court under Henry VIII encouraged ambitious men like Wolsey to get themselves noticed. He used the support of Richard Fox to gain promotion to the office of Royal Almoner, an official responsible for distributing left-over food from the palace kitchens to the needy poor who gathered outside each day. It was his organisational skills and his ability to guess what the King wanted to hear that allowed him to progress further. Since his accession Henry had been frustrated by the cautious advice of his father's ministers, especially in the field of foreign policy, where he wanted to make his mark. In 1512 the King entrusted Wolsey with the organisation of the following year's expedition to France. This meant organising transport, supplies and equipment for the 30,000-strong army which Henry proposed to lead himself. It was a big task, but Wolsey showed tireless energy and commitment to achieving it. The expedition went well and Wolsey was drawn into the peace negotiations which followed.

Henry was deeply impressed by Wolsey's efficiency in delivering success in Europe and engineered his rapid promotion to high office. By 1514 Henry was referring all major business to Wolsey, confident that it would be dealt with efficiently. Meanwhile Wolsey was angering all those at court who expected to have major influence over the King by being ruthless and discourteous to those at court with a high social rank.

Wolsey's rise to high office in Church and State

Within a few years Wolsey had accumulated ecclesiastical power to an extent that had never happened before in English history:

- **1513:** Became Dean of York and Bishop of Tournai (conquered in the French campaign that year).
- **1514:** Made Bishop of Lincoln and then Archbishop of York (the second highest post in the English Church).
- **1515:** Made Cardinal by Pope Leo X (a high-ranking position in the Catholic Church, above any English churchman); also became Lord Chancellor in Henry's government when William Warham resigned.

- **1518:** Appointed Papal Legate by Leo X (which allowed him to deputise for the Pope and exercise papal powers).

Wolsey's personality

It was accepted at the time that bishops were usually wealthy and worldly, but Wolsey came across as unusually proud and ostentatious. However, with such an impressive array of titles and positions, it was not difficult for Wolsey to elbow aside the King's noble advisers on the Royal Council and to become *alter rex* (the 'other king').

Wolsey's enemies – and he had many of these, including the Duke of Norfolk – came to see him as arrogant and vindictive. On the one hand, he flattered and apparently manipulated Henry, offering him lavish gifts and tokens while working him around to his ideas. At the same time, he used his legal powers as Lord Chancellor and a network of informants to intimidate anyone he saw as a rival. A good example of this was the treatment received by the Duke of Buckingham.

Source C The Venetian ambassador, Giustiniani, writing about Cardinal Wolsey in 1519.

The Cardinal is the first person who rules both the King and the entire kingdom. On the ambassador's first arrival in England he used to say to him, 'His Majesty will do so and so', but, by degrees, he began to forget himself and started to say, 'We shall do so and so'. Now he has reached such a height that he says, 'I shall do so and so'.

> What impression of Wolsey and Henry VIII is the Venetian ambassador in Source C trying to convey?

▲ Cardinal Wolsey. Wolsey is shown in the scarlet robes of a cardinal. He is holding a staff topped by a crown and in the other hand a piece of paper, thus showing he was the King's servant. It is the only known contemporary portrait (author unknown), but perhaps other portraits were destroyed after his fall from power.

Duke of Buckingham

The Duke of Buckingham, Edward Stafford, was the only man to hold the title of duke by the end of Henry VII's reign. In 1520 he was investigated by Wolsey after rumours that he had said in a private conversation that Henry might not be King for much longer. In 1521 he was ordered to London, arrested and imprisoned in the Tower. He refused to plead for his life, was tried for treason, and beheaded. Contemporaries believed, rightly or not, that Wolsey had played on Henry's insecurity to convince him to order these actions and had used Buckingham's fate as a warning to anyone who might be contemplating an attack on the cardinal's power.

Wolsey was certainly capable of taking revenge on anyone who offended him. He had been humiliated by Sir Amyas Paulet when he was a young priest, so on becoming Lord Chancellor, he summoned Paulet to London on a trumped-up charge and kept him there, demanding his daily attendance at the Court of Chancery for five years. The case was never heard, but the delays and expense virtually ruined Paulet.

Wolsey also amassed a large personal fortune and displayed his wealth ostentatiously. His household extended to over 500 servants and he usually travelled with a large escort of richly dressed attendants bearing his emblems and livery.

Source D From a report by the Venetian ambassador, Guistiniani, written in 1519.

He has a very great reputation – seven times more so than if he were the Pope. He has a very fine palace, where one crosses eight rooms before reaching his audience chamber, and they are all hung with tapestry, which is changed once a week. In his own chamber there is always a cupboard with silver vessels to the amount of 30,000 ducats [coinage used in Spain and elsewhere], this being customary with the English nobility. He is supposed to be very rich indeed in money, plate and household stuff. The archbishopric of York yields him about 14,000 ducats. From gifts, which he receives in the same manner as the King, he makes some 15,000 ducats.

Why is the Venetian ambassador portraying Wolsey in this way (Source D)?

Historians have tended to ignore many aspects of the fifteen years during which Wolsey ruled England with Henry. With hindsight, little appeared to change, compared with the establishment of the Tudors under Henry VII and the major changes in England in the 1530s with the Reformation and its consequences. The first major biography on Wolsey based on detailed research was by A. F. Pollard, published in 1929. Attention by historical researchers has focused much more on the periods before and after. However, recently, historians have been trying to establish the relationship between Wolsey and his master, Henry VIII, and whether that remained constant as Henry matured from a young man to middle age.

Wolsey and the Church

To what extent did Cardinal Wolsey seek to improve the Church?"

Wolsey was not just Henry's chief minister. He also pursued a career in the Church, ultimately as the Pope's representative in England. Henry supported him in this. Indeed, it was as a result of pressure from Henry and Wolsey that Pope Leo X made Wolsey a Cardinal. Henry's support was also important when Wolsey put pressure on the Pope to be appointed as a Papal Legate, first as a temporary position, and then in 1524, most unusually, he was granted the title of *Legatus a latere* (Papal Legate but with additional powers that meant he could act on behalf of the Pope). From this position, he was uniquely placed to give leadership or to reject those who wanted to reform the Church in England.

Condition of the Church in the 1520s

The condition of the Church in England is outlined in Chapter 1 (see pages 4–10). In essence, most people fully accepted Christian beliefs and there was substantial enthusiasm for religious devotion, as seen in the large-scale building projects that were taking place in the early 1500s. Most people, educated and uneducated, remained instinctively loyal to the Catholic Church and its teachings. On the other hand there was a definite strand of anti-clericalism, which Wolsey did nothing to reduce. With the advent of printing, more people became aware of the criticisms of taxes going to Rome to an extravagant Pope. People were aware of the shortcomings of the clergy, personified by Wolsey with all his pomp and ceremony, two illegitimate children (born in 1510 and 1512) and living openly with his mistress until 1519.

When the Reformation began in Europe, there were already those in England who would be sympathetic to Church reform. In the late fourteenth century John Wycliffe had been criticised for his beliefs that scripture was more important than the Pope and that there was too much emphasis on venerating the saints at the expense of personal piety. Descendants of his followers, known as the Lollards, survived in small numbers. Indeed, the Bishop of London in 1515 complained about their heretical views. They were to be found mostly in the south-east of England and in some other cities such as Bristol.

The other strand of dissent from Catholic beliefs stemmed from the events in Germany following Martin Luther's arguments that contradicted some key aspects of Catholicism – his 95 Theses – in 1517. He and other reformers published their beliefs, which stressed the Bible and criticised many Catholic rituals. Luther found that many people in Germany were willing to support him – partly for religious reasons and partly because what became known as Lutheranism could be used as a weapon against the Catholic Emperor, Charles V.

Source E Extracts from Luther's 95 Theses. These arguments consisted of 95 points that build up into an overall argument against the Pope's use of indulgences.

5. The Pope ... cannot remit any penalties other than those which he has imposed ...

21. Therefore those preachers of indulgences are in error who say that by the Pope's indulgences a man is freed from every penalty and saved.

24. It must needs be, therefore, that the greater part of the people are deceived by that indiscriminate and high-sounding promise of release from penalty.

43. Christians are to be taught that he who gives to the poor or lends to the needy does a better work than buying pardons.

62. The true treasure of the Church is the Most Holy Gospel of the glory and the grace of God.

NOTE-MAKING

In this section, write bullet points on what made Wolsey so powerful in the Church, and on what he achieved.

Papal Legate – Someone appointed by the Pope to act on his behalf in a particular country, usually for a specified purpose on a limited timescale.

William Tyndale

An early supporter of religious reforms along the lines outlined by Martin Luther, Tyndale strongly believed that the Bible should be available to all English people in their own tongue.

Luther's arguments criticising some aspects of Catholic beliefs and practices were reaching England by the 1520s, especially through merchants and traders. Ports in the south and east of England were exposed to Protestant literature because of trade with northern Europe. A group of Lutheran supporters, for example, met in Cambridge at the White Horse pub where they discussed Luther's theology. They were helped when **William Tyndale** started to publish parts of the Bible in English. Their numbers were small, but they assumed much greater importance when criticism became directed at the Catholic Church as part of Henry's attempt to gain a divorce. The protracted negotiations over the fate of Catherine of Aragon provided a forum for anyone's complaints against the Pope.

Wolsey and Church reform

At a time when the Reformation was underway in Europe and when there was clamour from some quarters for religious reforms, Wolsey did make some attempts although he did not see reforms as a major aspect of his work.

In his capacity as Papal Legate, Wolsey was able to instruct English bishops to carry out their duties more scrupulously and to order inspections of the quality of religious life in monasteries and other religious institutions. As a result, over two dozen religious houses were dissolved (closed down and their assets confiscated).

Wolsey was also interested in promoting religious learning to improve the quality of the clergy, partly funded by closing some monasteries. Papal permission for the monastic reform was obtained on condition that the money gained would be used to promote education. Indeed, in 1528 he drew up more plans for closing monasteries with fewer than six inmates and forcibly amalgamating those with under twelve, thus providing the starting-point for Cromwell in the next decade. He and his contemporaries saw nothing wrong in streamlining monasticism to make it more efficient and to benefit religious learning. It was not an attack on the concept of monastic life. While he was Papal Legate, he was responsible for removing from office eight unsuitable heads of monasteries. He planned to fund a school in his home town of Ipswich and to establish Cardinal College in Oxford, but he had fallen from power before these could be properly established.

As a cardinal representing the Catholic Church, Wolsey was strongly opposed to the spread of Protestant heresy in England. He encouraged Henry to take a stand against the new ideas of the German reformer Martin Luther, which led to public burnings of Lutheran texts. This started outside St Paul's in London in May 1521 when Wolsey was personally present, holding in his hand the unfinished manuscript of Henry VIII's book against Luther for which Henry was rewarded with the title 'Defender of the Faith' by the Pope. Several groups of people, mostly in universities, suspected of Protestant sympathies were arrested and punished, though no one was executed until 1530 after the fall of Wolsey. As recent historians such as Eamon Duffy and Christopher Haigh have argued, most people in England were content with Catholicism. Anti-clericalism was actually fairly limited. Therefore it was thought that the spread of Lutheranism could be stopped or at least limited, just as Lollardy had been a century before. Lutheran supporters were mostly seen as well-meaning people who had been wrongly influenced and who needed to see the error of their ways and to reform.

However, Wolsey's position in the Church did not always bring him praise. To some, he embodied everything that needed changing. He had already collected together a range of religious titles during his rise to power and he continued adding to them during the 1520s. He became Bishop of Durham in 1523 and Bishop of Winchester in 1529, both important positions which attracted good income. He was also appointed abbot of St Albans, one of the wealthiest monasteries in England. Of course, Wolsey could not hope to fulfil his religious duties in any of these posts, so he was permanently absent while a deputy acted for him. Because of this, Wolsey attracted criticism for the twin vices of absenteeism and plurality (the holding of more than one office at a time).

Source F From 'Cardinal Wolsey and the English Church' by Peter Marshall, Professor of History at Warwick University, published in *History Review*, 60, March 2008.

It is hard to dissent from the judgement of the historian Richard Rex (writing in 1992) that 'there is nothing in Wolsey's administration of the Church of England to justify in terms of reform the enormous legatine powers devolved on him from the papacy'. Wolsey was not the deeply corrupt, power-mad prelate of Protestant legend, but neither was he the kind of inspirational, reforming leader that English Catholicism needed if it was going to surmount the twin challenges of doctrinal rebellion and growing conflict between Church and State.

> From what you have studied, find evidence to agree or disagree with the judgement given in Source F.

Government under Wolsey

How effective was Wolsey's period of office as Chancellor?

Henry tended to leave Wolsey with day-to-day control of government, although Wolsey was careful never to assume that this meant that he could ignore the King. Indeed, he spent much of his time trying to keep Henry informed about what was going on while making sure that other courtiers did not replace him in the King's favour. A particular problem he faced was that Henry liked to surround himself with favourite nobles of his own age – his 'minions'. These men had access to the King's private rooms in the palace, so they could influence Henry from behind the scenes as well as prevent others from getting to see him.

Some of Wolsey's reforms of government were designed more to undermine potential political opponents, such as the minions, rather than to ensure good government. For example, in 1526 the Eltham Ordinances laid out methods for reorganising the chaotic finances of the Privy Chamber and for making the King's household more efficient. However, in reality, it appears that Wolsey was using these so-called reforms to reduce the influence of others at court and increase the control he could exert himself over the various aspects of government. Once he had achieved this greater control, the reforms were allowed to lapse. In general, Wolsey made few changes to the structure of government. Instead, he expended his energies in bringing about specific changes to aspects of royal policy that either dissatisfied him or which were not working to his or Henry's best advantage.

> **NOTE-MAKING**
>
> Make bullet-point notes on what Wolsey achieved as Chancellor.

Legal reforms

As Lord Chancellor, Wolsey was responsible for overseeing the legal system. His main concern was to tackle the problem of slow and often unfair delivery of justice. By 1516 he was already planning reforms to the system to improve matters. In particular he wanted to promote civil law, which was based on natural justice and evidence, rather than the common law which was based on precedent (that is, decisions on similar cases in the past).

The centre piece of his plans was a strengthened Star Chamber. Henry VII had established this court, which was staffed by members of the Privy Council, to deal out justice on his behalf, often in cases involving the nobility. However, it had not been particularly active, probably hearing only about a dozen cases each year. Wolsey used Star Chamber much more frequently to attack nobles and local officials who abused their power. He encouraged commoners to bring their complaints before the court and in doing so, increased the number of cases heard each year to about 120. This gave him the reputation of being a friend to the poor. In particular, he championed the laws against enclosure of land for sheep. He also used the Court of Requests to hear cases from poor people. It met in Whitehall in the Palace of Westminster (whereas under Henry VII it had been more tied to where the king was). It was popular because of the low cost of bringing a case and because decisions were reached quickly.

Source G From a report by the Venetian ambassador, Guistiniani, written in 1519.

He alone transacts as much business as that which occupies all the magistrates, offices and councils of Venice, both civil and criminal. He is thoughtful and has the reputation of being extremely just. He favours the people exceedingly, and especially the poor, hearing their cases and seeking to dispatch them instantly. He also makes the lawyers plead without charge for all paupers.

However, when the pursuit of justice for all clashed with his own interests, it was the latter that gained his attention. He was, after all, not a trained lawyer, and his interventions were resented by those who were. He did not seek to set up a new system, so his reforms were personal and unlikely to continue when he was not there. His modern biographer, Peter Gwyn, suggests that his interventions were piecemeal and not systematic, rather than tackling the issues as a whole.

Financial reforms

Shortage of money was a serious problem for Henry VIII. His father had made do by avoiding an expensive foreign policy, but this was not in keeping with the new King's desire to get himself noticed and respected by other rulers. Wolsey realised that existing forms of finance (see Chapter 1, pages 21–23) could not be exploited much further. In particular parliamentary grants, which were based on property taxes called fifteenths and tenths, had settled to a fixed sum, so were unlikely to rise much in the future. Indeed, with growing inflation (see Chapter 6, page 170) the sums raised were worth less and less in real terms.

In 1522 Wolsey organised a national survey to assess who could pay tax and how much. It was the first systematic investigation into national finances since the Domesday Survey of 1086. He used this to gain about £200,000 in forced loans in 1522–23. However, this was not enough in a period of inflation and expensive foreign policy.

To overcome this, Wolsey proposed a more flexible tax – a subsidy. This had to be approved by the House of Commons which met in 1523, but was based on income rather than property, similar to modern income tax. The subsidy did not raise as much as was hoped, and Wolsey also levied a tax on the Church.

In 1525, he proposed an 'Amicable Grant' from both the Church and ordinary taxpayers based on his valuations of their property. The reaction to this demand was to provoke the only significant rebellion in the first half of Henry VIII's reign.

Do you think Source G is giving an unbiased view of Wolsey's motives?

Amicable Grant

In March and April 1525 the government sent out commissioners to order the collection of the Amicable Grant. They were instructed to tax the laity at between one-sixth and one-tenth of the value of the goods they owned, and to tax the clergy at one-third of the value of their goods. They gave people just ten weeks to find the necessary money. Resistance was immediate and widespread, forcing Wolsey to begin admitting exceptions to the tax. As news of these spread, more regions demanded that they too should be exempted. Henry responded to the unrest caused by the tax by stepping in to suspend it. It was an embarrassing climb-down for both the King (who hoped to use the money raised for renewed warfare in France) and Wolsey.

Economic policies

It was not usual in the Tudor period for governments to have coherent economic policies, if only because there was little that could be regarded as a national economy and little that counted as widespread industry beyond shipbuilding and woollen production. However, Wolsey involved himself in the growing problem of enclosures. There had been tentative attempts to tackle the issue under Henry VII, but Henry had been too concerned not to annoy landowners unnecessarily while he was still vulnerable to opposition to sort matters out effectively. Wolsey had no such concerns and held the view that the conversion of arable land to sheep pasture by enclosing fields destroyed village life and jobs.

In 1517 Wolsey began a national enquiry to find out how much land was enclosed and what effects it was having. From this, legal cases were drawn up against landlords who were judged to have enclosed land without the proper permission. Further investigations were conducted in 1518, although opposition from landowners in Parliament in 1523 forced him to suspend these enquiries temporarily until 1526.

Foreign policy could easily disrupt trade – as happened in the late 1520s. Wolsey's alliance with France against Spain caused problems. England had little money with which to fight, and the main weapon was a trade embargo against Spain which controlled the Netherlands as part of Burgundy. This affected the English cloth trade very badly and coincided with the effects of one of the worst harvests (1527) of the period. There was widespread unemployment, the effects of which were made worse by the rise in prices that had set in during this decade (see Chapter 6, page 170). In 1526 Wolsey undertook a recoinage which increased the number of coins in circulation but reduced the weight of the silver coins. This debasement of the coinage stimulated exports, but contributed to the rise in prices as the coins were seen as worthless.

The later 1520s marked the first occasion in Tudor England where economic depression and price rises caused substantial suffering among the poor. Many riots had to be quelled in the spring of 1528 in the south east, East Anglia and the south west.

Wolsey and Parliament

Wolsey could easily be accused of trying to rule without Parliament, as only two were called – in 1515 and in 1523. The first caused problems for Wolsey over Hunne's Case and provided clear evidence of anti-clericalism, especially in the city of London; the second one was called only so that Parliament could agree to taxation as a result of the expensive foreign policy being pursued.

MPs only met when the King needed them, not as a right, and they met to carry out the King's wishes. Henry VIII next needed them in 1529 over his divorce.

KEY DATES: GOVERNMENT UNDER WOLSEY

1513 Wolsey in effect Henry's chief adviser

1515 Wolsey officially seen as chief minister when he became Lord Chancellor. Also appointed a Cardinal by the Pope

1517 Luther published his 95 Theses

1518 Wolsey appointed as Papal Legate

1523 Wolsey became Bishop of Durham

1525 Amicable Grant caused unrest in various parts of the country

1529 Wolsey became Bishop of Winchester

Hunne's Case

Richard Hunne was a respectable London merchant tailor. When his child died he refused to pay the usual mortuary fee to the Church. Hunne was arrested and put in the Bishop of London's prison. He was found hanged there, and a London jury returned a verdict of murder, adding that the Bishop was an accomplice. Parliament took up the case, and Cardinal Wolsey, as the senior representative of the Church in England, had to kneel before Parliament, begging forgiveness.

3 England's relations with foreign powers, 1509–29

This section becomes complicated because of the shifting political landscape:

- The changing situation in Europe, with changing alliances.
- The impact of the Reformation from 1517 onwards.
- The fear of the Ottoman Turks who were Muslim and gaining more control of the Mediterranean. In the 1520s the Ottoman Sultan, Suleiman the Magnificent, renewed campaigns in the Balkans and threatened to take Vienna. This was of major concern to Charles V and to the whole of Europe in general.
- Trying to establish the motives of Wolsey (and Henry) as to whether they primarily wanted to pursue war as a means to glory, or whether the primary aim was to establish long-lasting peace.

The map (Figure 1) on page 55 should help you.

The map (Figure 1) on page 55 should help you.

NOTE-MAKING

As you read this section, construct a timeline recording the main events and decisions during the period 1509–29. Then colour code the information to show when England was allied to Spain and when England was allied to France.

The challenge of foreign policy

Why was it difficult for Wolsey to succeed in foreign policy, and how did he try to achieve success?

Henry had won victories in France and Scotland in 1513. Although these gave Henry what he wanted in the short term – a quick military adventure to bring him popularity at home and respect abroad – it was hardly the beginning of a new era of English greatness in Europe. The campaigns had been expensive and had wiped out the surplus of money that Henry VII had so carefully gathered in his later years. It had also resulted in little real achievement beyond the satisfaction of defeating France. Tournai and Therouanne were not impressive spoils of war – Tournai was described as an 'ungracious doghole'.

The difficulty facing Wolsey was how to establish an effective role for England in European affairs. The resources at his disposal were limited. England could not compete in size or wealth with the French and Habsburgs monarchies. England was well placed to threaten the supply lines that the Habsburgs used to connect their scattered possessions in Spain and the Netherlands, or to threaten northern France, but she was relegated to a minor role whenever the focus of French–Habsburg rivalry shifted to the Italian peninsula. At the same time, Wolsey's survival as chief minister depended on him building Henry's reputation and delivering further victories.

Before Wolsey could discover the solution to this problem the European balance of power shifted with the deaths of King Louis XII of France in 1515, Ferdinand of Aragon in 1516 and the Holy Roman Emperor Maximilian I in 1519. Suddenly, Europe was populated with new, young monarchs who could compete personally with Henry to be the centre of attention.

The 21-year-old successor to the French throne, Francis I, showed this by immediately invading northern Italy to recapture Milan from the Habsburgs. His resounding victory over Swiss mercenaries in the Battle of Marignano gave him a reputation far in excess of what Henry had won by capturing Tournai. To make matters worse, the deaths of Ferdinand of Aragon and Maximilian I had allowed their grandson, the sixteen-year-old Charles, to assume the titles of King of Spain and Holy Roman Emperor in addition to his existing position as Duke in the Netherlands. Charles now commanded a vast empire stretching from the Americas through western and central Europe down into North Africa (see Figure 1). There was no chance that Henry could compete with Charles on an equal footing.

Wolsey's response to these changes was to create a new role in Europe for his master. Since Henry lacked the resources to wage war alongside these giants, Wolsey established England as the peacemaker between them. At the same time, he was careful not to ignore Henry's desire for military glory, especially at the expense of Francis I who was far too similar in character and ambition to Henry himself not to be regarded with jealousy.

Treaty of London, October 1518

Leo X, who had become Pope in 1513, had called for a general crusade to halt the spread of Ottoman power in Eastern Europe. There was little chance of this happening, but Wolsey saw in the scheme an opportunity to place England at the centre of European diplomacy. Rather than focusing on the crusade, he called for all the major powers of Europe to settle their differences and live under 'universal peace'. Over two dozen countries signed the resulting treaty, which committed them to avoid war or risk being attacked by the rest of the signatories. In this way, a crude balance of power was to be established across Western Europe which would prevent conflicts of the type seen since 1494 in Italy.

Ottoman power – The Ottoman Turks had become powerful by the fifteenth century and had begun to expand around the eastern end of the Mediterranean. They were Muslim and keen to spread their religion and build up an empire. Constantinople had been conquered in 1453. By the early 1500s the Ottoman Turks were expanding their control around the Eastern Mediterranean and threatening south east Europe.

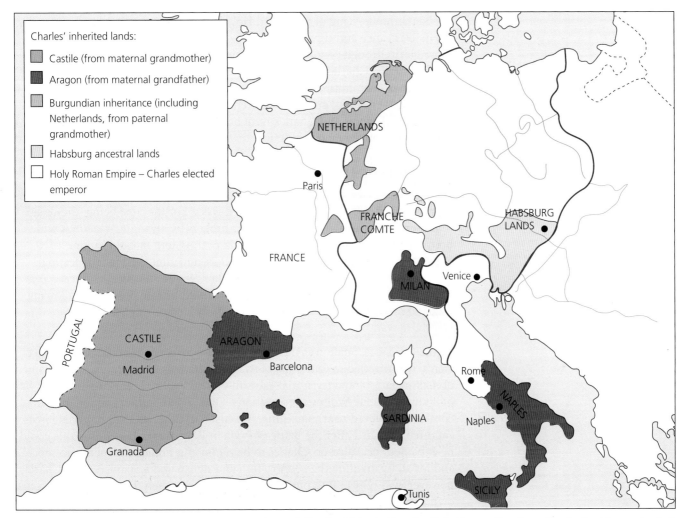

▲ Figure 1 Map of Europe showing the possessions of Charles V, including the Holy Roman Empire, after he had been elected Emperor in 1519. It also shows the areas of Italy that Charles controlled for most of his reign.

England was the pivotal point in this balance of power. Wolsey had arranged that each country should sign the treaty separately with England, rather than having everyone sign the same document. The treaty was, says historian Susan Doran, 'a glittering success', because it brought immediate fame to Henry, upstaged even the Pope and dispelled English isolation. Henry and Wolsey attempted to play out their roles as power-brokers in European politics for the next couple of years, but another turn of events – Charles becoming Holy Roman Emperor – again wrecked their plans.

Source H A view on the importance of the Treaty of London (1518). From *Europe and England in the Sixteenth century*, by T. A. Morris, (Routledge), 1998, p.160.

This Treaty of London did not last, and thus it has often been dismissed as a mere exercise in egoism. It remains probable, however, that Wolsey was sincere, and he had temporarily outflanked the Pope in his role as European peacemaker. If the prominence and prestige of the crown were the primary aims of foreign policy, then that policy reached its highest point in the Treaty of London.

In 1519 Charles was officially elected as Holy Roman Emperor, thus completing his dominance over Europe, and the Treaty of London's call for 'universal peace' began to look decidedly shaky. The problem lay in the change that Charles's election brought to relations with France. He was now ruler of the Netherlands, King of Spain and Holy Roman Emperor. His lands virtually encircled France and threatened to choke any efforts Francis made to win more glory through conquest. His election also threatened French control in northern Italy. Charles did not just inherit the title of emperor, but also his grandfather's commitments, one of which was to pursue the imperial claim to control over Milan, currently in French hands after Francis's victory at Marignano. Francis and Charles were now in direct opposition to each other and war was only a matter of time.

Support for the Habsburgs, 1520–25

Henry and Wolsey were gripped by the dilemma of having to choose one side over the other, when both choices carried risks. For the time being, they tried to preserve their image as neutral power-brokers by arranging meetings with both sides. Henry met Francis at the Field of the Cloth of Gold in June 1520 and also conferred with Charles twice, before and after the French meeting. Ultimately, though, Henry could not afford to remain shackled to a peace treaty that was so obviously collapsing, nor could he lose prestige by allowing England merely to stand on the sidelines and watch during any Franco-Habsburg war.

Of the two sides, Spain was the more attractive for a potential English alliance. Henry was married to Catherine of Aragon, Charles's aunt, and he still dreamed of making substantial territorial gains in France. In 1522, England declared war on France, despite Wolsey's reservations. Once again, military action on the continent achieved next to nothing, but cost a fortune. In 1525 imperial forces captured Francis I after the Battle of Pavia in Italy. Henry hoped that this could be exploited; he called on Charles to help him end French independence once and for all by dividing the country into an English and a Spanish zone. Charles, however, was reluctant to pursue English interests when they did not match his own and Henry again saw his plans thwarted.

Using events in the years 1509–18, what evidence is there that Henry's foreign policy was mostly a success?

Support for France, 1525–29

The results of English support for Charles in the early 1520s had disappointed both Henry and Wolsey. It appeared to them that Charles had used England to distract France but had given England nothing in return. In particular, Henry had felt that Francis's crushing defeat at Pavia had removed any obstacle to his long-held ambition to revive England's claims to the French throne. Charles's refusal to help infuriated him, but Henry was unable to raise the finances for an army to take action himself. Instead, Wolsey joined negotiations between France, the Pope, Venice and Florence for an anti-Habsburg alliance – the League of Cognac (1526), hoping still to play the peacemaker by using the talks to pressure Charles into being more reasonable.

Events soon dragged England into war against Charles, however. At the same time that Wolsey was trying to steer a course between France and Spain, Henry's decision to seek a divorce from Catherine of Aragon made neutrality impossible. Charles was Catherine's nephew, so was unlikely to view divorce proceedings favourably. Worse, Charles's army had followed up its victory at Pavia by taking control of most of the Italian peninsula, leaving the Pope a virtual prisoner. Since Henry required the Pope's approval for the divorce, Wolsey was forced to take a more direct stand against Charles. England and France concluded an alliance in 1527, and in 1528 both were at war with the Habsburgs.

The English contribution was again ineffectual, and in June 1529 Charles once again defeated the French at the Battle of Landriano. It was only at the last moment that Wolsey was able to ensure that England would be included in the resulting peace treaty, which was signed at Cambrai in August 1529. A fortnight later, Wolsey fell from power.

> ### KEY DATES: THE CHALLENGE OF FOREIGN POLICY
>
> **1518** Treaty of London
>
> **1519** Charles V, already King of Spain, elected Holy Roman Emperor
>
> **1520** The Field of the Cloth of Gold in France
>
> **1522** War declared against France
>
> **1526** League of Cognac, supporting France against the Habsburgs
>
> **1529** Treaty of Cambrai

ACTIVITY

Cardinal Wolsey's foreign policy aims have been the subject of some debate among historians:
- According to the early twentieth-century historian A. F. Pollard, Wolsey was keen to use England in the pursuit of the balance of power, but in particular wanted 'to hitch England to the Holy See'. He suggested that England matched the Pope's foreign policy, because Wolsey wanted to be rewarded with the title of cardinal and ultimately the Papacy.
- J. J. Scarisbrick, whose biography of Henry VIII in 1968 challenged Pollard's views, argued that Wolsey frequently did the opposite of what the Papacy wanted, and he doubted whether Wolsey really had serious ambitions to be Pope. He sought peace because war was expensive, and tried to achieve peace by allying with the strongest European power, so that no other country would dare attack.
- However, others take a more pragmatic line. Further analysis by historians since the 1970s has led to claims that Wolsey followed whatever path would bring him personal advancement and power (which meant satisfying both the King's need for glory and the Pope's interests). There was no coherent overall strategy and his priorities changed with changing circumstances.

Use the material in this section and your further research either to test some or all of these interpretations or to develop your own explanation of what Wolsey hoped to achieve.

NOTE-MAKING

Make notes on this section on the reasons for Henry's wish for a divorce and on the reasons why this was not achieved.

4 Henry's quest for a divorce

This section explains the close connection between the fall of Wolsey from power and Henry's increasing preoccupation with wanting a divorce from Catherine of Aragon. The relationship between the King and his powerful minister is then examined.

Wolsey and the King's divorce

Why did Wolsey fail to secure a divorce for Henry?

Wolsey's biggest challenge came in the late 1520s, when Henry decided that he needed to divorce Catherine of Aragon. It is possible that Henry was considering a divorce before he met Anne Boleyn. Catherine had failed to produce a male heir. However, Henry was apparently preparing his illegitimate son, born in 1519 and created the Duke of Richmond, to fill the role of heir-apparent. This makes it seem that a divorce from Catherine was not his priority at that moment.

What was Henry's priority – as with all monarchs of that period – was the need to establish the line of succession, preferably through an undisputed male heir. An illegitimate son might be accepted, although others with a lesser but legitimate claim could challenge the succession. At its worst it could lead to civil war, with the Wars of the Roses still fresh in people's memories.

By 1527 Henry had decided firmly that he wanted a divorce as he had become besotted with Anne Boleyn. Henry had spoken to Wolsey of the doubts about his marriage to Catherine as early as 1525, but the matter only became urgent in 1527 when Anne made it clear that she would not be Henry's mistress, causing Henry to be increasingly infatuated. A divorce would not be easy to obtain, however. The Pope, Clement VII, was very much under the control of the Emperor Charles V who was the nephew of Catherine of Aragon. Therefore neither Charles nor the Pope would be keen to support Henry's wish.

Wolsey tried three approaches to secure Henry's divorce:

1 Scriptural arguments

First, Wolsey drew up a complex line of argument based on the scriptures to justify the divorce in the eyes of the Catholic Church. He argued that the validity of Catherine's marriage to Henry in 1509 relied on Catherine's word that her first marriage to Prince Arthur had never been consummated. However, if this was not the case, Henry had been misled and the marriage had never been valid. This was based on a text from the Old Testament – Leviticus Chapter 20, Verse 16:

If a man shall take his brother's wife, it is an impurity; he hath uncovered his brother's nakedness; they shall be childless.

Henry became convinced that the lack of a legitimate male heir was God's punishment. He was living in sin and his conscience would not allow this to continue. Armed with this justification, Wolsey was confident that he could persuade the Pope to agree to the annulment. However, it was not that simple. Many theologians did not agree on Leviticus' meaning. Bearing in mind the practice of polygamy at the time it was written, many experts thought that it referred to not marrying your sister-in-law when your brother was still alive. After his death it was a man's duty to marry her and have children on his brother's behalf, as instructed in the book of Deuteronomy.

2 Diplomatic manoeuvres

The second line of attack was against Emperor Charles V. As Catherine's nephew he was unlikely to support a divorce and it was doubly inconvenient that at the moment Henry wanted it, Charles was in control in Italy. Wolsey tried to free the Pope from Charles's influence by using an alliance with France and the renewal of warfare in Italy to distract the Emperor. This policy failed, however, because Charles was too strongly entrenched in the Italian peninsula to be evicted by France.

3 Legal efforts

Finally, Wolsey hoped to side-step the whole problem of Charles V and his control over the Pope by holding the divorce hearings in England where he, as Papal Legate, would make the judgment. However, the Pope, Clement VII, was still concerned not to offend Charles V, so although he agreed to set up a commission to hear the divorce case, he sent Cardinal Campeggio to England with strict instructions to delay the hearing and to make sure that a decision was never reached. Wolsey had hoped that Campeggio would be co-operative – after all, he was already compromised by being the absentee Bishop of Salisbury. However, Campeggio was unwell, genuinely took months to reach England, and then wanted to do everything very thoroughly. Henry and Wolsey both became increasingly impatient.

When the court finally met in June 1529 to discuss the case, Catherine immediately refused to recognise it and appealed to the Pope to move the hearing to Rome. Since this offered him another opportunity to frustrate the divorce while not openly offending either Charles or Henry, the Pope agreed and the English court was wound up. As it did so, it became clear to Henry that Wolsey had run out of options for solving this problem. Wolsey's use to Henry had ended.

The fall of Wolsey

Why did Wolsey fall from power in 1529?

Wolsey had maintained his power and position because he served Henry well. When he ceased to do so, he fell from power. His two great failures were the collapse of his anti-Habsburg strategy in Europe, forced on him by the success of Charles V in Italy after 1525, and his inability to obtain the divorce for which the King had been waiting for two years. Neither of these objectives could be achieved at the time, but it was Wolsey who paid the price for failure.

In the summer of 1529 Henry used Wolsey's position as Papal Legate to accuse him of Praemunire – working in the interests of the Pope rather than his King. Ironically, it was his position as Papal Legate (which Henry had worked so hard to obtain for Wolsey) that was used against him. He was stripped of his powers and possessions and exiled to his diocese of York. Wolsey believed, perhaps correctly, that the King's mind had been poisoned against him by the supporters of Anne Boleyn at court, who blamed him for his failure to win approval for the royal divorce. There is evidence, explained in detail by David Starkey, that Wolsey had been losing control of the Royal Council in the late 1520s as Anne's father, brother and other supporters gained more influence there. This was exactly the kind of threat that Wolsey had always feared and tried to prevent by restricting access to the King. Now he was in no position to do so. It is certainly true that there was no love lost between Wolsey and Anne Boleyn's supporters, and it was easy for them to portray Wolsey as a papal official who was not really trying to obtain a divorce. However, there was a

> **Praemunire** – A Latin term used in medieval laws which made it a crime to use powers derived from the Pope to the disadvantage of the King or his subjects.

compelling reason for Wolsey to work hard to obtain the divorce – that is, his own political future – and there is plenty of contemporary written evidence to show that Wolsey was fully aware of this.

During the months that followed, Henry twice sent tokens of friendship to his former minister, raising Wolsey's hopes that he might be reinstated, but, instead, he was summoned to London in 1530 to answer further charges. Exactly why Henry acted then is not clear, but it was probably because he became convinced by Anne's supporters at court that Wolsey had been actively working against the divorce. Wolsey's ill-health led to his death on the journey southward, at Leicester on 29 November 1530, saving him the disgrace of being tried for treason. In a little over a year, the man who had apparently ruled England for the previous fifteen years was destroyed.

Why had Wolsey lost Henry's confidence by 1529?

There were four main factors that led to Wolsey's downfall:

1 His failure to secure Henry's divorce from Catherine of Aragon.
2 His failure to achieve Henry's aims in foreign policy – England was marginalised and isolated.
3 The fact that the Boleyn faction was hinting that Wolsey was delaying the divorce.
4 His reputation and personal ambitions.

Source I An assessment by G. R. Elton in his introduction to *Wolsey* by A. F. Pollard, (Collins), 1965.

Wolsey's long period of ascendancy proved essentially sterile ... Wolsey was not a creative or reflective man but an uncomplicated activist, a magnificent if often extravagant manipulator of what was available. And here lies some measure of redemption. To recognize that Wolsey contributed virtually nothing to the future is not to discard his present. For fifteen years he impressed England and Europe with his grandeur, his hard work, his skill and intelligence, and his very positive action in the affairs of the world. He often achieved what he set out to do, even if subsequent events showed his aims to have been mistaken and his solutions to have been patchwork. He made a great and deserved name, and his age would have been very different without him.

Interpretations: the relationship between Henry and Wolsey

Historians now generally agree that Henry was in charge, even when youthful, but that he recognised Wolsey's huge abilities and that often he allowed Wolsey full control to carry out policies. Therefore Wolsey only had independent decision-making when Henry sanctioned it. Consequently, the relationship was master and servant, with the servant bearing more power and influence than was normally the case.

Wolsey was completely aware that his power depended entirely on the goodwill of Henry, as proved in 1529. He had risen from the son of a butcher, his position at court depended entirely on Henry, and he was never going to gain full respect from noble families who upheld the hierarchical structure of society. After Henry had gained his divorce and the political reformation had occurred in the 1530s, it was natural for contemporaries and later historians to relegate Wolsey to the position of over-powering minister who acted despotically until he was ousted from power.

KEY DATES: THE FALL OF WOLSEY

1525 Henry started worrying about his marriage and the lack of a legitimate male heir

1527 Henry's marriage concerns actively discussed. Approach to the Pope and to Charles V

1528 Pope Clement VII agreed to send Campeggio to England to hear the case

1529 Case collapses. Wolsey stripped of his offices

1530 Wolsey summoned to trial, but died at Leicester on the way

---

Using your knowledge, write out a list of reasons or pieces of information that support the arguments in Source I. Then write out another list suggesting some disagreements.

Source J From 'Henry VIII and his Ministers' by John Guy, published in *History Review*, 23, December 1995.

For fifteen years Henry and Wolsey governed as a partnership. The king required a minister to accomplish his 'will and pleasure' and Wolsey triumphantly succeeded. Not everything was plain sailing. Tensions occasionally arose in the fields of military strategy and church patronage. But only rarely did Henry and Wolsey overtly disagree – as in the summer of 1521 when Wolsey was visiting Calais and was therefore unable to ride to Court, or in the spring of 1522 when he urged a surprise attack on the French navy, but Henry thought the plan too dangerous.

It follows from this interpretation that Wolsey, whom foreign ambassadors depicted as *'alter rex'* or 'second king', was more the loyal servant of the Crown than conventional historiography has suggested. That does not imply that Henry VIII knew or approved of everything Wolsey did, nor did it oblige Henry to stand by his minister when things went wrong. When Wolsey ... seemingly achieved 'universal peace' in Europe by a miracle of diplomacy, Henry was the first to claim the credit.

Source K From *Henry VIII* (Yale English Monarchs series) by J. J. Scarisbrick, (Yale University Press), 1997, pp.70–71.

For much of his career as Chancellor, it was Wolsey who alone guided English affairs. His quick, strong hands grasped everything because Henry seemed unable, or unwilling, to make the smallest decision himself. Who should attend upon the Princess Mary? What shall he reply to the regent of the Netherlands? ... All these Wolsey had to decide for him, for they were problems which this apparently helpless man, for all his bluster and swagger, could not resolve. Wolsey must be servant and master, creature yet impresario; he must abase himself and yet dominate, playing a part which only a man of superlative energy, self-confidence and loyalty could have endured. Yet the king who so often seemed to want nothing more than to dance and to hunt, and to have only the feeblest grip on royal duties, was also the man who, time and time again, could show a detailed grasp of foreign affairs and hold his own with, if not outdo, foreign ambassadors; ... who could pounce on something Wolsey had missed; ... assess a situation exactly, confidently overrule his minister ... There is no doubt that, at times, Henry was furiously involved in public business and in commanding partnership with Wolsey; and that he could break into his minister's conduct of affairs with decisive results.

Source L From *Cardinal Wolsey: Church, State and Art* by S. J. Gunn and P. G. Lindley (eds.), (Cambridge University Press), 1991, p.157.

The king took a more consistent and informed interest in foreign policy than in most other areas of government, and this both eased and complicated Wolsey's task. King and cardinal could work as a very effective double-act, using audiences with the king, 'simple and candid by nature', to encourage ambassadors frustrated by the cardinal's obstructiveness. Wolsey could use the king's disapproval as an excuse for refusing to contemplate concessions, or win goodwill from an ambassador by stressing the trouble he had had in persuading Henry to accept a proposal. Henry enjoyed lecturing envoys on such themes as the benefits of universal peace, but was equally happy to leave the grind of detailed negotiation to his minister.

ACTIVITY

There has been much discussion in the last half century about the exact relationship between the young Henry and his chief minister, Thomas Wolsey.

Study Sources J, K and L.
1 Construct a table to highlight the similarities and differences in what is said about the relationship between Henry and Wolsey in these three interpretations.
2 What are your own conclusions on the subject?

Chapter summary

- Henry VIII became King aged seventeen; and was a very different character from his father.
- In the early years of the reign were he implemented an active foreign policy against France and Scotland.
- Wolsey was dominant in Church and State by 1514 and this continued until 1529.
- As Chancellor, Wolsey carried out law reforms and attempted financial reforms.
- There was some anti-clericalism in the Catholic Church, but not as much as has sometimes been claimed.
- The Reformation in Europe began in 1517 under Martin Luther, and he gained some supporters in England in the 1520s.
- Wolsey, powerful as Cardinal and Papal Legate, did attempt some improvements in education and acted against Lutheran supporters and Lutheran literature.
- Foreign policy oscillated between allying with France and with Spain – doing what seemed best in English interests in the frequently changing European political scene.
- Henry VIII's wished for a divorce but he encountered difficulties because of the European situation.
- Wolsey, having failed by 1529 to gain a divorce for Henry, fell from power and died in 1530.

Chapter summary diagram

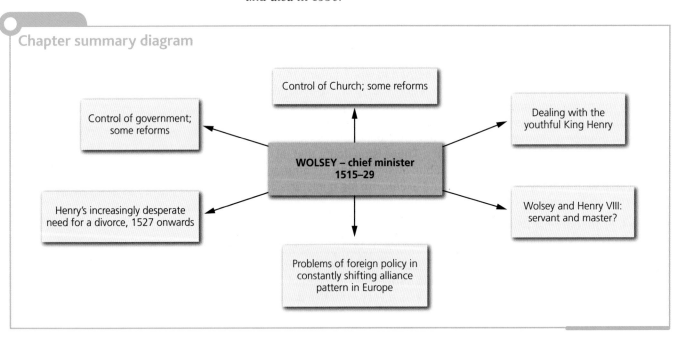

Control of Church; some reforms

Control of government; some reforms

Dealing with the youthful King Henry

WOLSEY – chief minister 1515–29

Henry's increasingly desperate need for a divorce, 1527 onwards

Wolsey and Henry VIII: servant and master?

Problems of foreign policy in constantly shifting alliance pattern in Europe

Working on essay technique: analysis

Analysis is a term that covers a variety of high-level skills including explanation and evaluation. In essence, analysis means breaking down something complex into smaller parts. This means that a clear structure which breaks down a complex question into a series of paragraphs is the first step towards writing an analytical essay.

Explanation

The purpose of explanation is to account for why something happened, or why something is true or false. An explanatory statement requires two parts: a **claim** and a **justification**.

EXAMPLE

If you are answering the following AS-level practice question:

'The most successful domestic policy in the period 1509–29 was Wolsey's legal reforms.' Explain why you agree or disagree with this view. (25 marks)

You might want to argue that one important example was Wolsey's increased use of the Court of Star Chamber, set up under Henry VII. Once you have made this point, and supported it with relevant detail, you can then explain how this answers the question.

For example, you could conclude your paragraph like this:

Claim ——• So Wolsey's increased use of the Court of Star Chamber was successful because •—Relationship he was able to use it to attack nobles and local officials who abused their power, and this meant that the monarchy had increased its control over the country.

Justification

The first part of this sentence is the claim while the second part justifies the claim. 'Because' is a very important word to use when writing an explanation, as it shows the relationship between the claim and the justification.

Evaluation

The purpose of evaluation is to weigh up and reach a judgement. Evaluation, therefore, needs to consider the importance of two or more different factors, weigh them against each other, and then reach a judgement. Evaluation is a good skill to use at the end of an essay because the conclusion should reach a judgement which answers the question.

> **EXAMPLE**
>
> Consider the AS-level practice question on page 63.
>
> If you were answering this question you might want to weigh up the extent to which Wolsey's legal reforms were the most successful or his financial reforms.
>
> For example, your conclusion might read:
>
> *Clearly, Wolsey's legal reforms were important because they represented attempts to control over-powerful nobles and local officials, and helped to establish a reputation that he was a friend of the poor. However, in the longer term his introduction of the Subsidy at a time of inflation to supplement the inflexible Fifteenths and Tenths proved to be important in helping to keep Tudor monarchs solvent. Therefore, the financial reforms might be seen as more significant in the longer term.*
>
> In this example the evaluation is helped by using a series of words (highlighted) that help to weigh up the importance of the factors – 'clearly', 'however' and 'therefore'. 'However' and 'nonetheless' are useful words as they can help contrast the importance of the different factors.

ACTIVITY

Again, consider the AS-level practice question from the example on page 63. Using your notes from this chapter:

1 Write a paragraph about the extent of success of Wolsey's legal reforms. Make sure the paragraph:
  a) begins with a clear point that clearly focuses on the question
  b) develops the point with at least three pieces of accurate detail
  c) concludes with explanation: a claim and a justification.
2 Write a conclusion to the essay in which you weigh up at least two factors (i.e. legal reforms and at least one other factor) and reach a judgement about the success of Wolsey's legal reforms by comparing that factor with the other(s).

PRACTICE A-LEVEL QUESTION

'The Catholic Church in England in the period 1485–1529 was criticised primarily because of the failings of its clergy.' Assess the validity of this view.   (25 marks)

Use the above question to practise all of the essay techniques that you have learnt so far.

Working on interpretation skills

Section A of the exam paper is different from Section B. Unlike Section B, it contains extracts from the work of historians, and is compulsory with no choice of question. Significantly, this section tests different skills. In essence, Section A tests your ability to analyse different historical interpretations. Therefore, you must focus on the interpretations outlined in the extracts. The advice given in this chapter on interpretations is for both the AS and the A-level exams.

- For the **AS exam**, there are two extracts and you are asked which is the more convincing interpretation (25 marks).
- For the **A-level exam**, there are three extracts and you are asked how convincing the arguments are in relation to a specified topic (30 marks).

An interpretation is a particular view on a topic of history held by a particular author or authors. Interpretations of an event can vary, for example, depending on how much weight an historian gives to a particular factor and whether they largely ignore another factor.

The interpretations that you will be given will be largely from recent or fairly recent historians, and they may, of course, have been influenced by events in the period in which they were writing.

Interpretations and evidence

The extracts given in the exam will contain a mixture of interpretations and evidence. The mark scheme rewards answers that focus on the *interpretations* offered by the extracts much more highly than answers that focus on the *information or evidence* mentioned in the extracts. Therefore, it is important to identify the interpretations.

- *Interpretations* are a specific kind of argument. They tend to make claims such as 'Mary was bound to fail in her bid to restore England to the Catholic faith'.
- *Information or evidence* tends to consist of specific details. For example: 'Mary's religious changes led to the deaths of nearly 300 people, burnt at the stake.,

Analysis of an interpretation

We start by looking at an individual extract and seeing how we can build up skills. This is the essential starting-point for both the AS and the A-level style of question on interpretations. The AS mark scheme shows a very clear progression of thought processes:

Level 5	Answers will display a good understanding of the interpretations given in the extracts. They will evaluate the extracts thoroughly in order to provide a well-substantiated judgement on which offers the more convincing interpretation. The response demonstrates a very good understanding of context. *21–25 marks*
Level 4	Answers will display a good understanding of the interpretations given in the extracts. There will be sufficient comment to provide a supported conclusion as to which offers the more convincing interpretation. However, not all comments will be well-substantiated, and judgements may be limited. The response demonstrates a good understanding of context. *16–20 marks*
Level 3	The answer will show a reasonable understanding of the interpretations given in the extracts. Comments as to which offers the more convincing interpretation will be partial and/or thinly supported. The response demonstrates an understanding of context. *11–15 marks*
Level 2	The answer will show some partial understanding of the interpretations given in the extracts. There will be some undeveloped comment in relation to the question. The response demonstrates some understanding of context. *6–10 marks*
Level 1	The answer will show a little understanding of the interpretations given in the extracts. There will be only unsupported, vague or generalist comment in relation to the question. The response demonstrates limited understanding of context. *1–5 marks*

Now study Extract A on page 66 and the practice question below, which is about Cardinal Wolsey.

With reference to the extract [A] and your understanding of the historical content, how convincing do you find the extract in relation to the success of Wolsey as the King's chief minister?

To help you answer this type of question you need to assess the interpretation in the extract. Carry out the activities on page 66 to help you to do this.

Extract A

Wolsey had the ruthlessness, the administrative skill, the reliance on new men and above all the absolute spirit of the renaissance prince. Although he was unseeing in an age of vision, an administrator rather than a creator, he was none the less a great man. He made his country famous abroad. The Emperor made no effort to fight for his aunt's cause. France and Spain neutralised one another and Henry was able to implement his reformation without any interference from abroad. At home Wolsey created a tremendous central authority in government for his master.

Adapted from *The Earlier Tudors* by J.D. Mackie, (Oxford University Press), 1987.

ACTIVITY

1 What is the argument for the interpretation in Extract A? Is it arguing that Wolsey was successful or not?

2 What evidence can you find in the extract to support the argument? What topics are mentioned to support the interpretation?

3 What do you know (that is, contextual knowledge) that supports these claims?

4 What contextual knowledge do you have to contradict these claims?

5 Using your judgement, are the arguments in support stronger than the arguments against, or vice versa?

Look back at the mark scheme on page 65, and see how your answers might match up to the levels shown there.

In relation to Extract A's assertions about Wolsey's successes, you should be able to find arguments both to support and to contradict. Remember, you can apply this approach when responding to other, similar, questions.

6 Consider the AS-level practice question below.

With reference to Extracts A and B and your understanding of the historical context, which of these two extracts provides the more convincing interpretation of the success of Wolsey as the King's chief minister? (25 marks)

Follow the same five steps for Extract B as you did for Extract A then compare the results of the two and come to a conclusion about which extract provides the more convincing interpretation.

Extract B

Henry VIII liked to shrug off responsibility for important decisions on his efficient but unpopular minister, Wolsey. The main business of government was to keep the peace and dispense justice; and this Wolsey did but little more. Wolsey's years seem tame compared to the bustling reforms of the next decade; but there is perhaps much to be said for mere stability. The failure of Wolsey's foreign policy in 1529 was hardly Wolsey's fault. There was little that England could have done to prevent Charles V's triumph in Italy – there was little that could therefore be done to secure Henry's divorce except by resorting to radical measures.

Adapted from *Peace, Print and Protestantism 1450–1558* (The Paladin history of England) by C. S. L. Davies, (Paladin), 1977.

Comparing two interpretations

As part of the building up of skills, we move on to comparing two interpretations. This is the format of the AS question, but will also be useful in the process of gaining confidence for A-level students.

Remember that the top two levels of the mark scheme refer to 'supported conclusion' (Level 4) and 'well-substantiated conclusion' (Level 5). For Level 4 'supported conclusion' means finishing your answer with a judgement that is backed up with some accurate evidence drawn from the extract(s) and your knowledge. For Level 5 'well-substantiated conclusion' means finishing your answer with a judgement which is very well supported with evidence, and, where relevant, reaches a complex conclusion that reflects a wide variety of evidence.

There is no one correct way to write the answer! However, the principles are clear. In particular, contextual knowledge should be used *only* to back up an argument. None of your knowledge should be 'free-standing' – in the question in Activity 6, for example, there should not be a paragraph saying what you know about the topic, unrelated to the extracts. All your knowledge should be used in context. For each extract in turn:

● Explain the evidence in the extract, backed up with your own contextual knowledge. In this example, for Wolsey being successful.

● Explain the points in the extract where you have evidence that contradicts Wolsey being a success.

Then write a conclusion that reaches a judgement on which is more convincing as an interpretation.

The break with Rome in the 1530s

3

When Wolsey fell from power in 1529 Henry VIII had made little progress in what he saw as his most important objective at the time – a divorce and the possibility of a legitimate male heir. Events moved slowly at first, but then at rapid speed. This chapter is concerned with the following key areas:

- The process of the break with Rome – Royal Supremacy
- Religious changes
- The opposition to religious change; social impact of religious upheaval
- Changes in Tudor government in the 1530s under Thomas Cromwell

The main focus can be phrased as a question:

Why was the 1530s such a momentous decade for the monarchy, the Church and government?

The events of the decade were extraordinary and largely could not have been foreseen in the last years of Thomas Wolsey's life. The results impinge considerably on the key questions of the specification:

- the consolidation and powers of the monarchy
- the way England was governed
- relationships with foreign powers
- the securing of the succession
- changes in English society and the economy, including the consequences of the dissolution of the monasteries
- long-accepted intellectual and religious ideas being challenged
- the importance of individuals in driving all this change, especially Thomas Cromwell.

CHAPTER OVERVIEW

When Wolsey fell from power in 1529, the direction of English policy towards obtaining a divorce for Henry appeared to be uncertain. Then after Thomas Cromwell had gained influence and, later, official positions under Henry VIII, government policy followed a clear direction. Cromwell and others around him realised that the Pope would never willingly grant a divorce. Yet Henry needed a divorce to marry Anne Boleyn – and this had to happen before the birth of any child so that it would be legitimate. Cromwell used Parliament to declare that England could take charge of the divorce proceedings without the approval of the Pope. This was achieved by Acts of Parliament that prevented Catherine appealing to the Pope's jurisdiction. Henry secured his divorce and control of the English Church.

However, any moves towards Protestant theology were slow, Henry himself helping to lead the resistance. There was little opposition to him just becoming head of the Church, and that was dealt with effectively. Meanwhile, alongside these important changes in the Church, Thomas Cromwell was engineering changes to the system of government to make it more efficient and centralised. Overall, the monarchy in the 1530s gained in power and authority.

NOTE-MAKING

Make notes in this section on the *stages* by which Henry achieved his divorce.

Sir Thomas More

1478 Born

1513 Began work on a history of the reign of Richard III which attacked the King for tyranny.

1516 Publication of first book of his major work, *Utopia*.

1528 Conducted heresy trials against suspected Lutherans (but intervention of Anne Boleyn protected some from execution).

1529 Appointed Lord Chancellor after the fall of Wolsey.

1531 Initiated further persecutions of Protestant reformers.

1532 Resigned after the King won approval for the 'Submission of the Clergy'.

1534 Refused to take the Oath of Succession recognising the legality of Henry's divorce.

1535 Convicted of treason and executed.

1 The Reformation Parliament and the establishment of Royal Supremacy

In November 1529 Parliament met to help the King achieve a divorce by putting pressure on the Pope. Within a few years Parliament had been used for far more – a revolution in the relationship between Church and State, and as a consequence increasing the role of Parliament in the government of England.

Slow progress on Henry's divorce, 1529–31

Why was progress so slow in these years?

The situation for Henry was complicated and, in his eyes, his divorce was urgent. His first attempts gained little, and some historians have dubbed these years as 'years without a policy'. This is harsh. Wolsey had tried and failed, but only because there was no easy solution. Most unusually, he was replaced as Lord Chancellor by a layman, Thomas More. More was less keen to be pragmatic and do whatever Henry wanted, regardless of Church teaching and the authority of the Pope. But he and other ministers did stumble towards the goal that Henry desired.

Sir Thomas More as Chancellor

Sir Thomas More was an able scholar, but he was a poor replacement for Wolsey as Lord Chancellor. More had a reputation for being a man who put his principles before everything else. He held strong humanist beliefs (see page 8), which he revealed in a number of books, most famously *Utopia* (1516). On the fictional island of Utopia, the natives live in a state of innocence. More used the arrival of visitors from the outside world as an opportunity to write a bitingly satirical contrast between real 'Christian' society and the fictional perfection of Utopia. One of his targets was the land-owning elite: More accused them of selfishly exploiting their tenants and allowing 'sheep to devour men' through the enclosing of land. More's book became a noted contribution to writings of the Renaissance period.

More's writings became a favourite with Henry VIII. He produced a history of the career of Richard III which helped to foster the myth of the Yorkist king as an evil, murdering monster. However, at court, More was deeply sympathetic to the plight of Catherine of Aragon and grew concerned at Henry's treatment of her and at the King's willingness to support those who wanted Church reforms as a way of obtaining his divorce. More was critical of some aspects of the Catholic Church, but like other humanists he remained convinced that reform could be achieved by steady persuasion rather than by drastic action. However, he was intolerant of anything that smacked of heresy and wrote viciously against Lutheran reformers and their beliefs. He was instrumental in the harsh persecution of reformers in 1528 and again in 1530–31 when he was Chancellor.

Perhaps the most marked difference between Wolsey and More was that, whereas Wolsey had been prepared to seize opportunities and to act flexibly in the interests of his royal master, More was a man of high and rigid principles, especially in religious matters. Since the question of the King's divorce remained unresolved when he became chief minister, this was to cause real difficulties in his relationship with Henry.

As Chancellor, More was able to attack Lutheran influences within the Church, but found his work frustrated by Anne Boleyn's presence at court and by the messy question of the royal divorce, which Henry saw as the central issue in 1530.

Anne Boleyn

Anne was the daughter of Sir George Boleyn, from a junior branch of the Howard Earls of Norfolk, intelligent, assertive and ambitious. Estimates of her character vary widely. Among those who disapproved of the divorce she was a 'goggle-eyed harlot'. Historians have accused her of 'domineering ways' that brought about her downfall, arguing that when Henry had won her sexually he became increasingly disillusioned with her assertive personality as well as her failure to produce a male heir. Her destruction in 1536 was brought about by Thomas Cromwell, who tortured her musician, Mark Smeaton, into a confession of adulteries and in the case of her brother George, incest, allowing her to be convicted of treason and executed by beheading with a sword.

Her recent biographer, E. W. Ives, has painted a different portrait, of an intelligent woman with a genuine interest in religious reform, who was betrayed by her husband and family and destroyed by the necessities of court politics and the problems of the succession. She was innocent of the charges of adultery. Arguments as to whether she deserved her fate seem to depend on the preferences and sometimes the prejudices of those who write about her. For the interested student, the best course is to read different interpretations, for example by Ives and Henry's biographer, J. J. Scarisbrick, and decide for yourself.

Attempts to progress the divorce question

Between 1529 and early 1532 Henry applied a number of measures designed to pressurise the clergy into supporting his case for a divorce. He was helped by the common ground he had with religious reformers wanting radical religious changes with their common view that the Church was the main obstacle to their ambitions. Thus Lollards, who were supporters of Luther (see Chapter 2,

▲ Sir Thomas More

▲ Anne Boleyn

On the rim of British coins today there are still the letters F. D. and D. G. Until recently the Latin words appeared in full – *Fidei Defensor, Deo Gratias* – 'Defender of the Faith by the Grace of God'.

Annates – A special tax paid by members of the higher clergy to Rome during their first year in office.

Excommunicate – The Pope had the power to cut off anyone from receiving the sacraments of the Church. This meant, in effect, cutting them off from God and salvation.

page 49), and some general anti-clericalism encouraged by humanist writings, all came together in support of Church reform. For the reformers, the problems facing the Church could only be solved by improving religious leadership. One way to achieve this was by strengthening royal power to protect and to develop the Church in England. During the 1520s Henry had opposed this idea and had even written a book, *In Defence of the Seven Sacraments*, which, by implication, showed support for the Pope's authority in Rome. For this service to the Church he had been awarded the title '*Fidei Defensor*' (Defender of the Faith) by the Pope.

However, as Henry's dispute with the Pope worsened, the ideas of the reformers began to prove more attractive. In 1528 William Tyndale (see Chapter 2, page 50) published *The Obedience of the Christian Man*, in which he argued that kings had authority from God which gave them responsibility for the souls as well as the bodies of their subjects, and that royal authority was supreme above any power within or beyond the boundaries of the kingdom. The book was banned in England, but Anne Boleyn had a copy sent to her from France, and brought it to Henry's attention. In addition, courtiers such as Thomas Cromwell had travelled extensively in Europe, where they would have become familiar with similar ideas. When Henry found himself obstructed by the authority of Rome and the Pope, he was not short of suggestions and ideas as to how he might remove these obstacles once and for all.

During Henry's campaign between 1529 and 1534 two clear objectives emerged. Initially, to obtain the divorce that he so desperately desired, he put pressure on the English clergy not to oppose him. He also put pressure on Pope Clement VII. Then, during these years, Henry moved from putting pressure on the Pope to challenging the Pope over who should control the English Church.

Historians are unclear, however, as to when the idea of taking control over the Church changed from being a vague threat in some of Henry's actions to an official policy. According to the historian Conrad Russell, for instance, the idea of divorcing Catherine without the Pope's permission was in Henry's mind as early as 1527, but he had to wait until conditions were right to carry out this plan. In particular, he had to delay until he could appoint to the higher clergy men who were likely to support him. This meant waiting at least until after the Archbishop of Canterbury's death. Warham was nearly 80 in the late 1520s (his exact date of birth is not known – c. 1450).

Other writers have seen more caution in Henry's policies. They point out that royal policies were applied very hesitantly. In the case of the prohibition of payments of annates, for example, the policy was suspended for a year and then only applied with the King's approval. This suggests that Henry still hoped to use the policy as a bargaining chip in his negotiations to get a divorce. Historians such as Geoffrey Elton and Christopher Haigh both use evidence such as this to suggest that Henry was unsure what to do and feared an open split with the Pope. To challenge the power of the Catholic Church so directly could have been dangerous to him. While there was an anti-clerical element in Parliament, the opposition to the Act against annates showed that this was not a commonly held view. Moreover, the Pope had the power to excommunicate Henry if things got too far out of hand. For a King, excommunication meant that oaths of loyalty taken by his subjects no longer applied, and that rebellion could be sanctioned, or even regarded as a duty, by the Church.

Henry divorces and becomes head of the Church of England

Why was Henry eventually successful in obtaining a divorce?

Whether or not Henry and his ministers had a clear plan, it was Parliament that was the essential tool that was used to put pressure on the clergy and the Pope. The series of moves listed in Figure 1 show how pressure was put simultaneously on the clergy and on the Pope.

Figure 1 Pressures on the clergy and the Pope, 1529–33.

Date	Pressure on the clergy	Pressure on the Pope
1529	Parliament was encouraged to voice anti-clerical feelings – Thomas Cromwell MP began collecting evidence of abuses.	
1530	Revival of medieval law of Praemunire – fifteen of the upper clergy were charged with supporting Wolsey's abuse of power against the King.	Scholars from Oxford and Cambridge were sent to European universities to find support for Henry's divorce.
1531	Henry 'pardoned' the clergy of crimes against him, but demanded that they should recognise him as 'sole protector and supreme head' of the Church. A compromise was reached: he was accepted as supreme head 'as far as the law of Christ allows'.	
1532	March: Thomas Cromwell introduced the 'Supplication Against the Ordinaries' into the House of Commons – a petition calling on the King to deal with the abuses and corruption of the clergy. Cromwell held no major office at this time, but was invited to join Henry's inner circle of advisers on the Royal Council. May: Henry demanded that the Church should agree to the 'Submission of the Clergy' – a document giving him the power to veto Church laws and to choose bishops, even if not approved by Rome. Resignation of Sir Thomas More accepted.	January: Act of Parliament passed (despite fierce opposition) preventing the payment of annates to Rome. Although the amount collected was not great, the banning of the payment was a significant attack on the Pope's rights over the clergy. The Act was suspended for one year. August: Death of Archbishop of Canterbury (William Warham). Henry asked the Pope to appoint Thomas Cranmer, a reformer with some Protestant views.
1533	January: Henry secretly married Anne Boleyn (now pregnant).	Act in Restraint of Appeals was passed by Parliament, denying Henry's subjects the right to appeal to the Pope against decisions in English Church courts. This law effectively prevented Catherine of Aragon from seeking the Pope's arbitration when the divorce case came before the courts.

Thomas Cromwell (1485?–1540)

Cromwell was born in about 1485, in Putney in London. Very little is known about his early life, but his origins were certainly humble. His father was probably a cloth worker and ale-house keeper. During his teens, Thomas seems to have been in some kind of trouble which led him to make his way to the Netherlands. He later described himself as having been 'a bit of a ruffian' in his youth. From the Netherlands he moved to Italy, where he served as a soldier, and where he probably came into contact with the radical political ideas which influenced his later life. After a period of service to a Venetian merchant, he returned to England in 1516, married, and found employment in the household of Cardinal Wolsey.

Wolsey seems to have recognised Cromwell's ability because, by 1519, Cromwell had achieved an important position in his household. Cromwell also learned enough about law to attend the **Inns of Court** (residences in London where barristers received training and where they could lodge while studying) in 1524 and to develop a successful legal practice. In 1529 he was elected as a Member of Parliament, in which capacity he played an active role in attacking abuses within the Church. Whether he was already known to the King, or brought to his attention at this time, he soon found himself in royal service and, in 1531, became a member of the Royal Council. Unlike many others, he combined this advancement with loyalty to his old master, Wolsey, until his death in 1530.

By 1532 Cromwell had effectively taken over the management of the King's divorce. Like Wolsey he realised that the key to success was to anticipate Henry's needs and to give him what he wanted. Also like Wolsey, he collected titles and promotions (this time outside the Church) rapidly. Between 1532 and 1536 he devised the strategy for the divorce and drafted a series of Acts that destroyed the power of Rome, created the Church of England and gave Henry unprecedented power and status as a monarch.

1532 Became Master of the King's Jewels, a position which gave him access to the King's private rooms in the palace.

1533 Became Chancellor of the Exchequer and Master of the Rolls (which gave him a leading role within the legal system).

1535 Appointed Vicar General (a government post which Henry created to give Cromwell the power to institute Church reform).

1536 Became Lord Privy Seal and Principal Secretary on the Royal Council; also rewarded with the title Baron Cromwell.

1540 Became Lord Great Chamberlain and Earl of Essex shortly before his fall.

Establishment of Royal Supremacy

What aspects of Church organisation and control were changed in the 1530s?

Parliament had been summoned in November 1529. The same Parliament still existed (not that it was meeting continuously) until 1536. A series of Acts of Parliament were passed defining the nature and organisation of the Church in England. These laws systematically stripped away the Pope's control and transferred power in key areas to the King. This was the Henrician Reformation as far as Henry was concerned – a political reformation over who controlled the Church.

Archbishop Thomas Cranmer (1489–1556)

Cranmer was one of the young scholars at Cambridge who joined the 'White Horse' group in the 1520s to discuss the exciting new ideas of Lutheranism coming from Europe. He was influenced by these ideas, but stopped short of embracing them to the point of becoming a heretic. Instead, his career took him to the royal court, where he became chaplain to Anne Boleyn's father. He wrote a defence of the King's desire for a divorce, using an erastian argument (which means that he justified divorce on the grounds that monarchs were the highest authority within their lands so could do as they pleased). Henry was impressed by Cranmer's moderate reformist ideas and saw in him a friend of about the same age and an ally against the power of the Pope.

When Archbishop Warham died in 1532, Henry asked the Pope to appoint Cranmer to fill the vacancy, even though he had never held a senior post within the Church. Henry was undoubtedly doing this to put further pressure on the Pope to give him his divorce, but he also saw the advantages of having a supporter as the leading English churchman.

Cranmer quickly proved to be a loyal friend. He authorised the much-desired royal divorce after the 1533 Act in Restraint of Appeals prohibited Catherine from challenging the matter before the Pope, and he accepted all the measures enacted during the reformation years of 1534–40. However, Cranmer also showed his Protestant sympathies by supporting the publication of the Bible in English and the efforts of Thomas Cromwell to move essential doctrines away from traditional teachings (see pages 77–78). Ultimately, however, Cranmer was a political servant of the Crown first and a churchman second. When Henry attacked the extent of reform by persecuting Lutherans and pushing the Six Articles Act through Parliament in 1539, Cranmer stood by when other Protestant bishops resigned. His loyalty to Henry allowed him to escape the traps set by the conservative faction during the 1540s and to survive as archbishop into Edward VI's reign.

Under the governments of Somerset and Northumberland a more Protestant atmosphere prevailed at court and Cranmer followed this mood in his wording of the 1549 and 1552 Prayer Books. At the same time, he spoke of trying to find a form of religion that would end religious disagreements and establish a permanent basis for faith. He consulted leading Protestant reformers and Catholic theologians from Europe, but never got to the point of setting out what this uniform faith should be. Privately, Cranmer supported moderate Protestant thinking, but respected and saw the value of some Catholic rituals – just as Elizabeth was to do in the settlement of 1559–63.

During Mary's reign, Cranmer suffered the consequences of his achievements in the previous reign. He had been too deeply involved in the writing of the Protestant Prayer Books to escape the Queen's distrust and was arrested on heresy charges. Ever the politician, Cranmer publicly renounced his Protestant 'errors' five times during his trial, but he was executed in 1556.

Source A From the opening of the Preamble to the Act in Restraint of Appeals, February 1533.

Where by sundry, old authentic histories and chronicles, it is manifestly declared and expressed, that this realm of England is an empire, and so hath been accepted in the world, governed by one Supreme Head and King, having the dignity and royal estate of the imperial Crown of the same, unto whom a body politic, compact of all sorts and degrees of people, divided in terms, and by names of spirituality and temporality, be bounden and own to bear, next to God, a natural and humble obedience; he being also institute and furnished, by the goodness and sufferance of Almighty God, with plenary [full], whole and entire power, pre-eminence, authority, prerogative and jurisdiction, to tender and yield justice … in all causes … without restraint to any foreign princes or potentates [powerful rulers]…

What is the opening of the Preamble (Source A) claiming?

Act in Restraint of Appeals

The Act in Restraint of Appeals was hastily passed in February 1533, the month after Henry's secret marriage to the now-pregnant Anne Boleyn, even though in the eyes of the Church he was still married to Catherine. It made clear that Henry's divorce case was to be heard in England and that Catherine could not appeal to Rome for her case to be heard there. The Preamble to the Act was used to make bold claims to justify what Henry, his ministers and Parliament were doing.

After the passing of the Act forbidding appeals to Rome, it was possible to make quick progress over Henry's divorce. A court was convened in May 1533 under Archbishop Cranmer. The arguments used were the ones used in the late 1520s that Catherine's marriage to Arthur had been consummated, and that this was prohibited in the Book of Leviticus. Therefore, Henry's marriage to Catherine was invalid, giving a respectable explanation to the fact that Henry had married Anne Boleyn four months earlier. In June 1533 the six months pregnant Anne was crowned as Queen, giving birth to Elizabeth in September.

Royal Supremacy by Act of Parliament, 1534

These changes were reinforced by the 1534 Act of Supremacy, which acknowledged the King as head of the Church, with all the rights this entailed to decide its organisation, personnel and doctrine. The word 'acknowledged' is key because the Act of Supremacy claimed that the King had always held the right to be head of the Church, and was now taking it up. This meant that Parliament was in no sense giving him the right (which it did not have the power to grant), but merely recognising it and setting up the framework to make it legally enforceable.

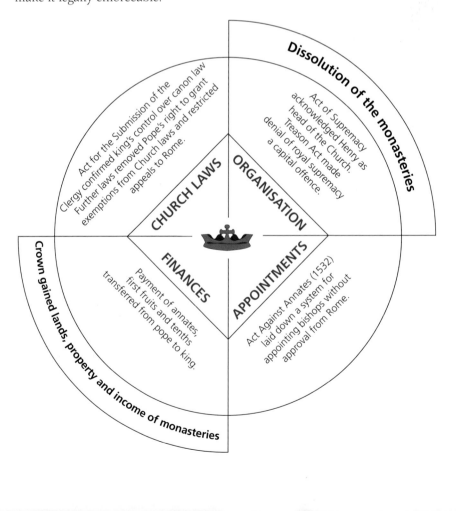

Figure 2 How the break with Rome affected Henry VIII's powers as King.

Albeit the King's Majesty justly and rightly is and oweth to be the supreme head of the Church of England, and so is recognised by the clergy of this realm in their Convocations; be it enacted by authority of this present parliament that the king our sovereign lord, his heirs and successors kings of this realm, shall be taken, accepted and reputed the only supreme head in earth of the Church of England called *Anglicana Ecclesia* ...

> How could the Act (Source B) claim that the clergy had already agreed?

To enforce the Act of Supremacy, a Treason Act made the denial of royal supremacy a crime punishable by death. It had been made clear that the monarch was in charge of the day-to-day running of the Church, and in 1535 Thomas Cromwell was appointed by Henry as Vicar General – that is, he was to act as Henry's deputy in his oversight of the Church's organisation and running. Henry was thus making instant use of his new position and title.

Implications of the Act of Supremacy

It might seem that this was a huge revolution, the Pope being replaced by the King as head of the Church of England. However, it is important to remember that medieval popes had seldom had much direct involvement in day-to-day decision making and control in England. Although Popes made appointments to senior positions such as bishoprics, it had long been accepted that the Pope confirmed the choice made by the King. Rome was rarely appealed to for legal decisions. Monarchs in various European states were gaining more powers over the running of the Catholic Church in their territories – with the encouragement of the Papacy in return for agreed taxation levies. Henry, through Acts of Parliament, had declared that the Church was under his control for its day-to-day management. Up to this point the only changes were political. No doctrines had changed at all up to 1536, and this reflected the role of Henry himself in controlling the process.

The importance of the Act in the short term was what Henry and Cromwell did next – especially with the dissolution of the monasteries. Soon the importance spread more to changes in doctrine which were approved by Parliament (where the monarch was a constitutional part). Indeed, it can be argued that the major consequence of royal supremacy in the longer term was in religious rather than political concerns.

KEY DATES: THE HENRICIAN REFORMATION

1529 Fall of Wolsey; Sir Thomas More became Chancellor; Parliament summoned

1530 Upper clergy charged with Praemunire

1531 Henry pardoned clergy in recognition of his position over the Church

1532 Act preventing payment of annates to Rome; submission of the Clergy; Cromwell became important as one of the King's advisers; Cranmer became Archbishop of Canterbury after the death of Warham

1533 Pregnancy and secret marriage of Anne Boleyn; Act in Restraint of Appeals; Henry's marriage to Catherine declared to be invalid; birth of Elizabeth

1534 Act of Supremacy; Treasons Act

1535 Cromwell became Vicar-General, overseeing Church on behalf of Henry; execution of Sir Thomas More

NOTE-MAKING

Divide a page into two columns. As you read this section make notes in the first column of what seemed to stay the same, and in the second column note down the Protestant influences on the Church.

Henry's wives

Catherine of Aragon: m. 1509; divorced 1533; mother of Mary; died 1536.

Anne Boleyn: m. 1533; beheaded 1536; mother of Elizabeth.

Jane Seymour: m. 1536; died in childbirth 1538; mother of Edward.

Anne of Cleves: m. 1540; divorced 1540.

Catherine Howard: m. 1540; beheaded 1542.

Catherine Parr: m. 1543; died 1548.

2 The extent of religious change in the 1530s

Having looked at the political reformation, we now need to study what changes there were to official religious belief and how they were implemented.

Spread of Protestant ideas

To what extent were Protestant beliefs replacing Catholic beliefs?

From 1529 onwards Henry had encouraged criticism of the Pope and the English clergy. He had allowed those who demanded reform to speak openly because it suited his purpose of pressurising the Pope into granting him a divorce. For the reformers this offered relief from persecution and the opportunity to influence the future of the Church in England. The King's divorce, the campaign to win support in the European universities, and the growing influence of sympathetic individuals such as Anne Boleyn and Thomas Cromwell, enabled the reformers to develop their ideas, increase support and gain influence within the government and the Church itself.

While Cromwell managed the campaign in Parliament, Anne drew Henry's attention to the work of Tyndale (see page 78), protected heretics like Robert Forman in London and encouraged the appointment of reformers to positions of power and influence within the Church. Her influence led to the appointment of Hugh Latimer and Nicholas Shaxton (who had been accused of heresy in 1531) to vacant bishops' posts, and to the selection of Thomas Cranmer as Archbishop of Canterbury in 1532.

By 1536 individuals who favoured some of Luther's reforms were firmly established in government. In spite of Henry's aversion to changes in doctrine, they appear to have been able to start influencing the religious debate at court. In addition, preachers such as John Bale, Edward Crome and Robert Barnes spread Protestant teachings in London, while Cranmer encouraged similar activities in Suffolk, Essex and Kent. The doctrinal reforms that occurred in the later 1530s further encouraged these reformers.

Henry's disillusionment with Anne Boleyn and her failure to produce a male heir did not affect the moves towards Protestantism. She was executed on trumped up charges of infidelity in 1536 and Henry married his third wife, Jane Seymour, who was from a family that leaned towards Protestantism. Unfortunately, that happy marriage ended in 1537 when Jane died after complications resulting from childbirth. She did, however, produce the male heir that Henry so badly craved.

Government propaganda supporting the Reformation

The government actively promoted the Reformation. One way it did this was the way in which preambles to Acts were phrased – for example, by appealing to the Bible and the early history of the Church, where temporal leaders had political control over the early Christian Church – for example, some Roman Emperors.

The reformers were also keen to draw a distinction between 'Potestas Jurisdictionis' (the right to exercise jurisdiction over the Church, which Henry claimed) and 'Potestas Ordinis' (the right to exercise spiritual power, which was still retained by the bishops).

In addition, after the break with Rome, some conservatives in theology were keen to appeal to the King to defend the Church against Protestant heresy, on the assumption that the King would fully support them. Some conservatives even published propaganda to emphasise the necessity of obedience to the sovereign. One of these was by Stephen Gardiner, the conservative Bishop of Winchester and one of the King's secretaries. He wrote a pamphlet with the title *'De Vera Obedientia'* ('True Obedience'). In it, he stressed the necessary hierarchy of obedience in society – wives to husbands, servants to masters. All must obey the ruler whom God has put in authority over them, and who in his person: *'representeth as it were the image of God upon earth'.*

Source C From Stephen Gardiner's book *De Vera Obedientia* (*'True Obedience'*), published in 1535.

Henry VIII King of England and of France, defender of the faith and Lord of Ireland, is granted ... by authority of Parliament, to call himself Supreme Head of the Church of England as well in name as in deed. Wherein there is no newly invented matter wrought, ... only to be more clearly expressed with a more fit term to express it by, namely, for this purpose to withdraw that counterfeit vain opinion out of the common people's minds which the false pretended power of the Bishop of Rome had for the space of certain years blinded them withal, to the great impeachment of the King's authority. Wherein surely I see no cause why any man should be offended that the King is called the Head of the Church of England rather than the Head of the realm of England ...

What is Gardiner's argument in Source C?

Other writers, encouraged by Cromwell, wrote more from a humanist or Protestant viewpoint. For example, Thomas Starkey's *Exhortation to Unity and Obedience* (1536) used the Bible as the sole source of authority. The Bible was clear on the necessity of obeying the temporal ruler.

Doctrinal reform

In the later 1530s, at the same time as the monasteries were being closed (see pages 78–82), Cromwell turned his attention to reforming the teachings of the Church. In 1536, as Vicar-General of the Church, he worked with Archbishop Cranmer to introduce some elements of Protestant beliefs. Both men had to tread carefully, as Henry's own beliefs were very conservative.

Cromwell issued Ten Articles of Faith, probably written by Cranmer but passed by Convocation (the parliament of the Church). The Articles stated that they had been: *'devised by the King's highness's majesty to establish Christian quietness and unity'.*

They included some distinctly Lutheran ideas (similar to those proposed by Martin Luther), but retained strongly Catholic elements. On some aspects the articles were vague. For example, the dead were to be prayed for, but there was no mention of purgatory. The wording of the Eucharist was Catholic, but Luther's views on gaining salvation by faith were also reflected.

These were enforced by two sets of Injunctions (or instructions) in 1536 and 1538, which ordered the clergy to follow the articles and explain them to their congregations. A *Bishop's Book* was published in 1537, offering interpretation and advice. Both the Injunctions and the *Bishop's Book* attacked the abuses and superstition that had come to be associated with the Church and encouraged Protestant reformers.

ACTIVITY

This official translation of the Bible into English was largely used in the Authorised Version of 1611. For example, 84 per cent of the New Testament is the work of William Tyndale. In his translation, he invented or popularised many words and phrases still in common use today, e.g. 'Judge that you be not judged'. Use the internet to research some more and see how many of them you use or have heard used.

What aspects of Catholic practices are being attacked (Source D) and why?

Also in 1537 the first official translation of the Bible into English was published. Cranmer had persuaded Henry to sanction this. It was based very much on the work of Tyndale but with contributions from Miles Coverdale. In 1538 a royal proclamation ordered that a copy should be placed in every parish church, to be read and examined by the congregation. The emphasis was very distinctly Protestant and against what were seen as Catholic errors.

Source D From the Second Set of Injunctions II and VI, 1538.

[Clergy should] exhort every person to read the Bible, as that which is the very lively word of God, that every Christian man is bound to embrace, believe and follow, if he look to be saved.

[Clergy should in sermon] exhort your hearers to the works of charity, mercy, and faith, specially prescribed and commanded in Scripture, and not to repose their trust ... in any other works devised by man's fantasies beside Scripture; as in wandering to pilgrimages, offering of money, candles, or tapers to images or relics, or kissing or licking the same ... or in such-like superstition.

These doctrinal changes were swift and significant. They created a climate for change that could not easily be reversed. In particular, the accessibility of the Bible to a wide range of people, each able to interpret and debate the word of God for themselves, laid the foundations for the variety of religious beliefs that were to appear later in the sixteenth century.

A swing back towards Catholicism in 1538–40

The official changes made in the years 1535–38 had been too fast for Henry. In addition, he required Catholic allies in Europe towards the end of the 1530s and needed to stress that the religious changes in England were extremely moderate. The swing back towards Catholic doctrines in 1538–40 also reflected the waning of Cromwell's influence, especially after Henry's opposition to Anne of Cleves becoming his fourth wife. The Catholic Howard family were gaining influence (leading to Henry's marriage later in 1540 to Catherine Howard). The head of the family, the Duke of Norfolk, was largely responsible for getting Parliament to agree to the Six Articles of 1539, which were largely Catholic in emphasis.

This setback for the Protestants proved to be temporary, but it was enough for two reforming bishops, Latimer and Shaxton, to resign their positions. As the articles had stated that clerical celibacy was to continue, Cranmer sent his wife (an ex-nun) to live with relatives in Germany.

Protestant reformers again gained the ear of Henry later in 1541 when the Howard family lost favour after Catherine Howard was discredited (she was executed in February 1542).

Political, social and economic significance of the dissolution of the monasteries

Why did Henry close the monasteries and seize their assets?

In the early sixteenth century there were at least 825 religious houses in England and Wales. Over 500 of these were monasteries, the others being nunneries and friaries. Many owned much land and employed many labourers, as well as providing livelihoods for those in villages nearby. By 1540 all these had closed – with huge implications for society and the economy as a whole as well as what was being assumed about religious beliefs and practices. It also provides evidence of how both monarch and Parliament were able to utilise their newly declared powers in the legislation of the earlier 1530s.

Causes of the dissolution

Once Henry was legally acknowledged as head of the Church in England, questions about accompanying reform of Church institutions needed to be addressed. High on the list of targets were the 825 or so monasteries, convents and other religious houses in England and Wales. In the Middle Ages these had been established as places where men and women could devote their lives to saying prayers on behalf of the souls of the living and the dead. As such, they had enjoyed a powerful reputation within the Church and had been treated with awe and respect. Monks, nuns and other members of the regular clergy who lived in these religious houses tended to set themselves apart from the communities close to which they were established, avoiding daily contact if possible. Nonetheless, monasteries played an important part in local life. They were places of shelter and sanctuary for travellers, sources of medicine and food for the needy and centres of education for the wealthy.

By the sixteenth century, however, the high regard in which they had been held had almost completely vanished. The number of regular clergy had declined to about 10,000 and some monasteries housed fewer than a dozen monks. Originally, the men and women who had dedicated their lives to prayer had lived simple lives but, over time, they had acquired servants to manage the day-to-day running of their houses and had accumulated luxuries by spending the money they received from renting out some of their land.

This decline gave Henry and Cromwell their first, but not their most important, reason for closing the monasteries. As head of the Church, the King could order inspections of any religious establishments. A survey was carried out, on Cromwell's orders, in 1535. It discovered that corruption and abuses were said to be common throughout the smaller monasteries of England and Wales, giving Henry the excuse he needed to close them (see Source E).

In reality, the level of corruption was probably not much worse than in the clergy as a whole. However, Cromwell had instructed his commissioners to find the most damaging pieces of evidence about each institution that they visited, even if that meant listening to unfounded gossip and rumours. Historians have tended to dismiss this official reason for the dissolution and have looked elsewhere for the causes:

Source E From the Act for the Dissolution of the Smaller Monasteries, 1536. This introductory paragraph sets out the official justification for the closure of these establishments.

Sin, vicious, carnal and abominable living is daily seen and committed amongst the little and small abbeys, priories and other such religious houses of monks, canons and nuns. The governors of such houses consume and waste the ornaments of their churches and their goods and chattels to the great displeasure of Almighty God and to the great infamy of the King's Highness and the realm.

- Monasteries were very wealthy institutions. In 1535 Cromwell, on Henry's instructions, commissioned a survey of the property and value of smaller monasteries, the *Valor Ecclesiasticus*. The survey revealed that these monasteries had the potential to double the Crown's annual income. At a time when Henry needed money to further his ambitions abroad, seizing the assets of the monasteries was an extremely tempting prospect.
- Seizure of monastic lands would also give the Crown additional property to distribute as a way of buying support from the nobility and gentry at a difficult time.
- Monasteries were permanent reminders of the Catholic Church. Although monks and nuns had been forced to swear an oath recognising Henry as head of the Church, they were potential centres of resistance to the royal supremacy.
- The primary role of monasteries – to pray for the salvation of souls – was not in keeping with the new Protestant theology of individual faith in God. For those critics of the Church who wanted genuine reform along Protestant lines, the monasteries were outdated and irrelevant institutions.

Process of dissolution

Cromwell adopted a three-part approach to ridding the country of its monastic traditions (see Figure 3 below). First, he gathered evidence to show that religious houses were unfit to continue. Second, he began to dissolve smaller monasteries. Finally, he moved to abolish the rest.

Figure 3 The process of dissolution – how Cromwell destroyed English monasticism, 1534–40.

Date	Cromwell's actions
1534	Act of First Fruits and Tenths allowed Henry to tax the Church. These were taxes previously paid to the Pope when a person was appointed (first fruits) and then one-tenth of their income every year.
	Act of Supremacy gave Henry the power to supervise and reform all religious establishments in England.
1535	Cromwell sent out commissioners to survey the value of monastic lands and properties and to produce a report, the *Valor Ecclesiasticus* (meaning 'Value of the Church').
	Cromwell sent out a second set of commissioners to investigate the moral and spiritual standards in the monasteries.
1536	Based on his commissioners' findings, Parliament passed the Act for the Dissolution of the Smaller Monasteries, which closed all religious houses with lands valued at under £200 per year.
	New commissioners were sent out to supervise the closures (provoking rebellion in Lincolnshire and Yorkshire – see pages 85–86).
1537–38	Closures continued, although some religious houses bribed officials to overlook them temporarily.
	The opposition of Carthusian monks to the dissolution of their establishments led to their execution on Henry's orders (see page 85).
1539	Parliament passed the Act for the Dissolution of the Larger Monasteries, extending the closures to all religious houses except chantries (small, private chapels where prayers were said for the souls of the dead).
1540	The Court of Augmentations was established, with Richard Rich as Chancellor, to handle the property and income from the dissolved monasteries.

Effects of the dissolution

Within the space of five years Cromwell had ended a tradition of English monasticism stretching back over five centuries. Historians use words such as 'vandalism' and 'plundering' to describe the methods used because religious houses had their valuables confiscated and melted down (whatever their worth as religious artefacts), including the lead from their roofs. Many of the impressive monastic buildings that had been a feature of the medieval landscape fell into disrepair and became crumbling ruins, while others were sold off to become houses for the wealthy.

The main beneficiaries of the dissolution were the King and the nobility. Henry's seizure of the lands and assets of the monasteries brought him great wealth. It has been estimated that the total value of the dissolution amounted to about ten per cent of the entire wealth of the kingdom, and this money came to Henry in one great transfer during the 1530s. For the next half century or so it was used to finance the kind of ambitious foreign policy which Henry had dreamed about at the start of his reign. In the longer term, it did little to help the monarchy's financial independence. As the cost of wars continued and escalated (because of greater commitments and rising inflation), Henry and his successors sold off monastic lands to raise money. The land was usually sold at full market value; very little was given to courtiers as rewards or favours. It was after the fall of Cromwell that land was sold off rapidly in the last years of Henry's reign. More than half of the monastic lands were sold off in the years 1543–47. In this way, the Crown lost control of these lands and the possibility of collecting taxes in the future.

Historians are still debating who bought the land from the Crown. It is a difficult question to answer because there is no clear national pattern. However, much of the property was bought either by members of the nobility to strengthen their existing regional holdings, or by the lesser gentry as a way of establishing their presence in a local community. For some writers, the growing visibility of the gentry class is the most important effect of the dissolution of the monasteries, because it illustrates an important change in society from the traditional ruling elite to a more widely-based ruling class. Protestants also benefited from the dissolution. For them, the closure of these strongholds of Catholic ritual dealt a great blow to the possibility of a return to Catholicism in England.

The main losers were the inhabitants of the monasteries and, to some extent, the local communities around them. For all their possible failings, monasteries did offer services to people living nearby which were not entirely taken over by other institutions after they closed.

Monks and nuns lost their work and their accommodation, although most received compensation in the form of pensions or one-off payments. One monk was still receiving a small annual pension until he died in 1607! About one-fifth of ex-monks managed to secure other paid positions within the Church in order to supplement their pensions. Unfortunately, the government was least generous to the friars and nuns who came from the poorest establishments. Despite this, historians have generally refused to link the dissolution to a rise in poverty, because the number affected in each local community was not that great and because there were other opportunities within the Church or in the homes of the great Catholic families for these people to take up.

LOOK AGAIN

Look back to key questions 4 and 5 on page viii and think how the dissolution of the monasteries had effects on society, the economy and on culture.

KEY DATES: THE DISSOLUTION OF THE MONASTERIES

1535 Cromwell sent out commissioners to survey monastic lands

1536 Act for closing smaller monasteries; Ten Articles and first set of Injunctions published

1537 First official translation of Bible in English published

1538 Second set of Injunctions, including English Bible in every church

1539 Act for closing larger monasteries; Six Articles published

1540 Henry's brief marriage to Anne of Cleves – then to Catherine Howard; Cromwell's fall from power and execution

1 How do Sources F and G differ in their view of the value and role of monasteries?

2 Both sources tell us something about the state of the monasteries before the Reformation. Why might a historian be cautious about using each of them?

3 If possible, research the results of the dissolution of a local monastery in order to build up a picture of the effects on the locality. This could equally be done for one of the monasteries where there are still plenty of ruins and much local evidence available.

Some writers point in particular to the effect of the dissolution on learning. Monasteries were places where great libraries of books had been built up over generations and where the sons and daughters of well-off families might go to receive part of their education. Evidence suggests that the great libraries were broken up, as books were taken by private collectors or simply burned. On the other hand some new cathedrals were founded from what had been religious institutions, for example, Peterborough Cathedral. In many other places the church within the monastery was retained as the local place of worship. Some schools that had been attached to monastic institutions re-opened. There are a few Henry VIII schools as a result. However, many of the King Edward VI schools that exist now in England are, in fact, re-foundations from earlier places of learning under the direction of monks.

Source F From a report by Richard Layton, one of Cromwell's commissioners, on a visit he made to the priory of Maiden Bradley in 1535.

I send you relics – God's coat, Our Lady's smock, part of God's supper – and all this from the priory at Maiden Bradley. There, you will find a holy father who has six children. His sons are all tall men who wait on him, and he thanks God that he never meddled with married women, but only with maidens (the fairest that could be got). The Pope, considering the holy father's fragility, has given him a licence to keep a whore.

Source G From the evidence given by Robert Aske, who protested against the dissolution of the monasteries. It comes from his examination after he had led a rebellion known as the Pilgrimage of Grace; quoted in *Tudor Rebellions* by A. Fletcher and D. MacCulloch, (Pearson), 1997.

The abbeys in the north parts gave great alms to poor men and have laudably served God. Now that they have been suppressed the divine service of Almighty God is much diminished and a great number of Masses are unsaid, much to the distress of the faith. The temple of God has been pulled down and the ornaments and relics of the church irreverently used. Many of the abbeys were in the mountains and desert places where people were in ungodly conditions and they gave people not only refreshment to their bodies but also spiritual refuge by their information and preaching. And such abbeys that were near the danger of the seas were great maintainers of sea walls and dikes, maintainers and builders of bridges and highways and other such things for the common good.

3 Opposition to religious change

NOTE-MAKING

Make notes on the individuals and groups who opposed the religious changes of the 1530s, and on why the government was able to deal with them successfully.

It is impossible to quantify, but many people in England were either suspicious of religious change or were totally opposed to it. We cannot know exactly what was happening. The nature of historical evidence means that we tend to know more about the activities and beliefs of the educated and famous rather than the ordinary illiterate villager or townsperson.

Opposition to change

Who opposed religious change, and why did they fail to prevent it?

The main problem facing those who were uneasy about events during the late 1520s and early 1530s was that it was unclear where matters were heading. There was no single great event to take a stand against until the break with Rome was made official by the 1534 Act of Supremacy. Even then, many people (including the Pope) assumed that the break was only temporary, until Henry could sort out his marital problems. So, religious conservatives were unable to mount a successful opposition to Henry's plans because, in the words of Christopher Haigh, *'they did not know that they were in "the Reformation"'*.

As a result, those opposing religious change mounted only a feeble resistance before 1534 and, although they reacted more vigorously afterwards, they had left the real challenge too late.

Resistance at court

Some individuals, including Sir Thomas More and old-established families such as the Howards, were very traditional in their beliefs. They were important people at Henry's court and tried to use their influence against the infiltration of Protestantism.

Sir Thomas More

Sir Thomas More (see page 68) was the most high-profile opponent of the royal divorce and the changes of 1534. He had replaced Wolsey as Chancellor for a brief period after 1529, but had fallen from royal favour when he showed reluctance to support Henry's plans to marry Anne Boleyn. In 1534 the Succession Act was passed. This made the children of Anne Boleyn the legitimate heirs to the throne. Catherine's daughter, Mary, was declared illegitimate because Henry's marriage to her had been declared invalid. More refused to swear an oath accepting this and was sent to the Tower of London. He refused to explain why he would not take the oath, but it seems likely that he felt that it would go against the Pope's authority. Although More wisely avoided incriminating himself, a trial rigged by Thomas Cromwell sealed his fate. According to evidence provided by Sir Richard Rich, one of Cromwell's supporters who was to become the head of the Court of Augmentations in 1540, More was alleged to have been overheard in prison saying that he did not accept Henry as head of the Church. This was slender proof of treason, but enough for the court, which ordered his execution. More had used passive resistance to signal his opposition to the changes going on around him, but he was too famous as a politician and too widely respected as a humanist to avoid persecution.

Source H From an account of the execution of Sir Thomas More, from *The Life of Sir Thomas More*, by William Roper (who was More's son-in-law).

And so the next day, being Tuesday, More's great friend Sir Thomas Pope came to him with a message from the King and his Council that he should suffer death before nine of the clock the same morning. 'Master Pope', said Sir Thomas More, 'for your good tidings I heartily thank you. I have been always much bounden to the King for the benefits and honours that he has from time to time most bountifully heaped upon me, and I am even more bounden to him for putting me into this place. And, most of all, I am bounden to his Highness that it pleases him so shortly to put me out of the miseries of this wretched world and therefore I will not fail earnestly to pray for him both here and also in the world to come.' 'The King's pleasure is further', said Master Pope, 'that you shall not use so many words'.

And so he was brought out of the Tower, and from there led to the place of execution. Where, going up to the scaffold (which was so weak that it was ready to fall), he said merrily to the lieutenant, 'I pray you, see me safely up, and for my coming down let me shift for myself'. Then desired he that all the people thereabouts pray for him, and to bear witness with him that he should now suffer death in and for the faith of the Holy Catholic Church. Which done, he knelt down and turned to the executioner with a cheerful countenance and said, 'Pluck up thy spirits, man, and be not afraid to do your work. My neck is very short, so take heed and do not strike badly, to save your reputation'. So passed Sir Thomas More out of this world and to God.

---

1 What does Source H reveal about More's character?
2 How can the account help to show why More was regarded as such a danger by the King?

Aragonese faction

Before 1534, those who opposed the attack on the Church generally expressed their concerns by being sympathetic to Catherine of Aragon in the matter of the royal divorce. Within the nobility, and at court, there was a personal following for Catherine among the 'Aragonese' faction. This consisted of a small group of nobles and courtiers, led by Henry Courtenay, Marquis of Exeter, and the northern Lords Darcy and Hussey, who supported Catherine of Aragon in the divorce question. Courtenay was a member of the King's Privy Chamber, while another supporter – Sir Henry Guildford – was the Comptroller [Controller] of the King's Household. From 1532, the stronger presence of Anne Boleyn and her supporters at court and the growing influence of Thomas Cromwell within the King's Council had largely silenced the Aragonese faction. However, they remained hopeful after the divorce that Catherine's daughter Mary would be recognised as Henry's heir. Her exclusion from the succession in 1536 helped to push Darcy and Hussey into supporting the rebellion known as the Pilgrimage of Grace (see pages 85–86) and their execution for treason. Courtenay did not become involved in the rebellion, but he did become linked to the activities of Reginald Pole, his distant cousin who was a descendant of the Yorkist kings overthrown by the Tudors. This association was enough to cause Henry to arrest Courtenay and to order his execution in 1539.

Resistance within the clergy

One bishop in particular stood out against Henry. John Fisher had been Bishop of Rochester since 1504. He had never shown any interest in world promotion or wealth. He studied and prayed and believed that Henry's actions against Catherine were totally wrong. He said so to Henry's face. However, Henry took a relatively lenient view until Fisher refused, like More, to swear the oath accepting the divorce. Fisher was imprisoned in the Tower. When the Pope declared that Fisher was to be made a Cardinal, Henry acted quickly. Fisher was accused of high treason, tried and executed. While Fisher was, in law, guilty, Henry's action gained support for Fisher's cause and provided evidence for accusations that Henry acted as a tyrant when it suited him to do so.

Elizabeth Barton, the Nun of Kent

Elizabeth Barton had been subject to visions since her teens, following an illness in 1525 and an apparently miraculous cure by a vision of the Virgin Mary. She had acquired local fame and been sent to a nunnery under the protection of Dr Edward Bocking, a Canterbury monk. By 1528 her visions had begun to focus on the King's marriage and she had warned of disastrous consequences if he abandoned his wife. Her threats continued and included telling the King to his face that he would be dead within a month if he divorced Catherine. The likelihood is that Elizabeth herself believed her visions, but those around her were playing a more political game.

By 1530 Bocking had developed Elizabeth's warnings into a wider campaign against changes in the Church, the influence of humanism and the Boleyn marriage, by encouraging pilgrims and publishing books describing her visions and the warnings they contained. Rumours were deliberately circulated about miraculous interventions, including the story that an angel had appeared while the King was at mass and seized the communion bread from his hands. Letters were sent to More and Fisher; links were established with Exeter (Courtenay) and Hussey, and with the Carthusian monks in London who were to prove a centre of resistance to the Royal Supremacy in 1534. All this suggested that an orchestrated campaign was being prepared.

Faced with this evidence Cromwell acted, and the nun and her mentors were arrested in September 1533. After a public humiliation at St Paul's Cross in London, where Elizabeth confessed that her visions were false, they were executed in April 1534. The judges could find no specific crime committed by Elizabeth, but the group were condemned by an Act of Attainder. While the nun's fate was tragic, her mentors had cynically exploited her fame for several years, and their attempts to co-ordinate a resistance movement represented a genuine threat that no government could afford to ignore.

Monastic resistance

By far the strongest clerical resistance to Henry came from the monastic orders. While the Cistercians and Benedictines, who owned the great rural monasteries dissolved after 1536, were not widely active, there were many examples of individual monks who preached against the divorce, the supremacy and the new heresies that came with them.

More significant, and certainly more organised, was the reaction of the widely respected London monks of the Carthusian order, who had remained closer to the strict ideals of monasticism. In 1532–33 they refused to accept the divorce and in 1534 resisted government pressure to agree to a declaration against the authority of the Pope. The government could not permit such defiance, and after the passage of the Treason Act, forced the Carthusians to submit, arresting the most reluctant and executing eighteen of them.

Resistance within the country

The government's success in containing opposition has led some historians to argue that resistance to the Henrician Reformation was both weak and minimal, never a serious threat to the King's position. In 1536, however, riots started in Louth in Lincolnshire. The townspeople were proud of their tall church spire which had been completed in 1515 and was nearly 300 feet high. Three sets of royal commissioners had visited the town within a few weeks of each other and there were wild rumours that the King or his ministers were going to close all the churches and that taxes were going to increase. The town also had a large monastery with a small number of

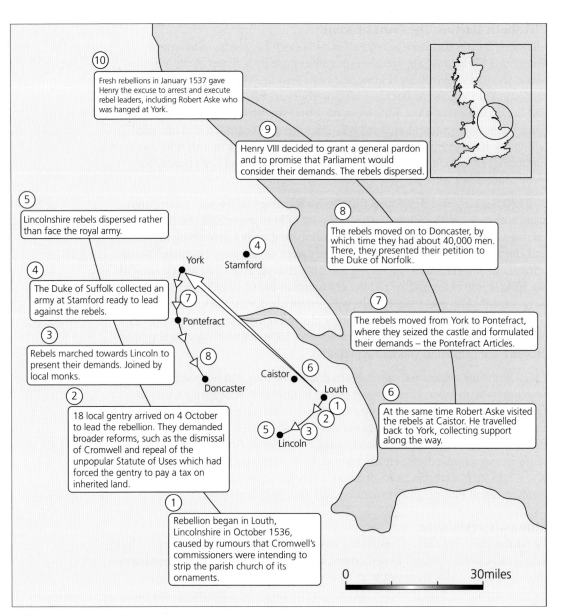

Figure 4 Course of the Pilgrimage of Grace, 1536–37.

10 Fresh rebellions in January 1537 gave Henry the excuse to arrest and execute rebel leaders, including Robert Aske who was hanged at York.

9 Henry VIII decided to grant a general pardon and to promise that Parliament would consider their demands. The rebels dispersed.

5 Lincolnshire rebels dispersed rather than face the royal army.

8 The rebels moved on to Doncaster, by which time they had about 40,000 men. There, they presented their petition to the Duke of Norfolk.

4 The Duke of Suffolk collected an army at Stamford ready to lead against the rebels.

7 The rebels moved from York to Pontefract, where they seized the castle and formulated their demands – the Pontefract Articles.

3 Rebels marched towards Lincoln to present their demands. Joined by local monks.

6 At the same time Robert Aske visited the rebels at Caistor. He travelled back to York, collecting support along the way.

2 18 local gentry arrived on 4 October to lead the rebellion. They demanded broader reforms, such as the dismissal of Cromwell and repeal of the unpopular Statute of Uses which had forced the gentry to pay a tax on inherited land.

1 Rebellion began in Louth, Lincolnshire in October 1536, caused by rumours that Cromwell's commissioners were intending to strip the parish church of its ornaments.

York · Stamford · Pontefract · Doncaster · Caistor · Louth · Lincoln

0   30 miles

Source I From *Tudor England* by John Guy, OUP, 1988, p.149.

The Pilgrimage of Grace was threatening because nobles, gentry, clergy and people combined forces, and because they shared an ideology. Indeed this revolt was neither a clash between different social groups nor a split within the governing class, but a popular rising by northerners in general.

monks that was being closed. The riots in Lincolnshire quickly spread across the whole of the north (see Figure 4). At the height of the rebellion the King's forces faced 40,000 'pilgrims' in arms. This was the most serious challenge to royal authority so far within the Tudor period. Study the map of the Pilgrimage of Grace (Figure 4) which shows the details of the events and the King's reaction.

Scale of resistance against the religious changes

Overall, it has to be said that the momentous social, economic and cultural changes resulting from the closing of all the religious houses caused little in the way of revolt. It used to be claimed by writers from a Protestant viewpoint that this was because most people were fed up with the shortcomings and scandals of the Catholic Church and welcomed the changes. However, this picture of a Church in crisis waiting to be reformed is a false one. The Church was in no worse a situation in the 1500s than it had been for at least a century and most ordinary people were not interested in the novelties of religious doctrine. What happened in church services in these years had not greatly altered – until the Bible in English appeared.

Cromwell had made sure that all the changes appeared legal – they were passed by Act of Parliament and therefore had the approval of the important people in each locality. The Treasons Act was an attempt to discourage opposition and, where necessary, the Act was used to silence opponents.

Once the process of dissolving the monasteries was under way, the heads of religious houses were given generous pensions and the monks a basic pension. The piecemeal process by which the monasteries were dissolved also reduced the scope for any opponents to mount a united opposition to what was happening.

KEY DATES: OPPOSITION TO CHANGE

1532 Resignation of Sir Thomas More

1534 Execution of Elizabeth Barton and others following an Act of Attainder

1535 Execution of Sir Thomas More and Bishop John Fisher

1535–40 Execution of eighteen Carthusian monks

1536–37 Pilgrimage of Grace

4 Royal authority and government in the 1530s

In the 1530s the nature and extent of royal authority changed. Through the process of obtaining a divorce, Henry had claimed powers at the expense of the Pope. Thomas Cromwell used the opportunity to institute reforms in the organisation of central government, though it is important not to exaggerate the extent of those changes.

Reform of government

How big a change took place to government, and with what effects?

One of the most contentious issues among historians over the past half-century has been whether or not Cromwell brought about changes in the structure of government that amounted to a revolution. Those who believe that he did regard Cromwell's actions as modernising the system of government into one that was distinct from the medieval idea of 'personal monarchy' (where the monarch was directly involved in decision making through his or her offices in the royal court), and which would be recognisable today as 'bureaucratic government' (where specialised departments and trained officials manage the routine matters of government).

The argument was originally made by Geoffrey Elton in 1953, in a book entitled *The Tudor Revolution in Government*. Since then, writers (including Elton himself) have watered down and modified some of his key arguments. Some of the historians who have challenged Elton have been his former pupils, especially David Starkey whose own detailed research on the period provides evidence that contradicts some of Elton's bolder claims. The result is a view of political reform in the 1530s which accepts that new institutions arose and that government expanded to cope with the changes brought about by Henry VIII's decision to break away from the Pope's control to get the divorce he needed. However, this view questions how far these changes were planned by Cromwell and how far the changes represented systems that were entirely new.

NOTE-MAKING

Your notes should focus on the changes to systems of government and on the extent of the changes in practice. You will see that there is not total agreement on this, and this needs to feature in your notes as well.

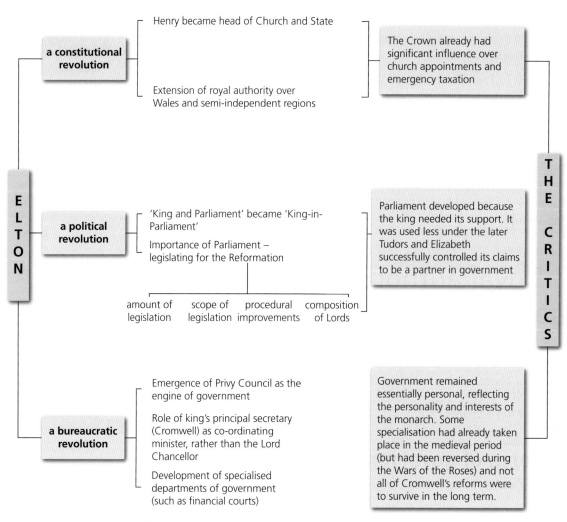

▲ Figure 5 Summary of the 'Tudor revolution in government' historical debate.

Royal Council

In the era of personal monarchy during Henry VII's reign, the King met regularly with his Royal Council of advisers. The council was a large group (although not everyone attended every meeting) which included leading noblemen, clergy and members of the King's household staff. During Henry VIII's reign a more professional Privy Council emerged. It was different from the old one because it contained fewer people, perhaps no more than 20 members, and was mainly composed of professionally trained lawyers and bureaucrats, rather than notables from the wider ruling class.

Historians disagree, however, about whether it appeared at all in the 1530s or was in fact a creation of the early 1540s after Cromwell's fall. It had also been suggested by Wolsey as a potential reform in 1526 – when one of his chief advisers was the young Thomas Cromwell. There was a move towards a smaller group of members in the 1530s which was important during the period of crisis in 1536–37 after the start of the Pilgrimage of Grace. However, it is doubtful whether the change in practice was extensive or part of a planned major change, as opposed to a reaction to particular circumstances.

Financial management

The Tudors had generally continued the system introduced by Edward IV of managing national finances not through the slow workings of the Exchequer and Treasury, but from offices in their private rooms in the palace – the Privy Chamber. This gave monarchs significant control over day-to-day decisions about all aspects of income and expenditure. Cromwell created new financial institutions alongside the Privy Chamber to manage the new revenues generated by the break with Rome. In all, four new departments were created:

- The Court of Augmentations – which controlled the land and finances formerly under the control of the Catholic Church.
- The Court of General Surveyors – which initially handled some of the ex-monastic land, but was soon amalgamated with the Court of Augmentations.
- The Court of First Fruits and Tenths – which collected money previously sent to Rome.
- The Court of Wards – the King had the ancient feudal right to collect money from the estate of a minor, under the age of 21, who had inherited.

So, by 1540, increasing specialism had apparently been introduced into the management of royal finances, although Cromwell recognised that the Privy Chamber remained an important part of the system and continued to work through it.

The King's advisers

As a result of the bureaucratic changes described above, professional administrators rather than untrained members of the nobility and clergy were needed to maintain the system. Both Wolsey and Cromwell represented this new breed of government official – hard-working and often from humble origins. Unlike the nobility, these men depended on the King for their promotions and titles, so formed an utterly loyal band of royal servants.

Power of the Crown

How much did the Crown increase its power in the 1530s?

Another feature of the debate about the significance of the 1530s has been what effect it had on the power and authority of the monarchy. In the introduction to the Act in Restraint of Appeals in 1533, Cromwell wrote that, historically, England was an empire and that everyone owed the King, ruling under God, total obedience (see page 74 for the preamble's wording). Cromwell's purpose in writing this was to set up the argument that Englishmen should not have the automatic right to appeal to Rome to give them judgments in religious cases, because the King was supreme in his own lands. However, the passage has also been taken to mean something more. Cromwell seems to be suggesting that England was an independent political body ('an Empire' that had been 'accepted so in the world') and that it was a single, unitary state, with all power derived from the monarch.

This view contrasted with the reality of England in 1533. First, the King was subject to the Pope's views in matters of religious doctrine and was supposed to seek the Pope's permission when choosing bishops and other high-ranking religious officials. Second, parts of England held 'liberties' which gave them semi-independent status. For example, Durham was governed by the Bishop as a semi-independent ruler. Another example was Wales which was no longer independent, but neither had it formally been made part of the English system of government. The consequence of these and other examples was that royal authority was spread unevenly across the country.

LOOK AGAIN

Evaluate the powers of the monarchy by 1540 compared with the description of national government on pages 20–21.

Statute law – Laws made by Parliament with royal consent. By the sixteenth century statute law was generally regarded as the highest form of law in England.

Proclamations – Decrees by the King on policy matters either falling outside the scope of parliamentary authority or made when Parliament was not in session to cope with an unusual circumstance or emergency. In 1539 the Proclamations Act gave these royal decrees equal force with parliamentary statutes, but also said that proclamations could not contravene existing statutes.

King-in-Parliament – The term 'King-in-Parliament' needs to be fully understood to avoid confusion. It does not mean the same as King *and* Parliament, which implies two separate powerful institutions. King-in-Parliament refers to government by the King, but implies that some of his functions, in particular the making of law, are carried out in Parliament rather than by the King alone. Through Parliament, the King could make statute law, the highest form of law: a statute (Act of Parliament) that had been agreed by both houses and signed by the King took precedence over any earlier law or custom and could only be changed by another statute.

Cromwell dealt with this by using the occasion of the break with Rome (which sorted out the first problem) to extend royal power more firmly across the kingdom. In 1536 an Act of Union with Wales reorganised local government in the principality and the borderlands of the marches (the border area between England and Wales). At the same time an Act against Liberties and Franchises removed and restricted the special powers exercised by regional nobles in the more remote parts of the kingdom, such as those held by the Bishop in the Palatinate of Durham. Cromwell's aim was not merely to limit the power of the magnates, but to provide consistent application of the law.

Role and importance of Parliament

How much did the function and power of Parliament change in the 1530s?

During the 1530s Cromwell used Parliament extensively to enact the legislation needed to legalise the break with Rome and to strengthen royal authority in outlying regions. Until then, Parliaments had not been a regular part of government, and although statute law had long been recognised as the highest form of law in England, kings were still able to make law by proclamation on many issues. The role of, and power exercised by, Parliament tended to depend on the state of royal finances. In the fourteenth and fifteenth centuries, when the Hundred Years' War was exhausting royal revenues, Parliaments had been called frequently and were able to exercise considerable influence over the choice of royal advisers and the measures taken by them. It should be stressed, however, that the House of Lords tended to take the lead and in many ways these Parliaments were an extension of noble politics. The restoration of royal finances under Edward IV and Henry VII had reversed this trend. Parliaments were rarely called and operated in partnership with the Crown. The expenses of Henry VIII's foreign policy under Wolsey had led to some friction with Parliament, and Wolsey chose not to call it unless it was unavoidable. There was, therefore, nothing to indicate the role that Parliament was to play in the 1530s when it was summoned at the time of the fall of Wolsey.

The Parliament that met in 1529 was to be unlike any that had gone before. It remained in being for seven years and passed a quantity and range of laws unseen before that point in parliamentary history. This stability and workload helped Parliament to develop its procedures and gave MPs a level of experience that was rare. For example, the process for passing a bill after three readings in both Lords and Commons became standard practice. Equally significant, Parliament legislated in areas of government and the Church where it had never previously been involved. By the end of the 1530s it was recognised that statute law made by the King-in-Parliament represented ultimate authority in England and Wales and could be applied to virtually any aspect of life and society. Moreover, if any future monarchs wished to change the laws that had been made, they would have to do so in co-operation with Parliament.

Cromwell chose to use Parliament in a way that his predecessors had not because he needed the status of statute law to strengthen the changes that he was making in Church and government. Parliament contained representatives of the 'political nation' – the governing class – on whom the King relied to make his policies happen. In the early 1530s the House of Lords contained 51 peers, 21 bishops and about 29 abbots, representing the nobility and the Church. The House of Commons had 310 members, 74 representing the English counties and 236 representing towns and boroughs.

The county members and some of the borough MPs were members of the lesser nobility, while borough members included merchants and royal administrators. With such a cross-section of the political nation present in Parliament, any changes it enacted were likely to be implemented smoothly, while any resistance from Parliament could be an early warning sign of trouble in implementing the King's wishes.

Composition of Parliament

The composition of Parliament changed considerably as a result of developments in the 1530s. After the dissolution of the monasteries the abbots disappeared and the number of bishops increased slightly with the foundation of four new cathedrals, while the number of peers increased to 55 by 1534. This meant that the clergy were now in a minority in the House of Lords. In the Commons, 14 new boroughs were given the right to elect MPs, while the increased status and importance of the chamber brought a growing tendency for gentleman landowners to seek election.

Chapter summary

- Henry VIII's divorce was gained through Parliament, not the Pope.
- Parliament was used to declare Henry VIII as Supreme Head of the Church.
- Government propaganda was used to justify Henry replacing the Pope.
- During the reign, religious change began to influence England as Protestantism was introduced.
- Archbishop Cranmer defined the beliefs of the Church of England.
- The dissolution of the monasteries was successfully accomplished.
- There were major consequences for the monarch, the Church and society following the dissolution of the monasteries.
- Some individuals such as Thomas More opposed the Reformation.
- The Pilgrimage of Grace, opposing aspects of religious change, was a potentially major rebellion.
- Thomas Cromwell was extremely important for the smooth running of government in the 1530s, though there are debates about the extent of the administrative changes he introduced.

Chapter summary diagram

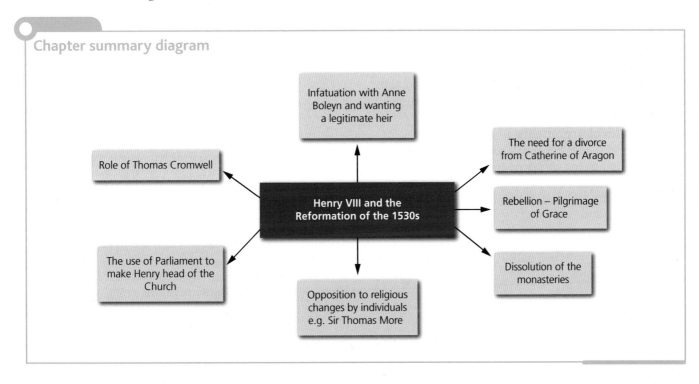

Working on essay technique: argument, counter-argument and resolution

Essays that develop a good argument are more likely to reach the highest levels. This is because argumentative essays are much more likely to develop sustained analysis. As you know, your essays are judged on the extent to which they analyse. The mark scheme opposite is for the full A-level. It is virtually the same for AS level. Both stress the need to analyse and evaluate the key features related to the periods studied. It distinguishes between five different levels of analysis (as well as other relevant skills that are the ingredients of good essays).

The key feature of the highest level is sustained analysis: analysis that unites the whole of the essay.

You can set up an argument in your introduction, but you should develop it throughout the essay. One way of doing this is to adopt an argument, counter-argument structure (see below). This approach will be very relevant on certain topics and questions where there are different opinions. We will first look at techniques for developing sustained analysis and argument before looking at the counter-argument technique.

Argument and sustained analysis

Good essays will analyse the keys issues discussed in the essay. They will probably have a clear piece of analysis at the end of each paragraph. This will offer a judgement on the question and is likely to consist of little or no narrative.

Outstanding essays will be analytical throughout. As well as the analysis of each factor discussed above, there will be an overall analysis. This will run throughout the essay and can be achieved through developing a clear, relevant and coherent argument.

High-level arguments

Typically, essays examine a series of factors. A good way of achieving sustained analysis is to consider which factor is most important, as in the example on page 93.

Level 5	Answers will display a very good understanding of the full demands of the question. They will be well organised and effectively delivered. The supporting information will be well-selected, specific and precise. It will show a very good understanding of key features, issues and concepts. The answer will be fully analytical with a balanced argument and well substantiated judgement. *21–25 marks*
Level 4	Answers will display a good understanding of the demands of the question. It will be well-organised and effectively communicated. There will be a range of clear and specific supporting information showing a good understanding of key features and issues, together with some conceptual awareness. The answer will be analytical in style with a range of direct comment relating to the question. The answer will be well balanced with some judgement, which may, however, be only partially substantiated. *16–20 marks*
Level 3	Answers will show an understanding of the question and will supply a range of largely accurate information, which will show an awareness of some of the key issues and features, but may, however, be unspecific or lack precision of detail. The answer will be effectively organised and show adequate communication skills. There will be a good deal of comment in relation to the question and the answer will display some balance, but a number of statements may be inadequately supported and generalist. *11–15 marks*
Level 2	The answer is descriptive or partial, showing some awareness of the question but a failure to grasp its full demands. There will be some attempt to convey material in an organised way, although communication skills may be limited. There will be some appropriate information showing understanding of some key features and/or issues, but the answer may be very limited in scope and/or contain inaccuracy and irrelevance. There will be some, but limited, comment in relation to the question and statements will, for the most part, be unsupported and generalist. *6–10 marks*
Level 1	The question has not been properly understood and the response shows limited organisational and communication skills. The information conveyed is irrelevant or extremely limited. There may be some unsupported, vague or generalist comment. *1–5 marks*

EXAMPLE

Consider the following practice question:

How far can Henry VIII's decision to dissolve the monasteries be explained by the Crown's financial problems that had developed since Henry VIII became king in 1509? (25 marks)

Introduction 1 addresses the question but does not develop an argument:

Introduction 1

During a period of inflation and an expensive foreign policy, Henry VIII desperately needed more money and there was a limit to what he could expect to be granted by Parliament. Getting control of the monasteries seemed an excellent solution to the problem. However, there were also other reasons why this major event occurred. These include the criticisms of the monasteries for their poor levels of devotion and the fact that the monasteries owed direct allegiance to the Pope who was no longer head of the Church in England.

This introduction could be improved by the introduction of an argument. An argument is a type of explanation. It makes a claim about the question and supports it with a reason.

A good way of beginning to develop an argument is to think about the meaning of the words in the question. With the question above, you could think about the words 'how far'.

Here is an example of an introduction that begins an argument:

Introduction 2

Getting control of the monasteries seemed an excellent solution to Henry's financial problems, and Henry as Head of the Church had the power to do so. However, this was not the main reason for the process of dissolution. The monasteries owed direct allegiance to the Pope who was no longer head of the Church in England, and the religious houses could become a centre for religious revolts against this. Henry VIII had previously been a loyal supporter of the Pope and had been given the title 'Defender of the Faith'. Now Henry had disobeyed the Pope in order to divorce Catherine of Aragon and marry again. Many monks rejected this carnal reason and argued that spiritual values included the acceptance of the authority of the Pope.

This introduction focuses on the question and sets out the main factors that the essay will develop. However, it also sets out an argument that can then be developed throughout each paragraph and is then rounded off with an overall judgement in the conclusion. It also introduces an argument about which factor was the most significant leading to the dissolution of the monasteries. This means that Introduction 2 is potentially better than Introduction 1, but it is important that it remains relatively brief and very concise.

Margin notes:

Clear focus on the question

Recognises that cannot just cover named factor

The introduction begins with a claim

Introduction continues with another reason

Concludes with outline of argument of most important reason

Counter-argument

You can set up an argument in your introduction as we have seen on page 93, but you should develop your argument throughout the essay. One way of doing this is to adopt an argument, counter-argument structure. A counter-argument is an argument that disagrees with the main argument of the essay. Setting up an argument and then challenging it with a counter-argument is one way of weighing up or evaluating the importance of the different factors that you discuss. Essays of this type will develop an argument in one paragraph and then set out an opposing argument in another paragraph.

ACTIVITY

Imagine you are answering the following A-level practice question:

'Changes in religion in the reign of Henry VIII up to 1540 occurred because of Cromwell.' Assess the validity of this view. **[25 marks]**

Using your notes from this chapter, one way to tackle this question would be to:

1 Divide your page as follows:

How Cromwell helped the process	Other reasons for changes in religion in the reign of Henry VIII

2 Consider the following points and place them either in the left- or right-hand column:
  – The Church was a wealthy institution and offered easy money for the King.
  – The Pope was unable to protect the Church from Parliament's decisions.
  – The Church had been criticised for its failings in morality.
  – The political reformation was achieved by Acts of Parliament which meant it was treason to oppose it.
  – Some supporters of Luther were influencing people's beliefs in England in the 1520s and 1530s, and there were small groups of Lollards. Humanists also supported some change.

  – The monasteries were a threat to Henry because they were under the control of the Pope.
  – Henry VIII controlled the process of the break from Rome because he needed to marry Anne Boleyn in order that their baby would be born legitimate.
  – Cromwell's careful wording of the Acts linked the political change of control to English national interests.
  – Cranmer was important for the way in which, as Archbishop of Canterbury, he steered changes in religious belief into the Church of England.

3 Now write a short argument that addresses the question of how important Cromwell's skills were. Remember, your argument must contain a statement and a reason.

4 Begin with the side of the argument that you agree with. Write two sentences that explain this side of the argument.

5 Now write two sentences for the side of the argument that you don't agree with. This is your counter-argument. Remember that it has to consist of a claim and a reason.

6 Use your original argument and counter-argument as the basis for writing two paragraphs in answer to the question.

Remember, you can apply this approach when responding to other, similar questions.

Resolution

The best written essays are those which contain sustained analysis. We have seen that one way of achieving this is to write an essay that develops a clear argument and counter-argument.

Next you should resolve the tension between the argument and the counter-argument. One way of concluding an essay is to resolve this debate that you have established between the argument and the counter-argument, as in the example on page 95.

EXAMPLE

Imagine you are answering the following A-level practice question:

To what extent was the reform of the Privy Council the most important development in government and administration in the reign of Henry VIII up to 1540? (25 marks)

A possible way to tackle this question would be to write one clear paragraph arguing that the Privy Council reform was the most important change and two paragraphs arguing against this. In an essay of this type you could then resolve the tension by weighing up the argument and counter-argument in the conclusion. In so doing, you can reach a supported overall judgement. For example, a possible conclusion could look like this:

In conclusion, the most important change was in the 1530s in the role of ● ——— **Begins with main argument**
Parliament. The process of Henry becoming Supreme Head of the Church had been achieved through Parliament, with the result that further administrative and doctrinal changes in the Church could only be made through Parliament.

Counter-argument contrast ——— ●However, aspects of administrative reform did have an impact as well, such as the developing role of the Privy Council. But the extent of these administrative ● ——— **Limitations of counter-argument**
changes have been criticised by historians since Elton first put forward his thesis, and not all the reforms survived Cromwell's period in office. Therefore,

Resolves tension ——— ●it can be argued that the changes in the function of Parliament was the most important long-term achievement. The 1530s marks the beginning of a Parliament that had gained responsibility for determining the religion of the country and a House of Commons that was becoming increasingly assertive towards the monarch as seen in the reign of Elizabeth and during the century of Stuart rule.

This conclusion evaluates the argument and counter-argument. It resolves the tension by identifying a problem with the counter-argument and reaching an overall concluding judgement in relation to the question.

The process of evaluating the argument and the counter-argument is helped by the use of words such as 'however' and 'nonetheless', indicating that the paragraph is weighing up contrasting arguments.

ACTIVITY

Imagine you are answering the following A-level practice question:

'Changes in religion in the reign of Henry VIII up to 1540 occurred because of Cromwell.' Assess the validity of this view. [25 marks]

Use the ideas on page 94 and the work you have already done on this question in order to complete the activities.

1 Answer the following questions:
   a) Which is stronger, the argument or the counter-argument? Why is it stronger?
   b) What are the flaws in the weaker argument?
   c) What strengths does the weaker argument have?
2 Having answered these questions write a conclusion that weighs up the argument and the counter-argument in order to reach an overall judgement. Use the words 'however', 'nonetheless' and 'therefore' to structure your paragraph.

Working on interpretation skills

The advice given here builds on the help given at the end of Chapter 2 (see pages 65–66).

For the AQA A-level exam, Section A gives you three extracts, followed by a single question. The wording of the question will be something like this:

'Using your understanding of the historical context, assess how convincing the arguments in these three extracts are in relation to …'   **(30 marks)**

The A-level mark scheme is very similar to the AS one on page 65:

Level 5	Shows a very good understanding of the interpretations put forward in all three extracts and combines this with a strong awareness of the historical context to analyse and evaluate the interpretations given in the extracts. Evaluation of the arguments will be well-supported and convincing. The response demonstrates a very good understanding of context. *25–30 marks*
Level 4	Shows a good understanding of the interpretations given in all three extracts and combines this with knowledge of the historical context to analyse and evaluate the interpretations given in the extracts. The evaluation of the arguments will be mostly well-supported, and convincing, but may have minor limitations of depth and breadth. The response demonstrates a good understanding of context. *19–24 marks*
Level 3	Provides some supported comment on the interpretations given in all three extracts and comments on the strength of these arguments in relation to their historic context. There is some analysis and evaluation but there may be an imbalance in the degree and depth of comments offered on the strength of the arguments. The response demonstrates an understanding of context. *13–18 marks*
Level 2	Provides some accurate comment on the interpretations given in at least two of the extracts, with reference to the historical context. The answer may contain some analysis, but there is little, if any, evaluation. Some of the comments on the strength of the arguments may contain some generalisation, inaccuracy or irrelevance. The response demonstrates some understanding of context. *7–12 marks*
Level 1	Either shows an accurate understanding of the interpretation given in one extract only or addresses two/three extracts, but in a generalist way, showing limited accurate understanding of the arguments they contain, although there may be some general awareness of the historical context. Any comments on the strength of the arguments are likely to be generalist and contain some inaccuracy and/or irrelevance. The response demonstrates limited understanding of context. *1–6 marks*

Notice that there is no reference in the mark scheme to *comparing* the extracts or reaching a judgement about which of the extracts is the most convincing.

Here is an A-level practice question (the extracts are on page 97 and guidance on how to answer it is on page 98):

Using your understanding of the historical context, assess how convincing the arguments in these three extracts are in relation to an analysis of the state of the Catholic Church in the reign of Henry VIII up to the time when Parliament met in 1529.   **(30 marks)**

Extract A

The church faced formidable difficulties by the early sixteenth century. The growth of an educated class of thinkers, the great impetus given to it by the printing press, the general scepticism about many of the devotional practices which the church encouraged or at least tolerated, the widespread resentment of church wealth, church privileges, church power; all this provided material which could be shaped into a revolutionary movement. Luther's protest was to weld these somewhat disparate trends into a rival system ... Lutheranism was far more intellectually and emotionally satisfying to the religiously committed than Catholicism. Catholicism was too much associated with the established abuses of the status quo.

Adapted from *Peace, Print and Protestantism, 1450–1558* by C. S. L. Davies, (Hart Davis), 1977, p154.

Extract B

Much of the evidence we have gives a favourable impression of the parish clergy, and much of it suggests that lay people were content with their priests. When churchwardens and other parishioners were invited to complain of their clergy at the visitations of bishops and archdeacons, they did so remarkably infrequently ... At Archbishop Warham's visitation of 260 Kent parishes in 1511–12, six priests were suspected of sexual offences (and another pestered a woman without success), and four priests were said to be ignorant. There were complaints of pastoral neglect from about one-fifth of the parishes, but that was rarely the fault of individual priests. It was much the same in the huge diocese of Lincoln. At visitations of over a thousand parishes between 1514 and 1521, only 25 allegations of sexual misconduct were made against priests ... There were 17 complaints that services were not regularly conducted, 12 that rituals were carelessly performed, seven that priests had failed to preach or visit the sick ... Though reformers might criticise, parishioners seemed satisfied.

From *English Reformations: Religion, Politics and Society under the Tudors* by Christopher Haigh, (Clarendon Press), 1993.

Extract C

Late medieval Catholicism exerted an enormously strong, diverse, and vigorous hold over the imagination and the loyalty of the people up to the very moment of Reformation. Traditional religion had about it no particular marks of exhaustion or decay, and indeed in a whole host of ways, from the multiplication of ... religious books [in everyday language], to adaptations within the national and regional cult of the saints, was showing itself well able to meet new needs and new conditions. Nor does it seem to me that tendencies towards growing lay religious sophistication and literacy, or growing lay activism and power in gild and parish, had in them that drive towards Protestantism which some historians have discerned. The Reformation was a violent disruption, not the natural fulfilment of most of what was vigorous in late medieval piety and religious practice.

Adapted from *The Stripping of the Altars: Traditional Religion in England, 1400–1580* by Eamon Duffy, (Yale University Press), 1992.

Possible answer

First, make sure that you have the focus of the question clear – in this case, the state of the Catholic Church in Henry VIII's reign, up to 1529 when Parliament met. Then you can investigate the three extracts to see how convincing they are.

You need to analyse each of the three extracts in turn. A suggestion is to have a large page divided into nine blocks.

Extract's main arguments	Knowledge to corroborate	Knowledge to contradict or modify
A		
B		
C		

- In the first column list the main arguments each uses.
- In the second column list what you know that can corroborate the arguments.
- In the third column list what might contradict or modify the arguments. ('Modify' – you might find that you partly agree, but with reservations.)
- You may find, of course, that some of your knowledge is relevant more than once.

Planning your answer – one approach

Decide how you could best set out a detailed plan for your answer. You could, for example:

- Briefly refer to the focus of the question.
- For each extract in turn set out the arguments, corroborating and contradictory evidence.
- Do this by treating each argument (or group of arguments) in turn.
- Make comparisons between the extracts if this is helpful. The mark scheme does not explicitly give credit for doing this, but a successful comparison may well show the extent of your understanding of each extract.
- An overall judgement is not required, but it may be helpful to make a brief summary, or just reinforce the level of understanding you have shown by suggesting which extract was the most convincing.

Remember that in the examination you are allowed an hour for this question. It is the planning stage that is vital in order to write a good answer. You should allow sufficient time to read the extracts and plan an answer. If you start writing too soon, it is likely that you will waste time trying to summarise the *content* of each source. Do this in your planning stage – and then think how you will *use* the content to answer the question.

Then the actual writing!

- Think how you can write an answer, dealing with each extract in turn, but making cross-references or comparisons (if this is helpful) to reinforce a point.
- In addition, make sure your answer:
  - shows very good understanding of the extracts
  - uses knowledge to argue in support or to disagree
  - provides a clear argument which leads to a conclusion about each extract, and which may reach a conclusion about the extracts as a whole.

Extracts that have an argument and counter-argument

Sometimes an extract will give opposing views within a paragraph – that is, an attempt at providing balance. The extract may reach a conclusion on which argument is stronger, or it may leave an open verdict. Look at Extract D.

Extract D

Improvements were being effected in the English Church in the later 15th and early 16th centuries. More graduates went into the Church; the learning of the parish clergy in most respects seems to have been adequate; more incumbents appear to have resided in their parishes; more bishops paid attention to their pastoral duties. Some monasteries kept abreast of humanist changes in education, while others achieved a new reputation for sanctity. Too frequently historians have overlooked these real gains in the late medieval church through their over-riding need to discover explanations for the acceptance of the Protestant Reformation in England later in the sixteenth century. Even so, for laymen jealous of the privileges of the clergy, laymen who wanted access to the scriptures without priestly mediation, these changes seemed far too little and came too late. Lollards did not long remain satisfied with the Christian humanism of Dean Colet; they went on to Robert Barnes, the Cambridge Protestant, who could supply them with a new translation of the Bible which they could read in English for themselves.

From *Church and People, England 1450–1660* by Claire Cross, (Harper Collins), 1976.

This extract presents:

- an argument that represents the thriving view of the Catholic Church
- contrary information suggesting that opposition to the Catholic Church was inevitable.

If this extract was being studied, your plan could highlight the balance within the extract and could seek to find evidence to support and refute both sides.

This would have to be reflected in your answer in relation to how convincing the arguments are. An extract that includes counter-argument as well as argument *could* be more convincing, but not necessarily so. It will depend on the context and your own knowledge which you are using in order to reach a judgement.

Henry VIII's last years

This chapter is mostly concerned with the 1540s, but traces English foreign policy from the mid-1530s onwards. The main areas examined are as follows:

● Relations with Scotland and other foreign powers; and involvement in Ireland.
● Factions at court; the fall of Thomas Cromwell.
● The succession.
● The impact of religious upheaval: continuity and change.
● An assessment of England at the time of Henry VIII's death.
● An assessment of Henry VIII as King – his achievements and his legacy.

Although this chapter is centred on the last years of Henry VIII's reign, inevitably in some respects it looks at his reign as a whole. Relations with Scotland and other foreign powers, especially France, need to be considered over all his reign. In Henry's mind the succession was constantly one of his top priorities, coupled with the direction and extent of religious change. By the end of his reign much had changed, but there was also failure, both personal and national. This detail reflects directly several of the key issues in the specification:

● How effectively was England governed?
● How did relations with foreign powers change?
● How was the succession secured?
● How far did religious ideas change and develop and with what effects?
● How did the English economy change?
● How important were key individuals?

The main question that emerges is:

To what extent was Henry VIII a monarch who could be proud of his achievements?

CHAPTER OVERVIEW

It is very easy to treat the last years of Henry VIII's reign as 'the declining years' of the monarch. Expenditure increased enormously in proportion with Henry's waistline! Foreign policy seemed to achieve little. Henry was constantly worried about the succession. Wars against Scotland and France did not enhance England's reputation, and the country was in danger of being marginalised from mainstream European politics. Financial and economic problems dominated the last few years.

Social tensions became worse, partly because of a rise in the population. At court, rivalry between factions for control of Henry and the succession came to dominate politics. There was also a tussle in and out of court over the beliefs of the newly created Church of England. There was a Catholic backlash in the 1540s against the Protestant reformers, but some decisive moves in a Protestant direction occurred just before Henry died.

Having been briefly married to Anne of Cleves in 1540 and to Catherine Howard in 1540–42, Henry then in 1543 married Catherine Parr, who provided some comfort and companionship for him in his last years. When Henry died in January 1547, his son Edward VI, aged nine, inherited the Crown.

1 England's relations with foreign powers

England's foreign policy was always heavily dependent on events and alliances within Europe, including Scotland. Henry VIII only turned his attention back to an active foreign policy in the late 1530s.

English foreign policy in the 1530s

What were the successes and failures of English foreign policy in the period 1536 to 1547?

Protestant allies

During most of the 1530s the main European powers were focused to the south. The Ottoman Turks under their warrior leader, Suleiman the Magnificent, had taken over most of the eastern Mediterranean and were threatening south-east Europe, including parts of the Holy Roman Empire and Spanish territories – both ruled by the Emperor Charles V. In 1529 the Turks had reached the gates of Vienna and besieged the city. In the mid-1530s they had threatened to control more of the eastern Mediterranean, including its strategically important islands and the North African coast, thus threatening southern Spain.

While Cromwell was focused on achieving control of the English Church and satisfying Henry's need for a new wife, the only attention paid to Europe was in dealings with the Pope. After giving up all hope of England returning to the Catholic Church, the Pope excommunicated Henry in 1538.

Meanwhile, England needed a suitable ally against the Catholic countries of Spain and France. In north Germany, part of the Holy Roman Empire, many of the princes had turned to Lutheranism, in part as a means of preserving their semi-independence from the Habsburg Emperor, Charles V. To help achieve this aim they had formed the Schmalkaldic League in 1531 and were looking for Protestant allies. Cromwell made overtures to the League but nothing was agreed about a possible alliance against the Habsburgs and France. The situation in Europe was very fluid in the later 1530s, which did nothing to help Cromwell's search for stable allies. Because Henry and his government had angered the Emperor Charles V over his divorce from Catherine, the natural ally to seek was France. However, nothing of significance was achieved – with the concentration in England being on the political and religious changes stemming from the process of the Reformation. Then in 1538 the threat to England became worse after a truce in the wars between those two nations – the Truce of Nice between Charles V and Francis I. There was fear of an invasion of England by an alliance of the two Catholic nations, with the backing of the Pope. This threat may well have influenced Henry in insisting on the publication of the Six Articles in June 1539, restating very clearly some key Catholic doctrines, in an effort to appease the Pope and Catholic countries.

In a bid to strengthen England's relationship with other Protestant countries in Europe, Cromwell arranged a marriage between the King and Anne, sister of the Duke of Cleves in Germany. Unfortunately, Cromwell had been badly misinformed about Anne's appearance, so when she arrived in England in 1539 Henry took a violent dislike to her and, although the marriage went ahead in January 1540, he refused to have anything to do with her. Divorce followed in the summer of the same year. By this time war was restarting between Charles V and the King of France, Francis I, and thus the Protestant alliance was not so necessary. The threat of invasion also receded.

Events in Scotland, 1540–47

During the 1540s, Henry again returned to the problem of the security of his northern frontier with Scotland. James V had intensified the potential threat his country posed by pursuing an actively pro-French policy. For example, in 1538 he married Mary of Guise, a relative of the French King. Henry attempted to negotiate an agreement with James which would have guaranteed England's security, but James refused, humiliating Henry in the process by failing to turn up for the pre-arranged talks.

By 1542, Henry was sufficiently concerned and irritated by events to send the Duke of Norfolk to attack the Scots. The campaign was a military success. On the English–Scottish border at Solway Moss (November 1542) the Scots army was defeated decisively. Over 1,000 Scots prisoners were taken. James V was not present at the battle as he was suffering from a fever, and he died within a week of the defeat, leaving the Crown to his week-old daughter Mary – known to history as Mary, Queen of Scots.

In the Treaty of Greenwich, Henry proposed to strengthen English influence in Scotland through the marriage of his son Edward to Mary, but this was too much for the Scots and the treaty collapsed. With it came the renewal of war as Scots nobles again looked to France for assistance in maintaining their independence from English control. In 1544 and 1545, the Earl of Hertford (reform faction leader and later Protector Somerset – see page 131) took the English army on a series of raids in the border region, especially on Edinburgh and Dunbar, with buildings burnt and people killed indiscriminately. People at the time referred to these attacks as Henry's 'rough wooing' of Scotland, but the Scots were only alienated further by them.

By his death, Henry had prevented Scotland and France from combining against him, but at great financial cost. Only repeated requests to Parliament for subsidies, reductions in the silver value of coins and the sale of monastic lands kept the Crown solvent. These short-term measures, however, contributed significantly to the financial difficulties of the mid-Tudor and Elizabethan periods.

Source A From 'Henry VIII and Scotland' by Gervase Phillips, *History Review*, 55, September 2006.

The novelist and historian George Macdonald Fraser once suggested that Henry was 'probably the worst enemy Scotland ever had'. When one considers the horrors he inflicted upon the Scottish people, particularly during 'the Rough Wooing', it seems a wholly plausible judgement. Paradoxically, though, Scotland never seems to have been Henry's primary concern. He did not envisage a united Britain; his occasional pursuit of dynastic union represented not a consistent foreign policy goal, but simply one means by which he might cow Scotland into forsaking the 'auld alliance' with France. The same objective lay behind his periodic claims of suzerainty [overlordship], his sponsorship of a pro-English faction within Scotland and the brutal military forays he sent across the border. The measure of his failure was not that he did not advance the cause of union, for he had little interest in such an outcome, but that, on his death, his policies had, in fact, driven Scotland ever closer to France.

What evidence have you to support the claims made in Source A?

English foreign policy in Europe, 1540–47

By 1541 Francis I and Charles V were at war again. In 1542 France allied with the Ottoman Turks against the Habsburgs. This, together with the English victory over the Scots in that year, encouraged Henry to enter the fray. He opted to ally with the Habsburgs against France. Under the agreement both sides promised to invade France within two years.

So in 1544 Henry (though physically severely limited in movement – for example, he had to be winched on to his horse) sailed with an army of 48,000 to Calais. Both he and the Emperor Charles V were supposed to march on Paris. They did manage to co-ordinate their arrival in France, but then both followed their own priorities, each blaming the other for not sticking to the attack on Paris. Henry, it seems, wanted to win glory for himself on his terms. He headed for Boulogne which he captured. Meanwhile, Charles and Francis signed a peace treaty at Crépy. The English fortified Boulogne, and Henry and most of his army returned home claiming a triumph. Francis threatened to invade England. The south coast was put on full alert and fortifications at St Mawes, Pendennis and elsewhere that had been hastily erected a few years earlier in the previous scare were reinforced. This was prudent considering the size of the French forces being assembled.

In fact, the attempt failed in 1545 – a mixture of French incompetence, adverse winds and the fact that the French did not have a base to use (unlike the English who had Calais). Boulogne's defences held out against the French attack. With a military stalemate, both sides were ready to talk about peace. The Treaty of Ardres was eventually signed in 1546. Henry kept Boulogne and was promised the renewal of payments of **pension money** from the French. It was agreed that if the French paid all the pension money outstanding, Boulogne would be returned to the French in 1554. Henry was confident that this was unlikely, given the previous history of these payments. Henry had gained an element of glory after the earlier failures within the reign. However, the war against France had cost £2 million – a huge sum which was paid for by large-scale borrowing, sale of monastic land and **debasement of the coinage**. Henry's expensive war left a legacy of increased inflation and debt for his children's reigns.

In Henry's defence, it can be argued that he achieved more (even if not much!) than either Francis or Charles over their long reigns. He did achieve victories over Boulogne and with the Treaty of Ardres. Judging him by the standards of the day, his priority was the acquisition of glory which was an essential part of the assumptions about kingship in this period. Through victory abroad, he enhanced the reputation of Tudor rule – even if undesirable consequences were the result.

English involvement in Ireland during Henry VIII's reign

Henry VIII regarded Ireland as a troublesome, rebellious part of his territories, just like the north of England, only worse. However, involvement there was also always closely connected with foreign policy.

Henry VII had had problems. The Irish leading family, the Fitzgeralds, had supported Lambert Simnel and Burgundy against the new Tudor King. Henry VII was successful, but real English control in Ireland was extremely limited, mostly to a small area near Dublin.

In 1536 Thomas Fitzgerald (Tenth Earl of Kildare) led a rebellion against the English Crown. The rationale was that Henry had become head of the Church and had therefore displaced the Pope. Fitzgerald announced his support for the Pope and for the Emperor Charles V. At this time, of course, any rebellion could have little to do with protests against Protestant doctrines as they had not been introduced in England at that time.

The rebellion was brutally put down and a more solid basis of government established to deter future rebellions and to prevent the country being used as

Pension money – An agreement dating from 1475 when Louis XI promised to pay Edward IV £10,000 per year. By this time the pension arrears totalled over £200,000.

Debasement of the coinage – A process whereby silver coins had their silver content reduced by substituting cheaper metals such as copper. By March 1545 the silver content was only 50 per cent of what it had been, and by March 1546 only 33 per cent. The process continued in the reign of Edward VI when it was only 25 per cent. The process allowed more coins to be circulated by the government.

a base for future foreign enemies of England. The Fitzgeralds lost their power as Lord-Deputies.

In 1540 Henry went further. A new kingdom of Ireland was declared. Anthony St Leger was sent as its first English governor. All lands in Ireland had to be surrendered to the Crown, with the promise of the return to their owners following pledges of loyalty to Henry. In return, some Irish lords were to be included in the Parliament in London. In practice the new governor only properly controlled a small part of the island around Dublin.

Therefore Henry set about establishing royal authority across all of Ireland. Principles of English common law were to be extended across the country. This process of breaking down feudal territories proved to be slow and was to take until the early seventeenth century to complete. It became known as the Policy of Plantations, which started on a small scale in Edward VI's reign and in Elizabeth's reign involved sending thousands of Protestants from England to Ireland. Much brutality was shown and executions were common (see Chapter 8, page 233).

Thus Henry's reign marked an important step in Irish history. Ireland was being moved from a clan-based Gaelic structure to a more centralised monarchical state, making it more typical of the rest of Europe. However, the Irish clung on to supporting the Pope and their Catholic faith at the same time as the Plantation settlers were Protestant in belief.

NOTE-MAKING

So, how far did Henry achieve his aims? Use the table in the Activity to provide evidence from Henry's entire reign. You will need to look back at Chapter 2 to remind yourself of details across the reign as a whole.

An assessment of Henry VIII's foreign policy

How successful was Henry VIII in achieving his foreign policy aims?

Henry was extremely knowledgeable on foreign affairs, as all foreign ambassadors commented. He did achieve successes at the beginning and end of his reign, but they were few. The long 'middle' period was dominated by his quarrel with the Pope over the divorce question and the repercussions that flowed from this in the 1530s over the process of the Reformation. The extent of his achievements in the 1540s, as explained above, is debatable.

England was not a powerful country in Europe and its geographical position on the edge of the continent made it superfluous to most of the trouble spots such as parts of Italy and the threat from the Ottoman Turks. Henry (and indeed Wolsey and Cromwell) were at the mercy of events and alliances made on the continent. Henry was also limited because of shortage of money to fight expensive wars.

KEY DATES: HENRY VIII'S FOREIGN POLICY

1540 Henry's marriage to Anne of Cleves

1541 Henry declared himself King of Ireland

1542 Battle of Solway Moss against Scots

1544 Invasion of France and capture of Boulogne

1544–45 'Rough wooing' of Scots

1546 Treaty of Ardres with France

ACTIVITY

Henry's aims in foreign policy	The extent to which Henry achieved his aims
Pursuing an active foreign policy against the French, reviving dreams of conquering France.	
Gaining honour and glory, in the style of medieval monarchs, especially against Francis I and Charles V.	
Maintaining good trade links with the Netherlands.	
Statesman – peacemaker of Europe.	
Securing his dynasty through foreign marriages.	

2 Factions at court and the succession

NOTE-MAKING

In this section your notes should focus on the causes and consequences of factionalism and include some examples.

From the late 1530s onwards factions were an important feature at court, as no single person or group enjoyed the total confidence of the King. In part, the jockeying for position reflected differences in attitudes towards the Reformation. In part those differences were being used to advance the interests of particular families and their relatives.

Growing factionalism in the late 1530s and the fall of Cromwell

Did Thomas Cromwell deserve his fate?

After the execution of Anne Boleyn and Henry's marriage to Jane Seymour, Cromwell appeared to be well in control. Moves towards Protestantism were being introduced and the monasteries were being dissolved (see Chapter 3, pages 79–82). The birth of a male heir in 1537 was exactly what Henry had been longing for.

Although the death of the mother, Jane, following complications after childbirth was a sorrow for Henry, it provided an opportunity for Cromwell and the Protestant reformers at court to encourage a foreign Protestant marriage. As France and Spain had signed a truce in 1538 there was the danger of a joint attack on England and a Protestant alliance seemed to provide some security.

Cromwell arranged a marriage between the King and Anne, sister of the Duke of Cleves in Germany. Unfortunately, Cromwell had been badly misinformed about Anne's appearance, so when she arrived in England in 1539 Henry took a violent dislike to her and demanded that the marriage should be cancelled. Although Cromwell complied, the fiasco weakened his relationship with Henry at a time when the King was already becoming unhappy with the tone of Cromwell's religious changes (see Chapter 3, pages 77–78).

Enemies at court

Cromwell had suffered a reverse over his religious reforms when the Six Articles were published in 1539, but Cromwell saw this as a temporary setback. Indeed, he might have survived if Henry had not publically shown his dislike of Anne of Cleves. Cromwell's enemies at court made good use of the collapse of the Cleves marriage in early 1540. Henry's distaste for Anne was heightened by his growing desire for Catherine Howard, the pretty, young and flirtatious niece of the Duke of Norfolk. The Duke was Cromwell's bitterest rival on the Privy Council and used this opportunity to poison Henry's relationship with his chief minister. Even so, Cromwell was temporarily in favour because in early 1540 he was created Earl of Essex – a huge elevation for a man who had been born with no connection with a noble family whatsoever. Clearly at that moment Henry did not intend to act against Cromwell.

However, as Cromwell worked towards securing the King's divorce from Anne, Catherine was instructed to spread rumours that he was not carrying out the task quickly enough. Norfolk knew that Henry was particularly keen to resist further changes in Church doctrine in the direction of Protestantism, and he suggested to Henry that Cromwell was protecting a group of Protestants in Calais (at that time an English possession).

Death of Cromwell, 1540

The fall of Cromwell came suddenly, but his power had always depended on his absolute obedience to Henry's wishes and his ability to provide Henry with the answers that he required. In 1539–40 his political skills failed him on both counts. The Protestant alliance, his own religious preferences and the Cleves marriage created the suspicion in Henry's mind that his chief minister was pursuing his own interests rather than his King's. This suspicion combined with Henry's embarrassment over the marriage fiasco to create a desire to punish Cromwell, which his enemies at court were well placed to exploit.

Although Henry was usually able to maintain control of the rival groups at court, it seems that on this occasion his anger at Cromwell and his desire for Catherine clouded his judgement. Certainly, he seems to have realised quite quickly that he had been deprived of his best and most faithful servant. Cromwell was executed after trumped up charges relating to introducing further Protestant changes and failing to enforce the Act of Six Articles were declared to have been proved by Act of Attainder. Cromwell was executed on 28 July 1540 – the same day as Henry married Catherine Howard.

What sort of person was Cromwell?

Cromwell used to be portrayed as a cunning, scheming man with no morality, out to get what he could. He was seen as a disciple of Machiavelli, the Italian writer whose philosophy of life has been (rather unfairly) summed up as 'the end justifies the means'. Historian Geoffrey Elton investigated Cromwell with detailed research which was possible because Cromwell had been a preserver of documents and when he was arrested in 1540 all his papers were impounded as potential evidence against him. Much of the material still survives. Other historians have followed in Elton's footsteps, but have not emerged with exactly the same view of the man.

To Elton, Cromwell was a brilliant public servant, a reformer of the government and someone who strongly believed in the rule of law. He was also a supporter of Protestant reforms – even when it would have been easier not to push against the wishes of Henry VIII. (In contrast, Archbishop Cranmer bided his time in the 1530s, either through prudence or cowardice, and only pushed when the tide had turned in favour of more Protestant reforms at the end of Henry's reign and in the reign of Edward VI.)

We have already considered Cromwell's role in government reforms (see Chapter 3, pages 87–89). Another of Elton's claims was that he was a supporter of the rule of law. Others have claimed that he was a tyrant working behind the scenes, with secret informers to spy on potential enemies and find evidence to justify their execution. Further research by other historians has shown Elton's view to be almost entirely accurate. There were lots of cases of treason in the 1530s, with 883 people charged but only 329 executed, and more than half of these were as a result of the Pilgrimage of Grace (see Chapter 3, pages 85–86). Cromwell is shown to have scrupulously followed the law, even when it meant him losing a case. When he did 'bend' the law, it was almost always when Henry was personally interested in the outcome and had made it clear to his chief minister that a guilty verdict was expected. There was harsh rule in the 1530s, but during the upheaval resulting from the Acts passed by Parliament there was little evidence of the use of terror or torture beyond the level that was accepted as commonplace in society at that time.

Cromwell's leanings towards Protestantism were sincerely held beliefs. He pushed Henry into agreeing to allow the Bible in English and Protestant reformers saw him as an ally. However, it is also true that he used his religious beliefs as a lever against the more conservative factions at court.

Cromwell was never able to enjoy the same exclusive role as Wolsey had done alongside Henry VIII. Partly, this is because Cromwell was serving a king who had outgrown his boyish enthusiasms and who wanted more control of policy – and not just over the divorce from Catherine. Cromwell proved himself invaluable to Henry when it came to drafting legislation in the years 1531–35 and guiding it through Parliament. He was then happy to enforce the legislation through the use of the Treasons Act of 1534.

The height of his power was after he had conspired with others at court to produce evidence against Anne Boleyn through the use of false testimony and torture. Her execution in 1536 also marked the loss of influence of her allies at Court. After this Cromwell was firmly in control with no immediate rivals, but he was not as secure as Wolsey had been. Cromwell's position relied on his control of rival factions, not from unqualified trust and support from the King. When in the late 1530s events at home and abroad conspired to undermine his position, his fall from power was swift.

Source B From *Peace, Print and Protestantism, 1450–1558* (The Paladin history of England) by C. S. L. Davies, (Paladin), 1977, pp.212–13.

Cromwell has traditionally been presented as a cold, calculating, businesslike, self-effacing, reliable subordinate, prepared to put up with any humiliation to grasp and retain power ... His reputation has suffered from the political executions which marked his ministry ... but the blame for them must fall at least as much on the king.

The image of a shrivelled bureaucrat is misleading. He was a cultivated if largely self-educated man who could more than keep his end up with a bevy of talented intellectuals – men like Thomas Wyatt the poet, Sir Thomas Elyot the educational theorist or a social and political thinker like Thomas Starkey. Cromwell had none of Wolsey's appetite for show ... Wolsey ostentatiously ran the government on behalf of the king; Cromwell was more concerned to keep up appearances, to give the impression of a subordinate who knows how to manipulate his master. There was certainly a meticulous attention to detail, whether drafting statutes, investigating the spread of seditious rumours and keeping his finger on the pulse of the localities or establishing government departments. Memoranda and agenda, preserved at length in the state papers, seem characteristic of his orderly business-like mind.

Source C An assessment of Cromwell's role compared with Wolsey's. From an essay in *The Reign of Henry VIII: Politics, Policy and Piety* by E. Ives, ed. D. MacCulloch, (Palgrave Macmillan), 1995, p.27.

Cromwell ... was not Wolsey in lay garb, and not merely because of his lower profile ... First, the shift of power back to the court, the immediacy of the king's matrimonial problem and its knock-on effects on foreign policy and finance meant that Henry, willy-nilly, was much nearer to decisions on detail than he had been. Second, the 1530s required a minister who would be pro-active, not reactive. Thirdly, Cromwell was in a different league from the Cardinal when it came to political originality. He needed to be. He did not have the advantages of age, European recognition and 'magnificence' which helped Wolsey to impress the king for so long. What is more, the greater involvement of the king meant that Cromwell's arrival did not marginalise the council attendant in the way Wolsey's had done. It was not enough, therefore, to mediate joint royal and ministerial directions to a team of councillors. Cromwell had also to manage an inner ring whose members saw the king more regularly than he did.

For each of Sources B, C and D, how convincing are the historians' views on Thomas Cromwell? Use your understanding of the historical context to explain your reasoning.

Source D The achievements of Cromwell – from the perspective of historians writing after research and publications by Professor Elton in the 1950s. From 'Thomas Cromwell: Brewer's boy made good' by Derek Wilson in, *History Today*, 62, December 2012.

Hitherto [i.e. before Elton's publications] Thomas Cromwell had been a rather shadowy, sinister figure and certainly a minister who bore no comparison with the more flamboyant Thomas Wolsey or the saintly Thomas More. Now he is acclaimed as the architect of the English Reformation and the brief era of his ascendancy (1532–1540) is portrayed as one of the most formative in the nation's history.

The last 50 years have seen great shifts in the reputation of this man about whom, despite his importance, we still know remarkably little. Indeed, it is the enigma behind the public figure which provides such rich pickings for novelists including most recently Hilary Mantel in *Wolf Hall*. Elton's presentation of Cromwell as an administrative genius who single-handedly transformed a medieval system of household government into a 'modern' bureaucracy was vigorously challenged by his peers. This somewhat esoteric debate over the nature of institutional change was significant in that it served to highlight the importance of the 1530s. England on the day after Cromwell's execution, we now realise, was a vastly different place from the England that had awoken to the news of Cardinal Wolsey's death.

Continuing factions, 1540–47

The last years of Henry VIII's reign were dominated by an intensification of the rivalry between the conservative and reform factions. The King's decision not to appoint a chief minister to follow Wolsey and Cromwell encouraged this development, as did Henry's increasingly poor health. This has led historians to question whether Henry was actually in control of events; some have downgraded the King's importance to that of a sickly bystander. It is difficult to know precisely how influential the King was between the fall of Cromwell and his death in 1547: some decisions towards the end of his life were clearly taken without his consent, while others show that Henry was still capable of wrong-footing his advisers. He succeeded in maintaining the authority of the Crown and achieved successes in France. Wherever the balance lies, it is important to understand that political development was being driven by the intensity of factionalism at court during this period.

What makes factionalism intriguing, especially in the 1540s, is that the King was fully aware of the manoeuvrings of his courtiers and even encouraged them. To some extent this was sheer egotism – the enjoyment of watching noblemen and counsellors fighting for royal attention – but it also prevented one view of politics from dominating and encouraged discussion of important matters such as religious change. This dimension means that it is difficult to discount completely the political importance of Henry, even in the last years of his reign, as the manipulator of courtly politics.

In 1540, the conservative councillors were able to feel self-satisfied and confident. They had recently won three key victories: the Six Articles Act had enshrined in law their belief that religious innovation should be limited; they had seen their greatest enemy, Thomas Cromwell, fall from power; and they had increased their access to Henry through his new wife, Catherine Howard (who was the niece of the Duke of Norfolk).

However, their success was to be short-lived. The first blow was the loss of Catherine. Although Henry was besotted with her (he called her his 'rose without a thorn'), there was a significant age difference between them – he was 49, she was 19. It was quickly obvious to all but Henry that she had other admirers at court and in 1541 the King was finally presented with the extensive evidence of her unfaithfulness. His response was fury: the men implicated in her adultery were executed and Catherine herself was beheaded for treason in February 1542. Although the Duke of Norfolk proclaimed his outrage at what his niece had done to his royal master, the incident did serious damage to the conservative group.

Worse was to follow. When the conservatives tried to break the friendship of Henry and Cranmer in 1543 by suggesting that the archbishop was dabbling in Protestant heresy, the King not only rejected these allegations against his friend, but put Cranmer in charge of the investigation into the claims. Henry also married Catherine Parr, a recently widowed lady, in July 1543. This was an important decision since Catherine was close to the Seymour family and was a Protestant sympathiser. She gathered scholars around her at court and allowed them to manage the education of Henry's youngest children, Edward and Elizabeth. Although the conservative faction struck out at her in 1546 by accusing members of her household of heresy, Henry supported his wife. This was to prove important as it ensured that Edward and Elizabeth were firmly in favour of Protestant reforms, as opposed to the Catholic views of their sister, Mary.

Succession Act of 1544

Well before his death, Henry took steps to ensure his son's safe succession. He had dealt with the lingering possibility of rival claimants by executing members of the Pole family and by his violent response to the Earl of Surrey's ham-fisted attempts to promote his family's interests. Henry had also ensured that the succession of Edward was secure in law. The Succession Act, approved by Parliament in 1543 but not given royal assent until February 1544, named Edward as heir, with Mary, then Elizabeth, as next in line should he fail to survive or to produce children. After that, the succession would go to the Suffolk family, thus ruling out the infant Mary Queen of Scots.

Factionalism and the succession, 1546–47

By the final year of Henry's reign the reform faction was dominant. Catherine Parr had survived and Edward Seymour had built his position at court both as Prince Edward's uncle and as a successful military commander in the war against Scotland. Sir William Paget was also well trusted by Henry VIII and was one of his chief advisers from 1545 onwards.

By contrast, the career of Gardiner, a leading bishop opposed to doctrinal reforms, was in decline. He had been accused by the reformers of suggesting that the Pope should be reinstated as head of the Church and only quick

Figure 1 Factions at court during the 1540s

Conservative faction	Reform faction
Accepted the break with Rome but opposed doctrinal changes.	Accepted the break with Rome, seeing it as an opportunity to introduce Protestant doctrines into the Church.
Led by the Duke of Norfolk (Thomas Howard) and Stephen Gardiner (Bishop of Winchester).	Led by Edward Seymour (Earl of Hertford and later Duke of Somerset) and Archbishop Cranmer.
Associated with: • passing of the Six Articles Act, 1539 • fall of Thomas Cromwell • Catherine Howard, Henry's fifth wife • plot against Cranmer (1543) • plot against Catherine Parr (1546)	Associated with: • foreign policy success in Scotland • fall of Catherine Howard • Catherine Parr, Henry's sixth wife • plot against Gardiner (1544) • arrest of Norfolk (1546)

thinking had enabled him to avoid the Tower. He had also made a crucial miscalculation by becoming embroiled in the plot against the Queen in 1546. This, together with a trumped-up accusation that he was refusing to grant some of his lands to the King, was enough to push him out of the inner circle of royal advisers. In the meantime, reformers occupied important positions at court.

In October 1546 Sir Anthony Denny, a keen supporter of religious reforms, was made Chief Gentleman of the King's Privy Chamber. As Henry's illnesses during his last months kept him largely confined to his private apartments, Denny's role became crucial. He tended to Henry's needs and spent much time with the King. He also decided whether Henry was fit to receive visitors and who should be admitted.

Sir Anthony Denny's position also gave him access to an important political instrument – the Dry Stamp. Instead of bothering the King with every trivial document that needed signing, the holder of the stamp could make an impression of the royal signature on to the paper, then ink in the outline to create an almost perfect copy of the King's handwriting. Using the stamp, the reform faction, led by Seymour and Denny, could legalise any document they chose – including an altered version of Henry VIII's will which it is thought Henry was too ill to approve. The revised will left the succession as Henry had agreed in the 1544 Succession Act, but added provisions that strengthened the power of the Regency Council established to rule on Edward VI's behalf. They published it shortly after news of the King's death.

While the reform faction worked its way into positions of authority at court, the conservative group was finally broken apart in December 1546 by the arrests on charges of treason of the Duke of Norfolk and his son the Earl of Surrey. Rumours had been circulating for some time that Surrey had spoken openly about his family's claim to the throne (a very sensitive issue given Henry's illness and the age of his only surviving son). To make matters worse, Surrey foolishly put part of the royal coat of arms of his ancestor King Edward I onto his own family emblem, despite having no official authority to do so. This seemed to suggest that his designs on the Crown were serious. Parliament passed Acts of Attainder against them. Surrey was executed a week before Henry's death. Norfolk escaped execution because Henry died on 28 January 1547 before giving the order. With the influence of both men eliminated, Bishop Gardiner removed from the Regency Council and Henry's will in their hands, the reform faction had triumphed.

By the terms of the will, the regency was to be managed by a council of sixteen men, named by Henry. The reform group dominated the membership of the council. Henry's death was kept secret while the leading politicians began to discuss how best to implement the regency. Henry's plan of government by committee was a clever way of protecting his son's interests, but it was too ambitious and unusual a scheme to work. The Earl of Hertford seemed the best placed for leadership. He was Edward's uncle, an important figure within the reform faction with a successful military career to commend him. Three days after Henry's death, the council appointed Hertford as Lord Protector, reviving the traditional idea of a regency led by someone close to the king-in-waiting. Following this, Hertford took the title the Duke of Somerset and used the power granted to the council in Henry's will to promote supporters with new titles and positions in government. Finally, Somerset began to appoint his own Privy Council, drawing on a wider circle of men than the will had envisaged. The transition from Henry's death to a Regency had been achieved peacefully with reformers in charge.

KEY DATES: FACTIONS AT COURT AND THE SUCCESSION

1540 Execution of Thomas Cromwell; Henry's marriage to Catherine Howard

1542 Execution of Catherine Howard

1543 Marriage to Catherine Parr; plot by conservative faction to arrest Cranmer

1544 Succession Act

1545 Sir William Paget became important member of Privy Council

1546 Sir Anthony Denny became Chief Gentleman of King's Privy Chamber; arrest of Norfolk and Surrey.

1547 Execution of Surrey; death of Henry VIII; regency for Edward VI dominated by reformers under Hertford (Duke of Somerset)

3 Position of the Church by 1547

By 1547 the Church of England had become established in its organisation under Henry VIII as Supreme Head, rather than the Pope. The monasteries had all been dissolved. However, in terms of doctrines, beliefs and practices the position was much less clear.

NOTE-MAKING

Notes in this section should focus on the balance between traditional Catholic beliefs and practices and Protestant innovations. One way to do this would be to highlight your notes in two contrasting colours.

Church of England by 1540

How much had the Church in England moved away from Catholicism by 1547?

The Six Articles Act of 1539 brought to a temporary end the gradual process of introducing Protestant beliefs. The Act reintroduced a strongly Catholic interpretation into Church services. It enforced the Catholic beliefs about the Eucharist where the bread and wine become the body and blood of Jesus (transubstantiation) and communion in one kind (bread) was only for the laity, and emphasised the seven sacraments of the Catholic Church (see Chapter 1, page 6) as essential for salvation, and the need for priests to remain celibate.

The reaction against Protestant ideas was another indication that the English Reformation would not progress as smoothly as some on the continent. At court, the fall of Thomas Cromwell in 1540 (see page 105) and the apparent success of the pro-Catholic conservative faction (see page 108) also seemed to mark a new stage in developments.

Developments in the last years of Henry VIII's reign

From 1540 until 1547 Protestants were mostly persecuted and their ideas attacked. However, they were not wiped out. Cranmer remained Archbishop of Canterbury, surviving attempts by the conservative faction to discredit him in the eyes of the King. Henry's last wife, Catherine Parr, also gave the Protestant movement renewed vigour. She maintained an interest in reforming ideas and encouraged the education of Prince Edward and Princess Elizabeth by Protestant scholars like Richard Coxe and John Cheke.

By Henry's death, the Reformation had reached a stalemate. The preaching of Protestant ideas was suppressed, but the country remained entirely separated from the Pope's control. The Bible was still available in English and limited reforms against the worship of saints and other superstitious practices had survived. Henry's Reformation had brought about the political consequences that he had desired, but had left English religion in an uneasy state – Catholicism without the Pope. The logic behind this position was weak. Henry had overthrown the Pope's power in England, but relied on bishops who preached the Pope's doctrines to maintain the split.

Thus there were many inconsistencies in this compromise and neither Catholics nor reformers were happy with the position.

Doctrines of the Church of England at the death of Henry VIII

The main doctrines of the Church of England remained Catholic:

- The Eucharist was seen as Catholic, including the belief of transubstantiation.
- Only the clergy were allowed to receive both the bread and the wine. Lay people only received the bread.

- All the seven Catholic sacraments remained in force.
- Confession of sins to a priest was seen as an essential part of devotion.
- English clergy could not marry – a problem for those who had married before this was re-imposed in 1540.
- Many of the processions and events of the Catholic Church remained.

However, some elements of Protestantism had been introduced:

- Although services were still in Latin, Cranmer had succeeded in 1545 in introducing some elements in English in 1545.
- The Great Bible of 1539 was the authorised English translation which replaced the Latin version.
- There was much less emphasis on saints and the laity were forbidden to go on pilgrimages to offer prayers to saints.
- The number of Saints Days had been greatly reduced to 25.

Religious beliefs in 1547

It is impossible for us to know exactly what ordinary people believed, since they have left no written record. Even if they had, we would have probably found the information confusing, because we tend to think in terms of 'Catholics' and 'Protestants'. However, at this time there were not two separate religious camps which split the country down the middle. It was not even inevitable that Protestantism as a separate Church would survive. There had been squabbles within the Catholic Church in previous centuries. Perhaps this would prove to be another example. Many people embraced some aspects of what we refer to as Protestant ideas – even if it was just appreciating the Bible in English. But only the educated and really devoted would have the time and inclination to understand and think through theological debates in a rapidly changing situation.

Luther had died in 1546, the year before Henry, and separate Lutheran churches and congregations had become established in parts of Germany and elsewhere. From the late 1530s another reformer, John Calvin (see Chapter 5, page 128), was preaching in Switzerland and France and gaining followers with beliefs that were more radical than Luther's. All these influences were reaching England, but at the same time most people were reluctant to abandon centuries-old traditions, especially those involving ceremonies and rituals. People were slow to embrace radical change unless there was a good reason to do so.

As explained in earlier chapters, it used to be argued by Protestant historians that most English people in the early sixteenth century despised the Catholic Church for its greed and other failings. However, evidence of actual religious devotion at the time suggests otherwise. Many people were slow to leave their long-accepted Catholic doctrines and this became clear when, in Edward VI's reign, rapid moves were taken in the Protestant direction and many communities were not enthusiastic in their support. Further evidence comes from the short reign of Mary which followed Edward's when Catholicism was temporarily restored without major controversy in many parts of the country away from London and the south east. Recently, historians have focused on accounts at the parish level rather than on Parliamentary legislation. Studies of the wording of wills and churchwardens' accounts show much continuing use of traditional Catholic language in the last years of Henry VIII's reign and beyond. Henry had been largely accepted as head of the Church, but widespread acceptance of Protestant beliefs was much slower.

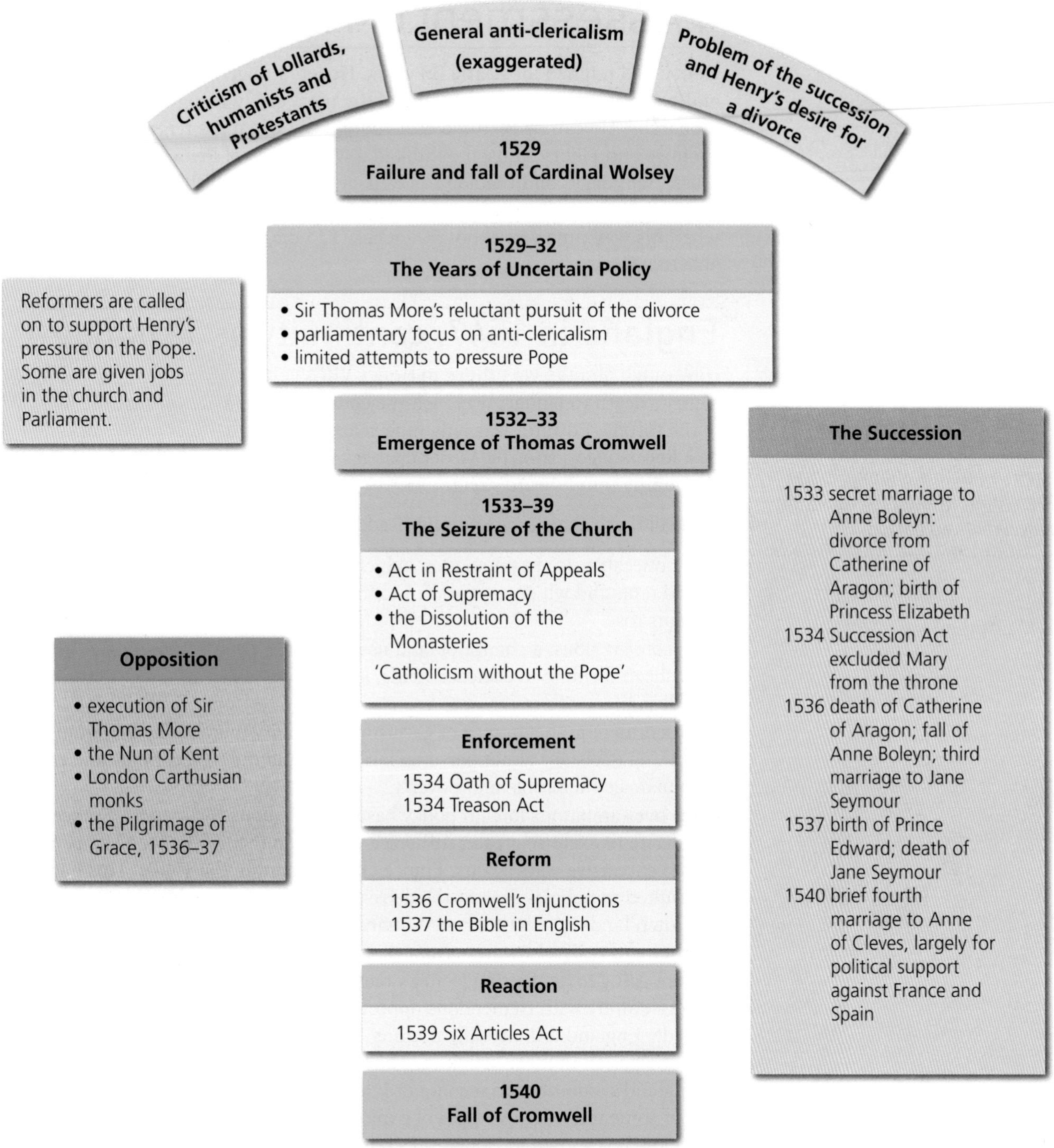

Criticism of Lollards, humanists and Protestants

General anti-clericalism (exaggerated)

Problem of the succession and Henry's desire for a divorce

1529
Failure and fall of Cardinal Wolsey

Reformers are called on to support Henry's pressure on the Pope. Some are given jobs in the church and Parliament.

1529–32
The Years of Uncertain Policy

- Sir Thomas More's reluctant pursuit of the divorce
- parliamentary focus on anti-clericalism
- limited attempts to pressure Pope

1532–33
Emergence of Thomas Cromwell

1533–39
The Seizure of the Church

- Act in Restraint of Appeals
- Act of Supremacy
- the Dissolution of the Monasteries

'Catholicism without the Pope'

The Succession

1533 secret marriage to Anne Boleyn: divorce from Catherine of Aragon; birth of Princess Elizabeth
1534 Succession Act excluded Mary from the throne
1536 death of Catherine of Aragon; fall of Anne Boleyn; third marriage to Jane Seymour
1537 birth of Prince Edward; death of Jane Seymour
1540 brief fourth marriage to Anne of Cleves, largely for political support against France and Spain

Opposition

- execution of Sir Thomas More
- the Nun of Kent
- London Carthusian monks
- the Pilgrimage of Grace, 1536–37

Enforcement

1534 Oath of Supremacy
1534 Treason Act

Reform

1536 Cromwell's Injunctions
1537 the Bible in English

Reaction

1539 Six Articles Act

1540
Fall of Cromwell

▲ Figure 2 Position of the Church, *c.*1540. The diagram shows how the changes had come about in the first decade of the Reformation in England. As explained in Chapter 3 (pages 76–78), Protestant beliefs had gradually been introduced under Cromwell and Cranmer, but only to the extent that Henry and the conservative faction of the council allowed.

4 Assessment of Henry VIII's reign

Henry had reigned for nearly 38 years. He left a huge impact on the country and he has, of course, become one of the most easily recognisable English monarchs. He can be pictured as a young king when his reign was full of promise and Henry himself exhibited a wide range of Renaissance interests in music, languages and theology as well as the more traditional ones of hunting and jousting. In contrast he is also known for his appearance in later years when his waistline was about 50 inches (125 cm) and when he was hardly able to walk.

Refer to the six key issues from the specification shown at the beginning of this chapter (page 100), to help you understand the overview of the period.

England in 1547: continuity and change

How much change was there in Henry VIII's reign?

Henry's death in January 1547 left the country vulnerable, because the heir to the throne, Edward, was only nine years old and this meant there would be a Regency government. Wider changes were also happening in these years, continuing into Edward's reign.

Some of these changes are summarised below:

- A noticeable rise in population, which put pressure on food supplies, jobs and rent, and which contributed to inflation because the price of essential items rose.
- In some regions, a change of land use from crop production in open fields to sheep-farming in enclosed fields, leading to the disruption of traditional village life.
- Resentment at the growth in government activity in everyday life, from making decisions about personal faith to regulating the economy and trying to manage the problem of poverty.
- An over-ambitious foreign policy based on a jealous rivalry with France and a desire to exercise greater influence in Scotland which had led Henry VIII into expensive wars against France and Scotland in the 1540s. This had resulted in policies such as the debasement of the coinage and the sale of Crown lands which threatened financial stability.
- Failure to realise how important the newly discovered parts of the world were going to be. During Henry's reign Spain and Portugal gained a huge empire with tremendous opportunities for developing international trade. England did virtually nothing, nor did the government encourage participation in these activities. The focus remained on European trade and England's ambitions to reconquer France. It was only in the reign of Mary that some interest in voyages of exploration started to be shown again after the interest shown in Henry VII's reign. Henry VIII's reign was one of lost opportunities.
- The gathering pace of religious debate. On the continent, Protestant faiths had emerged and were beginning to establish themselves in Germany, Scandinavia and Switzerland. In England, debate in universities and at court about the future shape of the Church and doctrine was beginning to widen out into the community. Although most people remained loyal to traditional religious ideas, Protestant influences were taking root in some parts of London and the south-east as well as in ports such as Hull which had trade links to Germany and Scandinavia.

On the other hand, the reign saw the flowering of humanism with the rapid development of printed materials. More of the land-owning classes were attending university where they received an education that reflected humanist thinking. Indeed, education, and not just lineage, was increasingly seen as being important. Education did not suffer much from the dissolution of the monasteries and new schools were being established, partly under the growing influence of Protestantism and its emphasis on learning. In any case, with the development of printing and the Bible being available in English, there was more incentive to learn to read. More of the gentry and nobility were sufficiently educated to take the lead in debates about the religious changes of the time. Government under Thomas Cromwell had been reorganised to aid greater efficiency. Lastly, the Tudor monarchy, because of events in the reign such as the Reformation and because of Henry VIII's personality, was much stronger and powerful than it had been at the beginning of the Tudor dynasty.

An assessment of Henry VIII as King

Henry succeeded in raising the profile of the monarchy. Royal ceremonies addressed both political and social functions. Administrators and courtiers were lavishly rewarded and artistic patronage at court was used to help create the image of the monarch as an unrivalled political leader. Jousts, tournaments and court festivals all contributed to Henry's control over noble rivals and to his ability to impress foreign visitors with his wealth and magnificence. All this was further exploited in Elizabeth's reign (see Chapter 7).

Henry succeeded in getting almost all the nation to accept that there were huge advantages in accepting and supporting Tudor government. Even the so-called crises of the next two short reigns could not shake the foundations of the Tudor regime that had become so well-established under Henry VII and Henry VIII.

How successful was Henry VIII?

Study Sources E, F and G.

1 For each, write out a summary of the main claims made about Henry VIII. Then put a tick or cross beside each to say whether or not you agree.

2 Now find evidence from your own knowledge to back up your ticks and crosses.

Source E The achievements of Henry. From *Access to History: Henry VIII and the Government of England* by Keith Randell (Hodder Education), 2001, pp.146–47.

Both the King himself and the orthodoxy of his time expected monarchs to be majestic. And that Henry indisputably was – even if some commentators would feel compelled to qualify the adjective with adverbs such as 'grotesquely'. It is true that some of the king's reputation for 'majesty' was created by good public relations work, as he was, for example, the first English monarch to arrange for copies of his portraits to be made in sufficient numbers for even those members of the elite who never came to court to be able to see how splendid he looked. But there is also plenty of substance to his reputation. Not only were there the high points, such as the Field of Cloth of Gold in 1520 [see Chapter 2, page 56], but there was also the routine reception of guests at his court (especially of groups of foreign envoys) which were internationally renowned for their extravagance and splendor – not least for the fine gifts that visitors took away with them ...

Nor was Henry's success in creating a reputation for majesty all window-dressing. It had important political implications ... Although kings had long begun the process of distancing themselves from their leading nobles by 1509, it was during the reign of Henry VIII that the development became virtually irreversible. The Duke of Buckingham and the socially superior members of the Pilgrimage of Grace were almost the last Englishmen for more than a century to challenge (even by implication) the concept that the monarch was very much alone at the head of the nation's political and social hierarchies.

Source F What Henry VIII bequeathed to his son, Edward. From *Sixteenth Century England 1450–1600* by Denys Cook in 'Documents and Debates' series, (Palgrave Macmillan), 1980, p.57.

King Henry VIII, the 'Stalin of Tudor England' (W.G. Hoskins) died and left to a sickly nine year old boy the crown. Henry bequeathed a heavy debt, a debased coinage, a shaken administrative system, an unsettled doctrine and a nation divided in religion. There was an uneasy truce with France and a war with Scotland. Within three days of Henry's death, Edward Seymour became protector of the realm, after a *coup*, engineered by himself. This raised the possibility of a factional struggle, complicated and intensified by religion, taking place against a background of acute social and economic problems ... Rents were increasing. Manufactures seemed to be declining and exports falling. Prices were high and rising, as was unemployment, and wages were inadequate. In the countryside there was universal discontent.

Source G An interpretation of Henry VIII's achievements. From *Henry VIII* by Professor J.J. Scarisbrick, (Eyre and Spottiswoode), 1968, p.498.

He had survived pretenders, excommunication, rebellion and threats of invasion, died in his bed and passed his throne peacefully to his heir. He had won a title, defender of the faith, which English monarchs still boast, written a book which is still, occasionally, read, composed some music which is still sung. He had made war on England's ancient enemies and himself led two assaults on France. For nearly four decades, he had cut an imposing figure in Europe, mattering to its affairs, bestriding its high diplomacy as few of his predecessors, if any, had done. He had defied pope and emperor, brought into being in England and Ireland a national Church subject to his authority, wiped about a thousand religious houses off the face of his native land, and of those areas of Ireland under his influence, and bestowed on English kingship a profound new dignity.

Chapter summary

- Henry was eager to fight France and to achieve glory, but his only glorious success was the capture of Boulogne.
- Scotland was a worry in Henry's reign because of its pro-French policy.
- Ireland was also a concern because it was Catholic and semi-independent and could always take the opportunity of supporting a foreign invasion of England.
- The fall of Cromwell in 1540 led to renewed factionalism.
- In the 1540s, there were tussles between religious conservatives and reformers.
- With a boy likely to inherit the throne, there were concerns about the succession, leading to the Succession Act of 1544.
- In the last months of Henry's reign the Protestant reforming faction triumphed over the conservative groups.
- The Regency Council after Henry's death was going to be dominated by Protestants.
- England in 1547 had significant political strengths but some economic and social weaknesses.
- How great was Henry VIII? – A continuing debate!

Chapter summary diagram

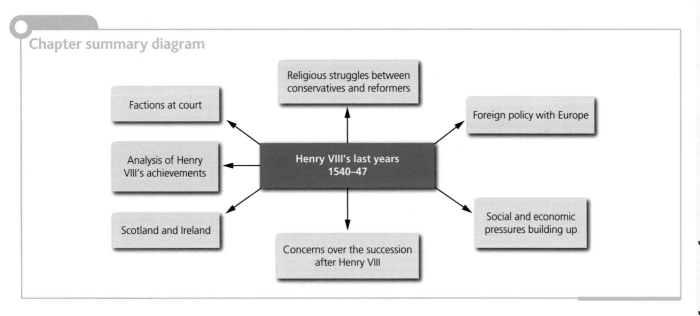

Working on essay technique: evaluation and relative significance

Reaching a supported overall judgement is an important part of writing good essays. One very important way to do this is by evaluating the relative significance of different factors, in the light of valid criteria. Relative significance means how important one factor is compared to another. This section examines how to evaluate and how to establish valid criteria.

Evaluation

The purpose of evaluation is to weigh up and reach a judgement. This means that you need to consider the importance of two or more different factors, weigh them against each other and then reach a judgement. Evaluation is a good skill to use at the end of an essay, because it helps support your overall judgement.

EXAMPLE

Look again at the following A-level practice question from Chapter 3 (page 95):

To what extent was the reform of the Privy Council the most important development in government and administration in the reign of Henry VIII up to 1540? (25 marks)

Look back at the sample concluding paragraph in Chapter 3, page 95. It would be possible to improve it by adding references to precise information so that the arguments are supported and not just statements. For example:

Begins with main argument → In conclusion, the most important change in the reign was in the role of Parliament in the 1530s. Parliament assumed responsibility for the Church, with the result that further administrative and doctrinal changes in the Church could only be made through Parliament. However, aspects of administrative reform did have an impact as well, such as the developing role of the Privy Council. ← *Counter-argument contrast*

Limitations of counter-argument → But the extent of these administrative changes have been criticised by historians since Elton first put forward his thesis, and not all the reforms survived Cromwell's period in office. The Privy Council itself as a separate distinct body did not survive the fall of Cromwell and was only resurrected in the reign of the boy-king Edward VI. There was no sudden distinct change in government bureaucracy that amounted to a revolution. Many 'medieval' practices remained until the nineteenth century. Therefore, it can be argued that the changes in the function ← *Resolves tension* of Parliament was the most important long-term achievement. The 1530s marks the beginning of a Parliament that had gained responsibility for determining the religion of the country, as seen in the reigns of the later Tudors with the frequent changes in Church doctrine, and a House of Commons that was becoming increasingly assertive towards the monarch as seen in the reign of Elizabeth and during the century of Stuart rule. Indeed, it can be claimed that the prominence of Parliament in the 1530s marked the beginning of the development of our modern Parliamentary democracy. Therefore, the reform of the Privy Council, because the changes in the 1530s were exaggerated, was not the most important development in the government and administration of the reign of Henry VIII.

In this example the evaluation is helped by using arguments with precise evidence that help to weigh up the importance of the different factors. Longer-term significance is also used to judge their importance, thus showing understanding of some key themes that run across the Tudor period.

In practice your conclusion would not be as long this because of the information and arguments that you have already included in previous paragraphs.

Relative significance

Clearly, the arguments above about Cromwell's reforms can be based on new evidence and new interpretations. The best essays will always make a judgement about which was most important, based on valid criteria. It is up to you to come up with valid criteria. Criteria can be very simple – and will depend on the topic and the exact question.

The following criteria are often useful:

- **Duration:** which factor was important for the longest amount of time?
- **Scope:** which factor affected the most people?
- **Effectiveness:** which factor achieved most?
- **Impact:** which factor led to the most fundamental change?

For example, in the essay title in the example on page 118 you could compare the factors in terms of their duration and their impact.

The conclusion on page 118 provides an example of what could be high-level work (if the essay was written in full with appropriate details) because it reaches an overall judgement and supports it through evaluating the relative significance of different factors in the light of valid criteria.

ACTIVITY

1 Now use the technique above to address the following A-level practice question:

How far can the foreign policy of Henry VIII be described as a success? **(25 marks)**

Think about the following when planning your answer to this question. The same points can be taken into consideration for other questions of this type:

- How will you define success?

- Identify four key areas in which Henry's foreign policy either failed, succeeded or had mixed success.
- Decide on the criteria with which you will judge the significance of these successes or failures.
- Write an argument in a sentence that summarises how far foreign policy in Henry's reign was a success.
- Support this by writing four more sentences specific to the areas you have chosen.
- Tip: Use words such as 'however', and 'nonetheless' to weigh contrasting points.

Working on interpretation skills: extended reading

The achievements of Henry VIII

Senior Lecturer, Lucy Wooding, summarises the strengths and weaknesses of the rule of Henry VIII.

Was Henry VIII a great king? Did he achieve important things, or did he waste the opportunities he had been given? Historians have never yet been able to agree. While he was still alive, Henry was at once feared by some and revered by others. After his death, as religious thinking polarised and Protestant opposed Catholic, it was even more difficult to assess. Henry had broken with the Papacy, abolished the hundreds of monasteries throughout England and published the Bible in English; yet he always proclaimed himself a Catholic, loathed Luther, upheld the seven sacraments of the Catholic faith and attended Latin Mass each day. Not knowing whether to cast him as a Protestant or a Catholic, John Foxe – the most influential Elizabethan historian, author of *Acts and Monuments* (better known as 'The Book of Martyrs') – described him as someone who was easily influenced, pressurised by wives or councillors into a series of contradictory policies. This view of Henry VIII as someone unpredictable and inconsistent was compounded by modern judgement that he was a lazy, inattentive ruler, who allowed first Cardinal Wolsey and later Thomas Cromwell, to run the country for him. Only recently have we begun to think again, realising that Tudor kingship was not so much about paperwork and council meetings as about courtly magnificence and artistic patronage, jousting and hunting, religious piety and military display, in all of which Henry VIII was ostentatiously assertive. We need to judge Henry VIII by the standards of his own time.

In 1485, when Henry of Richmond won the battle of Bosworth, nobody knew it was the beginning of the Tudor dynasty. Henry VIII, like his father, never forgot the civil war of the fifteenth century, always fearful that the 'Wars of the Roses' might start up again. So perhaps his most important achievement was to rule without challenge for nearly forty years and to pass the throne on to his son without bloodshed. Henry had six wives, not because he was self-indulgent, but because he desperately needed a son to inherit the throne. He had to wait nearly thirty years as king before Edward was born in 1537, when Henry was forty-six. Many of his more questionable actions, in particular the executions of his opponents, were because of this almost frantic desire to secure the succession.

Henry lived during the Renaissance, when scholars tried to rediscover the cultural heritage of ancient Greece and Rome, and revive the religious devotion of the early Christian Church. He was a great patron of artists, architects, scholars and churchmen, and played the part of a Renaissance prince with all his might, as a warrior, sportsman, musician, theologian and statesman, all at once. He built great palaces and fortifications, warships and colleges; he established parks and founded bishoprics, and he made England an important player in international politics. His meeting with the French king at the 'Field of Cloth of Gold' is a perfect example of his desire to be recognised for his military might and his role as peacemaker, his magnificence and his piety, all together. *35* *40*

Henry's need for security also lay behind his break with Rome and the 'Royal Supremacy', by which the king became head of the English Church, as our monarch still is today. Henry made this break, not because he opposed Catholicism, but because the Pope would not annul his first marriage to Catherine of Aragon, who could not give him a son. Many scholars of the time advised him that the Pope was really just the 'Bishop of Rome', who had become too ambitious and should be cut down to size. Henry also saw that heading the Church would mean a huge increase in his power and wealth. His publication of the English Bible in 1539 was to underpin his role; he wanted to govern just like an Old Testament king. Henry insisted he could do this without changing faith, but others thought that to break with Rome was to open the door to Lutheranism. Opposition to Henry's policies produced the largest rebellion of the sixteenth century, the 'Pilgrimage of Grace', when the north of England rose in revolt, only to be brutally crushed. Henry's most lasting legacy, therefore, was the opposite of what he intended. He left a country full of doubt, distrust and argument over the true form of Christianity, a conflict which would eventually claim the life of a king in 1649. In his attempt to increase the stability of the Crown, Henry set in motion events which would leave the country permanently divided. *45* *50* *55* *60*

**Lucy Wooding, Senior Lecturer in Early Modern History,
King's College, London**

ACTIVITY

Having read the essay, answer the following questions.

Comprehension

1 What does the author mean by the phrases:
   a) 'seven sacraments of the Catholic faith' (lines 8–9)
   b) 'Pilgrimage of Grace' (lines 56–57)?

Evidence

2 Using lines 33–43, list the ways in which Henry was seen as a Renaissance prince. Can you add any more from your own knowledge?

Interpretation

3 List the evidence you have to agree and/or disagree with the claims made in lines 22–32 about the reason why Henry had so many wives.

Evaluation

4 Write an essay analysing the extent to which you agree with this interpretation.

Key Questions: England, 1485–1547

The specification states that it requires the study in breadth of issues of change, continuity, cause and consequence in the Tudor period through six key questions. These have been either featured or mentioned at various points in the four chapters you have studied. The questions set in the examination (both the interpretation question and the essays) will reflect one or more of these key questions. Even though in the examination the questions may focus mostly on Henry VII or Henry VIII rather than the period as a whole, it is very useful to pause to consider developments across the wider time period you have studied so far, as this will help you to recognise and analyse change and continuity with a sense of perspective.

KEY QUESTION 1
How effectively did the Tudors restore and develop the powers of the monarchy?

Implies 'putting back to how it had been'. What does that mean in the context of Henry VII's reign?

Suggests extending or increasing. Can you relate this to Henry VII and Henry VIII?

What powers would monarchs of the sixteenth century expect to have? And over what?

Questions to consider:

- One of Henry VII's central achievements was the restoration of the powers of the monarchy. How did he achieve this?
- In the early part of Henry VIII's reign, was there any development of monarchical powers under Wolsey? Indeed, did Wolsey, through his own grandeur, detract from the young King's authority?
- Under Thomas Cromwell and the Reformation, did the power of the monarchy increase? (Think of the Church, the Act of Supremacy, Cromwell's tight control of the government.)
- Then in the last years of Henry VIII's reign, was there any real change? Indeed, was there a slight decline with competing factions in the council vying for favours and control?

Working in groups

Considering the two reigns as a whole:
1 Discuss the ways in which the Tudors restored the powers of the monarchy. How much of the success do you attribute to skill and how much to luck?
2 Discuss the evidence to suggest that the powers of the monarchy increased in this period.
3 Discuss the factors that limited the powers of the monarchy under the early Tudors.

How can you judge success? Is it just a lack of successful rebellions? Is it partly judged on the success or otherwise of royal propaganda?

Have you a clear idea of what Tudor government was like?

Questions to consider:

- Think of the personal control on government exerted by Henry VII. How did he use this to govern England? On whom did he have to rely? How important was the role of Parliament?
- What factors limited Henry VII's control over the country? Think of the nobles and remote areas. Think of the limited apparatus of government machinery. Consider the role of the Church.
- Under Cromwell, think of the changes in government organisation (e.g. the importance of the Privy Council and bureaucratic controls).
- Did the Reformation have any impact on how effectively England was governed?

Working in groups

Considering the reigns as a whole:
1 Discuss how effective central government was in governing England.
2 Discuss the limitations of local government for Henry VII and Henry VIII.
3 Discuss the evidence for and against the view that English people were mostly happy with the way in which their country was governed.

Think about what issues were likely to cause relations with foreign powers to change – marriage alliances, religion, trade, etc.

List the main foreign powers and their rulers.

Think about 'the succession' – why was it an important topic for each reign?

Questions to consider:

- Consider the problems for Henry VII with wars raging in Europe and having to decide on alliances – and therefore enemies. Why did England mostly favour a Spanish alliance?
- What role did Scotland play in England's relations with European powers? How much was this affected by events in Scotland rather than events in England?
- Under Wolsey, why was it difficult to have a consistent foreign policy? Think of what was happening in Europe in the 1520s.
- What effects did the Reformation have on England's foreign policy?
- What were the problems in securing the succession in 1509? And in 1547?

Working in groups

Considering the reigns as a whole:
1 Discuss what determined which country or countries England allied with and which England declared war on.
2 Discuss the role played by religion in determining foreign policy.
3 Discuss the role played by trade and the economy in determining foreign policy.
4 Discuss why the early Tudors were able to achieve undisputed successions.

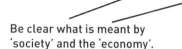

KEY QUESTION 4
How did English society and economy change and with what effects?

Be clear what is meant by 'society' and the 'economy'.

What would be the key indicators for judging change? Population? Prices? Unrest? Poverty and wealth?

Questions to consider:

- To what extent was society changing before and during Henry VII's reign?
- How did English society change as a result of the Reformation? For example, did the sales of monastic land make much difference to land ownership or to the poorer sections of society?
- Were agriculture and trade changing much in the first half of the sixteenth century? Why?
- What encouraged change in society and the economy? Think of inflation, population growth, discoveries of new lands beyond Europe and the development of printing.

Working in groups

Considering the reigns as a whole:
1 Discuss what factors encouraged change in society.
2 Discuss what factors encouraged tradition and stability in society.
3 Discuss what factors encouraged changes in agriculture, industry and trade.

KEY QUESTION 5
How far did intellectual and religious ideas change and develop and with what effects?

Make sure that you are in the world of the sixteenth century!

Does change mean 'different' or 'evolving'? Did this have effects on society?

Questions to consider:

- Think of the ways in which intellectual thought was developing through Humanism, the spread of the printing press and criticisms of the Catholic Church.
- What were the main differences in religious beliefs between the Catholic Church and the Church of England at the death of Henry VIII?
- In what respects was the Church of England not fully Protestant at the end of Henry VIII's reign?
- Once some English people embraced Protestantism, what were the effects for the country and its government?

Working in groups

Considering the reigns as a whole:
1 Discuss the changes in intellectual ideas and the extent to which they affected people's lives.
2 Discuss the differences between Catholic beliefs and those of Protestants. How far had Protestant beliefs been accepted by the Church of England by 1547?
3 Discuss the effects of intellectual and religious change. Were all classes of society affected?

KEY QUESTION 6
How important was the role of key individuals and
groups and how were they affected by developments?

How do you measure importance?
At the time? In retrospect?

Which individuals (apart from
monarchs) and groups will you
consider, and why?

What sorts of developments
were likely to affect individuals
and groups? Is it changes, e.g. in
religion, foreign policy, internal
events such as rebellions?

Questions to consider:

- Think of the key individuals, e.g. Morton, Wolsey, Cromwell, Cranmer. Summarise their contributions to the government of England and/or to changes that took place in the period.
- Think of key groups, e.g. nobles, early Protestants. How important was their contribution?
- How were key individuals affected by developments? Think of the fates of Wolsey and Cromwell in this period.
- Were groups also affected by developments? For example, the Merchant Adventurers were affected by changing trade patterns and the consequences of sailing expeditions. Think of your own examples.

Working in groups

Considering the reigns as a whole:

1 Compare the contributions of leading politicians under Henry VII and Henry VIII. Who made the most important contribution and why? This will involve discussing how you assess 'importance'.
2 Discuss what you understand by 'groups' that had influence in society. Which had the largest influence, and why?
3 Discuss why powerful politicians such as Wolsey and Cromwell so often ended up being executed.
4 Discuss which groups in society you think were most influenced by changes that happened in the reigns of Henry VII and Henry VIII. Explain why.

The Reigns of Edward VI and Mary

This chapter covers the 'little Tudors' between Henry VIII and Elizabeth. The period has been referred to as 'the mid-Tudor crisis', though this term is now largely discredited. The reigns of Edward VI and Mary are vital for understanding the reign of Elizabeth and were a period when some economic and social problems reached a peak. The chapter covers the following key areas:

- The reign of Edward VI – problems of strong government at the time of a boy king; relations with foreign powers; worries about the succession; changes in religious beliefs; rebellions; the social impact of religious and economic changes; developments in intellectual thought.
- The reign of Mary – re-introduction of Catholicism; marriage to Philip of Spain; issues over the succession; relations with foreign powers; continuing economic and social problems.

This content covers aspects of several breadth issues, but, with these short reigns, only parts of any development happened in a particular reign:

- The powers of the monarchy – in particular, problems of maintaining them effectively.
- Problems over relationships with foreign powers, especially Spain.
- Securing the succession when the country was divided over religion and with rival families.
- Changes in English society, especially concerning the economy.
- Intellectual and religious ideas changing and developing, leading to challenges to the monarch and the Church.
- The role of key individuals, such as Archbishop Cranmer.

The main question to be addressed is:

How stable was England in the period 1547–58 – in political control, in religion and in society?

CHAPTER OVERVIEW

Edward VI became King at the age of nine. This meant that there was a Regency Council, with leading nobles competing for positions of influence and power. Edward Seymour, Duke of Somerset, quickly took charge. He was replaced in 1549 by the Duke of Northumberland until Edward's death in 1553. Throughout the six years of Edward's reign there were problems over religious reform, economic problems arising from price rises and from enclosure of land and worries over foreign policy.

Mary (1553–58) ruled for five years and did her utmost, as the daughter of Catherine of Aragon, to return the country to Catholicism. She succeeded in part, with the help of her husband Philip of Spain, who became Philip II. Economic and social problems remained, but the reign tends to be known for its religious intolerance, leading to the deaths of nearly 300 Protestants. When Mary died in November 1558, Elizabeth succeeded.

1 Regency of Somerset, 1547–49

NOTE-MAKING

Using pages 127–33 make notes on the years 1547–49 under the different areas of Somerset's policies. Then highlight in different colours his apparent successes and failures.

England had had boy kings and regents before, not always with disastrous results. However, when Henry VIII died he left behind substantial problems for any ruler to deal with, and his uncle, Edward Seymour, who became Regent, was more experienced as a soldier than as a politician.

The Regency Council and Somerset

What were the achievements and failures of Somerset?

As explained in Chapter 4 (see pages 108–10), there was a struggle for control of the Privy Council in the last years of Henry VIII's reign. Edward Seymour, the Earl of Hertford (and soon to become Duke of Somerset), gained control of the Regency Council that was to rule on behalf of the young king.

The young Edward VI

Edward was born in October 1537, the son of Jane Seymour and third child of Henry VIII. Henry was delighted to gain a male heir, and Edward's life was precious. When he became King at the age of nine, he was the first to succeed to the titles of Supreme Head of the Church of England and of Defender of the Faith. Edward was very clever, especially at languages and theology. He seems to have been very serious – perhaps not surprising for a boy who had such an important position at such a young age. He impressed everyone with his learning and started training in outside activities as well, such as riding. Recent research has shown that by his early teens he was beginning to have significant influence on the Council's decisions, in particular over religious change. In 1552 he contracted measles and then smallpox, but recovered well. However, the following year he died of what used to be described as tuberculosis, but what can more accurately be described as a chronic infectious disease of the chest. In spite of what some historians have assumed, Edward was not particularly physically weak. Until spring 1553 there is no evidence that his early death was likely, never mind a foregone conclusion.

Protector Somerset

Edward Seymour's sister, Jane, had married Henry VIII in 1536. When the following year she gave birth to Henry's long-awaited male heir, Edward Seymour was guaranteed an important place in the royal household. He gained riches and titles, including Lord High Admiral and Lieutenant-General of the North.

He controlled the situation following Henry's death, taking charge of the Regency Council and gained the titles of Duke of Somerset and Lord Protector. He had important supporters within the Council who also wanted moderate religious reform to continue, and they combined to block those who were more conservative in their beliefs. Somerset also tried to implement social reforms following the bad effects on the peasants of land enclosures and price rises in Henry VIII's reign.

Among historians Somerset used to be thought of as the 'Good Duke' because he tried to help the poor. However, more recent assessments of him have stressed his weakness in making decisions and the fact that the country reached a major crisis by 1549.

To some extent he faced an impossible situation. As Lord Protector he had a lot of power (for example, he could issue proclamations in the King's name) but his position was by definition temporary until Edward came of age. All the problems he inherited from Henry VIII's reign were fraught with complexities.

Figure 1 Dilemmas facing Protector Somerset in 1547.

Decisions facing Protector Somerset's government	Why the government should take the decision	Why the government might regret the decision
Should the war with Scotland be resumed?	Henry VIII had revived this conflict partly to prevent France from using Scotland to weaken England. The weak succession in 1547 kept this danger alive. Over £2 million had already been spent on the war, for no real result. Could the new government afford to lose national pride by withdrawing now? Nobles and the gentry had raised forces and led troops in the campaigns of the 1540s. They were anxious to see the war continue to win personal fame. Could the new government afford to alienate these powerful families?	Henry VIII had already gone into debt and brought England close to bankruptcy to pay for the war. Could the country afford to continue? By attacking Scotland, it was likely that France would be drawn into the conflict. Could the government risk an invasion in the south while dealing with the Scots in the north?
Should religious reform along Protestant lines be encouraged officially?	The reform group dominated the council and key government posts. Could Somerset afford to do nothing? There was a Protestant minority in parts of the country, especially in London and the south-east, who were anxious to see further change. Could they be ignored?	In the regions, most people followed traditional Catholic rituals and practices. Would the government create open rebellion by using the law to change people's faith? Too much change might alarm the Catholic powers of Europe (especially Emperor Charles V) at a time when England was already at war with France and Scotland.
Should the government make economic and financial reform a priority?	There was good evidence of growing popular discontent over issues such as enclosure, price rises and the breakdown of traditional village communities. Action would perhaps satisfy people that something was being done.	Making changes, particularly to enclosure rights, would attack the gentry class on whom the government depended for support. Trying to improve national finances by raising taxes would certainly be unpopular and lose the new regime what support it could rely upon.

Martin Luther – Luther led the protest movement in Germany that started what we know as the Reformation. He criticised the practices of the Catholic Church and argued for some changes in religious belief (see Chapter 2, page 49).

John Calvin – Protestant reformer who developed more extreme ideas than Luther, in particular about some being pre-chosen (predestined) by God to be saved. Calvin also moved further away from the Catholic view of the Eucharist than Luther had done. For Calvin the remembrance of the Last Supper of Jesus with his disciples was really just that. The bread and wine were symbols, but Christ was spiritually present. Calvin gained many followers in Scotland where they became known as Presbyterians.

Religious reform, 1547–49

Somerset had personal sympathy with key Protestant ideas. As Lord Protector, however, he recognised the sensitivity in making religious changes and tried to adopt a moderate and cautious approach. He was happy that Thomas Cranmer, who remained as Archbishop of Canterbury, supported him in this. However, this cautious approach was not easy to maintain in the face of the pressures building up:

- As soon as news of Henry VIII's death reached the continent, exiled Protestants who had fled persecution in the 1530s and 1540s began returning from the Netherlands and Germany. They settled in towns and villages along the east coast, where their radical demands caused frequent clashes within the local community.
- The reform faction was in control of the government and keen to see reform get under way, but English bishops were split fairly evenly on whether to support further changes.
- The relaxation of press censorship (encouraged by the government) led to a massive increase in the number of pamphlets and writings against Catholicism and to the free circulation of the writings of Martin Luther and John Calvin, to the horror of religious conservatives.

At first, the government adopted a logical policy, which helped to stall for time. A full-scale enquiry into the state of the Church of England was launched, with commissioners sent out to investigate what was happening in every parish. In addition, measures were introduced which undid the Six Articles Act (see Chapter 3, page 78) and rules that provided for services and Bibles to be in English were strengthened. When Parliament met in November 1547, it was again used to enact religious change, but legislation did little more than to underline what was already happening. The Treason Act repealed the Six Articles Act and the heresy, treason and censorship laws which had stifled

▲ This is a famous depiction of the Edwardian Reformation. It is an allegorical painting, which means that it should not be seen as a literal likeness of any event, but contains messages and special meanings for its audience, in this case the triumph of Protestant 'truth' over Catholic 'error'. In bed, an ailing Henry VIII points to his successor, Edward, who sits on the throne beneath the royal coat of arms. Standing to Edward's left is Protector Somerset and seated next to him are members of the Privy Council. Through the window we can see people pulling down religious idols associated with Catholicism and burning them. The Pope has tumbled awkwardly at the front of the picture, hit by a copy of the Bible bearing the inscription 'The Word of the Lord Endureth Forever'. By contrast, the phrase 'All Flesh is Grass' is printed on the Pope's robe, thus questioning his claim to be head of a timeless Church. Frightened monks and priests flee the scene at the bottom left. Study the painting – in particular the faces of the people. How does the artist try to project his views on each person?

Chantries – Small religious houses endowed with lands to support priests who sang masses for the souls of the deceased – usually for the founder or other important people who paid in money or in kind. Chantries could also be chantry chapels within churches.

religious debate in the closing years of Henry VIII's reign. The Chantries Act abolished the Chantries, a logical step after the dissolution of the monasteries a decade earlier, because the main function of a chantry was to pray for the souls of the dead – a Catholic practice. However, it was done more to raise money for the Scottish war than for religious reasons.

It was not until that war was over that the government felt secure enough to take firm action to sort out the confusion over religious policy by passing the 1549 Act of Uniformity.

The Act was designed to impose a single (uniform) standard of worship across England in order to end the religious confusion and argument that had been growing since 1534. Among its terms were requirements that English was to be used as the language of worship and that congregations should be offered both the bread and wine during communion (this was a clear breach with the Catholic tradition of reserving the wine for the priesthood). However, it did not go so far as to create a full Protestant Church. Services were conducted along familiar lines (apart from the language) and by priests who dressed and behaved as always.

Source A From the Act of Uniformity, 1549.

Whereupon his highness [the king] by the most prudent advice ... to the intent a uniform quiet and godly order should be had ... has appointed the Archbishop of Canterbury, and certain of the most learned and discreet bishops, and other learned men of this realm ... having as well ... respect to the most sincere and pure Christian religion taught by the Scripture, as to the usages in the primitive Church, should ... make one ... order ... of common and open prayer and administration of the sacraments, to be ... used in his majesty's realm of England and in Wales; ... in a book entitled, 'The Book of the Common Prayer and Administration of the Sacraments, and other Rites and Ceremonies of the Church, after the Use of the Church of England':

... All ministers in any cathedral or parish church or other place within this realm ... shall, from and after the feast of Pentecost next coming, be bound to say and use the Matins, Evensong, celebration of the Lord's Supper, commonly called the Mass, and administration of each of the sacraments, and all their common and open prayer, in such order and form as is mentioned in the same book, and none other or otherwise.

Alongside the Act, Archbishop Cranmer introduced a new Prayer Book setting out the form that services should take. It was a masterpiece of vagueness. While not entirely denying the central Catholic idea that the priest transformed the bread and wine of the mass into the 'real presence' of Christ – His body and blood – the Prayer Book nonetheless gave the impression that the priest was simply commemorating an event, thus reassuring Protestants.

Summarise what the Act of Uniformity of 1549 was saying about the reasons for the Act and what it was intended to achieve (Source A).

1 Put the thoughts of Cranmer into your own words.
2 Use your knowledge from Henry VIII's reign and the early years of Edward's reign to give examples of:
   – resistance to change in religious practices
   – eagerness to change everything.
3 Can you think of examples in today's world where there are similar debates involving old versus new in matters of religion?

Cranmer's search for a compromise

Archbishop Cranmer searched for a compromise over the style of worship in the new Church of England. To that end, in the 1549 Prayer Book, he included an essay entitled, *Of Ceremonies, why some be abolished and some retained.* Part of it reads:

'*And whereas in this our time, the minds of men be so diverse that some think it is a great matter of conscience to depart from a piece of the least of their ceremonies (they be so addicted to their old customs), and again on the other side some be so new-fangle that they would innovate all thing, and so do despise the old so that nothing can like them except that it is new: It was thought expedient not so much to have respect how to please and satisfy either of these parties, as how to please God and profit them both.*'

During his brief time in power, Somerset dismantled the obstacles to religious change that had been erected by the conservative faction in the late 1530s while avoiding an open religious schism. The Privy Council hoped that these moderate reforms would satisfy the reformers without antagonising the religious conservatives too much, and that the large proportion of the uncommitted laity would accept what was happening. Given the weaknesses of the Regency government, the achievements of Somerset's religious policies were impressive, even though they did contribute to the causes of rebellions in 1549 (see pages 132–33).

Foreign policy under Somerset

Somerset was bound by Henry VIII's will which involved the arrangement of a marriage between Edward VI and Mary Queen of Scots. However, this was not wanted in Scotland and Somerset had to deal with the twin threats of Scotland and France. He hoped to isolate Scotland by agreeing an alliance with France. However, the French king, Francis I, died in 1547 and the new king, Henry II, was keen to assert himself. He renewed the Anglo–Scottish alliance and sent a fleet of warships with 4,000 troops to Scotland.

As a result, Somerset had to intervene in Scotland. He did so with a joint land and naval invasion. Somerset used Berwick as a base and invaded with 16,000 infantry and 4,000 cavalry, backed up at sea by a fleet of 30 warships and 50 supply ships. In the west an army of 2,000 marched from Carlisle across the border into Scotland, backed up with 500 cavalry. The Scottish army was large but poorly equipped compared with the English cannons and cavalry. A little way south of Edinburgh the Scots were defeated at the Battle of Pinkie. This gave Somerset control of all the border region, but success was limited as the English army was not strong enough to occupy the whole of Scotland.

As French troops continued to arrive in Scotland and Scottish nobles united against the English threat, Mary Queen of Scots, the heir to the Scottish throne, was moved to France with the intention of her being married to the heir to the French throne, who later became Francis II.

This meant that Somerset's costly foreign policy (£600,000) had cemented links between France and Scotland, with the prospect in the future of a marriage that would unite the two thrones. By 1549 Somerset had major concerns about what was happening in England. In the summer he withdrew troops from Scotland to deal with the rebellions that had broken out and also to protect the south coast against a possible French invasion.

Somerset has been much criticised. Although a good general, he was not decisive enough in leadership. However, he is not altogether to blame. He inherited a difficult diplomatic and military situation, leading to a war which could not be won.

Economic problems under Somerset

The reputation of the 'Good Duke' rested on his apparent desire to help those who had suffered from the consequences of the enclosure of land. A commission was established to investigate the legality of recent enclosures. Once more, government inspectors toured the country. Many poor families in the Midlands and the south had lost their lands and customary rights when landowners had converted fields from open strips for crop production into fenced-off pastures for sheep grazing. These families welcomed the commissioners and there was a real expectation that the commissioners would order a reversal of enclosure policy.

However, not everyone welcomed the arrival of enclosure commissioners. Gentry landowners who had made their wealth from sheep farming feared a loss of their livelihood, and were further angered by new laws, passed in 1548–49, which raised the tax on sheep and cloth.

The investigation of enclosures was a well-meaning policy, but led to frustration and fury among both rich and poor. The landowners feared that the drift towards enclosure of land would be reversed and this would severely limit their scope for enterprise and wealth creation. The poor had high hopes that the government was at long last on their side and would protect them against enclosures, but succeeding governments needed the support of the landowners to maintain law and order in the localities.

The really major economic problem was inflation which occurred in the first half of the sixteenth century and politicians of the period did not really understand this phenomenon. The biggest rises affected foodstuffs such as bread, cheese and meat. The rising population of the time did not help as more mouths to feed put pressure on agriculture and wages were failing to keep pace with rising prices. Both rising prices and population growth seem to have reached a peak in the 1540s, causing massive economic and social problems among the poorer classes, even when there was a good harvest. (For more details, see Chapter 6, pages 168–74.)

It was not surprising that by 1549 social unrest, fuelled by economic and religious concerns, led to rebellions in different parts of the country.

Western Rebellion, 1549

The first stirrings of popular rebellion can be seen well before summer 1549. As the government sent its agents out to check on the state of the Church and the progress towards limited reform from 1547, there were signs of resistance to change from local communities. The agitation was often instigated by concerns over religious change. However, other factors were also important. There were concerns, especially in the south-west, of gentry families gaining Church land after the Reformation and the dissolution of the monasteries, for their own use. This was coupled with more general social and economic discontent, as described above, over inflation, population increases and some changes in land use for sheep farming. In Helston in Cornwall, William Body was killed by a mob who resented his attempts to order the removal of traditional Catholic statues and images from local churches. In Somerset and Bristol mobs tore down the fences and hedges that had been erected to enclose pastureland. Similar stories of spontaneous local rioting were reported outside the south-west. Many of the riots were ill-focused and reflected a sense of desperation among the poorest classes. It was religion that provided the focus needed. The leaders of the revolt in Cornwall demanded the restoration of Catholic doctrines and practices, including the mass in Latin and a ban on the English Bible. The rebels described the new Prayer Book of 1549 as:

'but like a Christmas game … and so we Cornish men (whereo certain of us understand no English) utterly refuse this new English'.

The Western Rebellion grew out of these riots in Cornwall and Devon. When the government ordered that the new Prayer Book should be used in churches, groups were formed to resist and by mid-June a full-scale rebellion had begun.

The rebels gathered at Crediton, where they were met by a local landowner. He treated them unsympathetically and the accidental burning of part of the rebel defences prevented any chance of a quick settlement. The rebels then advanced past Exeter and set up camp. There was no attempt to march towards London to protest their grievances to the government; instead, the rebels brought the south-west to a standstill and waited for the government to come to them. News of the rebellion travelled slowly and Somerset almost certainly underestimated the seriousness of the situation at first. It was difficult, however, for the government to respond. Troops were needed to defend the north against Scotland and the coast against France. By the time the rebels had gained control of the lands around Exeter, the government also faced a second major protest in the east.

Kett's Rebellion, 1549

In Norfolk, there was a similar situation with widespread economic and social problems resulting from another bad harvest and rapid price rises, coupled with the mistaken belief that government ministers were profiteering from the situation in the absence of a strong king. Some of their demands (such as dismissing inadequate clergy and those who were non-resident) suggest that these rebels tended to be supporters of Protestantism and of Church reform, but that this was not their main motive. Gangs emerged in May and June 1549 to break enclosures. Robert Kett was one of the landowners whose property was attacked, but he agreed to end enclosure on his estates and offered to lead the rebels to secure their rights. Kett's Rebellion followed a similar pattern to the Western Rising. The rebels did not march towards London, but set up camp on Mousehold Heath, near Norwich. From there, they ran a largely peaceful campaign to end enclosures, improve local government and (unlike the Western Rebellion) secure better quality clergymen. At the height of the camp, Kett boasted that he could call on 15,000 men if the army attacked.

Fall of Somerset

The Western and Kett rebellions threatened a complete breakdown of government in two regions of England. In both cases, Somerset's response was slow almost to the point of paralysis. The western rebels were finally beaten by the royal army in mid-August, while the Earl of Warwick put an end to Kett's Rebellion at the end of the month in a bloody confrontation resulting in a combined total of 4,000 deaths from both sides. Neither revolt had forced a change in policy either on religion or enclosures, but they shook government to the core and gave those who were aggrieved at Somerset's style of leadership their opportunity to strike. Somerset was arrested on the orders of the council on 11 October and imprisoned in the Tower. He was released in February 1550 and was allowed to rejoin the Privy Council (his only real crimes had been incompetence and panic). However, rumours soon began to circulate that Somerset was gathering support to take power back from the council. He was arrested again and tried on charges of treason, specifically of plotting to assassinate some of his rivals on the council. He was executed in January 1552.

LOOK AGAIN

Compare the courses of the rebellions in 1549 with those of the Pilgrimage of Grace, 1536–37 (see pages 85–86).

KEY DATES: THE REGENCY OF SOMERSET, 1547–49

Jan 1547	Accession of Edward VI; Edward Seymour (Duke of Somerset) became Lord Protector
Sept 1547	English defeated Scots at Battle of Pinkie
Nov 1547	Parliament repeals anti-Protestant legislation of 1539 in Treasons Act; Act abolishing Chantries
1548	In the summer the French army landed in Scotland; Mary Queen of Scots moved to France
Jan 1549	Act of Uniformity and new Prayer Book; taxes increased on sheep and cloth
June 1549	Outbreak of Western Rebellion in Devon and Kett's Rebellion in Norfolk
Oct 1549	Fall of Somerset

2 Rule of Northumberland, 1549–53

The person who benefited most from Somerset's fall from power was the Earl of Warwick. He was the person who had led the troops which defeated Kett's rebellion, and he had supporters in government. However, he did not automatically slot in as the successor to Somerset. He had no direct link with the young King (Somerset was his uncle) and he had to work to gain sufficient support within the council. He gained the title of Duke of Northumberland, but it was not until February 1550 that he was fully in charge, with the title of Lord President of the Council. This was significant as he had to govern through the authority of the Privy Council.

NOTE-MAKING

In this section on Northumberland's rule, make notes on each area of policy. Then highlight in different colours where he was apparently successful and where he appeared to fail.

Northumberland

How successful was Northumberland in solving the problems which faced England in 1549?

Northumberland used to be seen as a ruthless opportunist, but now it is generally recognised that he was working in very difficult circumstances. The most serious public disturbances in the sixteenth century had just occurred, and there was still much unrest after bad harvests and a slump in the cloth trade in the early 1550s. Therefore, his policies were somewhat different from those of Somerset.

Religious changes under Northumberland, 1550–53

In these years Protestant reformers had by far the most influence in the government and changes were made which took the English Church firmly into a very Protestant position. Reformers continued to flood into England – and many were quite extreme in their views. Some were Calvinists with definite beliefs about government on earth needing to be modelled on Biblical teaching (as had been set up in Geneva) and the need for godly lives, involving strict morality. Others were concerned with social reform and a more equal distribution of wealth.

Northumberland, in securing his dominant position in the Privy Council, was keen to support people with radical views. How much he actually agreed with them is a matter of debate. Some think he was merely being opportunist in sealing his position following the downfall of Somerset.

Conservatives lost their prominent positions, e.g. Gardiner, a prominent pro-Catholic, was imprisoned in the Tower of London. Another conservative, Bishop Bonner of London, was deprived of his diocese and Ridley, an enthusiastic reformer, appointed in his place. Several other new reforming bishops were appointed.

In January 1552 Parliament assembled. A comprehensive programme of religious reform was discussed and laws were passed.

- Treason Act – it became an offence to question the Royal Supremacy or any of the beliefs of the English Church.
- The Second Act of Uniformity – it became an offence for both clergy and laity not to attend Church of England services. Offenders were to be fined or imprisoned.
- The 1552 Prayer Book removed all traces of Catholicism and the mass. The significance of the Eucharist (now referred to as the Last Supper) was reduced, with more emphasis on it being a commemorative ceremony.

- In 1553 instructions sent out to bishops told them to ensure that altars were replaced by communion tables, and that clergy should not wear vestments when taking services.
- An attack on Church wealth – partly motivated by government needs – meant that commissioners began the removal of all gold and silver plate still held in parish churches. This process had only just begun when Edward VI died.

As a result of the above, by summer 1553 the Church of England was definitely Protestant. The 42 Articles drawn up in that year listed its doctrines, influenced by Calvin as well as Luther. However, although the doctrines were Protestant, the hierarchy and government of the Church of England remained the same, with its archbishops, bishops and dioceses.

Source B From the Treason Act of 1552.

Be it therefore enacted by the assent and consent of our Sovereign Lord the King and the Lords spiritual and temporal and the Commons of this present Parliament assembled, and by authority of the same, that if any person or persons, after the first day of June next summer by open preaching, express words ... that the King ... is an heretic ... or usurper of the crown ... shall suffer forfeiture of goods and imprisonment during the King's pleasure for the first offence; forfeiture of profits of lands and spiritual promotions for life and of all goods and perpetual imprisonment for the second offence; and the penalties of high treason with forfeiture of lands and goods for the third offence ...

1 Explain why the Treason Act placed the King, even though he was only aged fourteen at the time, at the centre of the explanations (see Source B).
2 What do you think the third penalty means?

Religious beliefs under Edward VI and the influence of humanism

What did the people of England think? There is no agreement on this. When Mary became Queen and enforced Catholicism, many were happy to acquiesce. Many landowners seemed to favour Protestantism (perhaps influenced by their gaining of monastic land!) and there was much enthusiasm for Protestant reforms in and near London as a result of more direct influences from Protestant areas of northern Europe through trade and travel. However, for many others there was acceptance rather than enthusiasm. Many, especially the uneducated, did not like the disappearance of familiar ceremonies and did not approve of the strict limitation of the number of Holy Days in the year to twenty-five.

However, at the same time, among the educated elite another strong influence was at work – humanism (see Chapter 1, pages 7–10). This had been flowering at Cambridge University and elsewhere since the early sixteenth century, and it gained a new impetus in the reign of Edward VI. Some of the works of Erasmus were translated into English and published in Edward VI's reign. Originally humanism had not been either 'Catholic' or 'Protestant'. Before Luther's protest in 1517, the question would have been unthinkable. By the reign of Edward VI, some humanists, such as Bishop Gardiner, were very definitely conservative in their theology. However, many, especially the younger ones, were not, and humanist ideas became linked with the emerging Protestant doctrines being introduced in the reign.

This became linked to developments in education. Richard Cox, a Protestant humanist, was one of Edward VI's tutors. Roger Ascham and William Grindal (future Archbishop of Canterbury) served as tutors to the future Elizabeth I. Humanism was becoming the focus for the development of religious thought and its ardent followers in Edward VI's reign became the core of the ruling group at the beginning of Elizabeth's reign.

Metrical psalms – psalms translated into English poetry and set to hymn tunes.

Humanists were, as educated people, keen to spread their knowledge. This led to an explosion in publishing in the mid-sixteenth century. Several volumes of metrical psalms were published to reflect Calvinistic expectations of music in church services. Various clergy published theological books written in beautiful Tudor prose. One famous example is the publication of 'Sermon of the Plough', preached at St Paul's in 1548 by Hugh Latimer. His writing reflects Protestant ideas but also stresses social morality – the notion of the people of England all being part of a commonwealth, needing to work together for the common good. Latimer became the focus of the 'Commonwealth Men' who denounced greedy landlords and sought a fairer deal for the poor in society.

In conclusion, it is accurate to paint a contrast between the educated elite, many but not all of whom were firmly Protestant in theology, and the remainder of the population where the extent of acceptance of Protestant theology is far from certain.

Foreign policy under Northumberland, 1549–53

Northumberland changed direction in foreign policy almost completely. He was willing to sacrifice influence in Scotland in order to concentrate on urgent internal problems in England. He also realised that future friendship with France might be valuable if the main enemy was seen as Spain and the Holy Roman Empire, both ruled by the Emperor Charles V who was a hard-line Catholic. This was at the time when the Counter-Reformation was just starting in Europe, where Catholic countries were seeking to regain ground lost to the Protestants.

Counter-Reformation – An offensive against Protestantism, taken by the Catholic Church centred on Rome. It started with the Council of Trent which first met in 1545. Catholic doctrines were re-stated in order to provide clear arguments against Protestant doctrines. Jesuits and the Inquisition were trained to convert people back to Catholicism (see Chapters 7 and 8 for more details).

Therefore in 1550 a peace treaty was signed with France – the Treaty of Boulogne. It represented an English defeat. Boulogne and Calais had been English possessions. Rather than succeed in Henry VIII's vision of extending English territory in France, Boulogne had to be given up to the French. The English also had to remove their remaining garrisons from Scotland, and after lengthy negotiations the border between England and Scotland was restored to what it had been before Henry VIII's Scottish campaigns. On the positive side, an alliance with France did agree on the future marriage of Edward VI and Henry II's daughter, Elizabeth.

Relations with Charles V were mostly bad. He was angry about the move towards more extreme Protestantism that was being implemented in England.

Economy, trade and exploration

Following the expense of Somerset's war, the government had no money and had to borrow heavily from European bankers. William Cecil, Secretary of State, and Thomas Gresham from the Treasury were put in charge of financial planning. This included the sale of chantry lands to start paying off loans. Successive debasements of the coinage under Henry VIII had encouraged inflation, so the coinage was called in and re-issued with the silver content the same as it had been in 1527. Even so, more Crown lands had to be sold off and the government decided to increase revenue by raising Customs and Excise rates.

There were other pressing social and economic problems in addition to finance:

- Population figures continued to rise, putting more pressure on food supplies and on prices.
- Poor harvests in the early 1550s made grain prices rise rapidly.
- There was considerable social unrest after the popular uprisings of 1549.
- The cloth trade with the Netherlands, which was very important to textile workers, was suffering problems. There was a sudden drop in exports in summer 1551 due to a temporary problem with trade at Antwerp and this led to increased unemployment among textile workers in East Anglia and the west of England.

Northumberland's policies therefore reflected these problems:

- The sheep tax of 1548 was repealed in 1550.
- A new Treason Act of 1550 re-imposed censorship which helped restore law and order.
- Even though there was little pressure to enclose more land, anti-enclosure legislation was enforced and the unpopular enclosure commissions ended. Acts were passed to protect arable farming.
- A new poor law was passed in 1552. This made parishes responsible for raising money to look after the deserving poor.

In addition, with the uncertainties of trade with Europe, Northumberland encouraged the expansion of trade routes. By 1553 English ships were trading as far as the Gold Coast in West Africa. English ships were not advanced or strong enough to sail round the Cape of Good Hope to get to India or China, but there was interest in renewing the search for a north-east passage round the north of the American continent. In 1552 a company was set up, supported by city merchants and members of the Privy Council, and led by Sebastian Cabot. In May 1553, Sir Hugh Willoughby set out to find a route. He and two of the ships perished, but his second-in-command, Richard Chancellor, succeeded in reaching the port of Archangel and established diplomatic links with Ivan IV, the Tsar of Muscovy. The Muscovy Company was founded to encourage trade between the two countries. This was the beginning of English exploration, which continued in the reign of Mary and flourished in the reign of Elizabeth. (See Chapter 8, pages 228–32.)

How well-governed was England in the reign of Edward VI?

Many of the problems faced by Somerset, which led to his ultimate disgrace and execution, were not actually his responsibility – they were inherited from the reign of Henry VIII. Somerset did have the advantage of being Edward's uncle but he failed to act decisively on a range of issues, allowing discontent to simmer and grow, leading to rebellions. Northumberland on the other hand had no close link with the young monarch, but he did seem to be well in control with support from the Privy Council and stability was being restored. Some recent historians have praised his efforts in adverse circumstances. For example, D. Hoak has said:

'The Duke appears to be one of the most remarkably able governors of any European state in the sixteenth century.'

However, the international situation was still very threatening, and at home Northumberland's position became weak with the deterioration of Edward's health in the spring of 1553.

Succession crisis of 1553

In spring 1552 Edward VI caught and survived both measles and smallpox. However, in January 1553 the first signs of a more serious illness affecting his chest appeared. It was clear that, short of a miracle, the fifteen-year-old would not live to be crowned king. Under the terms of the 1544 Succession Act, Edward's heir was the Princess Mary. This posed a problem for the Northumberland government: Mary was a committed Catholic and had drawn close to her cousin, the Emperor Charles V. If she succeeded to the throne, the policies pursued since 1550 would be swept aside along with the men who had promoted them. To protect both himself and the Protestant faith, Northumberland tried to alter the succession before Edward died. He based his plans on two facts:

KEY DATES: THE RULE OF NORTHUMBERLAND, 1549–53

Oct 1549	Fall of Somerset; power struggle to replace him
Feb 1550	Earl of Warwick (becoming Duke of Northumberland in 1551) emerged as leading minister; became Lord President of the Council
Mar 1550	Peace of Boulogne with France; Scotland closely linked with France
1551	Strengthening of currency after effects of debasement; failed harvest and collapse in value of cloth exports
Jan 1552	Somerset executed
Mar 1552	Second Act of Uniformity
May 1553	Marriage of Northumberland's son to Lady Jane Grey
Jul 1553	Death of Edward VI; Lady Jane Grey proclaimed queen under terms of Edward VI's will; failure of coup and succession of Mary Tudor
Aug 1553	Execution of Northumberland

1 Mary had been made illegitimate when Henry VIII's marriage to Catherine of Aragon had broken down. Similarly, Elizabeth had also been made illegitimate by the collapse of Henry's marriage to Anne Boleyn. Although both women had been officially restored to the succession, these changes had been damaging.

2 Henry VIII's will had directed the succession towards his own children, but had not set aside the claims that his younger sister's family might make. From these two strands, Northumberland decided to ensure that Edward's will did not pass the Crown to either Mary or Elizabeth, but to Lady Jane Grey (who married Northumberland's son in May 1553, six weeks before Edward's death).

Edward VI agreed with this plan – some recent research suggesting that he was a keen instigator – but it is clear that he wanted to protect the Protestant faith. He signed his agreement days before his death in July 1553, aged fifteen. Northumberland had not had time to prepare properly for the succession of Lady Jane Grey, who 'reigned' for nine days before Mary was crowned queen.

The events of 1553 showed that, for most people, it was important that God's rightful choice of monarch – Mary – should take the throne rather than a usurper. Moreover, there was still significant support for traditional ways outside London, so the provinces backed Mary to succeed. The fact that Mary was Catholic and Lady Jane Grey Protestant seems to have assumed little importance. The Privy Council only agreed to support Northumberland after much cajoling, and because it was the dying King's wish. The only local authorities outside London to back Lady Jane Grey were Berwick on the Scottish border and King's Lynn in East Anglia. Northumberland quickly saw the lack of support for the change in succession, and he himself ended the attempted coup when he surrendered to Mary near Cambridge. Very soon he, his son and Lady Jane Grey were all in the Tower of London. The events surrounding Mary's succession illustrated both how vulnerable the country could be to political disruption and yet how secure the Tudor dynasty had actually become. The only successful coup against the Tudors lasted just nine days.

Mary was initially reluctant to execute Jane Grey because she recognised her as an innocent pawn in Northumberland's plans, but she also realised that the pretender queen would continue to represent a hope for English Protestants as long as she remained alive. Confirmation of this came in the form of an attempted rebellion led by the Duke of Suffolk, Lady Jane Grey's father. For this reason, she was convicted and beheaded on the charge of treason. Northumberland and other ring-leaders had already been executed within weeks of their arrest.

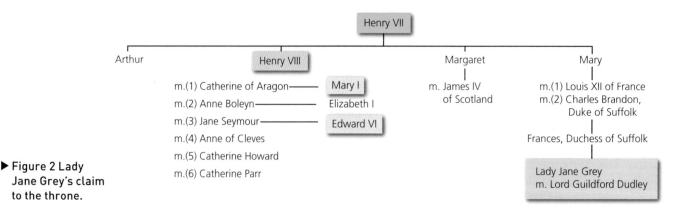

▶ Figure 2 Lady Jane Grey's claim to the throne.

3 Reign of Mary Tudor, 1553–58

Mary became the unquestioned queen of England after Lady Jane Grey and her supporters gave up their attempt to change the succession. At her accession Mary was popular, but by the time she died, five years later, her popularity had greatly declined. This section will investigate the reasons for this change.

Mary's policies and how she became unpopular as queen

How much support did Mary have for her policies?

Mary threw away the genuine wave of support that carried her to the throne because she failed to realise that the country had undergone significant change for about a generation, and that altering direction in any of these areas had to be done slowly and cautiously. Instead, Mary appeared to be impatient to make changes. She interpreted the popularity which greeted her succession as a sign that her subjects were welcoming the return of Catholicism rather than as a reaction against Northumberland and Lady Jane Grey. In this way, her sharp reversal of the religious policies promoted by the reformers during the 1540s and early 1550s and her equally dramatic decision to marry her nephew Philip, heir to the Spanish throne, turned her early popularity into doubt and dislike in the minds of many Englishmen.

Religious reform

The major aim of Mary's reign was to reinstate traditional Catholic doctrines, services and ornaments in the Church. As a child, Mary had been brought up by her mother, Catherine of Aragon, as a strict Catholic. When her father had manipulated religion to divorce her mother, and when he had denied the authority of the Pope and seized control over the Church for himself, Mary had been horrified. She saw the break with Rome as a sinful act and was determined to correct it. The destruction of Church property and the rewriting of the Prayer Book had only confirmed her desire to put things right and to restore the old religion.

Changes in legislation

Parliament met in October 1553. The obedient majority of the House of Commons passed the First Act of Repeal which swept away all the religious legislation approved during the reign of Edward VI. The doctrine of the Church of England was restored to what it had been at the death of Henry VIII. Mary was persuaded by her advisers not to try to achieve more at that time.

However, when Mary felt more secure and after the return of Cardinal Pole from exile in Catholic Europe to England in November 1554, Parliament met and passed the Second Act of Repeal in January 1555. This abolished all doctrinal legislation passed since 1529. Since this included the 1534 Act of Supremacy, it meant the reinstatement of the Pope as head of the Church. It did not, however, mean the restoration of Church lands and property, for this was too complex and too divisive an issue to be resolved easily. However, using Parliament to change religious doctrines also meant that MPs had, since the Reformation started, gained a decisive role over religion.

NOTE-MAKING

In this section on Mary I, make notes about the key events and policies under each sub-heading. Arrange your notes in two columns – one for aspects where she succeeded in her aims and the other for her failures.

Source C From the Second Act of Repeal, passed by Parliament in January 1555.

Whereas since the 20th year of King Henry the Eighth of famous memory, ... much false and erroneous doctrine hath been taught, preached and written, partly by divers the natural-born subjects of this realm, and partly being brought in hither from sundry other foreign countries ... hath been sown and spread...

By reason whereof ... we do declare ourselves very sorry and repentant of the schism and disobedience committed in this realm ... And that we may as children repentant be received into the bosom and unity of Christ's Church [i.e. Catholic Church] ...

... [To accomplish this] we do repeal all laws and statutes made contrary to the said Supremacy and See Apostolic during the said schism...

Do you find it surprising that this Act (see Source C) was passed by Parliament with little opposition? If so, why?

Although there was opposition to this sudden change of direction, Mary remained convinced that Protestantism lacked the deep roots in English culture that would allow it to survive. Having achieved the reunion of England with the Catholic Church, government policy now divided into two distinct strands – education and persecution. To ensure that Catholicism took root once more, emphasis was placed on better training and supervision of parish priests. Bishops were instructed to set up local training schools and to make regular visits to observe the work of priests in their area. National decrees laid down the standards expected from priests and new editions of the Prayer Book and Bible were issued for guidance.

Royal authority and Mary's policy of persecution

It is the policy of persecution that has in the past been much more widely reported by historians, giving rise to the Queen's reputation as 'Bloody Mary'. Leading Protestant churchmen, including Archbishop Cranmer, were arrested and others replaced by committed Catholics. Within a year of Mary's succession, the senior clergy had been purged of Protestant elements and work had begun on ordering parish priests who had married to either give up their families or leave their jobs. Once Parliament had revived the heresy laws which had operated during Henry VIII's reign, Protestants who would not renounce their faith were burned at the stake in their local community as a warning to others. The executions began in February 1555 and claimed both high-ranking victims such as Cranmer and many ordinary people who were unable to escape abroad. About 300 suspected Protestants were burned in total. Mary's government was asserting its royal authority – but no more than her father's government had done in the 1530s and 1540s when faced with what was seen as heresy then.

Source D A description of the burning of bishops Latimer and Ridley in Oxford in 1555. From *Book of Martyrs* by John Foxe, first published in 1563.

Then the smith took a chain and fastened it about both Ridley and Latimer's middles. Then his brother brought him gunpowder in a bag and tied it around their necks. Then they brought a faggot [a bundle of sticks], kindled with fire and laid it down at Ridley's feet. Latimer turned to him and spoke in this manner: 'Be of good comfort, brother Ridley, and play the man. We shall this day light such a candle by God's grace in England as I trust shall never be put out'. And so the fire being kindled, Latimer cried out, 'O Father of heaven, receive my soul' and reached to the flame as if embracing it. After he had stroked his face with his hands, and, as it were, bathed them a little in the fire, he soon died, with very little pain. But Ridley lingered longer by reason of the badness of the fire, which only burned beneath him. He asked for them to let the fire come to him, saying 'I cannot burn'. This was apparent for after his legs were consumed, he showed his other side towards us, shirt and all untouched by flame! In which pain he suffered till one of the standers-by moved the faggots. When Ridley saw the fire flame up, he leaned himself to that side. And when the flame touched the gunpowder, he was seen to stir no more, but burned on the other side, falling at Latimer's feet.

140

Foxe was an exiled Protestant. Studying Source D, why is Foxe's work such effective propaganda for Protestants?

▲ The burning of bishops Latimer and Ridley, from an illustration in John Foxe's *Book of Martyrs* which documented the Marian persecutions.

The death of Cranmer in 1556 – burnt at the stake in the centre of Oxford – was particularly significant. He had been the guiding force behind the introduction of Protestantism from 1533 when he had become Archbishop of Canterbury through to the end of Edward VI's reign. Under Mary he had recanted – that is, accepted that supporting Protestantism was an error – but then he decided to stand by his religious convictions. Mary, who hated all that Cranmer had been responsible for, did not wish to see him burnt to death, but believed she had no option when he withdrew his recantation.

Mary regarded the executions as necessary to cleanse the country of Protestant heresy. Her advisers were less convinced. As the death toll mounted, signs of opposition to the policy began to appear. By executing her subjects in such a graphic way in their own community, Mary inadvertently turned many into public heroes. Instead of frightening people back to Catholicism, the burnings raised questions about what was so powerful and important about Protestantism that people were prepared to die for it. This was picked up by English Protestants who had fled abroad. They produced propaganda which associated Catholicism with intolerance and an over-powerful government, and helped to undermine Mary's popularity. However, it is possible to overstate the effects of the burnings. Beyond London, there is little evidence of strong reactions. Much of the history written since the reign of Mary has been too heavily influenced by the propaganda of Foxe and others in the succeeding reign of Elizabeth when Protestantism was restored.

Source E From a letter by Simon Renard, the imperial ambassador in London, writing to Mary's husband, King Philip II of Spain, February 1555.

The people of London are murmuring about the cruel enforcement of the recent acts of Parliament on heresy which has now begun, as shown publicly when a certain Rogers was burnt yesterday. Some of the onlookers wept, others prayed to God to give them strength, perseverance and patience to bear the pain and not to recant; others gathered the ashes and bones and wrapped them in paper to preserve them; others threatened the bishops. The haste with which the bishops have proceeded in this matter may well cause a revolt. Your Majesty might inform the bishops that there are other means of chastising the obstinate at this early stage, such as secret executions, banishment and imprisonment. The watchword should be *secure, caute et lente festinare* [to hasten safely, cautiously and slowly].

1 Where might you expect Renard's religious sympathies to lie (Source E)? Why?

2 Is this source useful for studying reactions to Mary's religious policies?

The Spanish marriage

Mary came to the throne aged 37 and unmarried, raising the possibility that her reign would be no more than an interlude before her Protestant younger sister, Elizabeth, took the Crown. Mary reasoned that if Catholicism was to survive beyond her reign, she must marry and produce an heir – the age-old Tudor problem. As Catherine of Aragon's daughter, she was close to her Spanish relatives and had been considered a possible wife for Charles V. In 1553, she discussed the possibility of marriage to Charles's son, Philip, with Simon Renard, the imperial ambassador and a close personal friend. The two worked out the details of the marriage alliance without consulting the Privy Council. Because of this, the scheme was a disaster in the making because Mary did not take into account the likely reaction of her subjects to the plan.

Opposition to the marriage

Opposition to the marriage centred on two concerns. First, Philip was a staunch Catholic. Protestants feared that he would add strength to Mary's determination to reverse the Reformation in England. Second, Philip was heir to the throne of Spain and its vast empire in Europe and the Americas. It was assumed – correctly – that he would use England as a tool to further Spanish ambitions and would have little regard for the interests of the country. There was also the question of how France would react if England and Spain drew together so closely, and what this would mean for relations with Scotland.

Although Mary was desperate to marry Philip (who was her cousin once removed), she was careful enough to limit his power within England. By the terms of the marriage agreement, Philip was to be called King, but he had none of the powers associated with the title. He was also forbidden from bringing foreigners into English government and had no claim to the throne in the event of Mary's death. In effect, the agreement created a marriage of convenience and wisely limited the damage that could be done to English interests.

Nonetheless, Mary pressed ahead with the marriage, which took place in July 1554. She always valued the relationship with Philip more than he did. Once he became King of Spain in 1556, Philip paid Mary only one brief visit and that was largely to persuade her to join him in waging war against France. The extent of Mary's desperation and self-delusion about the state of the marriage can be seen in the two apparently false pregnancies that she had in 1554 and 1557.

Wyatt's Rebellion, February 1554

In early 1554, when the plans for Mary's marriage to Philip of Spain were being made, Sir Thomas Wyatt, a member of the gentry in Kent, was planning what has been rather romantically seen as a nationalist, Protestant rebellion against Mary. As news of Mary's plan to marry Philip of Spain leaked out from the court, Wyatt and others plotted to overthrow the Queen and to replace her with Edward Courtenay, the great-grandson of the fifteenth-century Yorkist King, Edward IV (and the only male claimant to the throne to hand). Courtenay, to strengthen his thin connection to the Tudor Crown, was to marry Princess Elizabeth.

The rebellion has often been conveniently labelled as anti-Catholic and anti-Spanish. It is true that, in spite of agreements made in the marriage contract that Philip would have no power over English internal affairs, there was a lot of xenophobia in the country. Wyatt probably feared that the government would be controlled by Spain or at least by Spanish interests.

◄ A painting celebrating the marriage of Mary Tudor to Prince Philip of Spain, 1554.

It is also true that the rebels supported Protestantism. This religious motive was identified as the cause of the rebellion in a book written by John Proctor immediately afterwards. But this book was commissioned by the government, with the intention of putting the focus on religious discontent in order to divert attention away from the unpopular marriage.

There were also particular circumstances in Kent that encouraged unrest. The cloth industry had been in decline for some time, creating a lot of economic hardship. People were able to use the situation to air their grievances. Local politics also caused instability, with some gentry families jockeying for positions of influence in the county and at court.

The original plan was for four rebellions against Mary to begin in March 1554: one in Devon where the Western Rebellion had taken place; one in Leicestershire led by Lady Jane Grey's father; one on the Welsh border; and one in Kent, led by Wyatt. However, it was difficult to keep these plans secret and the plotters had to advance their timetable to the beginning of February to maintain the element of surprise. Three of the four uprisings simply failed to materialise. Only Wyatt was able to gather sufficient men – about 3,000 in total. He marched his rebel army into London but found London Bridge closed against him. In the confusion that followed, Wyatt failed to convince Londoners to join him and the rebellion collapsed within a week.

LOOK AGAIN

Compare Wyatt's rebellion with the Pilgrimage of Grace (pages 85–86) and the Rebellions of 1549 (pages 132–133) in terms of:
- their causes
- the severity of the threat posed.

Unlike the Western Rising and Kett's Rebellion of 1549, Wyatt's actions were serious because he threatened the capital, although the failure of the City to support him meant that the danger posed by the rebels was reduced. However, Mary came to realise that as long as Lady Jane Grey was alive she posed a threat because she could be used as a figure-head in any future rebellion. Mary ordered the execution of Wyatt, Lady Jane Grey and her husband and about a hundred other conspirators. Princess Elizabeth was also arrested on suspicion of complicity, but released after no solid evidence could be found to implicate her.

Foreign policy under Mary

Although few Englishmen wanted it, the natural outcome of Mary's marriage was war. Philip had made no secret of wanting England's help against France in what turned out to be the final stages of the struggle between the Spanish Habsburgs and the French Valois monarchy. He put Mary under considerable pressure to declare war. By doing so, Mary undid the diplomacy of Northumberland and put English foreign policy back onto its traditional anti-French footing. She declared war on France in June 1557 and sent troops across the Channel to join her husband's forces. Together, they achieved victory in the battle of Saint-Quentin, but Spain was too exhausted financially to follow this up.

Within a year, France had not only recovered but had seized Calais from the English. Although this would have been impossible to defend in the long term, this was a terrible blow to national pride, for Calais represented the last outpost of the great medieval empire that had included England and half of France. It severed England from the continent and seemed to symbolise the limited role that the country could play in European affairs. For Mary personally, it was a humiliating example of how her marriage had become more of a convenience for Spain than for England. Popular feeling was such that, when she died ten months later in November 1558, few people mourned her.

Mary's reputation

It is very tempting to leave the story of Mary's reign at that – misjudged religious and foreign policies which sacrificed English interests to win the approval of Spain – and to portray Mary as something between a sad victim and a self-deluding idealist. Her government also had to contend with the consequences of bad harvests of 1555–57 which led to much malnutrition and some starvation among the poor, and with virulent outbreaks of plague starting in 1556 and continuing into Elizabeth's reign.

Thus concentrating only on the problems would ignore the achievements of her reign. These have been overshadowed by the high-profile disasters, but are important if we are to gauge the extent of the 'mid-Tudor crisis' in the 1550s. Behind the scenes, a quiet strengthening of government and royal finances was taking place:

- The role of the Privy Council in managing the daily running of government was becoming more established, and committees were used to deal with specialised issues (such as the war against France).
- Efforts were made to make revenue collection more efficient (Northumberland had begun this campaign in 1552 by setting up a royal commission) by transferring more responsibility to the Exchequer.
- A new Book of Rates was introduced in May 1558 to improve Crown income from customs duties.
- Plans were drawn up to revalue the currency after the 'Great Debasement' of the 1540s.

Book of rates – All goods leaving the country were taxed and the income passed to the Crown as part of ordinary revenues. The Book of Rates (1558) set out the level of tax on a wide range of products but had not been updated since the beginning of Henry VIII's reign and therefore took no account of mid-Tudor inflation. The effect of updating rates was to treble Crown income from customs duties, but provoked hostility from the merchant community since the new rates coincided with the collapse of the cloth market.

Mary's government has also been credited with reviving England's great military and naval tradition, providing Elizabeth with the means to resist Spain later in the century. During the Northumberland regime, standards of maintenance of the royal fleet had been allowed to slip, and a number of ships had been decommissioned, leaving Mary with just three serviceable warships. A major programme of rebuilding and refitting was begun under Mary and by 1558 there had been a return to the fleet level of that at the end of Henry VIII's reign. The government also modernised the army. The 1558 Militia Act laid down a system of Commissioners of Muster with responsibility for organising the recruitment of regional militias in wartime, while the Arms Act of the same year established better procedures for supplying weapons to the royal forces.

In spite of the above, Mary is still often labelled a failure. It is true that Protestants were burnt at the stake, but more were killed under Cromwell in the 1530s. Compared with what was happening in places in Europe, her policy was relatively moderate. Rebellions happened throughout the century – and she defeated Wyatt and his followers with ease. She suffered some divisions within her Privy Councillors, but so did other Tudor monarchs. Her foreign policy, though ill-advised, was no more foolish than some other expeditions in the Tudor period. It is possible to conclude that, if she had lived longer and had had time to establish her rule, and to show that she could manage without being dominated by her husband (who was frequently absent anyway), perhaps her reputation would not be so 'bloody' and more sympathy would be shown.

Source F From *Reform and Reformation, England 1509–1558* by G.R. Elton, (Harvard University Press), 1977.

It has become something of a commonplace to assert that Mary Tudor was the most attractive member of her family – kind, long-suffering, gentle, considerate. The evidence of her recorded words hardly bears this out; it shows her rather to have been arrogant, assertive, bigoted, stubborn, suspicious and rather stupid. She was ill-prepared to be England's first woman sovereign. She had ever been her mother's daughter rather than her father's, devoid of political skill and unable to compromise. Her persistent attachment to the papal Church and religion made her exceptional even among those who watched the Reformation with misgivings and reluctance. Humanism had passed her by as much as had Protestantism. Thirty-seven years old in 1553, she seized a power rightfully hers for the exercise of which she was utterly unsuited.

> With reference to Source F and your own knowledge, how convincing an interpretation of Mary do you find the arguments?

KEY DATES: THE REIGN OF MARY TUDOR, 1553–58

July 1553	Mary proclaimed Queen
Jan 1554	Marriage Treaty with Spain
Feb 1554	Wyatt's rebellion
July 1554	Mary married Philip of Spain
Jan 1555	Papal supremacy of Church restored; Edwardian reforms abolished
Feb 1555	First executions of Protestant heretics
Jan 1556	Philip became King of Spain
March 1556	Execution of Cranmer
Sept 1556	Worst harvest of sixteenth century (following very poor harvest of 1555)
June 1557	War against France to support Philip II
Jan 1558	Loss of Calais
Nov 1558	Death of Mary; smooth accession of Elizabeth I

4 To what extent was there a mid-Tudor crisis?

As you have worked through this chapter, you will have begun to decide for yourself if the evidence is sufficient to suggest a mid-Tudor crisis. To come to a judgement you will have to engage in what examination boards call a 'synoptic' activity. This means that you will have to use knowledge and skills drawn from across the whole of your study of the Tudor period, rather than from just one section of it. So, your judgement will need to be taken in the light of information about Henry VIII's reign in the 1530s and 1540s (Chapters 3 and 4), the reigns of Edward VI and Mary (this chapter), the beginning of Elizabeth's reign (Chapter 6), and the wider religious, social and economic changes of the Tudor period (Chapter 6). You will also need to think about why historians have come to different conclusions about the same events. Some of the reasons which you might consider are given below.

- Some historians (e.g. Whitney Jones) focus on one aspect of the mid-Tudor period, such as religious change or the structure of government. Do these different interests lend themselves to different conclusions?
- Some writers (e.g. David Loades and Robert Tittler) have studied the 1540s and 1550s in the light of what had already happened in Henry VIII's reign; others judge the crisis years in view of what Elizabeth went on to achieve. How can these forward-looking and backward-looking perspectives lead to different conclusions?
- Historians may have personal views, particularly of the treatment of Protestants in Mary's reign, or the general plight of the poor at this time. Can historical judgements, particularly on dramatic or controversial subjects, ever be free of personal opinion?

The interpretations of older generations of historians (broadly meaning anyone writing before the 1950s) have gradually been reversed by so-called 'revisionist' writers. Traditionally, the 'Little Tudors' – Edward VI and Mary I – received far less attention than Henry VIII and Elizabeth I. Their reigns were short and their achievements few. Although Protector Somerset was hailed as the 'Good Duke' for his attempts to continue the Reformation and improve the social and economic conditions in England, the Duke of Northumberland was characterised as a self-seeking and ruthless politician. Mary I's reign was often dismissed as simply disastrous. She transacted an unsuitable marriage, lost England's last continental possession and nearly wrecked the Protestant Reformation.

More recently, writers have found more positive things to say about the period 1547–58, and many discuss the mid-Tudor period in a slightly wider context to include the last years of Henry VIII's reign and the beginnings of Elizabeth's. They have noted that government was never in serious danger of collapse during these years and that many of the reforms credited to Elizabeth were in fact foreshadowed by Northumberland and Mary. For these reasons, historians such as David Loades and Robert Tittler have downplayed the idea of a mid-Tudor crisis, although they still recognise the difficult social and economic conditions of the time.

Chapter summary

- The Duke of Somerset (1547–49) and Duke of Northumberland (1549–53) led Regencies on behalf of Edward VI who became King at the age of nine.
- England became more Protestant, at first slowly, and then at a faster pace with the 1552 Act of Uniformity and Prayer Book.
- England suffered the dangers of rebellions with France allied to Scotland.
- Social and economic problems caused price rises and difficulties with overseas trade.
- Rebellions in 1549 threatened the Crown.
- The attempt on the death of Edward VI in 1553 to change the succession to Lady Jane Grey failed.
- Mary married Philip of Spain (Catholic) but failed to have children.
- Mary attempted to restore Catholicism, but could not achieve restoration of Church land.
- Leading Protestants were persecuted; some were burnt at the stake.
- Mary's successes (e.g. in reforms) tended to be overshadowed by her increasing unpopularity – made worse by propaganda after her death.

Chapter summary diagram

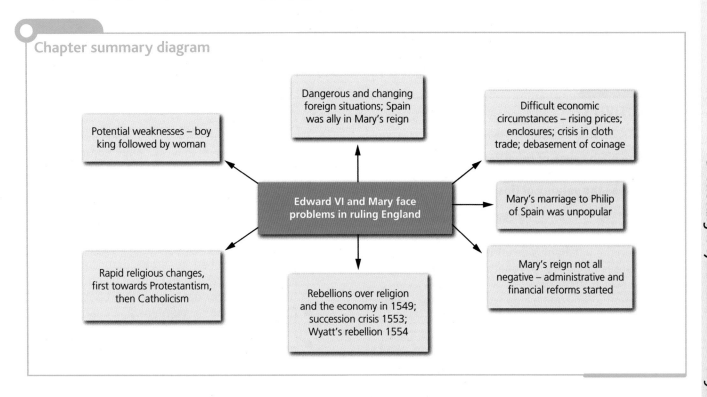

Working on essay technique

Remember the skills that you built up in Chapters 1–4 on essay writing. The main headings were:

- **Focus and structure:** Be sure what the question is on and plan what the paragraphs should be about.
- **How to write a focused introduction:** Be sure that the introductory sentence relates directly to the focus of the question and that each paragraph highlights the structure of the answer.
- **Deploying detail:** Make sure that you show detailed knowledge – but only as part of an explanation being made in relation to the question. No knowledge should be 'free-standing'.
- **Analysis:** Think of the wording of an answer in order to strengthen the explanation.
- **Argument and counter-argument:** Think of how arguments can be juxtaposed as part of a balancing act in order to give contrasting views.
- **Resolution:** Think how best to 'resolve' contradictory arguments.
- **Evaluation and relative significance:** Think how best to reach a judgement when trying to assess the relative importance of various factors, and possibly their inter-relationship.

ACTIVITY

Consider the following A-level practice question.

'The main cause of rebellions in the years 1536 to 1558 was religious disagreements.' Assess the validity of this view. **(25 marks)**

1 On the top of a large sheet of paper write out the title.
2 On the left-hand side jot down the main topic areas (in this case, rebellions) that you might cover in an answer.
3 On the right-hand side transform these ideas into a basic plan for an answer. Think of the structure. In outline, what evidence is there that rebellions were caused by religion? Which appear to be caused primarily by other factors, and what were they?

4 Then look at the list of essay writing skills above. See how they can fit into your plan. Some, such as an introduction, will be there automatically.
- Introduction – is it simple or could it be complex? Does it do more than introduce? Does it highlight the structure of the answer?
- Where can you add specific details to your plan so that you show a range of knowledge?
- Does your plan successfully feature analysis and evaluation? Are you sure it will not lead to a narrative or descriptive approach?
- Can you balance arguments and counter-arguments?
- Can you reach a judgement which 'resolves' any conflicting arguments and which assesses the relative importance of the various factors.

Working on interpretation skills

In earlier chapters of the book you were given the opportunity to develop skills in answering interpretations questions. It is probably a good idea to re-read the advice given earlier in the book at the end of Chapters 2 (pages 65–6) and 3 (pages 96–9) before you answer the practice A-level question that follows.

> Using your understanding of the historical context, assess how convincing the arguments in these three extracts are in relation to the existence of a mid-Tudor crisis from 1538 to 1558.
>
> (30 marks)

Extract A

The picture we see of Henry VIII towards the end of his reign is a very different image from that which started his reign. Gone is the picture of confidence and virility. Instead, we see the bloated face of a man who had lived an extremely tempestuous life ....

Henry had done his best to fulfil his role as warrior-king. The victory at Boulogne would live on in popular memory for the rest of the century. However, Henry had provoked real hostility in his personal life – his rejection of Catherine of Aragon and his series of new wives hardly matched his father's fidelity.

It is hard to see Henry VIII in a very positive light, both as man and as king ... Henry talked a good game – his own church, warrior-like-posing in foreign fields, monuments built to his own magnificence. But when asked the question 'What has Henry VIII ever done for you?', the peasant in the field might well have been lost for words ...

From *The Early Tudors: England 1485-1558* by D. Rogerson *et al*. (Hodder) 2001, p.184.

Extract B

The concept of a mid-sixteenth century crisis in England is now considered to be difficult to maintain. This is certainly true if by 'crisis' it is implied that the whole of the country, and all the people, were experiencing a crisis continuously between 1547 and 1558. Indeed, it is only really possible to say that the country as a whole and some sections of society underwent very short-lived crises at times between these dates. If this is the case, most historians would consider that this was normal for any country at any time. Mid-Tudor England faced a variety of problems. Many of these arose from the political, social and economic consequences of the political and economic breakdown at the end of the late Middle Ages. Others, like the reactions to the English Reformation, can be seen as very short term. A few, such as the succession crisis of 1553, were responses to immediate events. At no time, even in 1549, was the country in danger of collapse, and for most people life went on as normal.

From *Edward VI and Mary: A Mid-Tudor Crisis?* (2nd edn.) by Nigel Heard, (Hodder Education), 2000, p.158.

Extract C

[In the traditional interpretation] Mary was portrayed as a politically naïve zealot whose reintroduction of Catholicism was widely unpopular. In particular, her burning of Protestants as heretics backfired, as she inadvertently turned them into martyrs and was subsequently labelled by Protestant propagandists as 'Bloody Mary'. Her Catholicism led her into domestic and foreign policy disaster as she stacked her Privy Council with Catholic nonentities ... Mary was lucky to survive the Wyatt Rebellion, which the Spanish Match provoked. Marriage to Philip then led to English involvement in the Spanish–French war, which disastrously culminated in the loss of the last English possession in France: Calais ...

This picture of the mid-Tudor period apparently reveals a country lurching from crisis to crisis. Given the link between religious and political opposition, and the way in which economic discontent fuelled rebellion, the case for a full-scale structural crisis appears to be a strong one.

From *Elizabeth I: Meeting the Challenge, England 1541–1603* by John Warren, (Hodder Education), 2008, pp.5–6.

The beginning of Elizabeth's reign, 1558–63

The brevity of the two reigns of Edward VI and Mary, coupled with the religious and economic problems that featured in those eleven years, meant that Elizabeth inherited the throne in difficult circumstances. Elizabeth had to address urgent problems in religion and foreign policy, and social and economic problems were also prominent at the beginning of her reign. This chapter takes the opportunity to look across the century at issues such as price rises, population growth, poverty and vagrancy. As such, several key issues of breadth are directly relevant:

- How Elizabeth was able to stabilise the powers of the monarchy.
- How Elizabeth dealt with threats in foreign policy in the first years of her reign.
- How she gambled over the succession by not marrying.
- How England changed substantially during the sixteenth century socially and economically.
- How religious ideas developed in the Elizabethan Settlement and the results of those ideas; the key groups who were affected, such as Catholics and Protestants and the poor.

The main questions to be addressed in this chapter are:

How successful was Elizabeth in establishing herself as queen in the first few years of her reign?

and

In what ways did economic and social issues affect life in Tudor England?

CHAPTER OVERVIEW

Elizabeth was cheered at her coronation; she showed the ability immediately to gain the support of the crowds as well as her courtiers. She re-introduced Protestantism through Parliament in 1559 with the Act of Supremacy and Act of Uniformity. The re-established Church of England was relatively moderate in its Protestant doctrines but still with a traditional Church hierarchy. Her foreign policy represented a careful balancing act involving Spain, France and Scotland – all potential or actual enemies. The question of a marriage assumed importance immediately as foreign princes saw the opportunity for a useful alliance.

The chapter also investigates the economic and social issues that were important in Tudor England, both for the government and for the people as a whole. The price rise, most acute in the 1520s, 1540s and 1590s, was not understood; in its severity it was a new phenomenon. Population growth produced tensions within society, especially when poor harvests occurred, leading to Elizabeth's government passing a succession of laws which culminated in the Poor Law of 1601.

1 Elizabeth's accession

Hindsight is wonderful. Elizabeth reigned for over 44 years and the triumphs of her reign have been celebrated ever since. However, in her first few years as Queen she had to prove that she was capable of ruling and able to secure a settlement in religion that was amenable to the majority.

Elizabeth's life before 1558

What do we know about Elizabeth's character as it developed, before she became Queen in 1558?

Elizabeth's early life was traumatic. When she was born in September 1533, her father was hugely disappointed. He had expected and wanted a son. When she was less than three her mother, Anne Boleyn, was accused of sexual misdemeanours, including with her own brother, convicted of high treason and executed. Henry remarried and Parliament changed the succession to the heirs of his new marriage, making Elizabeth and her older sister Mary bastards – that is, not eligible to inherit the throne. Elizabeth, of course, would have been too young to have understood fully what was happening at the time, and she was in any case being brought up by governesses at the court. However, the events must have had an impact on her as she grew older and learnt about them.

Her father died in 1547 when she was thirteen. This would not have been a traumatic event though, as death through 'old' age was expected and Henry had been a remote figure in her life. In fact, in the last years of Henry's reign Elizabeth had enjoyed a stable environment around the court of his last wife, Catherine Parr, who took her under her wing. It was at this time that Elizabeth developed her religious beliefs – moderate Protestantism within the Church of England that her father had created. Indeed, it is noteworthy that Henry and his councillors allowed his daughter to be brought up in the Protestant faith when he was strongly resisting most changes from strict Catholic doctrine. Elizabeth was also legitimised when she was named third in line of succession in the Succession Act of 1544.

It must have been strange for Elizabeth when her nine-year-old brother became King, but soon someone else became the centre of her attention. The Duke of Somerset, Edward Seymour, became Lord Protector on behalf of Edward. He had a younger brother, Thomas Seymour, who, after the death of Henry VIII, married Catherine Parr. Remember that Edward and Thomas were both uncles of King Edward, being brothers of Jane Seymour. Catherine Parr became pregnant. Thomas resented the power and wealth that his brother enjoyed and started to flirt with the young princess while she was living with them in their house, Chelsea Manor. Thomas was attractive in looks and manner and Elizabeth enjoyed his attentions. Indeed, in modern terminology, she probably developed a crush on him. Thomas was allowed liberties that were not at all accepted in sixteenth-century court etiquette, such as visiting Elizabeth's bedchamber when she was in bed. Tragically, Catherine died a few days after giving birth to a daughter and Thomas appeared to encourage rumours that he was thinking of marrying the princess Elizabeth.

The Duke of Somerset saw his brother's intended action of marrying the second in line to the throne as a direct challenge to his own authority. Lord Thomas was arrested, accused of high treason and executed. Elizabeth feared for her own life and claimed that she had not been party to Thomas's plans.

NOTE-MAKING

In considering Elizabeth's early life, make notes on the events and circumstances that would have had a major influence on her.

Following investigations, this was accepted – partly because there was nothing to be gained for pursuing a case against an heir to the throne who on her own posed no threat to the present government and who had declared her total loyalty to the young King's authority and to the Protestant religion. However, it is commonly accepted by historians that this episode left a huge impression on the fourteen-year-old Elizabeth. Emotionally, she was always cautious with men. It is claimed, without any direct evidence, that this episode explains why she never married.

Elizabeth played no part in the plan to change the succession in 1553 to Lady Jane Grey. However, the accession of Mary I in July 1553 immediately caused Elizabeth a problem – namely, her sister's Catholic faith and the determination to impose this on her subjects. Very soon in the reign a group of gentry plotted to overthrow Mary and place Elizabeth on the throne. Wyatt's Rebellion in January 1554 (see pages 142–43) was quickly ended and the ringleaders executed. However, Elizabeth's position was perilous. She almost certainly had played no part in encouraging the plot, but she was arrested and taken to the Tower of London, entering through the Traitors' Gate. Elizabeth expected the worst; Mary, her sister the Queen, refused to see her. Elizabeth languished there for two months and was then taken to a country house in Oxfordshire where she was under virtual house arrest for the remainder of Mary's reign. Pressure was put on Elizabeth from time to time to accept the Catholic Mass, but she was learning to keep her thoughts and beliefs to herself – a trait that she exhibited on many occasions when she became Queen.

Elizabeth's character

Elizabeth's life up to the age of 25 provides several hints as to major events that determined her character and historians have been quick to psychoanalyse her. In addition, she is said to have inherited traits from her father, such as his quick temper as well as the way she could charm people. It has even been claimed that she inherited her grandfather's miserliness in her reluctance to spend money. However, this could just as easily have been realistic frugality.

Elizabeth had been brought up with all the training expected of a princess and possible heir to the throne. She was cultured in the arts, music, literature and languages. She studied theology, was keen to promote the Bible in English and did not believe in some central Catholic doctrines such as transubstantiation. She took great pride in her clothes and loved ornaments and jewels. Elizabeth learnt quickly as a young queen that her appearance and demeanour helped to symbolise her importance and status. However, we have to take contemporary descriptions of her with some caution, with reports by ambassadors being written for specific purposes.

1 What can you learn from Sources A and B about Elizabeth's appearance?

2 Use the internet to study some of the well-known portraits of Elizabeth. A good place to start would be the National Portrait Gallery website (www.npg.org.uk). How do the descriptions above compare with the portraits you have seen?

Source A The Venetian ambassador describes Elizabeth near the beginning of Queen Mary's reign. From *Calendar of State Papers, Venetian, Vol. V.*

She is now about twenty-one years old. Her figure and face are very handsome, and such an air of dignified majesty pervades all her actions that no-one can fail to suppose she is a queen.

Source B A different Venetian ambassador describes her two years later. From *Calendars of State Papers, Venetian, Vol. VI.*

She is now twenty-three years old ... Although her face is comely rather than handsome, she is tall and well-formed, with a good skin. Although swarthy, she has fine eyes and above all a beautiful hand of which she makes great display.

Elizabeth's accession and coronation

How did Elizabeth consolidate her position as Queen in the first year of her reign?

Part of the Tudor myth is that the whole nation greeted the accession of Elizabeth with unreserved joy. Indeed, from the early 1570s the anniversary of the accession was celebrated as a public holiday and from 1576 it was added to the list of holy days. It is true that the death of Queen Mary was greeted with relief by many people, but there were also fears about how the young Queen Elizabeth would cope. England faced many immediate problems over religion, foreign policy, trade and lawlessness, made worse by rising prices and trade recessions. There was also the question of finding a suitable person for Elizabeth to marry in order to produce an heir to guarantee the succession.

England in 1558

The belief that England was a weak country in 1558 was reflected in some contemporary writings.

Source C From a document by Armigal Waad, Clerk to the Privy Council, summarising the problems confronting the government at Elizabeth's accession.

The Queen poor, the realm exhausted, the nobility poor and decayed. Lack of good captains and soldiers. The people out of order. Justice is not executed. All things are dear. Divisions among ourselves. Wars with France and Scotland. The French king bestriding the realm, having one foot in Calais and the other in Scotland. Steadfast enmity but no steadfast friendship abroad.

Source D From a letter by Sir Thomas Smith, a Protestant and one of Elizabeth's councillors, writing in 1560 about the situation at her accession.

I never saw England weaker in strength, men, money and riches. As much affectionate as you know me to be to my country and countrymen, I assure you I was then ashamed of both. They went to the wars hanging down their looks. They came from thence as men dismayed and forlorn. At home was nothing but fining, heading, hanging, quartering and burning; taxing, levying, beggaring, and losing our strongholds abroad.

Elizabeth's advisers

Elizabeth moved cautiously but decisively. Fortunately for her, Cardinal Pole, Mary's chief adviser, had died the same day as the Queen. That allowed her flexibility to choose her leading advisers.

The Privy Council had grown in size during the reign of Mary to 40 or 50 members. Elizabeth was determined to have a smaller council, with a preference for people who had shown loyalty to the Tudor dynasty, either through personal service to her or because they came from an established family. Elizabeth was able to build up a core of professional men who enjoyed her confidence and therefore they tended to serve for long periods.

NOTE-MAKING

In this section your notes should focus on the problems Elizabeth faced on her accession and how she initially made a good impression as a young queen.

What evidence do you have from the reign of Mary to support or contradict the report to the Privy Council (Source C)?

How useful is Source D, bearing in mind the author and what you know of the situation in 1558?

Of Mary's Privy Councillors, 11 out of 30 were reappointed. The most notable was the Marquess of Winchester who had been Lord Treasurer since 1550 and had therefore served under two monarchs already. Elizabeth appointed nine new councillors, the key appointment being Sir William Cecil, aged 38, as her Principal Secretary. He served her for the next 40 years. His brother-in-law, Sir Nicholas Bacon, became Lord Keeper.

Elizabeth's coronation: consolidation of power, 1559

Elizabeth's coronation in January 1559 was a splendid occasion. The rejoicing contrasted with Mary's coronation when there was only restrained applause and some jeering – though some of the accounts may, of course, be subject to religious bias! She was welcomed wholeheartedly by the citizens in her procession through the city and greeted by orations and pageants, most with a strong Protestant flavour. Elizabeth appeared welcoming and open in her demeanour and this further pleased the crowds. The following day, 15 January 1559, Elizabeth was crowned and anointed by Owen Oglethorpe, the Catholic bishop of Carlisle, in Westminster Abbey. She then came out of the Abbey to be presented to the people amidst a deafening noise from loud instruments and drums.

Source E The splendour of the Queen's coronation. From *Elizabeth I, Queen of England* by Neville Williams, (Sphere Books), 1971, pp.54–55.

For the Queen herself the most splendid robes imaginable were devised. On the eve of the coronation, when she drove in state through the City of London, Elizabeth appeared in a [gown] made from twenty-three yards of gold and silver tissue with fur trimmings and a lace of silk and gold. During the coronation she changed her robes twice. Her parliament robe was of crimson velvet with a fur of powdered ermines. Her Robes of State were of purple velvet … On her head in the procession to the Abbey she wore a hat of crimson velvet, embroidered with Venice gold and a few pearls … All the trappings for the procession were newly produced too … Elizabeth I has had a bad reputation among historians for parsimony, but it is quite clear that nothing was stinted at her coronation. Comparatively few would be able to witness the actual crowning, but countless Londoners and other subjects would see the various processions and spectacles.

How did Elizabeth use her coronation to help consolidate her power and gain acceptance as Queen (see Source E)?

▲ Elizabeth's coronation portrait.

2 Elizabeth's religious settlement, 1558–63

It is not clear what proportion of the population were convinced Catholics in 1558 – or, indeed, how many were determined Protestants. Many people, largely the uneducated, would have opinions somewhere between the two extremes. It is probable that many liked some aspects of Protestantism, such as the use of the English language and not paying taxes to Rome, but they also enjoyed the traditional rituals of the Catholic Church. Elizabeth had to determine how to establish a stable Church that most people could accept. Failure to achieve this would threaten wars fought over religion, as were happening across Europe.

NOTE-MAKING

Notes here should concentrate on the difficulties of reaching a religious settlement.

What shaped the religious settlement?

Was the religious settlement of 1559 primarily influenced by Elizabeth's personal wishes?

Elizabeth had to act quickly to avoid confusion. At the same time as the religious settlement she had to consider Parliament's views and also be aware of the precarious situation in England's foreign dealings with Spain, France and Scotland.

Elizabeth's religious views

Working out precisely what Elizabeth's personal religious views were is a difficult task. As Queen, she was conscious of the impression she made on others, especially at the beginning of her reign, so she was careful not to give too much support for just one point of view. Added to that is the problem that Elizabeth's priorities concerning the Church were shaped much more by political considerations than by any religious ones. She wanted to establish a settlement of religion which would heal divisions between Catholics and Protestants and maximise her own control over the Church, rather than creating something which necessarily reflected her personal theology. Like most people of the time, Elizabeth subscribed to the view that there could be no peace between different faiths, and that their mutual hostility would destroy national unity and lead to unrest and civil war.

Nonetheless, there are clues that her preferences were for Protestant ideas. As the daughter of Anne Boleyn she had grown up connected to a family sympathetic to religious reform. Her education had been conducted by teachers such as Sir Roger Ascham who were knowledgeable about Lutheran ideas. Although Elizabeth was forced to live as a Catholic during her sister Mary's reign, incidents during her first years as Queen have been used by historians to argue that she was a genuine Protestant. Within a month of becoming Queen and before the national religious settlement was reached she forbade priests in the Royal Chapel to elevate the host (a point in the Catholic Mass when the priest held up the communion bread, transformed into Christ's body). She was also apparently furious when the Dean of St Paul's Cathedral presented her with a copy of the Prayer Book containing illustrations of saints.

However, there were also signs that Elizabeth liked some traditional teachings. In particular, she enjoyed some of the comforting ornaments of the Catholic Church such as the crucifix, candles and church music. She also supported the traditional view that priests should devote their lives to God and not marry. One of the major disagreements she had with Matthew Parker, her first

Archbishop of Canterbury, concerned an instruction she issued forbidding any clergyman to live with his wife on cathedral grounds or in a college. To hold such views while supporting more radical ideas about faith was not surprising. Religious change had been going on in England for all of Elizabeth's life so it was probable that, as an intelligent person, she should find some aspects of that change more acceptable than others.

Influences on the religious settlement

The Elizabethan settlement took shape in 1558–59, and its essential parts were in place within six months of the new Queen's accession in November 1558. This does not mean, however, that the process of settlement was easy.

Influences at home

Faced with high hopes and expectations from both Catholics and Protestants as soon as she became Queen, Elizabeth issued a Royal Proclamation in December 1558, in which she insisted that there should be no preaching:

'… other than to the gospels and epistles and to the Ten Commandments in the vulgar tongue … or to use any other manner of public prayer, rite or ceremony in the church but that which is already used in her Majesty's own chapel, and the Lord's Prayer and the Creed in English, until consultation may be held by Parliament.'

This happened the following month, January 1559, when both sides of the religious spectrum had high hopes.

The first attempt to introduce bills into Parliament was wrecked by the opposition of the Catholic bishops appointed under Mary and some noblemen in the House of Lords, who formed a solid Catholic voting block. They objected to the attempt in the legislation to bring back the Protestant Prayer Book of 1552 and to the prospect of the Church being headed by a woman.

Influences abroad

In political terms, Elizabeth had to proceed with care. England was still at war with France and unable to rely completely on the support of Spain. While the population of London had demonstrated massive support for a Protestant settlement, opinion elsewhere was less clearly in favour and the north of England remained deeply conservative. Beyond the northern counties lay Scotland, still firmly allied to the Catholic French, and whose young queen was wife of the heir to the French throne and next in line to that of England. Any alteration of religion in England, therefore, was bound to have an impact on England's relationship with France, Spain and Scotland.

Elizabeth was helped in getting agreement on a settlement because of two events around Easter 1559. The first was the signing of the Peace of Câteau-Cambrésis between France and Spain. This drew the long-running wars between them to a close and ended English military action against France. The second was a government-sponsored debate between Protestant and Catholic clergy at which some of the Catholic bishops made the mistake of suggesting that they did not accept Elizabeth's authority over them, allowing her to arrest and imprison two of them.

Once Parliament reassembled after Easter, it was a little easier to steer legislation through. Elizabeth made some concessions over her title and the wording of the Prayer Book and put considerable pressure on the noble members of the Lords to back her. This, plus the imprisonment of the two bishops in the Tower, gave her a majority of one vote.

> **Peace of Câteau-Cambrésis**
> A peace treaty which brought an end to half a century of periodic fighting between Spain and France.

NOTE-MAKING

The striking aspect of the religious settlement of 1559–63 is its achievement of a compromise between the rival viewpoints of Catholics and Protestants. Before moving on to look at the effects of the settlement on these religious groups, check that you have understood this by listing the ways in which the new Church tried to attract support from both sides, using the following headings:
- Control of the Church
- Structure of the national Church
- Appearance of churches
- Religious doctrine.

Religious settlement of 1559

What shape did the Elizabethan Church settlement take, in its theology and in its organisation?

In one momentous year the shape of the Elizabethan Church was determined. Many of its features lasted for several centuries and the present-day Church of England still shows its influence.

Act of Supremacy, 1559

The issue of control over the Church was settled by the Act of Supremacy in May 1559. It re-established the English monarch as head of the Church, although Elizabeth chose to be titled 'Supreme Governor'. In effect, her status was the same as that which had been held by Henry VIII and Edward VI, but by choosing a less controversial title than 'Supreme Head' she was able to satisfy those people who still regarded the Pope as the rightful head of the Church or who felt that it was wrong for a woman to hold the top position.

The Act of Supremacy also required all churchmen to swear an oath of loyalty to their new Supreme Governor. To make sure that the change of leadership was truly being accepted at parish level, commissioners were sent out to investigate and a new court was established – the Court of High Commission – to prosecute those whose loyalty was suspect.

Organisation of the Church of England

Beyond the change of leadership, little else was altered about the national organisation of the Church. England would continue to have two archbishops – Canterbury and York – as it had done during Catholic times, and bishops would remain. This form of organisation did not appear in any of the Protestant churches in Europe, where much more emphasis was placed on each congregation organising itself.

Act of Uniformity, 1559

The Act of Uniformity of May 1559 set out rules about the appearance of churches. Essentially, it said that any practices which had existed in 1549 when the first Prayer Book had been issued should still be followed. So, although the altar was replaced by the more Protestant communion table, Catholic artefacts such as crosses and candles could be placed on it. The Act also set out what priests should wear to conduct services, another nod towards Catholics, since Protestants felt that what mattered were the words being spoken, not what the preacher looked like. By keeping a Catholic appearance to the church, those who drew up the settlement made probably their wisest move. They judged, correctly, that most people were less concerned with theological disputes over precisely what went on during the communion service, so would accept the introduction of mildly Protestant ideas about worship; but they would find abrupt changes to the appearance of their church jarring.

Source F From a report by the French ambassador de Maisse, written in 1597.

As for the manner of their service in church and their prayers, except that they say them in the English tongue, one can still recognise a great part of the Mass, which they have limited only in what concerns individual communion. They sing the psalms in English, and at certain hours of the day they use organs and music. The priests wear the hood and surplice. It seems, apart from the absence of images, that there is little difference between their ceremonies and those of the Church of Rome.

To make sure that there was uniformity of worship, attendance at church was made compulsory. Anyone failing to attend could be fined (though the fines were small and not usually imposed) and the money collected distributed to the poor. Attendance at Catholic Mass, rather than the communion service of the Church of England, was treated as a serious offence, with a heavy fine. Anyone saying Mass could face the death penalty.

Royal Injunctions of 1559

It was impossible to set out all the regulations governing the reformed faith in a single Act of Parliament, so further instructions – the Royal Injunctions of July 1559 – were issued. There were 57 instructions, including rules that:

- preachers had to be licensed by a bishop before they could begin preaching
- preachers had to preach at least one service each month or lose their licence
- every church had to display a Bible written in English
- pilgrimages were to be outlawed
- no more altars were to be destroyed.

1559 Prayer Book

The form of worship to be followed was set out in the Act of Uniformity. As its name suggests, its purpose was to establish a single agreed set of doctrines throughout the country, ending the quarrels between Protestants and Catholics. To achieve this, a new Prayer Book was issued which set out the way that services should be conducted. In fact, the Book of Common Prayer issued in 1559 was a fusion of the two Prayer Books issued in Edward VI's reign. It amalgamated the moderate language of the 1549 book with the more openly Protestant words in the 1552 book. This might sound confusing, but it worked brilliantly as a compromise between what Protestants and Catholics wanted to hear when they worshipped.

Meaning of the bread and wine

Central to disagreements between Catholics and Protestants was the question of what happened to the bread and wine during the Mass. For Catholics, the priest transformed the bread into Christ's body and the wine into Christ's blood so that anyone consuming them would be taking God's presence directly into themselves, allowing the cleansing of sin and spiritual renewal. Protestants adopted a different line. To a greater or lesser extent the different Protestant reformers believed that the bread and wine were important symbols of Christ's presence. This meant that the bread and wine could be used to create a moment of great intensity for the celebrant, but not necessarily more.

In the English Reformation a careful course was eventually picked between these two interpretations, as these extracts from different Books of Common Prayer show.

The 1549 Book of Common Prayer instructed the priest to use the following form of words:

'The body of our Lord Jesus Christ which was given for thee, preserve thy body and soul unto everlasting life.'

The more Protestant 1552 Book of Common Prayer changed the phrase to:

'Take and eat this in remembrance that Christ died for thee, and feed on him in thy heart by faith, with thanksgiving.'

And in 1559, the Elizabethan Book of Common Prayer struck a balance by requiring priests to say:

'The body of our Lord Jesus Christ which was given for thee, preserve thy body and soul unto everlasting life, and take, and eat this, in remembrance that Christ died for thee, feed on him in thine heart by faith and thanksgiving.'

NOTE-MAKING

Based on your notes on pages 156–62, consider the following question:

Was the Church of England in 1559 more Protestant than Catholic, or more Catholic than Protestant?

Thirty Nine Articles of 1563

A single act of Parliament could not completely set out a new faith for the country, however. In the following years, the Convocation of the Church set about the task of producing a definitive statement of what 'Anglicanism' meant. The result was the Thirty Nine Articles of faith, published in 1563 and made law in 1571, which still remains the essential statement of belief in the Church of England today. The Thirty Nine Articles, like the rest of the settlement, welded together parts from the different Protestant and Catholic traditions into a whole that was acceptable to as many people as possible.

Reactions to the settlement at home

Elizabeth hoped that the settlement would calm the tensions that had been growing since Henry VIII's reign and allow England to avoid the sort of religious warfare that had been seen in the German states of the Holy Roman Empire during the 1550s and which could be seen in France at the start of the 1560s. She had good reason to be optimistic: reaction among most Catholics and Protestants to the changes was muted. It has been estimated that around 400 of the clergy lost or resigned their livings because they would not accept the settlement. Virtually all the Catholic bishops appointed by Mary refused and were dismissed, but this gave Elizabeth the opportunity to make new appointments which created a leadership within the Church that was enthusiastic about her reforms. Compared to the 800 or so Protestants who had fled abroad in Mary's reign, the scale of refusal between 1559 and 1563 was minimal.

However, localised opposition was evident from the start. Some ministers simply ignored the new Book of Common Prayer and stuck to the traditional Catholic form of worship, while a survey of Justices of the Peace in 1564 found that only about half of them could be relied on actively to support the settlement. Some of the strongest reaction in England was against the financial side of the settlement and the seemingly minor issue of what priests wore to conduct services.

Act of Exchange, 1559

Like her father, Elizabeth viewed the Church as a treasure box to be used by the monarch. The disastrous war against France under Mary, and problems with Scotland at the start of Elizabeth's reign, had created a dangerous shortage of money in the royal treasury. Elizabeth followed Henry VIII by taking taxes that were traditionally paid to Rome into her own coffers, repealing Mary's reinstatement of such taxation. However, she also adopted a more controversial policy. In the Act of Exchange, Elizabeth was allowed to take over property belonging to bishops and to force them only to rent land to her. In practice, the Act was often used more as a threat to keep in line bishops who were critical of the settlement than as a means of gaining more land and property, which might explain its unpopularity.

Foreign reactions to the Church settlement

Elizabeth was also concerned about the reaction from abroad. Both France and Spain were Catholic powers and could pose a threat to the settlement. In the event, neither showed much inclination to be critical. France was becoming absorbed in civil war and Philip II of Spain was prepared to give Elizabeth the benefit of the doubt. Neither he nor the Pope saw the changes in England as permanent and hoped that Elizabeth could be persuaded to return the Church to Rome.

In 1559 Philip offered to marry Elizabeth. It was more of a gesture than a genuine offer and was designed to keep open the hopes of Catholicism being maintained in England. However, as the 1560s progressed, Elizabeth began to regard Spain as more of a threat. During this decade the international balance of power was destabilised by events which left English foreign policy reeling.

French–Scottish dimension

Events in 1559 also complicated the international situation. Mary, Queen of Scots, was already married to Francis II, the heir to the French throne. They became king and queen when Henry II of France was killed in a tournament held to celebrate the Peace of Câteau-Cambrésis. This solidified the alliance between France and Scotland and was a threat to Elizabeth, especially as Mary also had a claim to the throne of England, being a grand-daughter of Henry VII. Indeed, in the absence of Elizabeth producing an heir, Mary was the rightful person to succeed the throne, assuming that Henry VIII's last will was ignored (see Chapter 4, page 110).

Meanwhile, in Scotland a group of Protestant nobles led a rebellion against the French Catholic regent in Scotland, Mary of Guise, who had been ruling Scotland ever since the death of her husband, James V, in 1542. She had been ruling on behalf of her daughter, Mary, Queen of Scots, ever since she had inherited the throne at the age of six days. William Cecil persuaded Elizabeth to send in secret limited arms and money to them. However, in 1560 a peace settlement (the Treaty of Edinburgh) was reached and the French troops stationed in Scotland were withdrawn. After this treaty had been signed, another complication arose when the young French king, Francis II, died suddenly.

This meant that Mary returned to Scotland as Queen but a widow. Who she married next was of vital concern to English interests. In fact, her eye went in the direction of Lord Darnley, who had himself a distant claim, through his mother, to the English throne.

While Elizabeth's councillors were worrying about the situation in Scotland, in 1562 the French state collapsed into civil war between rival groups of nobles and their clients for control of the Crown. Charles IX had ascended the throne aged 10, with his mother, Catherine de Medici, as regent. Catholic families, including the Guises, were ranged against Huguenot families, led by the Prince of Condé. Although a weakened France was good news for Elizabeth because it removed that immediate threat, it also tipped the balance of power decisively towards Catholic Spain.

Huguenot – The name given to Protestants in France who were followers of John Calvin.

Elizabeth was always cautious in making decisions, but even she embraced the idea of intervening in support of the Huguenots. Her favourite, Robert Dudley, was totally behind the project, keen to project himself as a statesman. The hope of Elizabeth, Dudley and other ministers was that, in return for support for the Huguenot rebels, it might be possible to recover Calais as an English possession.

In the Treaty of Hampton Court (September 1562) England promised loans and military aid to the Huguenots. English troops, led by Dudley's brother, the Earl of Warwick, captured Le Havre. But then the focus changed from helping the Huguenots towards trying to exchange Le Havre for Calais. The Huguenots were disillusioned with this, reached a temporary truce with the Catholics, and planned to oust the English from Le Havre. In fact they were helped by an outbreak of plague in Le Havre, and the town was surrendered in June 1563. The Peace of Troyes was signed in 1564 between the English and French governments.

The whole episode showed how there was no clear thinking in English foreign policy at this time. Elizabeth herself came to realise that ill-defined campaigns were unlikely to succeed, even if being fought in the name of religion. She was also acutely aware of the potential problems in assisting rebels against a legitimate monarch. The results of this episode made her even more cautious in foreign policy later in her reign.

Influence of the Council of Trent

The deliberations of the Council of Trent finally ended in 1563, having begun nearly twenty years before in 1545. The council was a meeting of Europe's leading Catholic clergy to discuss the future of the Church. Ominously, the council produced a series of hardline decrees ending the possibility of a peaceful compromise with Protestants. It also reflected a more general reinvigoration of Catholicism within Europe – against both Protestants and the Muslim Ottoman Turks who were threatening the western Mediterranean at this time. Some wanted Elizabeth excommunicated, but others, including Philip II, hoped to be able to persuade Elizabeth to change the religious settlement. However, Elizabeth became concerned at the threat of either or both France and Spain attacking England.

Significance of Philip II ruling the Netherlands

Philip II also ruled the Netherlands – vital for English trade. In 1563 Philip banned the import of English cloth to the Netherlands. Officially, this was to protect the Netherlands against infection by plague from England, but the ban reflected annoyance that the balance of trade had turned in England's favour while Elizabeth turned a blind eye to piracy in the Channel and to English merchants spreading Protestant ideas in the Netherlands. Elizabeth responded by banning all imports from the Netherlands, but both sides backed down and normalised trade relations in 1564.

So in the first years of her reign Elizabeth saw the signs of a dangerously powerful Catholic Spanish monarchy behind these events. Her response was to search for a way of containing the might of Spain without overextending her limited resources. In the end, Elizabeth was forced by events to make war against Spain, but by that time she was facing a country with the image but not the substance of a superpower.

KEY DATES: THE RELIGIOUS SETTLEMENT OF 1559

Nov 1558 Elizabeth I succeeds to the throne

1559 Elizabeth's coronation; Act of Supremacy; Act of Uniformity; Royal Injunctions; Prayer Book of 1559; 1559 Treaty of Câteau-Cambrésis

1560 Treaty of Edinburgh; death of Francis II – Mary, Queen of Scots, a widow, returns to Scotland

1563 Council of Trent reasserts strict Catholic doctrine; Thirty Nine Articles published

---

3 Marriage and the succession: Elizabeth's dilemma

The reigns of Elizabeth's brother and sister had been short. There was no guarantee, especially in sixteenth-century England, that Elizabeth's reign would be long. Therefore the dual topics of her marriage and the succession were important from the very outset of her reign. So, while stability appeared to be achieved over religion, there were serious concerns over the urgent need to settle the succession – and the first step for that would be for Elizabeth to agree to a suitable marriage.

Problems of marriage for Elizabeth

Why was Elizabeth reluctant to marry, in spite of the pressure she faced?

The question of Elizabeth's marriage was deemed urgent. She was already 25 years old and would, in normal circumstances, already have been married off to some European prince as part of England's foreign policy. Now she was Queen, and many people felt – but did not always voice – discomfort at the idea of a female ruler. Was this not directly contrary to the natural order of things and God's laws?

In fact, as already explained earlier in this chapter, Elizabeth's rule was accepted – but only as second best. The problem would be solved by finding Elizabeth a suitable husband. He might then co-rule with Elizabeth and, hopefully, there would soon be a male heir to guarantee the succession.

The main difficulty was in deciding who that husband might be. Elizabeth's early vague answers on the subject of marriage were taken by her councillors to reflect common sense. Keeping foreign suitors waiting made for good diplomacy when England faced several threats from abroad. If the potential husband was foreign, that might help establish or reinforce England's alliances. However, there was the danger of England becoming a satellite of the husband's territories. If the husband was English, there was the danger of upsetting the balance of power within the English nobility. There was also the vexed question of religious beliefs – Catholic or Protestant? Once Elizabeth had established her religious settlement (see pages 156–62) it became clear that England was to be moderate Protestant in belief, but with a degree of latitude allowed to those who were either more extreme Protestants or those who hankered after Catholicism. Any marriage might well upset the delicate balance that had been achieved in Elizabeth's religious settlement.

Possible suitors, 1559–62

Suitors from Europe

The first volunteer to marry Elizabeth was Philip II of Spain. He assumed, naively, that Elizabeth would be pleased to gain political continuity and stability. He wanted England to work with Spain in the struggle against France. He also wanted to ensure that France, through Mary Queen of Scots, did not gain influence in England – including being recognised as heir to the throne. Elizabeth was evasive and Philip quickly recognised that this political match was most unlikely to happen. Instead, he made other suggestions.

NOTE-MAKING

Your notes should focus on the reasons why Elizabeth did not marry in the early years of her reign.

John Knox

Many of the feelings against a female ruler were reflected in a pamphlet published in late 1558 by the Scottish Protestant reformer, John Knox. His literal reading of the Bible led him to protest against women rulers – 'the monstrous regiment of women'. The work had been aimed against the ruling Catholic Marys – Mary, Queen of Scots, and Mary of England. However, Mary of England died while the pamphlet was being printed and when it appeared in England for people to read it was assumed, wrongly, that it was aimed against Elizabeth.

Two of Philip's cousins were the Austrian archdukes Ferdinand and Charles, who were the younger sons of the Holy Roman Emperor. Ferdinand would certainly not be suitable because he was seen as a staunch Catholic who was unable to compromise. His brother, Charles, was a possibility. It is accepted now that Elizabeth had no intention of marrying him, but diplomatic channels were kept open for nearly a decade. The aim was to make sure that the Habsburgs remained friendly towards England.

Prince Eric of Sweden fancied his chances. He was Protestant and was the heir to the Swedish throne. Elizabeth returned his friendship and she and people at the court benefited from many lavish gifts that were bestowed. However, she had no intention of marrying him – and there would be little benefit anyway in terms of European diplomacy.

Suitors from England

During 1559 rumours were rife in England about possible eligible bachelors from among the nobility. One was the Earl of Arundel, but he was Catholic. One leading member of the gentry class was Sir William Pickering, who spent many hours with Elizabeth in 1559. However, the friendship was never anything more – at least, in Elizabeth's eyes – because there was nothing to be gained politically from her marrying a member of the gentry.

In Elizabeth's view there was only one serious contender – Robert Dudley – and this was in spite of the fact that both his father and grandfather had been executed. His grandfather had been executed at the beginning of Henry VIII's reign as the penalty for becoming too powerful under Henry VII. His father paid the price of trying to change the succession in 1553 to avoid a Catholic monarch.

Dudley was 27 years old and began in 1559 to monopolise Elizabeth's attention. This drew much unfavourable comment from those at court and beyond. Dudley's wife, Amy Robsart, was ill, and it was assumed that, if she died, he and Elizabeth would marry. By 1560 it was clear that there was serious romance. Then in September 1560 Amy Robsart was found dead with a broken neck at the bottom of a flight of stairs. The circumstances appeared to be suspicious as the servants had been sent away before the accident happened. There were wild rumours that Dudley had hired killers; some of the rumours included Elizabeth in the conspiracy. It appears that Elizabeth's chief secretary, William Cecil, did nothing to dispel the rumours as he believed Elizabeth should be available to be used in the coming years as a marketable pawn in the European marriage market. It is also likely that any marriage involving Dudley would mark the end of Cecil's career ambitions at court.

Historians have been divided in opinion ever since on whether a crime had been committed. In fact, it does not matter. What is important is that Elizabeth eventually came to see – after several weeks of anguish – that such a marriage would be impossible after the death of Dudley's wife in those circumstances. They remained close friends for the rest of his life until his death in 1588, just after the Spanish Armada had been defeated. Dudley is commonly accepted as being the love of Elizabeth's life. He was created Earl of Leicester in 1564.

Smallpox

In October 1562 at Hampton Court Palace Elizabeth was taken ill with what was thought to be a bad cold. However, within a few days it was clear that she had contracted smallpox. There was a serious epidemic at the time and a substantial proportion of sufferers were dying. Elizabeth recovered, but it brought home to everyone the importance of agreeing Elizabeth's marriage and a succession to the throne. If Elizabeth had died, England could easily have descended into a civil war.

The House of Commons petitioned the Queen when it met again in 1563. Elizabeth's answer was evasive:

'And though I am determined in this so great and weighty a matter to defer mine answer till some other time … yet I have thought good to use these few words … to show you that I am neither careless nor unmindful of your safety in this case.'

Marriage and international diplomacy

From 1563 onwards it gradually became obvious that Elizabeth's preferred policy was not to marry. She was simply playing for time, whether dealing with petitions from Parliament or foreign ambassadors making a case for an advantageous marriage to an eligible European. It became almost a game, and continued on and off well past the age when Elizabeth would have been capable of bearing a child (see Chapter 7 for details of arguments with the House of Commons in 1566 and later years). Negotiations with the Archduke Charles resumed in the later 1560s. In 1579 – when Elizabeth was in her mid-forties – the Duke of Alençon was welcomed to England. Elizabeth was still able to use her charms to dabble in courtship where the real purpose was to aid international diplomacy.

Contenders for the succession

In the absence of Elizabeth providing her own heir, there was no obvious contender for the succession. There were no more descendants of Henry VIII. Any English contender would come from the daughters of Henry VII (see Figure 1).

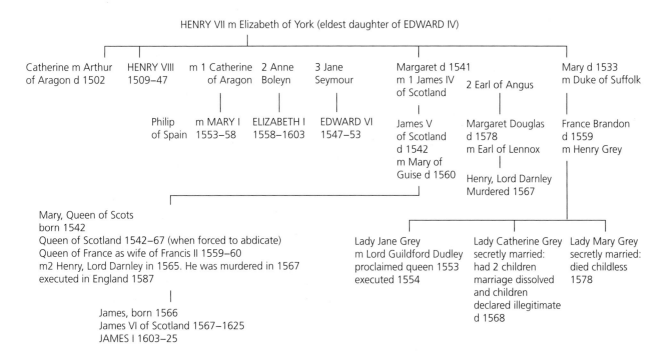

▲ Figure 1 The Tudor succession.

- The main Stuart claim derived from Henry VII's daughter, Margaret, who had married James IV of Scotland. The granddaughter of that marriage was Mary who had become Queen of Scots at the age of six days, on the death of her father, James V. She had briefly been Queen of France when married to Francis II (1559–60) but had then returned to Scotland. She was staunchly Catholic and after upheavals in Scotland finished up fleeing to England in 1568 to seek help from her cousin Queen Elizabeth who kept her confined, not knowing what to do with her (see Chapter 8).
- Another Stuart claim was from Margaret's second marriage after the death of James IV to the Earl of Angus. Their daughter, also called Margaret, had married the Earl of Lennox. This was a weaker claim, but it was more acceptable to some than Mary Queen of Scots.
- The Suffolk claim came from the marriage of Henry VII's younger daughter, Mary, to Charles Brandon, Duke of Suffolk. Their daughter Frances married Henry Grey, and they had three daughters. The eldest, Lady Jane Grey, had already been executed (see Chapter 5, page 144). The other two sisters, Catherine and Mary, had claims to the throne, and were both Protestant.

In practice, as Elizabeth lived to be almost 70, a series of deaths simplified the situation. The only practical possibility that remained was the son of Mary Queen of Scots, James VI of Scotland. However, Elizabeth's longevity was not a foregone conclusion and many hours were spent worrying and debating what should happen in the event of the Queen's death. It was not at all obvious that the eventual succession would be peaceful and almost universally accepted.

Elizabeth had been criticised by some historians for putting her own personal interests before those of the nation by refusing to marry. However, a case can also be made for her procrastination. By keeping options open, she helped England's diplomacy in Europe at a time when the country was threatened by a dominant Spain and by the need to build up trade relationships with as many countries as possible. If she had made a decision about the succession in the middle of her reign, and, for example, disallowed Mary Queen of Scots, it would have been extremely likely that there would not have been unanimous agreement on any of the alternatives. Those councillors and MPs who wanted to establish certainties over the succession were probably asking the impossible. Just because it served her own self-interest and was criticised by her councillors and MPs, this does not mean it was a bad policy.

Source G The Spanish ambassador in England, De Feria, wrote to Philip II immediately after the death of Mary in 1558. He outlined what he saw as the likely scenario for marriage for the new queen, Elizabeth. From *Elizabeth I* by G. Regan, (Cambridge University Press), 1988, p.35.

Everybody thinks that she will not marry a foreigner and they cannot make out whom she favours, so that nearly every day some new cry is raised about a husband. They have dropped the Earls of Arundel and Westmoreland and say now that she will marry William Howard's son or Pickering ... They will look with more favour on the Archduke Ferdinand than on your Majesty, when they have made up their mind to accept a foreigner, because they think he will always reside in the country, and will have no quarrel with France ...

How accurate was the Spanish ambassador in his arguments about Elizabeth's likely course of action in the first years of her reign (Source G)?

4 Social and economic conditions in the mid-sixteenth century

Society was undergoing substantial change in the mid-sixteenth century. This was partly the result of religious upheavals, but there were also economic and social factors, such as rising prices, population growth and changes in the pattern of trade. These have already been outlined in Chapter 5 (see under Somerset, pages 131–32 and Northumberland, page 134).

These changes seemed to increase in pace in the middle decades of the century, but it is important here to see them in the wider perspective of the whole Tudor period.

NOTE-MAKING

Notes can be made in tabular form. Organise a page in two columns. In the left column, put 'Nobility', etc., and in the right column list the main characteristics of each social class.

Mid-Tudor society

What were the main divisions within Tudor society?

On the basis of the 1549 rebellions and political instability of the mid-sixteenth century, historians have tended to assume that there was a social crisis at all levels of society. However, the basic stability of the hierarchy of Tudor England suggests otherwise. The church hierarchy was still intact and the monarch, helped by the ruling classes, maintained law and order with few exceptions. There was social mobility, but it was limited and probably became less easy to advance through education towards the end of the century. Women were very limited in scope for advancement, except occasionally through marriage. For men, the main routes were through land ownership, gaining a position of status in a town, for example, as a merchant, or through one of the professions. Economic status was not always the same as social status. For example, professions provided social status, but not necessarily wealth. Merchants might gain wealth but not necessarily social status.

LOOK AGAIN

Look at Key Question 4 on page viii. Compare what you read about society and the economy on pages 2–4 of Chapter 1 with developments outlined in this section. List the main changes or developments in the Tudor period.

Nobility and gentry

It is true that there were tensions that arose from the rising population and the redistribution of land following the dissolution of the monasteries. It used to be argued that the basic cause was the aspirations of the rising gentry class, encouraged by Crown appointments, clashing with the traditional nobility. In fact, the number of nobles and gentry remained fairly constant between 1500 and 1550. The gentry class made up about one per cent of the population – about 4,500 families according to Wolsey's survey in 1524. The number of gentlemen (those below the gentry class) did increase, but probably in line with population growth as a whole. The redistribution of Church land following Henry VIII's assumption of control of the Church's land and wealth, and the consequent dissolution of the monasteries, had mostly reinforced the existing positions of nobility and gentry. Only a small amount of land appears to have passed into the hands of new landowners.

It is true that some old noble families fell from power – usually because of royal disfavour (e.g. the de la Pole family who were Yorkist supporters) or the failure to produce a male heir – but this was normal in any century. However, the number of peers remained similar – 51 in 1547 and 55 in 1603. They continued to hold roughly 10 per cent of the land available for cultivation. Henry VIII created the most new peerages in the 1530s – mostly for political reasons, to ensure that lay peers in the House of Lords could outnumber the bishops. Most of the new creations under Henry were successful courtiers or soldiers. Hence there was some scope for upward mobility on merit for a few families. However,

Elizabeth's policy was to limit the number of new creations and rely as much as possible on the old families. The main exception was Lord Burghley who served her for 40 years.

Some of the 'greater' gentry started to rival the aristocracy in land, wealth and power – again, nothing new, but a little more in evidence in the sixteenth century because of the particular political background. The leading gentry families had the status of knights. The number changed from about 300 to 600 during the Tudor period, but the large increases were more to do with successful soldiers being dubbed knights on the field of battle rather than the active policy of the monarch. Indeed, Elizabeth was sparing in the number that she personally created, in spite of the upward aspirations of many landed families. Knights owned slightly less than the 10 per cent of the nobility.

Changing expectations in society also tended to help the gentry class. Their numbers increased during the Tudor period – but not much at the expense of the nobility. Indeed, the overall increase in numbers of gentry masks the fact that many families died out or became impoverished and lost status. Together with the nobility, they were the prominent local landowners who dominated society in the localities. Those who rose often benefited from the acquisition of positions at court and gaining offices, or made fortunes in trade or in the law. Land-owning provided status but not necessarily wealth. The gentry were often at the centre of the increased interest in learning, greatly helped by the printing revolution. Many could read and studied new literature from England and from Europe. Some saw themselves as intellectually superior to the 'lazy' nobility who relied on their inheritances and their traditional status.

Lower orders of society

Popular uprisings might suggest social conflict and crisis. In fact, in any century there were tensions. In the fifteenth century, because of depopulation after the Black Death, living standards for the poorest had become less bleak. Economic pressures in the sixteenth century led to a fall in living standards for those groups of society. The population had risen from something like 2.3 million in the 1520s to about 3 million in the 1550s. The surplus of available labour led to wages not keeping pace with inflation. Increased numbers put pressure on food supplies. It is thought that about 50 per cent of the rural and urban poor lived at or below subsistence level. When the harvest was bad, as in 1549, there was substantial suffering.

However, there were opportunities for some. The number of wage labourers increased as more opportunities arose in local industries and in trade. For example, mining of iron and coal provided employment for some, as did weaving, but these opportunities were limited to particular locations, thus encouraging geographical mobility.

Therefore when considering a possible crisis in society, it is essential to look at the long-term situation and to see any short-term changes as relatively minor fluctuations from the long-term trend.

The economy in mid-Tudor England

In what ways did the economy cause stress and tension in mid-Tudor England?

The economic situation in mid-Tudor England was shaped primarily by changes in society and in international trade. The actions of monarchs often made little difference, partly because the problems were only partially understood.

Population growth

Population levels started to rise in the Tudor period. The population had reached a low point of about 1.5 million in 1470, but had risen to 2.3 million in the 1520s. As you can see in Figure 2, this increased to nearly 3 million by mid-century, and then there was a slight decrease in the 1550s. By the end of Elizabeth's reign the population had reached 4 million.

Exactly why the growth occurred is not known. Diseases such as influenza, cholera, malaria and typhus, as well as the Bubonic Plague, were all still common, especially in cities and towns in the summer months. It is possible that younger people were building up more immunity. It is also possible that epidemics, though still feared and with terrible consequences, were less common during the 1540s. Then during the 1550s there were fresh virulent outbreaks of plague in 1551 and 1552 and of influenza in 1556 and 1558, which can account for the slight fall in the 1560s.

Another difficulty in assessing the evidence is the large differences in population density across England. The comparatively well-populated south-east, with London and other towns, was always likely to suffer more from pestilences.

Bad harvests, usually caused by abnormally wet summers, were always likely to have an effect on population figures. For example, when population was growing at its fastest rate in the 1540s, it is noticeable that there were good harvests from 1537 to 1542 and from 1546 to 1548. Then at a time when the population probably dipped in the 1550s there were bad harvests from 1549 to 1551 and from 1554 to 1556. Often poor harvests coincided with epidemics being at their worst.

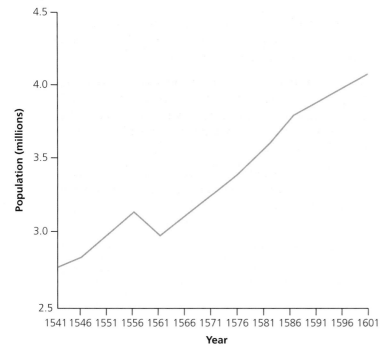

NOTE-MAKING

Notes here can concentrate on the causes and effects of population growth and inflation.

Remember that the causes were not understood at the time and historians are not fully in agreement now, but the effects were obvious for all to see.

1 What does Figure 2 show?
2 What social problems might be indicated by Figure 2?

◀ Figure 2 English population change, 1541–1601.

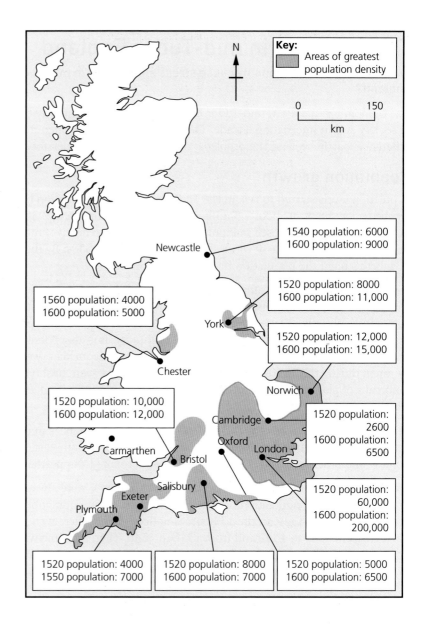

○ What does Figure 3 suggest about the population of England in the sixteenth century?

Figure 3 Population distribution in ▶ the sixteenth century.

Inflation – An increase, usually over a long period, of a wide range of prices and services.

However, it is necessary to be cautious in seeking to establish a neat pattern of cause and effect. All statistics quoted are estimates. There was much regional variation. One area suffered appalling weather while another did not – just as happens in this country in the twenty-first century with localised flooding and disasters. All the latest research suggests that the effects of enclosure have been exaggerated. In good weather there was still plenty of farmland to support the population. Indeed, before the Black Death of 1348–49, the population in the country had been substantially larger than it was in the 1550s.

Inflation

In very rough terms, inflation over the course of the sixteenth century was about 400 per cent, though not all prices rose to the same extent. Prices had already doubled between 1500 and 1550 and the effects were bound to have contributed to social unrest and problems within society. In that half-century prices rose most in the 1520s and 1540s.

People at the time were very uncertain about the causes of inflation. To them it was a new phenomenon. Historians used to have simple explanations – but the evidence does not fit well, as shown in Figure 4 on next page.

Figure 4 An analysis of the possible causes of Tudor inflation.

Cause	How this factor explains inflation	Evaluation of this factor
Government spending	Henry VII spent money cautiously, but later Tudors increased spending, especially on foreign wars. This put more money into circulation as the government bought clothing, provisions, weaponry and ships for wars against France and Scotland.	Government spending was only a small part of national economic activity.
Debasement of the coinage	To generate more money for foreign wars, Wolsey instituted the first debasement of the coinage in 1526–27 (i.e. lowering its value by reducing the percentage of real silver or gold). Governments between 1544 and 1551 made successive devaluations. Reducing the silver content forced people to ask for more money to yield the same metal value.	The 'Great Debasement' coincided with the steeper price rises of the 1540s, but the reminting of coins in the early years of Elizabeth's reign undermines this factor's importance in explaining later periods of inflation – especially the 1590s.
Increases in the circulation of bullion within Europe	The discovery of silver in the Spanish Empire led to an influx of precious metals into Europe from the mid-sixteenth century. This new quantity of silver did not just remain in Spain – it was used to pay troops in Italy and the Netherlands, to repay debts to bankers in Germany and by merchants importing items into Spain. The greater quantity of money in circulation meant that prices could rise as there was surplus purchasing power.	Although the discovery of the largest deposit of silver in the Americas came in 1545, large-scale importing did not occur immediately, so the timing of this factor does not easily explain why inflation began in England as early as the 1520s. Also the greater circulation of silver was more likely to affect merchants importing luxury items, such as European wines or fine cloths, but it was the price of domestically produced grain that rose the most.
Bad harvests	Crop failures decreased the amount of available food, forcing prices to increase.	Bad harvests caused temporary shortages of foodstuffs, so it is difficult to see why this should explain the continuous price increases of the sixteenth century, or why there was inflation in industry as well as agriculture.
Land sales	More land came onto the open market for sale after the 1530s (see Chapter 3, page 81). The ensuing scramble to buy among the nobility, gentry and wealthy merchants forced up land prices.	The timing of the opening up of a Tudor land rush fits the beginnings of inflation and would have had an effect on rents, but land sales only affected the privileged few and cannot easily explain inflation in a wide range of commodity prices.

Modern economic historians favour an explanation that starts with population growth – but this does not explain the marked rises in particular decades. Nor does it explain why marked population rises in other centuries did not lead to price rises. It is thought that farmers in the 1520s were concentrating more on wool production rather than responding to the needs of food for the growing numbers of people. Debasements of the coinage can help explain the big price rise of the 1540s, and the prevalence of epidemics in the 1550s, with less pressure on food supplies, can help to explain why inflation was less of a problem in that decade. In other words a combination of circumstances led to inflation under the Tudors, with the poor being hit the hardest.

Problems of the poor in the mid-sixteenth century

To what extent did the Tudors understand the social problems of the poor, and how did they react?

Tudor governments were right in seeing an increasing problems in the middle of the sixteenth century – roaming unemployed men, usually described as vagabonds, and an escalation of petty crime. Inflation, population increase, debasement of the coinage, bad harvests and the effects of the dissolution of the monasteries on lay workers all played their part (see Chapter 3 for details).

171

NOTE-MAKING

The focus of note-making here should be on listing the different attempts to alleviate the problems experienced by the poor.

Write out a table, with dates in the left column and the main details of the laws passed, on the right.

Tudor legislation in mid-sixteenth century England

Tudor governments were slow to act simply because it was not an established field of activity. The Church, monasteries, families and charitable houses had been deemed sufficient. When the government felt compelled to take action, measures were piece-meal and ill-thought out. For example, in 1552 attempts were made to reduce begging by making beggars register and be given permission to beg. If they begged without a licence, they were to be whipped and returned to their parish of origin and fined.

In 1563 another attempt was made to reduce the numbers of so-called vagabonds roaming the countryside. The Statute of Artificers (that is, apprentices) was ambitious in its scope. It aimed to enforce potential workers to take on seven-year apprenticeships, tied to a particular place, thereby restricting freedom of movement. It also aimed to fix prices and wages. In essence, the government was accepting responsibility in principle for what had been regulated by the medieval guilds controlled by the masters of each trade or activity. The local Justices of the Peace were given responsibilities for carrying out the Act by having powers to punish and send culprits back to their original parishes.

In the mid-sixteenth century, the only distinction drawn between categories of poor was between the impotent poor (people unable to work because they were too young, too old or had a disability) and the idle poor (those fit to work but not working and seen as undeserving). There was no distinction between the lazy and those who were genuinely seeking work.

The severity of the problem varied from one decade to another, in relation to the peaks of inflation and population growth, but the principle of government intervention had been accepted.

▲ The punishment inflicted on those caught begging without a licence. © A beggar is tied and whipped through the streets, c. 1567 (woodcut).

Tudor legislation in 1572, 1576, 1597 and 1601

Later developments in laws dealing with the poor in Elizabeth's reign are summarised here. You should bear this mind as you work through Chapters 7 and 8.

The big change was in 1572 when an Act of Parliament made a distinction between those who were genuinely unemployed and the 'idle poor'. Some local areas had already started charities to provide for the 'deserving', but in 1572 the Poor Relief Act made donations to local authorities compulsory. In 1576, Houses of Correction were set up to punish those who refused to work.

When social problems again became acute in the 1590s (due to inflation, poor harvests, high taxation and the effects of war against Spain) more action was taken. Governments were afraid of riots and rebellions, as had occurred in 1549. There were food riots in London and the south east in 1595 and in East Anglia in 1596–97. These spurred the Privy Council into taking further action, especially with the effects of continuing bad harvests which were causing greater distress.

The Poor Law Act of 1597 confirmed the compulsory poor rate, but also required the setting up of pauper apprenticeships to train boys until 24 and girls until 21. More houses of correction were to be built so that the able-bodied poor could be put to work. The 'impotent poor' were to be provided for in alms houses or poorhouses. Vagrants were still treated in the same harsh way as before. This 1597 Act was repeated, with slight changes in 1601. The Poor Law Act of 1601 remained the basis of England's treatment of the poor until the nineteenth century. A clear distinction had been made between the lazy and other unemployed people, but there was no real acceptance that many were unemployed and unable to support themselves through no fault of their own.

Figure 5 Tudor Poor Law legislation.

Date	'Impotent poor'	'Idle poor'	'Genuine unemployed'
1495	All beggars punished by being placed in stocks, then whipped and returned to parish of origin.		
1531	Allowed to beg in their parish if they obtained a licence; fined if they begged without a licence.	Whipped and returned to parish of origin; fined if they begged without a licence.	
1536	Money to be raised through voluntary contributions to assist impotent poor.	Whipped and returned to parish of origin; fined if they begged without a licence. Children found begging to be taken from parents and put to work.	
1547	Funds collected through churches to support impotent poor; houses to be built to accommodate poor.	Anyone unemployed for more than three days classed as vagrant. If convicted of begging, branded and given to informant as a slave for two years. For a second conviction, further branding and lifelong slavery. Death penalty for third offence.	
1552	Compulsory census and registration to reduce unauthorised begging, attempts made to persuade more people to make contributions.	Whipped and returned to parish of origin; fined if they begged without a licence. Children found begging to be taken from parents and put to work.	
1563	If people refused to make contributions they could be taken to court and imprisoned.	Whipped and returned to parish of origin; fined if they begged without a licence.	
1572	Compulsory contributions to poor relief. Overseers of the poor appointed by the parish to help organised poor relief.	Punishments for vagrancy increased: whipping and ear bored for first offence, with criminal charges for further offences.	Some classes of people excluded from punishment – recognised for first time as 'deserving poor'.
1576		'Houses of correction' to be set up to punish those who refused work.	JPs required to buy raw materials to provide work for those who were able.
1597	Powers of overseers of poor carefully defined – included finding work for able poor.	Whipped and returned to parish of origin. Each county had to have at least one house of correction to which persistent beggars could be sent.	Tools and materials to be provided for those able to work. Children to be apprenticed to a trade.
1601	Earlier laws brought together and reissued with some amendments.		

The effects of these Elizabethan Acts of Parliament were limited. In practice, more help was provided by charitable giving for poor relief than through compulsory levies. On the other hand there were no rebellions as serious as those in the mid-century and food riots were limited in scale and frequency. That might suggest that some of the legislation reflected a degree of panic on the part of the Privy Council, with an exaggeration of the scale of the problem overall. Tudor society was essentially stable by the standards of the time and Tudor rule was successfully continued by the Stuarts.

Source H Different sorts of poor people. From *Description of England* by William Harrison, published in 1586.

With us the poor is commonly divided into three sorts, so that some are poor by impotency, as the fatherless child, the aged, the blind and lame, and the diseased person that is judged to be incurable; the second are poor by casualty, as the wounded soldier, the decayed householder, and the sick person visited with grievous and painful disease; the third consisteth of thriftless poor, as the rioter that had consumed all, the vagabond that will abide nowhere but runneth up and down from place to place, and finally the rogue and the strumpet.

1 In your own words, explain the three different sorts of poor people as described in Source H.

2 Using the information in the last section of this chapter, how accurate is this description in terms of how the Tudors saw society at that time?

3 How did Tudor legislation attempt to deal with each category?

Chapter summary

- Elizabeth made a very favourable impression at her accession and coronation, 1558–59.
- Elizabeth's upbringing had a profound effect on her personality and attitudes.
- The Church of England was recreated with the Acts of Supremacy and Uniformity in 1559.
- The Protestant beliefs of the Church of England were set out in the Thirty-nine Articles, 1563.
- Elizabeth's had many suitors – but would she marry?
- The succession would be contested if Elizabeth failed to produce an heir.
- Population growth had major effects on society and the economy.
- The causes of inflation are still debated; the effects are more clear cut.
- There was much focus on the poor with the effects of population growth and inflation.
- Attitudes towards the poor changed during the Tudor period.

Chapter summary diagram

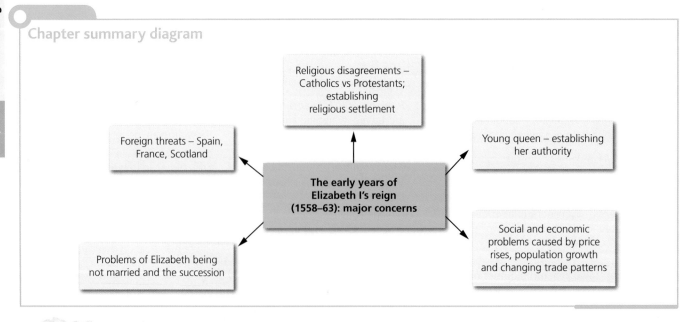

Working on essay technique

Remember the advice from Chapters 1–4 and the summary provided at the end of Chapter 5 and consider this A-level practice question.

'The crisis faced by the Tudors in the years 1540–63 was primarily caused by economic factors.' Assess the validity of this view. (25 Marks)

This is a complex question, which can be approached in different ways. One way, for example, would be to:

- Identify 'the crisis faced by the Tudors'. How did it manifest itself? Instability of government? Rebellions? Decline of influence overseas?
- What were the causes?
  - Economic (price rise, trade problems, etc.)
  - Social (land ownership, poverty, population growth, bad harvests, etc.)
  - Religious (see-saw of religious changes)
  - Political (primarily uncertainties over the succession; rival noble families)
- Investigate whether the word 'crisis' is helpful or an exaggeration.

Follow the stages outlined in the activity on page 148 at the end of Chapter 5.

This essay title encompasses a wide area, both in breadth and chronologically over nearly a quarter of a century. There is absolutely no opportunity to describe anything. Events will need to be referred to – but with snippets of precise detail to avoid superficiality.

In particular, this essay allows for complexity including arguments and counter-arguments, because the interpretation provided in the quotation:

1 Gives you a reason for a crisis – and there are also others to be considered.
2 Makes the assumption that there was a crisis – the extent of which can be debated.

This complexity can be reflected in your introduction and/or your conclusion. The subject also gives you the opportunity to show awareness of different historians not always agreeing. This might be because of:

- different opinions on which factors were most important
- a different emphasis on how the various factors inter-relate.

So, for example, in this question:

- Some historians have been keen to stress the existence of a mid-Tudor crisis, and, in so doing, probably exaggerating it.
- It is possible to inter-relate the issues in different ways, e.g. did the policies of Somerset and Northumberland reflect economic and social concerns, or did they help to make them worse?

Working on interpretation skills: extended reading

How skilful was the young Elizabeths as Queen?

Dr J. P. D. Cooper assesses the threats to Elizabeth's reign and her skill at addressing them.

Writing in the early 1560s, Sir Thomas Smith described the monarch as 'the life, the head, and the authoritie of all thinges that be doone in the realme of England'. *De Republica Anglorum* pictured subjects approaching the royal presence bareheaded, 'in adoration and kneeling'. But as Smith explained,
5 this did not mean that England was an absolute monarchy. Queen Elizabeth exercised her power through Parliament, where Lords and Commons came together to consult, to pass laws and to vote taxes. The young Elizabeth's skill as a ruler would be tested by her ability to find, and subsequently to maintain, a political and religious consensus after years of uncertainty and
10 conflict. As a woman surrounded by men, she would also need to ensure that her own voice remained dominant among the many clamouring to advise her.

Elizabeth's first decision, to appoint William Cecil as her principal secretary, was one of her wisest. Cecil had been a loyal friend during the
15 dangerous years of Mary's reign. In the words of his biographer Stephen Alford, he possessed 'the best political mind of his generation'. Minister and monarch didn't always see eye to eye, notably over the question of Elizabeth's marriage, but in other respects their partnership brought a welcome stability to government. The 1559 peace treaty with France, and
20 English support for the Protestant Lords of the Congregation in Scotland, effectively neutralised the 'auld alliance' which had threatened England for generations. Mary Queen of Scots was deposed in 1567 and fled to England the following year, placing her fate in Elizabeth's hands. If the English military expedition to Le Havre in 1562–63 ended in surrender
25 and humiliation, then it also signalled the need for reform in the army; the forces mustering against the Spanish Armada in 1588 would be stronger as a result.

Smith referred to the monarch as 'the governor of the common wealth', and it was in the same terms that Elizabeth defined her supremacy over
30 the church. Taking the title 'supreme governor' of the Church of England, rather than supreme head as Henry VIII and Edward VI had been, enabled Elizabeth to side-step her critics without degrading the power that she wielded in practice. The 1559 Book of Common Prayer played down conflicting interpretations of the Eucharist by combining the Protestant
35 formula from Edward VI's second Prayer Book, implying that the service of Holy Communion was an act of remembrance, with a more traditional form of words emphasising Christ's sacrifice on the cross.

Was this Elizabeth's own doing? The Queen's personal religious opinions have foxed generations of historians, although it would not now be easy to argue, as Wallace MacCaffrey once did, that Elizabeth was, 'coldly – at times, hostilely – indifferent to religious concerns'. Elizabeth had been a Protestant figurehead during Mary's reign, and she did a lot to promote the English Bible and remove Catholic imagery from parish churches. But she also patronised sacred music in Latin and kept a silver crucifix in her chapel, to the dismay of her more Protestant advisors. Whatever her inner belief, Elizabeth's implacable defence of the religious compromise agreed by Parliament in 1559 confirms that she appreciated the political value of a moderate Protestant settlement.

Elizabeth's achievements during the early years of her reign, her shrewd collaboration with Cecil and the skill with which she negotiated tensions in church and state, are not really in doubt. She had also begun that conversation with the broader population, through progresses and pageantry and elaborate speeches, which ultimately matured into a nation-wide culture of loyalty and celebration. On one key issue, however, historians remain as mystified as Elizabeth's own subjects. Why didn't the Queen marry and settle the succession? Was it a conscious decision on Elizabeth's part, to preserve her independence and freedom of movement (a position favoured by feminist and gender historians), or else an accident of politics (as the sustained diplomatic campaign to marry into the French royal family, apparently taken seriously by Elizabeth, might imply)? Susan Doran points out that Elizabeth's own opinion was only one factor in the equation; the inability of her councillors to agree among themselves may have been just as important. If the succession was going to be secured, it had to be soon. Every year that passed increased the risk that Elizabeth might die in childbirth. By 1569 Cecil was writing to the Queen that the threats to her rule were 'many, great and imminent'. With Catholic rebellion and conspiracy on the near horizon, he was right to be worried.

Dr John Cooper is Senior Lecturer in History at the University of York, specialising in sixteenth-century Britain. He is principal Investigator of the AHRC project 'St Stephen's Chapel, Westminster, Visual and Political Culture, 1292–1941'

ACTIVITY

Comprehension

1 Explain the meaning of the following:
   a) 'Auld alliance' [paragraph 2, line 21]
   b) 'Governor of the common wealth' [paragraph 3, line 28]

Evidence

2 List the ways in which Elizabeth is said to have shown good judgement as Queen in the first few years of her reign.

Interpretation

3 Use your knowledge to question whether Elizabeth was as successful in the first years of her reign as the interpretation suggests.

Evaluation

4 Assess how successful the young Elizabeth I was in consolidating the powers of the monarchy compared with her brother and sister, Edward VI and Mary, in their reigns.

Elizabethan England: Queen, government and changing religious ideas

This chapter focuses on Elizabeth's rule in England during the next four decades from 1563 to 1603. The important foreign policy aspects, including the threats posed by Mary Queen of Scots, are dealt with in detail in Chapter 8, though they will be mentioned here when relevant to domestic affairs.

This chapter therefore deals with the following parts of the specification:

● Elizabethan government: court, the arts, ministers, parliament, factional rivalries.
● Religion: development of Puritanism, continuing Catholicism, the Church of England by 1603.

Several of the key questions in the specification are directly relevant, especially those concerning the monarchy and the government. The role of individuals and groups is also very relevant in terms of Elizabeth and her ministers and also groups such as Parliament, Catholics and Puritans. The section on the Elizabethan court and culture relates to the changes and developments of intellectual and religious ideas.

The reign of Elizabeth is often seen as a Golden Age. The main question that emerges for this chapter is:

Does Elizabeth I deserve her reputation as the Queen of a Golden Age?

CHAPTER OVERVIEW

Elizabeth created an image of herself as Queen, even more so than Henry had done so as King. This was achieved through elaborate court ceremonies and protocol, and through the way in which Elizabeth portrayed herself to the courtiers and the population as a whole. She also patronised the arts, leading to a flourish in literature, music, art and architecture. Yet relations with Parliament were often difficult, with continuing concerns about the succession and foreign policy, as well as domestic issues over freedom of speech, religion and financial quarrels over taxes and monopolies. Although the Elizabethan religious settlement was a triumph of statesmanship at the beginning of the reign, there were ongoing disputes. The minority of Catholics wanted the restoration of their religion and looked to Mary Queen of Scots and to Philip II of Spain for support. Some Protestants thought that the Church of England needed further purifying and this led to disputes between the Church of England and those who wanted to take the reformation further. The Golden Age was partly tarnished.

1 Elizabeth and her court

Elizabeth used her charms as well as her intellect to dominate and control life at court. She recognised that some believed that she could not be head of the Church (since there was no scriptural authority for women to take doctrinal decisions). She understood that some objected fundamentally to the notion of a female ruler. The Presbyterian leader in Scotland, John Knox, had no doubts on the matter, as seen in Source A below. (See also Chapter 6, page 163 for more on John Knox.)

Source A From *The First Blast of the Trumpet against the Monstrous Regiment of Women* by John Knox, published at the end of 1558.

To promote a woman to bear rule, superiority, dominion or empire over any realm, nation or city, is repugnant to nature, contumely to God, a thing most contrarious to His revealed will and approved laws; and finally, it is the subversion of good order, or all equity and justice.

Knox was the leader of the Protestant Reformation in Scotland and had been a strong critic of Mary I who he believed lacked the authority to enact religious changes. The same arguments could now be used against Elizabeth.

Therefore, Elizabeth had to be able to impose her will in a male-dominated society. Historians generally agree that Elizabeth was a very effective ruler. Although she was over-cautious at times and had to be pushed into making critical decisions, her image was that of a woman who had put her country before her personal needs and who protected England as a mother protects her family.

Elizabeth's image-making

What methods did Elizabeth and her ministers use to enhance her image as Queen?

Elizabeth needed to promote a strong image with perfect health and strength. In public she was keen to be seen dancing with ambassadors or leading the chase when on horseback and out hunting. The reality was a little different. She was prone to occasional fainting fits and suffered frequently from headaches. She was apparently very short-sighted, which must have made both public occasions and private reading difficult. She often suffered from chronic toothache – a problem that was common at the time with those who, instead of eating fresh fruit, thought it was healthier to preserve the fruit in a sugary syrup before eating it.

It was therefore extremely important that Elizabeth's image was carefully cultivated.

- She travelled the country on 'royal progresses' – at least 25 during her reign – staying in the homes of leading families and meeting her subjects to show the human face of the monarchy. Progresses were accompanied by much spectacle for the entertainment of the masses, such as fireworks displays, street decorations and a royal procession.
- She deliberately toned down the extravagance at court, not only to save desperately needed money but also to portray herself as careful and hard-working. She made it clear that she would sooner spend money on public needs than on new palaces. Where possible, she relied on extravagant gifts from courtiers who wished to impress her. In 1563 Parliament voted her an allowance for the court of about £40,000 each year, which was

NOTE-MAKING

Make brief notes on each of the ways in which Elizabeth was able to project her image.

179

Source B From a report of the Queen's royal progress in 1568 by the Spanish ambassador.

She was received everywhere with great acclamations and signs of joy, as is customary in this country; whereat she was extremely pleased and told me so, giving me to understand how beloved she was by her subjects and how highly she esteemed this, together with the fact that they were peaceful and contented, whilst her neighbours on all sides are in such trouble. She attributed it all to God's miraculous goodness. She ordered her carriage to be taken where the crowd seemed thickest, and stood up and thanked the people.

Bearing in mind that the Spanish ambassador was representing the Catholic country of Spain, why might his attitude towards Elizabeth (Source B) be surprising?

never enough, especially with rising prices. Elizabeth always had to make up the difference out of her income – another reason to be careful in spending money.

- Every day thirteen poor men at the palace gates were given a small sum of money (5 old pence – about 2 new pence). Giving to the needy continued all year, but was at its peak around Easter.
- Elizabeth did, however, maintain separate 'wardrobes' at Whitehall, Windsor, Hampton Court and the Tower. She indulged in expensive fineries, especially Italian silks and satins.
- Courtly rituals were emphasised, for example at mealtimes. There were elaborate rituals later in the reign surrounding Elizabeth processing to church. Outdoor rituals included jousting tournaments at which the Queen's champion competed in her honour. Such rituals were often medieval in origin and were designed to focus attention on Elizabeth as the provider of honours and glory. There were tiltyards for jousting at Greenwich, Hampton Court and Whitehall. At Whitehall Elizabeth built an enclosed gallery for spectators. As the reign progressed, the most important jousts were held on the anniversary of her accession.
- Elizabeth's reluctance to commit herself to marriage was also turned into positive propaganda. As the 'Virgin Queen', she reminded the country that her priority was politics. There is little doubt that she benefited from the associations people drew between her image and the Catholic image of the Virgin Mary.
- Other female icons were borrowed to flatter Elizabeth. From popular Renaissance culture came the image of Astraea, the Greek virgin-goddess who was the last of the gods to leave the earth. Mythology suggested that Astraea's return would bring a new age of prosperity and stability, which Elizabeth's propagandists converted into the illusion of the Queen ushering in England's 'Golden Age'. She gained the title of Gloriana after the publication of Edmund Spenser's poem *The Fairie Queene*, in which Gloriana represented Elizabeth.
- Dances at court and staged masques were used as part of the ritual (see page 187). Portraits and paintings drew on classical themes, well known through the spread of the Renaissance, to reinforce positive images of the Queen as the provider of peace and plenty.
- To control the representation of her image, Elizabeth ordered in 1563 that all paintings of her were to be modelled on portraits supplied by her 'Sergeant Painter'. Production of unauthorised images was prohibited and offending items destroyed. This meant that a standard image of the Queen appeared in nearly all paintings, unchanging over the decades, even though Elizabeth grew thinner and more arthritic, and began to lose her looks, hair and teeth.

All this propaganda mostly reached the upper sections of society in a direct way (e.g. seeing the portraits) but the whole country was influenced by word of mouth, including from the clergy in their pulpits.

Because of the extent of this Elizabethan image-building, it is difficult to get a truthful picture of what Elizabeth was like. She was certainly hard-edged, demanding much from her courtiers and impatient with people who failed her. She deliberately created a masculine personality to command her courtiers, but at the same time used the fact that she was a woman to charm them and throw them off-balance. It was a skilful combination and one which allowed Elizabeth to rule over a court which was more loyal and united than any since the 1520s.

▲ *The Armada Portrait*, painted shortly after the event, attributed to George Gower (1540–96). This portrait shows a youthful and commanding ruler, when in fact Elizabeth would have been 57 years old at the time. What aspects of the *Armada Portrait* suggest Elizabeth's power and authority?

Role of the court

What was the importance of Elizabeth's court in enhancing her authority?

The royal court was the hub of social and political life, as it had been throughout the Tudor period. Under Elizabeth, however, the ritualisation of courtly life blurred its political and social functions, leaving a spectacular atmosphere that befitted the 'Golden Age' of royal propaganda. Elizabeth did not merely promote men who were loyal to the Tudor dynasty. Courtiers who attracted and flattered her were also brought into government. The most famous example is Robert Dudley (see page 183).

NOTE-MAKING

In the following section (pages 181–186) list the ways, with brief details, that Elizabeth used the court to project her image and keep control over the country.

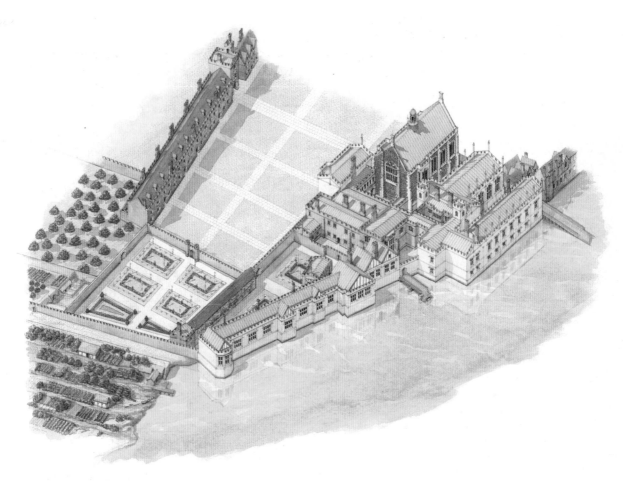

▲ Whitehall as it was in the sixteenth century.

LOOK AGAIN

Think how the role of the court had evolved since the accession of Henry VII.

The royal court incorporated both government offices (such as the Privy Council and the Chamber, which met in rooms in the palace) and the Queen's personal household. It was a place where the business of government was conducted and was at the same time the private household of the Queen. To achieve social status and future titles or lands, nobles had to be seen at court. To ensure that government ran smoothly, royal officials had to attend court to secure royal permission for their actions. This explains why the social and political functions of the court overlapped.

Elizabeth inherited fourteen principal residences in London and the south of England. Some had come into royal possession after the disgrace of a former minister. For example, Whitehall and Hampton Court had both become royal residences after being owned by Wolsey. Greenwich, her birthplace, remained her favourite residence.

The Queen's main palace was at Whitehall. The Palace had three blocks which contained gardens, tennis courts, the official rooms for the Privy Council, a guard room, a great hall and the state apartments which included Elizabeth's rooms. Whitehall was not Elizabeth's favourite palace, but she spent a lot of time there, except in July and August when the plague was most likely to hit the city.

The royal household employed nearly 1,500 people from the Lord Chamberlain to the herb woman. Most received a diet or daily allowance of food and drink, as well as candles and firewood. Royal servants were paid little and relied for most of their income on tips which had to be paid by people who wanted access to court. The domestic staff were organised in departments, each with its own strict hierarchy, such as the Robes, the Pantry, the Bakehouse and the Woodyard.

Robert Dudley, Earl of Leicester (1532–88)

Although Dudley was the son of the late Earl of Northumberland, Elizabeth's interest in him stemmed from the close relationship the two enjoyed (it has been suggested that Dudley was her personal choice for a husband). This is corroborated by one visitor to the court (see Source C below).

Source C From a record by James Melville, the ambassador of Mary Queen of Scots, written during the 1570s.

She [Elizabeth] took me into her bed-chamber, and opened a little cabinet, wherein she kept many little pictures wrapped within paper, and their names written on with her own hand upon the papers. Upon the first that she took up was written, 'My Lord's Picture'. I held the candle and pressed to see which picture was so named. She appeared loath to let me see it; yet I prevailed for a sight of it, and I found it to be the Earl of Leicester's picture.

It is telling that Dudley gained so many promotions so quickly, entering the Privy Council at the relatively young age of 30. His relationship with Elizabeth

was volatile – he disagreed sharply with her on some policies and voiced his concerns openly, and his relationships with other women caused public arguments with the Queen. Nonetheless, he was a capable and trustworthy minister. As Earl of Leicester he controlled large areas of land and used patronage at court to promote the careers of men with similar views to his own.

Leicester was leader of the more radical group of politicians at court and in the Privy Council. He supported active policies to defeat Catholicism at home and abroad and grew frustrated at the Queen's caution and Lord Burghley's opposition. Among the policies Leicester favoured were:

- Further reforms to the Church along the lines suggested by Puritans.
- Stronger persecution of English Catholics, especially after news of their plots to replace Elizabeth on the throne with Mary Queen of Scots.
- Active military intervention to help the Huguenot and Dutch rebels.
- An alliance with France against Spain.

1532 Born, son of the Earl of Northumberland.

1550 Married Amy Robsart.

1554 Sentenced to death under suspicion of his role in Lady Jane Grey's coup, but pardoned by Mary.

1557 Distinguished himself at the Battle of Saint-Quentin against France.

1559 Appointed Master of the Horse; made a Knight of the Garter.

1560 Suspicious death of his wife – rumours that Dudley had ordered her murder.

1562 Joined the Privy Council; advocated military intervention in France to assist the Huguenots.

1564 Made Earl of Leicester.

1585 Commanded the expeditionary force to aid the Dutch rebels.

1586 Angered Elizabeth by accepting the title of Governor of the Netherlands; brought back to England.

1588 Appointed to lead part of the royal army against the possible Spanish invasion, but died before the Armada arrived.

System of patronage

Elizabeth had a strong appreciation of the need to gain and to retain the loyalty of the politically important members of Tudor society. This could be achieved partly through the astute use of patronage, which was central to the operation of the court. Elizabeth bestowed these favours carefully, and to a wide circle, so that goodwill was maintained. Elizabeth's aim was to ensure that as many nobles and gentry as possible were bound through patronage in loyalty to the Crown, and then there would be relatively few who would lend support to plots against her. This was to prove important at various points during her reign – for example, the Rebellion of the Northern Earls in 1569 (see page 200). This was reflected in the advice given by William Cecil, Lord Burghley and Elizabeth's Chief Secretary, in 1579 (see Source D, page 184).

Source D From advice given to Queen Elizabeth by William Cecil, Lord Burghley.

That you gratify your nobility and the principal persons of your realm to bind them fast to you with such things [i.e. patronage gifts] ... whereby you shall have all means of value in your realm to depend only upon yourself.

The Crown controlled appointments to offices in local and central government, the Church, the law and the royal household. In addition, the monarch had land and titles to distribute, as well as economic benefits such as the right to collect taxes. The key to power, position and wealth, therefore, was the Queen.

The most valuable patronage was the grant of office, and these varied from high positions in society to lower positions such as household servants and working in a stable at court. It has been estimated that a large proportion of the politically active class held some office, great or small, under the Crown. The importance of patronage extended to what has been called secondary patronage. For example, those who had acquired office found that their office gave them the right to make various appointments. Thus even more people were tied, albeit indirectly, to showing loyalty to the Queen.

Another form of patronage was carried out with the grant of pensions or favourable grants of land. Occasionally land was sold outright, but Elizabeth had learned from the mistakes of her father's reign and realised the importance of keeping hold of as much as possible. Therefore favours involving land were bestowed by leasing land at a low rent, often to important politicians.

Monopolies were a lucrative form of income for the recipient who had the sole right to manufacture or sell a particular item, such as sweet wines and the mining of tin. However, they were unpopular as they prevented competition and there were frequent complaints in the House of Commons towards the end of Elizabeth's reign.

Elizabeth saw the dangers of being too liberal with another form of patronage – the grant of titles. She realised that they were most valued if not given too freely. For example, Elizabeth only granted eighteen peerages during her reign, and at her death in 1603 there were fewer nobles than there had been in 1558. Elizabeth was able to maintain control in the male-dominated atmosphere at court and could keep rivalries under control. Her chief secretary, Burghley, kept a careful eye on the whole patronage scene to ensure that there was a wide distribution that encompassed as many of the politically-interested as possible.

Factional rivalries

Historians have commented on the domestic peace during Elizabeth's reign. At the beginning of her reign, William Cecil (later created Lord Burghley) held most sway at court. He controlled most patronage and policy. However, by the mid-1560s

---

In your own words, explain the advice that William Cecil was giving to Elizabeth (Source D).

Monopolies – Such rights were granted by Royal Charter, declaring that a particular group of merchants had the sole legal right to make or to import a commodity such as soap or sugar. Monopolies were unpopular because they were often granted in everyday products, allowing the group of merchants who controlled the monopoly to fix prices at artificially high levels to make a profit.

he had rivals. Dudley was created Earl of Leicester in 1564 and he was extremely ambitious on his own behalf – both in politics and in his ambition to marry the Queen. A third potentially powerful figure at court was the Earl of Sussex, a relation of the old-established Howard family. He returned from the army stationed in Ireland (see Chapter 8, page 233) in 1565. The Earl of Sussex became a Privy Councillor, was able and represented the old aristocracy. He had the support of the Duke of Norfolk, the only dukedom that had survived into the reign of Elizabeth.

The complex plot involving Leicester and some supporters at court in the late 1560s who had the idea of getting the Duke of Norfolk to marry Mary Queen of Scots (see Chapter 8) led to what we know as the Northern Rebellion in 1569. Leading figures in the north tried and failed to restore Catholicism and Norfolk was disgraced and executed in 1572. Elizabeth eventually accepted Leicester's protestations of innocence.

In the 1570s and 1580s there was generally much more co-operation between courtiers. Cecil became Lord Burghley in 1571 and he had a considerable following at court, simply because he had access to much patronage and the ear of the Queen. Leicester also had a large following, and he and the Queen remained on close, friendly terms.

A third influential and trusted adviser was Sir Christopher Hatton. He was the younger son of a country gentleman and was charming and loyal. Elizabeth seemed to favour him as a courtier and developing politician, simply because of his charming manner and his genuine intention of serving the monarch rather than himself. Indeed, Hatton's seeming close friendship with Elizabeth caused jealousy from others, including Leicester. For example, when Hatton was ill, in 1573, Elizabeth visited his bedside daily. Then when he was recovering she sent him to the Netherlands to a spa for treatment, under the care of her physician, Dr Julio.

In the 1580s Walter Raleigh became a special favourite of Elizabeth. Apart from his experience as a soldier in Ireland, charming manners and good looks, he was very clever and had a quick wit. He wrote poetry and charmed the Queen – even though he was twenty years younger than she was. The famous story of Raleigh laying down his cloak for the Queen to avoid the mud is most certainly an invention, but it does capture Raleigh's character and chivalrous outlook, which extended to his enthusiastic encouragement of expeditions to America to establish trade and colonies (see Chapter 8, page 228). Other courtiers such as Christopher Hatton were jealous of the attention that Elizabeth devoted to Raleigh.

Sir Francis Walsingham was the other person at court with huge influence. From 1573 to 1590 he was one of the Queen's Principal Secretaries, and his big desire was to see the emerging Church of England adopt more radical Protestant views and practices. This ensured his loyalty to the Protestant Queen and his hatred of Catholicism and its foreign supporters. In the 1580s he developed an extensive spy network that was used very successfully to trap Catholic supporters of Mary Queen of Scots.

During Elizabeth's reign, therefore, there were different groups of courtiers and government officials vying for attention from the monarch. These often became factions – that is, groups who aimed to work together for their common cause (e.g. moving the Church of England further away from Catholicism and more towards Puritanism – see Chapter 6). But these factions were also working for the good of the country and the monarch. Although they often disagreed about the best way to achieve the Queen's aims, they were not generally disloyal. By maintaining the close support of men such as Burghley and Leicester over such long periods, Elizabeth brought stability to courtly politics and for most of her reign avoided the destructive factionalism that had beset the final years of her father's reign and the crisis year of 1549.

LOOK AGAIN

Think how factions at court functioned in different ways during the Tudor period.

Source E From 'Loyalty to the Crown' from *New Worlds, Lost Worlds: The Rule of the Tudors, 1485–1603* by Susan Brigden, (Penguin), 2000, pp.363–64.

The Tudors had succeeded in their ambition that loyalty to the Crown replace loyalty to the old nobility. The ancient nobility had yielded power – though very far from all their power – to a service nobility which owed its advancement to royal favour and employment at court ... The new world of the court had become the centre of power, patronage and stability, and everyone who mattered in the realm was drawn to it ... The Queen had herself portrayed in gowns embroidered with eyes and ears, as symbols of her ceaseless vigilance over her people.

This period of stability at court ceased at the end of the 1580s. Leicester died in 1588, Walsingham in 1590 and Hatton in 1591. Burghley lived until 1598, but was a semi-invalid from 1592 onwards and had increasingly little influence.

Thus court politics became more divisive in the last years of Elizabeth's reign. The young Earl of Essex captivated the Queen and gained huge influence over patronage as well as politics. In the background, Robert Cecil, son of Lord Burghley, was emerging as the competent politician, and he was made Chief Secretary in 1597. The disintegration of a system based on the court and the Privy Council in the last years of Elizabeth's reign have seen some historians suggest that this marked the beginning of the breakdown in government consensus which led to civil war in 1642. Others have argued that the last years of Elizabeth's reign merely marked an unfortunate episode which could have easily been corrected, as in the mid-Tudor period when court factionalism had been prominent and then strong government was restored.

Elizabeth and the arts

How did Elizabeth use the arts to enhance her image as Queen?

Elizabeth's reign coincided with a great flowering of the arts in England. She cannot be given total credit for this phenomenon but she was a discriminating patron, keen to show support even if not always with money. Her courtiers were encouraged by her to favour art, music, literature and the theatre. Life at court reflected these interests. Noblemen, who in previous reigns might have stayed in their localities, sometimes festering grievances, were encouraged to come to the capital. By 1590 half of the English peers had town houses in London, mostly on the Strand or nearby. Many more rented houses that they used in some of the winter months.

Elizabeth was keen on outdoor events, including hunting and shooting. Sometimes tournaments would take place, and from 1572 an annual tournament was held to mark the day when Elizabeth succeeded to the throne. She loved horse riding and continued to ride very fast until the last years of her reign. She could compete in riding with the excellent horseman, Robert Dudley, her Master of Horse in the early part of her reign.

She was a skilled musician and could play several instruments including the virginals (an early keyboard) and the lute. She spent money quite lavishly on music, and encouraged musicians and composers. The famous Elizabethan composers, William Byrd and Thomas Tallis, were employed at the Chapel Royal. She spent over £1,500 each year on music. The Chapel Royal included gentlemen and children to sing at services, and over 60 instrumentalists, including seventeen trumpeters. Elizabeth was very keen on dancing, especially the galliard and the volta which were both energetic dances and helped to keep her fit until she was no longer able to perform them. The pavane was less energetic and much favoured by Elizabeth later in her reign.

In particular, in the evenings at court there were entertainments. Elizabeth loved watching plays, masques and other dramatic performances. The masque, originally a masked dance with miming, had developed into something closer to modern ballet. Masques were presented with elaborate costumes and scenery by the Master of the Queen's Revels. The performance was interspersed with songs and poems. They were staged using themes that enhanced the image of the Queen and were often designed to impress foreign visitors to court.

Elizabeth had her own company of actors, The Queen's Players. Robert Dudley also had his own company and would pay them to perform before the Queen.

Near the end of her reign Elizabeth showed an interest in William Shakespeare, an emerging playwright in the 1590s. His company of players, the Lord Chamberlain's Men, performed *Twelfth Night* at court one Christmas. It is said that Shakespeare wrote *The Merry Wives of Windsor* because Elizabeth had said that she would like to see Falstaff in love.

Attitudes towards Elizabethan theatres

Elizabeth's patronage of the theatre was particularly important because the Puritans in London in the 1590s were waging a propaganda war against the evils of the London theatres that had developed since the 1570s.

Here is a simplified extract from a letter from the Lord Mayor of London to the Privy Council in July 1597:

'Plays give opportunities to the ungodly people that are within this city to assemble themselves. They are places for vagrant persons, masterless men, thieves, horse-stealers, whoremongers and other idle and dangerous persons to meet together. They also draw apprentices from their ordinary work to the great hindrance of trade. In time of sickness it is found by experience that many, having sores but not yet sick, take occasion for recreation by hearing a play, whereby others are infected.'

Reflecting the Queen's own interest in drama, the Privy Council in 1600 agreed that plays should be encouraged, with necessary precautions taken:

'It is considered that the use of such plays, not being an evil in itself, may with good order and moderation be suffered in a well-governed state. As Her Majesty is pleased at some times to take delight and recreation in the sight and sharing of them.'

Some of the leading nobles, perhaps taking their cue from the Queen, also promoted the theatre. Indeed, Shakespeare relied on patronage from members of the nobility – and it was he who, more than anyone else, helped to create the Tudor propaganda picture of stable and successful rule.

One famous example which, it is alleged, reflected the powerful influence of the theatre, occurred in 1601. The Lord Chamberlain's Men were persuaded to stage a performance of Shakespeare's *Richard II* just before the Earl of Essex staged his infamous and doomed revolt. However, the staging of the play, involving the deposing of Richard II, failed to rouse the London mob against their Queen and Essex paid the price (see Chapter 8, page 234–35, for details of this rebellion).

The dramatists also engaged in their own propaganda, for example, Thomas Nashe in 1592:

'When people argue that plays corrupt common people, that's false, for no play they have encourageth any man to tumults or rebellion, but lays before such the gallows, or praiseth or approveth pride, lust, whoredom, drunkenness, but beats them down utterly. Men that are their own masters (such as gentlemen of the court) spend their leisure time in the afternoons on gaming, harlots, drinking or seeing a play. Is it not then better they should choose the least evil, that is plays?'

The first theatre, named The Theatre, was built in 1576, followed by the Curtain, the Rose and the Swan, before the most famous, The Globe, was opened in 1599. The flourishing of theatres in London reflected both official encouragement from the court and also the growing interest in the Renaissance. Many of the courtiers and government officials were very literate and had studied Greek and Roman writers. Elizabethan authors referred to them and Italian writers frequently and assumed that their readership would understand the references. In other flourishing aspects of the arts such as architecture and painting, much use was made of achievements and attitudes from the Ancient Classical period. Writings also showed the influence of the wider world, both helped by widening horizons through the development of printing and the discovery of new land and civilisations beyond Europe.

Intellectual and educational developments under Elizabeth

Under Elizabeth, Renaissance thinking and writing flourished. Printing continued to mushroom, with 2,760 books published in Elizabeth's reign up to 1579 and 4,370 from 1580 onwards. The extent of their influence depended, of course, on the ability to read. Literacy levels have been much disputed. It is clear that many could read but not write (fewer than 20 per cent of the population could sign their name). However, there were more opportunities to learn to read in Elizabethan England – and the printed word provided a powerful incentive to do so. The Reformation provided another incentive. In Elizabeth's reign Catholics and Protestants relied equally on the printed word.

The number of schools founded per decade in Elizabeth's reign was fewer than in the 1550s, but the combined effects of these developments provided opportunities, especially for families who were just below the privileged classes. In fact, the opportunities declined a little towards the end of the century with less charitable giving to found or maintained schools as a result of the economic depressions of 1586–87 and 1594–98. This in turn may have led to a lowering of literacy rates in the 1590s. However, the trend towards higher rates of literacy was still upward, especially in the city of London where many printing presses were centred.

Many of the books published reflected the humanist background of the Renaissance from earlier in the century. English writers referred frequently to Greek and Roman authors as well as publications from Italy. Works by Plato and Aristotle were used to argue for virtue in public life and for virtuous men to seek public office. More works by Classical Roman scholars were translated into English. For example, the educated could read the major writings of Tacitus – the *Histories* and *Life of Agricola* (published 1591) and the *Annals* and *Description of Germany* (published 1598). Thus Elizabeth had at her court many of the finest trained minds available in England, and as a consequence was the centre of much philosophical debate stemming from Classical and Renaissance literature.

LOOK AGAIN

Think of the importance of printing in encouraging the spread of intellectual and religious ideas throughout the Tudor period (Key Question 5).

2 Elizabethan government

Elizabethan government developed from the systems that had either evolved or were created during the reign of Henry VIII. Much of the central government was based on life at the court. Local and regional government increased in importance through the Justices of the Peace and other networks of local control.

The Privy Council

Why was the Privy Council important in Elizabeth's reign?

The Privy Council had been established as an advisory and co-ordinating body during the reign of Henry VIII. Its composition was determined by the monarch, from whom its power derived. Membership of the Council had grown to between 40 and 50 people during Mary I's reign to contain the heads of major government departments, representatives of the greater nobility and the Crown's personal favourites. On her accession to the throne, Elizabeth was expected to change the personnel of the council in line with the different priorities and supporters that she had, but Elizabeth also reduced it to under 20 members to make it easier to manage and to reduce the power of the traditional nobility.

LOOK AGAIN

Compare this section with Chapter 4 (pages 87–91).

▲ William Cecil

William Cecil, Lord Burghley (1520–98)

There is general agreement that William Cecil was the greatest of Elizabeth's ministers. He worked with the Queen for most of her reign, first as Secretary of State, then as Lord Treasurer from 1572 to his death in 1598. His family pedigree was relatively undistinguished, but he demonstrated a talent for administration which brought him to Elizabeth's attention in 1550 when she appointed him to oversee her estates. Much of his later career continued to be associated with financial management, but he exercised a much wider influence, counterbalancing the younger and more headstrong Earl of Leicester. Like Elizabeth, Burghley was essentially a conservative and a stabiliser. He promoted policies which attacked religious extremism, whether from the Puritans or Catholics, and sought to preserve England's independence abroad by treading a careful path between France and Spain. This policy brought him into conflict with Leicester who favoured a more openly anti-Spanish and anti-Catholic policy.

1520 Born in Lincolnshire, son of a minor Welsh family who had supported Henry VII's claim to the throne.

1535–41 Educated in humanist and Protestant ideas at Cambridge.

1543 Became an MP.

1550 Appointed Surveyor of the Queen's Estates.

1550–53 Acted as Secretary of State in Northumberland's government.

1553 Fell from power when Mary came to the throne.

1558 Career revived under Elizabeth when she re-appointed him Secretary of State.

1561 Appointed Master of the Court of Wards and Liveries.

1568 Earl of Leicester and the Duke of Norfolk plotted to reduce his influence at court.

1571 Awarded the title Baron Burghley.

1572 Became Lord Treasurer.

1598 Died.

Source F From an unflattering description of Burghley by the Spanish ambassador in the 1570s.

The principal person in the Council at present is William Cecil, now Lord Burghley. He is a man of mean sort, but very astute, false, lying, and full of all artifice. He is a great heretic and such a clownish Englishman as to believe that all the Christian princes joined together are not able to injure the sovereign of his country. By means of his vigilance and craftiness, together with his utter unscrupulousness of word and deed, he thinks to outwit the ministers of other princes.

How useful is this description of Burghley (Source F)?

What do the examples given in Figure 1 tell us about how Elizabethan government worked?

Personnel

Few of the pro-Catholic courtiers that Mary had installed on the Privy Council survived her death. Elizabeth's preference was for people who had proven their loyalty to the Tudor dynasty, either through personal service to her or because they came from an established family. The number of nobles was significantly reduced, as was the trend under Mary of appointing members of the Church on to the council. In their place Elizabeth built up a core of professional men who enjoyed her confidence and so tended to serve for long periods, improving the effectiveness and unity of the council. Not all historians have seen this as an advantage. Christopher Haigh, who has been the leading critic of Elizabeth's achievements, has pointed out that by largely excluding the nobility and the Church, Elizabeth made the Privy Council unrepresentative of the ruling elite as a whole, undermining its value as an advisory body and provoking resentment among courtiers at the restriction in their opportunities to advance in government. He also suggests that the Council's narrow membership limited the range of debate and tended to produce a co-operative body unlikely to challenge the Queen.

Functions of the Privy Council

The traditional functions of the Privy Council were maintained under Elizabeth, although the workload expanded considerably because of the need to administer the Elizabethan Church and the country's complex foreign policy. Broadly, the Council had four main roles:

● It offered advice to the monarch. One of the key areas of debate was policy towards the Netherlands because there was no agreement among councillors on the best course of action to check the growth of Spanish power in the region.

● It administered public policy. The Council maintained a network of contacts at national and local level through which its instructions were implemented (see the diagram of Elizabethan government, page 193).

● It co-ordinated the work of the different elements of government.

● It acted as a royal court of law through the prerogative courts which Privy Councillors staffed.

Of these functions, the advisory role was the most dramatic, because it sometimes brought councillors into direct confrontation with the Queen. However, the more important part of the Council's work was undoubtedly its daily administrative duties, since these kept the whole machinery of the Elizabethan state operating. The range of policy areas that the Council managed can be glimpsed from the minutes of its meetings (see Figure 1).

Figure 1 Examples of the routine work of the Privy Council.

Date	Example
July 1565	Instructions to the major and city corporation of Newcastle regarding the arrival of German miners.
Jan 1567	Instructions to the Treasury to settle debts for two plays the Queen had attended at Christmas.
June 1570	A request for the transfer of a prisoner to the Tower for torture to investigate his part in a murder.
Feb 1574	Instructions for the recall of licences issued to corn sellers in Berkshire, Bedford and Hereford who were suspected of price fixing.
Aug 1574	Requests for the mustering of troops in readiness for intervention in Ireland.
Nov 1574	Instructions to arrest Catholic troublemakers in Lancashire.

Part of the increase in the variety of the Council's work can be explained by the growth in the number of petitions (requests for help from individuals) it received. Rather than rely on the legal system, those with enough money and influence approached the Privy Council directly with their grievances. Although councillors tried to discourage this practice, they were inevitably drawn into settling these private disputes as part of their administrative control of local life. The result of the increased workload facing the Elizabethan Privy Council was a growth in the number and duration of meetings. During the crisis years of the 1590s, when England was at war with Spain and facing economic problems at home, the Council often met six full days a week, compared to the three half-days that were typical at the start of Elizabeth's reign.

Significance of the Privy Council

Judging whether the Privy Council managed government policy depends on which aspect of its work is being considered. This was still an age of personal monarchy, where the Queen was expected to take important decisions and to have the final say. In some policy areas, such as determining the succession, taking firm action to support the revolt of the Netherlands and dealing with Mary Queen of Scots, the Council was unable to exert much pressure on Elizabeth. These matters concerned the Queen personally, or were areas that fell within the royal prerogative, and she tended to guard her right to decide such questions jealously, even if that meant being slow and over-cautious in reaching a decision. However, she was not unreasonable and a well-argued case could sway her. So too could threats of resignation, especially by her most trusted councillors early in her reign. William Cecil, for example, used this tactic to pressure the Queen into military action against Scotland in 1560 (see Chapter 6, page 161).

Local and regional government

How was local and regional government organised in order to provide effective control for Elizabeth's government?

You will see from the examples of the work of the Privy Council on page 190 that a large portion of routine administration involved issuing instructions to those who implemented royal policies in the regions. Since the government lacked the equivalent of a modern professional civil service (and the money to buy one), it relied on men of standing in the local community to act as its agents. The growing tendency of the government to interfere in local communities (to instruct the parish priest on how to conduct his services or to arrange poor relief, for example) was an important – but not always welcome – trend during the sixteenth century. Increasing the scope of government activity inevitably involved placing more work on this unpaid governing class. This group accepted the heavier workload because of the prestige and influence its role carried within the community.

Justices of the Peace

The key figures in local government were the Justices of the Peace (JPs). They were appointed from the ranks of the gentry or from wealthy families and the merchant elite in towns. Their responsibilities included maintaining the rule of law by settling disputes and punishing offenders and administering a range of government policies, including the Poor Laws (see Chapter 6, page 173). Under Elizabeth the trend towards appointing more JPs continued; it has been estimated that there was an average of 50 per county by 1600. However, whether this number made local government any more effective is questionable. JPs were in the difficult position of having to live in the communities they administered. Not surprisingly, then, there were accusations that some ignored policies that they knew would be unpopular locally or used their position for personal profit against local rivals.

Source G From instructions issued to Elizabethan JPs.

Know that we have assigned you to be our Justices to keep our peace and to keep and cause to be kept all ordinances and statutes published for the good of our peace. Further, we assign you to inquire of all and every felonies, poisonings, enchantments, sorceries, magic, trespasses, engrossings and extortions whatsoever, and all other crimes and offences, and of such men as go or ride armed in assemblies against our peace in disturbance of our people. Also of such as lie in wait to maim or kill our people, and of innkeepers and all others who in weights and measures or in selling offend against the ordinances and statutes published for the common good, and of such sheriffs, bailiffs, stewards, constables, keepers of jails and other officers as are lukewarm, remiss or negligent in the performance of their duties. And to hear and determine all felonies and to correct and punish the same by fines, ransoms, forfeitures and otherwise.

Source H From examples of work done by JPs in the West Riding of Yorkshire, 1597–98.

An order prohibiting Adam Hutchinson and Thomas Hodgson of Barnsley from operating alehouses because they 'are men of bad behaviour' who 'do maintain ill rule in their houses'.

An order requiring the parish of Halifax to provide poor relief for an abandoned baby left in the village of Southerham.

An order preventing brewers from selling ale at prices above one penny for two pints, unless they had a special licence from the JP.

An order requiring larger landowners in the parishes of Leeds to send horses and labourers to help repair the road from Leeds to Wikebrigg.

An order that Thomas Stringar should be whipped back to his home parish of Wenbridge as punishment for sheep rustling.

WORKING TOGETHER

Shakespeare sometimes satirised local government officials. Look at *Henry IV, Part 2* and the role of Justice Shallow.

1 What does Source G suggest about the preoccupations and concerns of the authorities in Elizabethan England?

2 How useful is the information in Source H in helping a historian to judge the work of Justices of the Peace?

Lord Lieutenants

In Elizabeth's reign, another type of local official grew in status. Lord Lieutenants had been responsible for raising local militias during Henry VIII's reign, but under Elizabeth they acquired additional duties. In the second half of her reign, a Lord Lieutenant was appointed permanently in nearly every county, usually from one of the most distinguished families (which in many cases meant someone already sitting on the Privy Council). He was expected to manage the raising of troops, but also to supervise the work of JPs and to report local events to the Privy Council. The title – which still exists today – carried considerable prestige, as did the office of Deputy Lieutenant, created in the 1560s, to share the workload.

Beneath these impressive figures lurked a massive group of parish officials, each with their own little responsibilities. This might be to distribute poor relief, to look after the day-to-day affairs of the parish church, to arrest troublemakers, to repair local roads or to catch rats. The variety of work going on at a grassroots level should remind us that 'government' was a lot more sophisticated than it might first appear.

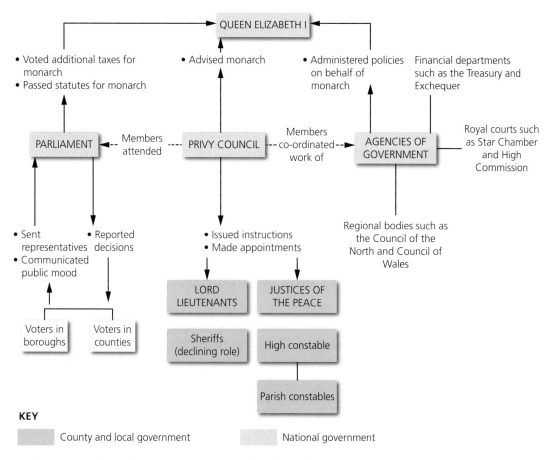

KEY

County and local government   National government

▲ Figure 2 Structure of government in the reign of Elizabeth I.

LOOK AGAIN

Compare the role of Parliament under Henry VII with its position under Elizabeth.

3 Elizabeth and her Parliaments

In Chapters 3 and 4, we looked at how Henry VIII's need to legalise the break with Rome in the 1530s increased the scope and importance of parliamentary work. During the reigns of Edward VI and Mary, Parliament had continued to be used to enact religious changes, including the important doctrinal statements contained in the Act of Uniformity in 1549, and had been involved in legislating to manage social and economic change. So, by 1558, it had become embedded within the political system to a degree that would have been unrecognisable to Henry VII. That is not to say, however, that Parliament had necessarily become more powerful in the process. It was still primarily an instrument to support royal policy. It was summoned and dismissed in accordance with the monarch's needs and had little power to initiate policies. Instead, it advised the monarch, voted extra taxation in emergencies and turned royal policies into laws.

Relations between Elizabeth and her Parliaments

How amicable were relations between Elizabeth and her Parliaments?

In Elizabeth's long reign, members of the House of Commons sometimes clashed with the wishes of the Queen. Some historians have carried out research on those disagreements and tried to trace the origins of conflicts between Crown and Parliament that developed under the Stuarts, leading to the civil wars of the 1640s and which ended with the execution of Charles I. Historians such as Professor J. E. Neale were writing in the 1940s and 1950s when the British Parliamentary system was still regarded as a shining model for other emerging democracies in the world to follow, with its peaceful evolution over the previous three centuries. This so-called 'Whig view' of history assumed that history was concerned with progress and viewed English history in this light. It was easy to look back and see the seeds of the constitutional conflicts of the seventeenth century that led to civil wars in disputes that occurred in the previous century.

Evidence for growing conflict between Crown and Parliament

Professor Neale found plenty of evidence to suggest that the growing legislative importance of Parliament encouraged factionalism among MPs. The Commons had become a forum for decision making akin to the Privy Council and royal court.

This was particularly the case in religious matters, where the competence of Parliament to enact changes to both the structure and doctrines of the Church had become established in the reign of Henry VIII and then in the succeeding reigns of Edward VI and Mary. Some MPs attempted to use Parliament to reform the Anglican Church, created in 1559, along more radical, Puritan lines.

To do this, they used Commons time to debate the condition of the Church, extending their previously weak privileges of free speech.

Parliament's influence was also increased by the Crown's financial problems. Elizabeth tried to control spending and to increase traditional sources of revenue (see pages 197–98), but was forced to rely heavily on parliamentary subsidies during the years of war against Spain. This gave Parliament financial leverage over the Crown, but also provoked angry exchanges at the demands that the government was making at a time of inflation and economic hardship.

The following pieces of evidence are among those used in support of a growing tendency towards conflicts.

- By the end of Elizabeth's reign, over half of MPs had a university education or were trained lawyers. This helped to create a more self-confident Parliament which was able to argue more strongly against the Crown.
- 1566: MPs angered Elizabeth by discussing the succession question.
- 1563–66: A Puritan party – what the historian Sir John Neale described as the 'Puritan Choir' – emerged as a group of at least 40 MPs who appeared to be fairly organised to press for more religious reforms to take the Church of England further away from Catholicism.
- 1576: Peter Wentworth was imprisoned in the Tower for demanding greater freedom of speech.
- 1586: Norfolk election case – the House of Commmons asserted its right to settle a dispute over the result of the election, even though this was traditionally the Lord Chancellor's responsibility.
- 1584: Puritan members of the Commons reacted with fury to Archbishop Whitgift's attack on godly preachers who wanted reforms to 'purify' the Church of England.
- 1593: MPs discussed a bill to reform the Church, using their claim to free speech. Elizabeth ordered Lord Keeper Pickering to read out a statement to them setting out the extent to which she was prepared to allow free speech. While she recognised that MPs should not be prevented from discussing legislation, the Queen insisted that this did not extend to matters other than legislation which interested them.
- 1601: Parliament clashed with the Queen on the issue of monopolies. MPs successfully refused to grant her additional taxes for the war against Spain unless she agreed to withdraw many of the licences that had been issued.

Evidence against conflict between Crown and Parliament

Recently, a number of these arguments have been challenged by historians who prefer to stress co-operation rather than conflict in the Crown's dealings with Parliament. This was the view of Professor Geoffrey Elton in the 1960s and 1970s, and other historians such as M. A. R. Graves. According to this view, opposition in Parliament was infrequent and disunited, never posing a serious challenge to Elizabeth's authority. Moreover, there was a considerable measure of agreement on most issues between the elite who sat in Parliament and those who directed policy at court. Where disagreements existed, they did not signify a crisis within the ruling elite, but were usually a working out of policy on issues of religion and foreign matters that resolved rather than created conflict. Unlike Charles I in the 1630s, Elizabeth never had any intention of ruling without Parliament.

The following specific pieces of evidence can be cited in support of down-playing the notion of frequent conflicts.

- Only thirteen Parliaments were summoned during Elizabeth's reign, and each sat for short periods – the average was ten weeks per session. For much of the time, Elizabeth ruled through the Privy Council and its machinery of government without the need for parliamentary legislation.
- It is true that Elizabeth used her powers to stop the progress of some Parliamentary bills – that is, her veto – but this was not usually a last attempt to block something that was unwelcome to the Queen. It was usually on the grounds that the bill had defects and her ministers realised that it needed to be redrafted. Many of these bills appeared in later sessions of Parliament and were passed without comment. Sometimes a bill was vetoed because it was realised that it would have unintended consequences. Only a few were vetoed because they were unwelcome to Elizabeth and these concerned Puritan reforms or a requirement for action against Mary Queen of Scots.
- The Commons was an important training ground for future Privy Councillors, a place where political fortunes could be made by catching the attention of the Queen.
- The Commons did not press its demands to settle the disputed Norfolk election of 1586 and conceded the right of the Lord Chancellor in this matter.
- Elizabeth resisted all attempts by Parliament (and the Privy Council) to force her to marry or name a successor.
- The 'Puritan Choir' was a less united and powerful group than Neale has suggested. Religious opposition to the Elizabethan Settlement was not sustained throughout the reign, but flared up in response to particular events (as in 1584). It also failed to bring about any changes.
- Although individual MPs like Wentworth railed against the limitation on their freedom of speech, there was no general support to win this right given Elizabeth's absolute opposition to it.
- Elizabeth summoned most of her Parliaments to obtain money. On nearly every occasion, she received the grant that she asked for.
- Much of the work of the Commons involved legislating on uncontentious issues, such as land disputes and town charters. This mundane work performed the important function of creating an outlet for local matters to be resolved quickly and without violence.
- The House of Lords was at least as important in the sixteenth century as the House of Commons. For example, at least one-third of MPs were, in effect, nominated by a lord, with no actual election. Some of the Queen's chief ministers, such as William Cecil (Lord Burghley) had seats in the Lords, not the Commons. Government influence in the Commons was achieved through the presence of 'lesser' ministers such as Sir Christopher Hatton.

Figure 3: The main issues discussed in Elizabeth's Parliaments. These varied from session to session, according to the current situation at home and abroad. Remember that most of the bills introduced were on local issues introduced by individual MPs. The topics listed here are the ones that were potentially contentious. (NB. Finance and religious issues are dealt with later in this chapter. Mary Queen of Scots and foreign policy are dealt with in Chapter 8.)

Date	Issue discussed in Parliament
1559	Religious settlement
1563 and **1566–67**	Marriage and succession
	Voting money for foreign policy
	First calls for further religious reform from Puritans
1571	Religion, following Papal Excommunication in 1570
	Mary Queen of Scots (in prison since 1568 in England)
1572, 1576, 1581	Mary Queen of Scots and Catholic threats
	Wentworth and free speech
1584–85	Jesuit priests, Puritans
	Foreign threat from Spain
1586–87	Mary Queen of Scots
	Puritans
	Freedom of speech
1589	Financial requests for continuing war against Spain
	Puritanism
1593	Religion
	Finance
1597–98	Economic and social problems
	Finance; monopolies
1601	Finance for foreign policy, including Ireland
	Monopolies

Problem of royal finances

How serious were Elizabeth's financial problems?

Elizabeth ruled at a time of inflationary pressure on the economy. The prices of basic commodities rose, but so too did those of goods that the government consumed, such as iron for shipbuilding or provisions for the army. To remain solvent or to stand any chance of pursuing an active foreign policy, the Crown had to increase its revenue. Mary Tudor had already begun the process of examining how to achieve this (see Chapter 5, page 144) and Elizabeth largely continued and developed this work. Between 1558 and 1603 royal income increased by approximately 50 per cent, just enough to keep pace with price inflation, but not enough to afford prolonged war against Spain after 1585. Revenues were raised by exploiting traditional sources of income rather than by innovating:

- The new Book of Rates introduced at the end of Mary's reign increased the income from customs duties on exports. The recovery of the cloth industry after the crash of the 1550s also helped to generate taxes.
- As head of the Church, Elizabeth claimed income from a variety of religious sources, such as the 'first fruits' tax on all new ecclesiastical office-holders.

NOTE-MAKING

Make notes on (a) the causes of financial problems, and (b) the ways in which the government tried to keep Elizabeth solvent.

- Parliament was approached to grant additional subsidies to finance foreign policy.
- Crown lands, some appropriated from the Church in the 1530s, were sold off to raise £800,000.
- Monopoly rights to produce or import particular products were sold to merchants.

Elizabeth also attempted to control expenditure. Part of her cautious approach to foreign policy, especially to direct military action in support of French or Dutch Protestant rebels, stemmed from her recognition that she lacked the money to sustain a war against Spain. Like Henry VII, Elizabeth tried to conserve her finances by using diplomacy rather than open combat. Other methods of saving money included underpaying officials and delaying the appointment of bishops when positions became vacant (so that the Crown could collect Church taxes).

Source I From a speech by Chancellor of the Exchequer, Sir Walter Mildmay, addressing the House of Commons in 1576, explaining Elizabeth's financial problems.

But lest peradventure that some members [of the House of Commons] may judge that the financial contribution granted by us five years ago might suffice for many years without any new; I dare assure you for the acquaintance I have with her Majesty's affairs, that the same hath not been sufficient to answer [cover] the extraordinary charges [expenditures] since then, not even half, and her Majesty hath supplied the rest out of her own revenues not sparing herself to serve the necessity of the realm ...]

> How was Sir Walter Mildmay trying to explain the need for the House of Commons to grant more taxation (Source I)?

At first sight, these policies seem to have been successful. Although Elizabeth left the Crown in debt, she had enough money to defend England against the vastly superior military strength of Spain when war broke out in the last two decades of her reign (see pages 224–27). Some historians, however, have been more critical of these policies and have pointed out that Elizabeth's failure to transform radically what was essentially her father's financial system left the Crown underfunded. They also challenge the idea that the growth in income was a success, arguing that Burghley, the Lord Treasurer for much of the reign, was inefficient at extracting the maximum value from the Crown's assets. (See also Chapter 8, pages 236–38, for a description of the state of England in 1603 when Elizabeth died.) Looking beyond Elizabeth's reign, modern historians also note that financial weakness was a principal reason why the Crown was forced to rely on Parliament in the seventeenth century. Since this created tension in the relationship between Crown and Parliament and ultimately contributed to the civil wars of Charles I's reign, it is tempting to see Elizabeth's caution as one of the long-term causes of this conflict, a connection suggested by A. G. R. Smith (see Source J).

Source J From *The Emergence of a Nation State: the Commonwealth of England, 1529–1660* by A. G. R. Smith, (Longman), 1984. Smith suggests that Elizabeth's financial policies:

... left Burghley's successors in the office of Lord Treasurer in charge of an old fashioned financial machine which brought the government a much smaller proportion of national resources than it might reasonably have enjoyed. Even more important, perhaps, it accustomed the landed and trading classes to a situation in which they paid a very small part of their income in taxation. When they were called on to give more under the early Stuarts their reluctance and resentments caused major difficulties for the crown.

4 Elizabeth: Religion and religious ideas

The Elizabethan Church Settlement of 1559 (see pages 158–61) appeared at the time to be a triumph of moderate common sense over bigoted extremist views. It appeared to satisfy the wishes of the vast majority and reflected the mood of the nation in desiring a period of stability. However, in matters of religion, deeply held convictions are not easily put aside, and it was not long in Elizabeth's reign before it became clear that the compromise of 1559 was not accepted by all. Some wanted to purify the Church of England of 'Popish' elements of worship and doctrine. Others wanted the restoration of the traditional religion under the Pope, with all the ceremonies and beliefs associated with it.

This section provides details of how the Catholic threat and Puritan influences developed during Elizabeth's reign. Although you do not need to know all the narrative details, it's important to understand how religious issues affected foreign policy, dealings with Mary Queen of Scots, relations with Parliament, the issue of the succession and so on. You also need to be able to write about how religious developments reflected both change and continuity, and how this led to the situation at the end of Elizabeth's reign.

Catholic threat in England

How successful was Elizabeth in maintaining a unified Church of England?

In the first decade of her reign Elizabeth clearly hoped to win over the English Catholics to her compromise Church. Public celebration of the mass was forbidden, but little was done to limit private worship. Recusancy laws were passed to force attendance at church, but Elizabeth hoped that, by keeping many traditional ceremonies, she could make the new Church of England an acceptable alternative for all but the most dedicated Papists.

Catholicism in the first decade of Elizabeth's reign

Elizabeth's government moved cautiously against possible Catholics, or Recusants as they were known. Fines were imposed for those not attending the Church of England services. There were fines or confiscation of land for anyone persuading a priest to say the Catholic Mass. Any priest conducting a Catholic service could be imprisoned. The penalties were deliberately relatively severe, but not harsh as Elizabeth had no intention of creating martyrs.

It appeared at first that Catholicism had little support after Elizabeth's accession. Although most of Mary's bishops refused to accept Elizabeth's religious changes and were deprived of their positions, few parish priests refused the Oath of Supremacy. However, this does not mean that they were all wholeheartedly behind the Church of England. Regional surveys show that in some areas (e.g. Lancashire) there was substantial support for Catholicism. It is true that not many fines for non-attendance were collected, but that was due to the failure to collect them. Many clergy in the 1560s led worship that contained traces of Catholicism, for example, by using Latin rather than English. Historians such as Christopher Haigh have found plenty of evidence of this in their local studies.

This cautious policy stemmed from the Queen herself. Often she had to silence the more radical Protestants who spoke out against Catholicism. Remember that it was also in this decade that Foxe's *Book of Martyrs* was first published,

> **Recusant** – The term recusant applies to those who refused to attend their parish church on a regular basis. Attendance was made compulsory by Parliament and anyone who failed to go was fined, initially 1 shilling (5 pence) for each failure. This was a significant amount of money for anyone below the gentry and may be one reason why Catholicism lasted longer within the gentry and nobility.

cataloguing all the horrors of the Protestant burnings in Mary's reign (see Chapter 5, Source D, page 140). The Parliament of 1563 passed a more strict law against office-holders such as lawyers and MPs who refused the Oath of Supremacy, with a second refusal carrying the death penalty. Any priest saying Mass would be sentenced to death. However, these laws were not fully implemented – on the instructions of Elizabeth herself to Archbishop Parker. No one was asked a second time to subscribe to the Oath; therefore, there was no death penalty. No Catholic priest was executed for saying Mass until 1577 – and this harshness reflected the huge change in the international situation by then.

Change of policy towards Catholics, 1567–72

Between 1567 and 1572 Elizabeth found it increasingly difficult to sustain her tolerance. A number of events at home and abroad changed the image she had of English Catholics as a discontented group into a positive threat to her survival:

- In 1567 the Pope showed his hostility to the Religious Settlement by instructing English Catholics not to attend Anglican Church services.
- In 1567 the Spanish Duke of Alba was sent to the Netherlands to put down the rebellion that had broken out there against Spanish Catholic rule. The presence of 10,000 Spanish troops just across the Channel from southern England raised fears that Spain might be intending to force England back to Catholicism.
- In 1568 Mary Queen of Scots arrived in England seeking sanctuary. She seemed to represent all the worst scenarios of English foreign policy – the Catholic contender for Elizabeth's throne; a Catholic successor if Elizabeth had no heir herself; a focus for the traditional hatred of Scotland; and someone who would encourage a French–Scottish alliance against England.
- In 1568 a seminary (training college) for priests was founded by William Allen in Douai in the Netherlands to train missionaries to go to England to support Catholics.

Source K From a report in the Spanish state papers, dated 28 December 1579, a decade after the setting up of the seminary at Douai.

The number of Catholics, thank God, is daily increasing here, owing to the College and seminary for Englishmen which your Majesty [Philip II] ordered to be supported in Douai, from where there has come in the last year (and from the College of Rome) a hundred Englishmen who have been ordained there, by which means a great number of people are being converted, generally persons who have never heard the truth preached before. These priests go about disguised as laymen, and although they are young men, their good life, fervency and zeal in their work are admirable.

- In 1569 leading Catholic northern nobles, led by the Earls of Northumberland and Westmorland, rebelled against Elizabeth. The background to this was a conspiracy for Thomas Howard, Duke of Norfolk and a Catholic sympathiser, to marry Mary Queen of Scots. At the very least this would help Mary to be seen as first in line to succeed Elizabeth and ensure the restoration of Catholicism. The Earls of Northumberland and Westmorland had been in touch with the Pope and Spain with the intention of securing military backing in support of Norfolk and Mary.
  Elizabeth I learnt of the plan for the marriage and quickly forbade it. Norfolk begged for mercy from the Queen and was sent to the Tower. Rather than come to meet Elizabeth, Northumberland and Westmorland led a rebellion. The rebels entered Durham, replaced the Protestant communion

How reliable about the strength of Catholic support do you think Source K is likely to be?

table in the cathedral with Catholic symbols and restored the Catholic Mass. The rebels failed to gain much support, except in North Yorkshire, and a government army marched north to meet them. The rebel leaders fled to Scotland.

- In 1570 the Pope finally excommunicated Elizabeth. Pius V hoped to encourage other Catholics to join the rebellion. In doing so, he declared that all Catholics were free of any oaths of loyalty to her. Any Catholic obeying her would also incur the sentence of excommunication. This provided direct encouragement to Catholics in England and abroad to oppose Elizabeth's rule. It provided a justification for rebellions centred on Mary Queen of Scots and for Catholic Europe to wage war on England.
- In 1571 the Ridolfi Plot was uncovered which planned to murder Elizabeth and replace her with Mary (see Chapter 8, page 217).
- In 1572 Catholics in France slaughtered Protestants during the St Bartholomew Day celebrations and brought the religious wars there to a temporary end. Elizabeth feared that France would now turn its attention to heresy in England.

Despite this list of problems, Elizabeth was cautious about provoking an outright confrontation with English Catholics. A new Treason Act was introduced in 1571 making the denial of Elizabeth's supremacy or the importation of the Pope's order of excommunication acts punishable by death, but, beyond that, she consistently blocked attempts by the more aggressively Protestant MPs to increase penalties for recusancy or attendance at mass.

Source L From The Papal Bull of Excommunication, February 1570.

... Elizabeth, the pretended queen of England ... having seized the crown and monstrously usurped the place of supreme head of the church in all England ... has followed and embraced the errors of the heretics ... We declare her to be deprived of her pretended title to the aforesaid crown.

▲ An engraving of one of the attempts to assassinate the Queen. This image should be read like a cartoon because it shows a number of events. In the left panel the would-be assassin is arrested. In the centre, the Queen is shown safe on the throne. On the right, the remorseful assassin commits suicide before his trial by drinking poison.

Jesuits

Founded in 1534, the Society of Jesus, or the Jesuits as its members were more commonly known, was a religious order dedicated to serving the Pope. Jesuits underwent rigorous spiritual training to emerge as dedicated enemies of anti-Catholic beliefs and used their influence as educators to the rich and powerful in Europe to mount an effective counter-attack against Protestantism.

Edmund Campion (1540–81)

Edmund Campion was one of the first Jesuits to work as a Catholic missionary in England. He arrived in secret in 1580 and travelled to Lancashire, which had the greatest concentration of Catholics who would not accept the Anglican beliefs of Elizabeth's Church. There, and later in London, he preached in the homes of important Catholic families, disguising his identity and using safe houses to avoid arrest. Although this afforded him some protection, the government was sufficiently concerned about the threat of the Jesuits to use spies to locate, arrest and execute him in 1581.

Why were Edward Campion and others brought to trial? What was their defence?

Catholicism in the 1570s

In many ways the decline of Catholicism in England from the 1570s was brought about by the Catholics themselves rather than by Elizabeth's actions. By forbidding them to attend church the Pope exposed Catholics to fines for recusancy that few could afford and forced them to choose between their loyalty to Rome and loyalty to friends and neighbours, because in many ways the parish church lay at the centre of village life. Attacks by foreigners on Elizabeth, such as the excommunication order and the plotting by Ridolfi and others, were not popular with English Catholics, who could see a difference between Elizabeth as the illegitimate head of the Church and Elizabeth as their rightful monarch. Most landowners were happy with the stability of Elizabeth's reign. Elizabeth had inherited the throne lawfully through Parliamentary statutes. If her right of inheritance were to be questioned, so could the inheritances of landowners. Social stability was much preferable to anarchy.

Arrival of the missionary priests

A 'new Catholic' emerged in the mid-1570s with the arrival of Catholic priests, specially trained, from Europe. They mostly came from Douai in the Netherlands where there was a Catholic seminary, founded by William Allen, an Englishman. It was created for Catholics in England who could be trained as priests for England (see Source K, page 200). The first four priests arrived in England in 1574. By the 1590s there were over one hundred. They moved around in secret, living with Catholic families.

In 1580 another wave of priests began to arrive – the Jesuits. They were specially trained members of the Society of Jesus which focused on missionary activity. The first two, Edmund Campion and Robert Parsons, began building up a network of safe houses, often with specially-constructed priest hiding holes.

Source M A report of the trial of Edmund Campion, from *Chronicals of England, Scotland and Ireland* by Raphael Holinshed, (1577).

On Monday, being the twentieth of November, Edmund Campion, Ralph Sherwin, Lucas Kerbie, Edward Rishton, Thomas Coteham, Henry Orton, Robert Johnson and James Bosgrave were brought unto the high bar at Westminster where they were severally and together indicted upon high treason. When they convicted them of these matters (which with obstinacy they still denied), they came to the intent of their secret coming into this realm, which was the death of her Majesty and the overthrow of the kingdom. 'Yea,' saith Campion, 'never shall you prove this, that we came over either for this intent or purpose, but only for the saving of souls, which mere love and conscience compelled us to do, for that we did pity the miserable state of our country.

Reactions to the Catholic threat, 1580s and 1590s

In the 1570s the Douai priests were not initially seen as a major threat. However, by the late 1570s, and with deteriorating relations with Spain and the continued presence in prison of Mary Queen of Scots, the government was forced into action. Several priests were executed for denying the royal supremacy.

The Jesuits were seen as fanatics and therefore more dangerous. Campion was executed in 1581. Parliament when it met wanted to impose severe penalties on any Catholic worship. After several attempts, Parliament agreed on an Act in 1581 'to retain the Queen's Majesty's subjects in their due obedience'.

Penalties were harsh. Saying Mass incurred a fine of 200 **marks** and a year's imprisonment. Failure to attend church incurred a fine of £20 a month – sums that ordinary people could not afford.

With Mary Queen of Scots still being a focus for discontented Catholics, there were more plots. One was the Throckmorton Plot in 1583 where French Catholics planned to invade England in support of English Catholics, the expedition being paid for by Spain and the Pope. It was easily defeated, but Elizabeth came to agree with Parliament that the situation was critical.

In 1585 an even more extreme Act was passed – 'Against Jesuit seminary priests and other disobedient persons'. Catholic priests were to leave the country within 40 days. Even their continued presence in England would be deemed as high treason. In Elizabeth's reign nearly 150 Catholic priests were executed, most of them under this Act. This was very closely linked to the drift to war with Spain in the mid-1580s and the pressing need for Elizabeth to act against Mary Queen of Scots (see Chapter 8).

With a combination of harsh laws and the wish of most Catholics to remain as loyal subjects of the Crown, Catholicism became less of a threat. In some parts of the country, especially among the landed classes, Mass was still practised in secret. The strongholds were mostly in North and West Yorkshire, South and West Lancashire, Herefordshire and South Wales. But there was little enthusiasm for plots against Elizabeth.

How much the seminary priests achieved in keeping Catholicism alive until the next reign is a matter of dispute. Some historians have argued that Protestantism had nearly wiped out Catholicism until the priests arrived and gained converts. Others have argued that the success of Protestantism at the beginning of Elizabeth's reign has been exaggerated, with the government not seeking to pry too much into what happened in some of the great houses of England. Whichever view is held, it is true that Catholicism was surviving in the 1590s, often based on gentry households and a few of the nobility. However, among the ordinary people Catholicism appears to have had less support. The Catholic cause was not helped in the late 1580s and 1590 with disputes between the Douai priests and the Jesuits. The Jesuits were firmly behind Spain's plans to invade England; the Douai priests urged caution in supporting Spain because Philip II was not just fighting against England in the cause of Catholicism. He had his own agenda centred on power and wealth.

Overall, then, Elizabeth's cautious policy towards Catholics seems to have been a success. She gained the instinctive loyalty of almost all her subjects, including the landowners who had most to lose if they rebelled. It is estimated that in 1603 perhaps ten per cent of the population had Catholic sympathies, but that only two per cent were active recusants.

Who were the Puritans?

To what extent did the Puritans threaten the stability of the Church of England in the reign of Elizabeth I?

Just as the Elizabethan Church settlement had offended hardline Catholics, it also was rejected by some Protestants. Inevitably, by creating a Church which drew on both traditions, the settlement included elements that some Protestants found difficult to accept because the restored Church of England, though Protestant in theology, was so traditional in its structure and rituals. 'Puritans' wanted to purify the Church of its papal elements.

Marks – Two-thirds of a pound (in pre-decimal currency, 13s 4d).

KEY DATES: CATHOLICISM IN ELIZABETHAN ENGLAND

1567 Pope forbade Catholics to attend Anglican services

1568 Arrival of Mary Queen of Scots in England – imprisoned; foundation of Catholic seminary at Douai to train priests for England

1569 Revolt of the Northern Earls

1570 Excommunication of Elizabeth by the Pope – not well received by many English Catholics

1571 Treason Act against bringing the letter of excommunication into England; Ridolfi Plot

1580 Arrival of Jesuit missionaries such as Campion

1581 Execution of Campion

1583 Throckmorton Plot against Elizabeth

1585 Act against Jesuits and Seminary Priests that assumed Catholic missionaries were automatically guilty of treason

1587 Execution of Mary Queen of Scots

1588 English Catholics rejected call to support Spanish Armada

The word 'Puritan' has often been used as a term of abuse or at least with negative connotations, such as Puritans seen as the enemies of all forms of enjoyment. It is therefore important to see why some Protestants were genuinely dissatisfied with the 1559 settlement, hoping that this would be a stepping-stone towards further Protestant reforms.

In particular, they opposed the survival of bishops within the new order, arguing that they were an invention of the Pope to maintain his power rather than a creation of the early Christian Church. These Protestants also examined the Bible for other evidence that the shape of the English Church was not that ordained by God and discovered that, among other things, making the sign of the cross during baptisms and the wearing of clerical vestments had no scriptural authority.

This sort of hardline stand against Catholicism within the English Church, together with a desire to create a simpler, more biblical form of worship, characterised the Puritan tendency. From the outset, we must be careful not to think of the Puritans as a 'group' because there was no real organisation among them. They held various shades of opinion about what they would and would not accept about the Elizabethan settlement and about how far they wanted further religious reform to go. However, all shared the belief that the English Reformation had not been completed in 1559 and, because of this, they threatened the stability of the Elizabethan settlement just as effectively as Catholic recusants.

In practice, there were three main strands of Puritan thought in Elizabeth's reign:

- The **moderate Puritan** strand, which reluctantly accepted the structure of the Church and pressed for reform of beliefs and religious practices along the lines of the European churches.
- The **Presbyterian** strand, which called for a thorough reform of the structure of the Church and the simplifying of faith and ritual, especially as Presbyterianism was well established in Scotland.
- The **Separatist** strand, which broke away from the national Church to pursue its own radical Protestant reformation, on a parish-by-parish basis.

Early stages of Puritanism in Elizabeth's reign

Puritanism pre-dated the Elizabethan settlement. The educated elite of merchants, lawyers and craftsmen had been influenced in the 1520s by the teachings of Luther and other continental reformers who had criticised the state of the Catholic Church (see Chapters 1 and 2). They had used arguments that would have been recognised by their grandchildren in the 1570s. Since then, in the last years of Henry VIII's reign and Edward VI's reign, Calvin's influence had been keenly felt in England, especially with its emphasis on predestination and the notion of the godly elect (see Chapter 5, page 128). So the Puritan element in society began to voice its concerns at the nature of the Church settlement devised in 1559 before the ink was even dry on the Acts of Supremacy and Uniformity. Complaints that the settlement was too Catholic came to a head during the discussions in Convocation (the Church parliament) about the Thirty Nine Articles of faith in 1563 (which were passed by only one vote) and in the Vestiarian Controversy of 1566.

Vestiarian Controversy

Vestments were the special clothes worn by the clergy during services. As part of the drive towards uniformity, Elizabeth wrote to Archbishop Parker (Archbishop of Canterbury) in 1565, reminding him of the need to ensure that all clergy were following the religious practices set out in the Injunctions of 1559. In 1566 Parker issued a Book of Advertisements which set out what was expected, such as those receiving communion kneeling, not standing. In particular, in terms of dress code he insisted on the surplice and cope (i.e. long cloak) as standard apparel. In London, thirty-seven clergymen refused to follow this instruction and were suspended. Although the incident might seem trivial to modern eyes, it symbolised an important point at the time. The vestments chosen by Parker were very similar to Catholic clothing, and so offended Protestant preachers who were forced to wear them. Their refusal raised the further question of how far the Queen's authority as Supreme Governor of the Church extended. Parker wanted to compromise – indeed, he had watered down the requirements in his Book of Advertisements. He recognised that the Bible did not prescribe particular clothing, and was forced to fall back on the requirements being the Queen's wishes as Supreme Governor of the Church. The controversy rumbled on with no conclusion and no explicit support from the Queen who had no wish to provoke enemies at a time when the threat from Catholicism was growing (see previous section, pages 199–203). Archbishop Parker remained, working as a scholar, as Archbishop of Canterbury until his death in 1575.

Presbyterian demands in the 1570s

It was a series of lectures by the Professor of Divinity at Cambridge University, Thomas Cartwright, in the spring of 1570 which brought the radical dimension of Puritanism to national, and royal, attention. In his lectures Cartwright argued for the abolition of bishops and called for a form of Church government based on that developed by the reformer John Calvin in Geneva. Calvin had established a structure in which control was exercised by the minister of each church, helped by respected elders of the community. This model, argued Cartwright, could be adapted to fit the parish system in England and could be given national cohesion through Calvin's other idea of having regional committees and a national assembly of the whole Church. Such a system, known as a Presbyterian model of the Church, was said to be closer to the form of organisation justified in the Bible.

Elizabeth's reaction to Cartwright's ideas was open horror. The Presbyterian system involved abolishing bishops and left very little room for a 'Supreme Governor'. If she had any doubts about the revolutionary implications of this sort of change, she had only to look to Scotland, where the introduction of Presbyterianism in the 1560s had been accompanied by the overthrow of Mary Queen of Scots.

In practice, Cartwright had little practical influence, but the matter was debated in the House of Commons in 1571 when Thomas Strickland tried to suggest changes to the structure of the Church of England, but most of the bishops were horrified, as was Elizabeth. As a result, the Thirty Nine Articles of 1563 were formally approved by Parliament and this meant that clergy had to accept those articles as a condition of gaining an appointment in the Church.

In 1572 another writer, John Field, published *Admonitions to the Parliament*. The book argued that a Presbyterian Church structure was the only one sanctioned by the Bible: that the terms ministers, elders and deacons come from scripture; there is no mention of bishops. In an additional pamphlet Field denounced the Book of Common Prayer as 'Popish'. He was imprisoned for a year as a result.

Source N From A View of Popish Abuses yet Remaining in the English Church by John Field, 1572.

[The Book of Common Prayer] is an unperfect book, culled and picked out of that popish dunghill, the Mass book, full of all abominations ... In this book we are enjoined to receive the Communion kneeling, which has in it a show of popish idolatry ... The public baptism ... is also full of childish and superstitious toys ... marking the child in the forehead with a cross.

What aspects of Catholicism is John Field criticising in Source N?

Source O From Peter Wentworth's speech in the House of Commons, 8 February 1576.

I have never seen in any Parliament but the last the liberty of free speech in so many ways infringed, with so many abuses offered to this honourable House. The Queen said that we should not deal in any matters of religion, except what we receive from the bishops. Surely this was a doleful message; for it meant, 'Sirs, ye shall not deal in God's causes, no, ye shall in no way advance His glory'. It is a dangerous thing in a prince unkindly to abuse his or her nobility and people, and it is a dangerous thing in a prince to oppose or bend herself against her nobility and people, yea against most faithful and loving nobility and people.

1 Why would the Queen be angry with Peter Wentworth's speech (Source O)?
2 Was Elizabeth justified on grounds of religion in rejecting each of the points in Source P?
3 What are Elizabeth's reasons for banning prophesyings (Source Q)?

However, other events meant that disputes between the Church of England and Puritan groups quietened down for a while. In particular, in 1572 the massacre of thousands of Huguenots (French Protestants) in Paris on St. Bartholomew Day horrified all Protestants in England. The continuing threats from Spain and from Catholic priests beginning to arrive in England also meant that all Protestant groups had a common cause. The Queen herself did not want religious change. In 1576 she gave explicit instructions that Parliament was not to debate religious matters without her permission, and imprisoned Peter Wentworth in the Tower when he challenged her (see Source O).

Archbishop Grindal and the 'prophesyings'

Outside Parliament, the government became alarmed at the spread of 'prophesying'. Prophesyings were generally well-organised gatherings of clergymen at which young or unlicensed preachers could practise their art and receive advice from their more experienced colleagues. Many of the gatherings had the full support of the local bishop, although these meetings did not always show the influence of Presbyterian views on the structure of the Church. Their main emphasis was on educating the clergy and laity. However, those opposing the meetings could argue that the Puritan clergy were able to increase the number of competent preachers at their disposal and get around the tight licensing laws.

In 1576 news reached Elizabeth of some unorthodox preaching at a prophesying in Southam, in Warwickshire. She ordered her new Archbishop of Canterbury, Edmund Grindal, to suppress prophesyings, but he consulted other bishops and came to the conclusion that the meetings were not dangerous. He therefore refused to accept the Queen's instructions and, for good measure, lectured her about the importance of this sort of work in spreading the word of God and ensuring the well-being of souls.

Source P From a letter by Archbishop Grindal to Queen Elizabeth I, 1576.

I and others of your Bishops have found by experience that these profits come from these exercises [prophesyings]:

1. The ministers of the Church are more skilful and ready in the Scriptures, and apter to teach their flocks.
2. It withdraweth their flocks from idleness, wandering, gaming etc.
3. Some suspected of doctrinal error are brought to open confession of the truth.
4. Ignorant ministers are driven to study, if not for conscience then for shame and fear of discipline.
5. The opinion of laymen about the idleness of the clergy is removed.
6. Nothing beateth down Popery more than that ministers grow to such a good knowledge by means of these exercises.

Elizabeth did not respond well to this godly instruction. She had Grindal placed under virtual house arrest in his residence at Lambeth Palace and for the remaining seven years of his life he was unable to function as leader of the Church. Meanwhile, Elizabeth issued direct orders to her bishops that prophesyings were to stop.

Source Q Elizabeth's instructions to the bishops banning prophesyings.

In sundry parts of our realm there are no small number of persons which, contrary to our laws established for the public divine service of Almighty God and the administration of the holy sacraments within this Church of England, do daily devise, imagine, propound and put into execution sundry new rites and forms as well by procuring unlawful assemblies of a great number of our people out of their ordinary parishes ... which manner of invasions they in some places call prophesying and in some other places exercises ... we will charge you that the same forthwith cease. But if any shall attempt, or continue, or renew the same, we will you not only to commit them unto prison as maintainers of disorders, but also to advertise us, or our council, of the names and qualities of them, and of their maintainers and abettors.

Whitgift's attack on Presbyterianism in the 1580s

The 1580s saw the purging from the national Church of its Presbyterian elements. In 1583 Edmund Grindal died and Elizabeth appointed a devout Anglican, John Whitgift, to replace him. Whitgift, who was known affectionately by Elizabeth as 'my little black husband' because of his sombre clothing, shared many of Elizabeth's views and prejudices (he was unmarried, for example). He had no sympathy with the Puritans and was determined to enforce uniformity.

He immediately issued Three Articles that would have forced all ministers to swear an absolute acceptance of bishops and of all that was contained in the Prayer Book and the Thirty Nine Articles. The result was uproar, and within weeks about 300 ministers had been suspended in the south of England alone. Letters of complaint from local gentry enabled many of these men to be reinstated, but the tone of the new Church administration had been set. Over the next few years strict controls were enforced to end prophesyings and suppress any other developments of Presbyterian practices.

Source R From the Three Articles of 1583.

That none be permitted to preach, read, minister the sacraments, or to execute any other ecclesiastical function unless he consent and subscribe to these Articles following:

That her Majesty, under God, hath, and ought to have, the sovereignty and rule over all manner of persons born within her realms, either ecclesiastical or temporal, soever they be.

That the Book of Common Prayer containeth in it nothing contrary to the word of God, and that he himself will use the form of the said book prescribed in public prayer and administration of the sacraments, and none other.

That he alloweth the book of Articles, agreed upon by the archbishops and bishops of both provinces (Canterbury and York), and that he believeth all the Articles therein contained to be agreeable to the word of God.

> Why was each of these three articles in Source R thought to be important at the time?

Development of 'classes' in the 1580s

The word 'classes' is the plural of 'classis' which was the term used for regional meetings to which congregations sent representatives for discussion on issues. There is evidence that these developed in some areas of the country in the 1580s. It would be tempting to believe that the development was in response to Whitgift's hard line on Prophesyings and Presbyterianism, as the informal organisation suggested a structure that resembled that of the Presbyterian Church in Scotland. The evidence suggests that many of these meetings were broadly 'Puritan' in nature and were genuine attempts to discuss and to educate clergy and lay people. Most clergy accepted Whitgift's Three Articles, having no desire to upset the established social structure of society in which the Church of England had a central role.

Similarly, in the Parliament of 1586–87 there were demands, led by the MP Anthony Cope, for the introduction of a Calvinist Prayer Book, which assumed a Presbyterian Church structure, to replace the Book of Common Prayer. Cope and some of his supporters were dispatched to the Tower. While MPs showed some sympathy with genuine Puritan grievances (in some cases siding against over-zealous bishops), there was little support for any change to the structure of the English Church. This was reflected in the country as a whole, and where some areas, such as large parts of the south-east, showed Puritan sympathies, other parts tended to be close to Catholicism. Nowhere was there widespread support for a Presbyterian Church structure.

Separatist movement

Because Protestantism insisted that the Bible was the only source of religious teaching and that it should be made available to all in their own language, the separate development of individual churches was always a possibility. In England, some congregations did follow that path, using isolated, voluntary gatherings to explore the Bible and to reach their own conclusions about the direction their faith should take them. Evidence of early Separatists is notoriously difficult to gather since their activities were illegal and therefore secret. The experience of persecution under Mary had certainly created some Separatist groups, but hope of real reformation under Elizabeth meant that the vast majority of Elizabethan Puritans were, and remained, members of the national Church. By 1583, however, it was clear that they were not going to bring about reform by remaining within the Anglican Church, so small groups of Separatists began to emerge.

Brownists

The Brownists are one of the best documented of the Separatist groups. In 1580 an impatient reformer named Robert Browne had established a Separatist congregation in Norwich. After a brief spell of imprisonment he left England and settled in Holland where he wrote *A Treatise of Reformation Without Tarrying For Any*. In it, Browne argued that the Church of England was corrupted by its Catholic traces and lack of moral discipline. He said that true Christians should leave it in favour of separate, voluntary gatherings of 'saints' who would exercise proper discipline. In 1583 John Copping and Elias Thacker were hanged for distributing Brownist pamphlets.

Marprelate Tracts, 1588–89

The Separatist movement reappeared in 1588–89 in the form of the scurrilous Martin Marprelate Tracts, a bitter written attack on the Church and the bishops that used foul language and abuse to make its case. The pamphlets were anonymous and printed in London. Although Puritans like Thomas Cartwright were horrified by the tracts and hurriedly disassociated themselves from them, the reaction of both the authorities and public opinion allowed the Privy Council to bring about the final destruction of organised Puritanism.

Cartwright and his associates were hauled before the Court of High Commission and forced to reveal what they knew about the remnants of the prophesyings movement. Government propaganda linked Puritanism to Separatism, and Separatism to treason. In 1593 Parliament was persuaded to pass an Act against Seditious Sectaries which allowed the authorities to execute those suspected of being Separatists.

The emergence of Separatists and the publication of the Marprelate Tracts had provided the ammunition the government needed for an all-out attack on Puritanism. However, it was more difficult to eradicate it as a force in English religious thought, as is seen in the early years of Stuart rule. Hence it is possible to argue that, although the Puritans were seen as a nuisance to Elizabeth's government, their main importance was to be in the Stuart period.

KEY DATES: PURITANISM

1566 Vestiarian Controversy under Archbishop Parker

1570 Cartwright's lectures

1571 Strickland failed to get Parliament to consider changing the structure of the Church of England

1575 Appointment of Grindal as Archbishop of Canterbury

1576 Elizabeth ordered Parliament not to discuss religious matters without permission; suppression of prophesyings and suspension of Grindal for defending them; Peter Wentworth imprisoned

1580 Brownist congregation established in Norwich

1583 Appointment of Whitgift as Archbishop of Canterbury heralded renewed attacks on Puritanism

1587 Cope and others sent to Tower because they argued in Parliament for a Presbyterian Church structure

1588–89 Publication of Marprelate Tracts

1593 Act against Seditious Sectaries

5 Church of England by 1603

The material in this chapter suggests that the new Anglican Church was assaulted by both Protestants and Catholics during its first half century of life. Yet both of these attacks had failed to move the Church from the direction set out in the 1559 settlement.

Reasons for the survival of the Church of England

- Elizabeth had a strong interest in maintaining the 1559 settlement because she saw it as the best way to create both religious and political stability. Her opposition to Puritans meant that they found it difficult to use parliamentary means to change elements of the settlement.
- Elizabeth was aided, after 1583, by John Whitgift, her Archbishop of Canterbury. His uncompromising support for Anglicanism gave her a powerful ally against radical elements within the Church of England.
- The establishment of the Court of High Commission gave the authorities a means to prosecute religious radicals, and laws such as the Treason Act acted as a deterrent to those thinking of reacting against Anglicanism.
- Radicals, by definition, put forward extreme views. Most people accepted the middle-of-the-road approach of the Church of England, with its traditional Catholic appearance and its doctrines which put more stress on personal fulfilment through faith; they disliked the 'innovations' proposed by the Puritans. Because of this, radicalism was not as widespread as might be suggested by the events of the period.
- Peer pressure was important. Attendance at Anglican services was made compulsory from 1559 and fines were introduced to enforce this. In small communities non-attendance was the subject of gossip and could lead to isolation from the rest of the village.
- Catholicism in England was discredited by its association with rebellion against the legitimate monarch and by its undertones of foreign (Spanish and papal) control.
- Events in Europe during Elizabeth's reign – bitter divisions between Puritan minorities and their Catholic rulers in France and the Netherlands resulting in civil wars – reminded Englishmen of the dangers of encouraging religious disagreements.
- By 1603, the Anglican Church had influenced the attitudes of two generations of English people. During this time the religious authorities had made the Church's position more secure by discussing and defining its essential beliefs and by using a licensing system to monitor the quality of the clergy.

Robert Hooker and The Laws of Ecclesiastical Polity, 1593

Anglicanism survived because it had powerful support and because it offered an acceptable compromise between the extremes of Roman Catholicism and Puritanism. Its supporters gradually developed its theology and were able to establish a credible justification for it. The most effective case for the Anglican Church was made by Richard Hooker in *The Laws of Ecclesiastical Polity* in 1593.

Hooker accepted that the Church of England represented a compromise between the Catholic tradition and the ideas of continental reformers, but

LOOK AGAIN

Look at Key Question 5 on page viii. How far had religious ideas changed and developed during the Tudor period?

argued that this was far from being a mere convenience. Instead, the Anglican 'middle way' represented the true Christian faith, built on medieval tradition and enjoying continuity from the early Church. He said that the unnecessary and superstitious additions made by the medieval papacy had been stripped away to reveal the essentials of early Christianity required for salvation. These essentials were relatively few and simple – faith in Christ based upon reading the Bible and commemoration of Christ's sacrifice on the cross. Other matters such as the nature and conduct of ceremonies and the extent and role of decoration were 'matters indifferent', which could safely be left to the discretion of the monarch and the bishops. Hooker viewed the bishops as not essential to the Church, but accepted them as a convenient and effective way of organising it. For the sake of order and Christian unity the existing ceremonies should be accepted and enjoyed for the decency and order that they provided.

The 1559 settlement had been shaped by political concerns, but time, practice and the authority of tradition had finally enabled it to establish a genuinely Anglican identity that many wished to defend. Catholicism had declined and the attachment that many people had to its ways had been transferred to the Anglican Church. Puritans had pushed too hard and too fast for radical change and had been defeated because of this. Even so, the divisions that Elizabeth had inherited had not healed entirely, and these divisions became wider later in the next century.

In Elizabeth's reign, in political terms, the establishment of Anglicanism had been a success. England had avoided the destructive civil wars over religious identity and choice that had affected France and the Netherlands. Elizabeth had emerged as a strong and independent monarch, partly because she was not bound to the wishes of the Pope and partly because governorship of the Church gave her important powers of patronage as well as a new source of authority over her people.

Shortcomings of the Church of England

In religious terms, the change to Anglicanism produced more mixed results. It did not necessarily answer the criticisms of the clergy that had helped to begin the demand for reformation in the 1520s. Set against the high standards that the Puritans demanded of their ministers, the Anglican Church seemed to contain the same moral laxity that had tainted Catholicism.

Source S From a Puritan *Survey of Ministers* conducted in Essex in 1586.

Mr Ocklei, parson of Much Bursead: a gamester.

Mr Durdent, vicar of Stebbing: a drunkard and a gamester and a very gross abuser of the Scriptures (witnesses: Mr Denham, Mr Rogers, etc.)

Mr Durden, parson of Mashbury: a careless man, a gamester, an ale-house haunter, a company keeper with drunkards and he himself sometimes drunk (witnesses: Richard Reynolds, John Argent, etc.)

Mr Cuckson, vicar of Linsell: unable to preach, he hath been a pilferer.

Source T From a report to the Royal Council concerning the state of religion in Lancashire and Cheshire in the early 1590s.

Small reformation has been made in Lancashire and Cheshire as can be seen by the emptiness of churches on Sundays and holidays. The people so swarm the streets and alehouses during service time that many churches have only the curate and his clerk present. The people lack instruction for the preachers are few, most of the parsons unlearned and no examination is made of schools and schoolmasters. The proclamation for the apprehension of Jesuits, seminaries and mass priests is not executed.

1 What do Sources S and T suggest about the state of the Church of England and its clergy during Elizabeth's reign?
2 On what grounds might you be cautious about using these sources as reliable evidence?

Protestant historians saw much to congratulate in the Elizabethan Church settlement, although Catholic writers have been more critical. They have pointed out evidence of ruthlessness in the application of policies and have questioned the wisdom of the whole settlement given the divisions it caused. More recent historians have given a more qualified view of Elizabeth's policies over religion. The explosiveness of Puritanism in the seventeenth century rocked the Church – but it was re-established after the Civil Wars with a structure and set of beliefs that were virtually unchanged from 1559. This has lasted, with some modernising, into the twenty-first century.

KEY DATES: THE CHURCH OF ENGLAND

1559 Re-establishment of Church of England by Act of Parliament

1583 Whitgift became Archbishop of Canterbury

1593 Hooker's *The Laws of Ecclesiastical Polity* published

1603 Death of Elizabeth I

Chapter summary

- Elizabeth's image-making and propaganda methods had a huge effect on how contemporaries viewed her and her reign.
- The court and patronage were an important aspect of royal control over the nobility.
- Elizabeth played an important role as patron of the arts, leading to what is known as the Elizabethan Renaissance.
- Cecil, Lord Burghley, was important in helping to maintain stability and reduce factionalism for nearly 40 years.
- Parliament had an important role in religion and finance, but there were many disputes over issues such as Elizabeth's non-marriage, religion, monopolies and the succession.
- Finance became an important issue, with inflation and Elizabeth's foreign wars from 1585 onwards.
- There was a perceived Catholic threat following the excommunication of Elizabeth and the arrival of Catholic priests including Jesuits in England.
- Puritans wanted to purge the Church of England of Catholic practices.
- Many Puritans wanted a different Church organisation either on the Presbyterians model, or as Separatists.
- The Church of England was developing its own ethos and style with the Queen as Supreme Governor.

Chapter summary diagram

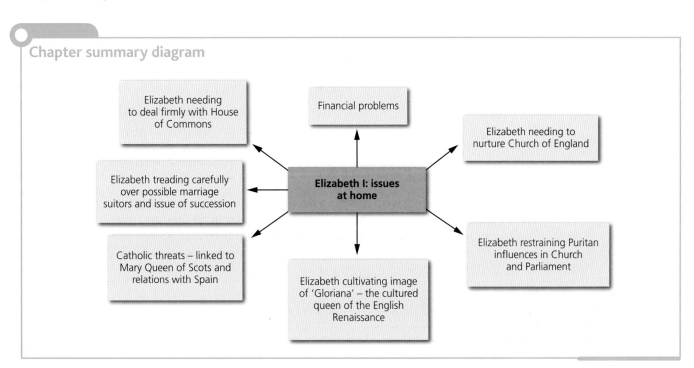

Working on essay technique

So far in the advice given the skills being developed could help a student to write a good essay.

To write an outstanding essay though, all the same skills are needed. In addition:

- all those skills outlined in previous chapters are shown at a high level
- a good understanding shown of issues and concepts (which might on this breadth paper include showing awareness of longer-term perspectives)
- an excellent understanding demonstrated of the historical context, with precise factual information.
- a conclusion that contains a well-substantiated judgement.

In the context of this chapter, there are plenty of opportunities in answering questions about the reign of Elizabeth I to show awareness of broad issues that run through the century – even if it is sometimes a brief comment comparing Elizabeth with her father, Henry VIII.

EXAMPLE

So in the context of Elizabeth I, and the last of the key issues on the role of individuals and groups, consider this A-level practice question:

'It was Elizabeth's influence that was the most important for the development of the arts in her reign.' Assess the validity of this view.

(25 marks)

As you have learnt already (and practised!), you are looking for aspects of developments where she had a huge input and areas where she did not.

There are various aspects in this chapter – and also in Chapter 6 – that you might wish to consider:

- Life at Court; patronage
- The Arts (keen supporter of music, theatre, etc.).
- Importance of other factors and influences – social structure, printing, effects of Renaissance, role of nobility, etc.

In order to achieve Level 5, you need to demonstrate the following characteristics:

- Precise details (names, dates, specialist terms, etc.).
- Clear planning, including a substantial conclusion that leads to a judgement.
- Showing clear understanding of the reign by linking aspects – not treating every aspect as separate.
- Showing breadth of knowledge and understanding, with possible brief references to developments earlier in the century.

You might wish to write a detailed plan for this essay title and then look at the AQA mark scheme for analysis of essay questions (see Chapter 3, page 92). Check that what you have done seems to have reached at least Level 4, and then consider whether it has qualities that suggest that a mark within Level 5 is appropriate.

Working on interpretation skills

At the end of Chapters 2 (pages 65–6), 3 (pages 96–9), and 5 (page 149), there have been sections on interpretations. In the A-level examination Section A you are given three sources and asked to evaluate their reliability.

First, have a look back at the advice in these chapters. Remind yourself of the skills that are being tested. Then study the three extracts below on the theme of Elizabeth and her Parliaments and carry out the activity that follows.

Extract A

In the view of the Tudor sovereigns – and Elizabeth held it to the end – parliaments were summoned to do three things, and three things only: to vote such taxes as were required, to legislate on topics submitted to them, and to give advice on policy when asked. Elizabeth's parliaments certainly fulfilled these functions. Each session was called with some principal object in view ... (However) it was during these sessions that the House of Commons began to grope towards another, and rival, conception of its functions, and in the process to join issue with the Crown. That issue is epitomised in the immortal words 'freedom of speech'...

'Matters of state' could come up only on the royal initiative. Unfortunately, the two questions which touched Members most keenly were by this definition 'matters of state'... Succeeding parliaments went on urging the Queen to ease her subjects' minds by marrying or naming a successor, or at least by disposing of the claim and person of Mary Stuart.

From *Tudor England* by S. T. Bindoff (Penguin), 1950, pp.221–23.

ACTIVITY

Having read the extracts, and using the advice given in previous chapters, make notes on the content, using your knowledge to decide what you agree with and what you disagree with. In practice, it may sometimes be partial disagreements – that is, disagreeing with the emphasis or tone. Then answer the following practice question.

Using your understanding of the historical context, assess how convincing the arguments in these three extracts are in relation to Elizabeth's relations with Parliament during her reign. **[30 marks]**

Extract B

Some historians have argued that Parliament became politicized under Elizabeth; ordinary MPs, especially puritans and common lawyers, according to this view, ventilated their "opposition" to her conservatism. But this interpretation endows the House of Commons with a preconceived status and fails to recognise the influence of the Lords in an aristocratic age. It also falsely presupposes that 'adversary politics' prevailed in the sixteenth century. ... Those who have posited the 'rise' of the Commons have studied Tudor Parliaments from the perspective of a determinist interpretation of the 'origins' of the Civil War and Interregnum. By seeking the origins of the Stuart conflict in the so-called 'apprenticeship to future greatness' of the Elizabethan House of Commons, the leading exponent of this interpretation [J.E. Neale] was driven to manufacture a 'puritan choir' supposedly operating within Elizabeth's early Parliaments.

From *Tudor England* by John Guy (OUP), 1988, p.320.

Extract C

'[In 1601 Elizabeth's] touch was as sure as ever. Before Christmas her words to the deputation in the Council Chamber were in print and later generations were to call it her "golden speech", for she had here put into words, without attempting a definition, the essence of that remarkable relationship between sovereign and people in the golden age of monarchy that passed with her death ... The Commons had responded loyally with voting four subsidies and eight fifteenths and tenths ... Before they dispersed to their homes for Christmas, she gave members ... a masterly survey of policy during the forty-four years as queen, a statesman's swan-song, for with taxation voted for the next four years she knew, surely, she would be unlikely to survive to address another Parliament.'

From *Elizabeth I, Queen of England* by Neville Williams, (Weidenfeld and Nicholson), 1967, p.348.

Conflict and exploration in Elizabeth's reign

This chapter completes the remaining aspects of Elizabeth's reign that are listed in the specification. One main focus is foreign affairs, and this looks at:

- the continuing issues over religion and the succession
- the complications surrounding Mary Queen of Scots
- deteriorating relations with Spain.

The chapter also features the last years of Elizabeth's reign and analyses the state of England at the time of her death in 1603.

This content relates in particular to some of the key questions:

- How effectively did Elizabeth consolidate and develop the powers of the monarchy?
- How did relations with foreign powers change and how was the succession secured?
- How important was the role of Elizabeth and other individuals and groups?

As well as looking at the state of England in 1603, the central question we will focus on in this chapter is:

How successful, and why, was Elizabeth in dealing with foreign threats to her rule?

CHAPTER OVERVIEW

The opening section of this chapter traces the life of Mary, Queen of Scots, in France and Scotland and her disasters over husbands. Her flight to England led to nearly 20 years of imprisonment, during which time there were various plots in which she was an active participant against Elizabeth. Her execution only occurred when Elizabeth had run out of other options.

During the same years relations with Spain deteriorated, primarily over religion and trade, including the activities at sea of English privateers. A state of war existed between England and Spain from the time that English troops invaded the Spanish Netherlands, with Spain retaliating with the Spanish Armada of 1588. English seamen did well out of plundering the Spanish Empire and Elizabeth encouraged voyages of exploration. Nearer to home, the policy of establishing plantations in Ireland continued with, from the English point of view, considerable success.

Throughout Elizabeth's reign the question of the succession loomed large (see Chapters 6 and 7). In the second half of her reign Elizabeth had become too old to produce an heir. Elizabeth herself refused to discuss the question of the succession.

1 Mary Queen of Scots

Mary Queen of Scots dominated the middle section of Elizabeth's reign from the time of her flight into England in 1568 to her execution in February 1587. Here we consider her importance in an overall context, taking fully into account England's foreign policy and the attitudes and actions of England's neighbours, as well as the effects that she had on politics and religion in England.

Mary in France and Scotland

Why was Mary Queen of Scots seen as a threat to Elizabeth in the years before she fled to England?

Mary had been Queen of the Scots since she was one week old, but had spent much of her childhood in France. She returned to Scotland when she was in her late teens. Whether in France or in Scotland, Mary was seen as a threat to Elizabeth's position as Queen of England.

Mary as a young queen

1542 Mary was born, the only child of James V of Scotland; her father died when she was a week old, leaving the country at war with England. Scottish nobles ruled the country on behalf of the infant Queen. If Edward VI of England had lived longer than he did, one plan was that the young Mary would have been married to him. Both were descended from Henry VII.

1548 Mary was taken to France to be educated at court by her mother, Mary of Guise, and was brought up as a Catholic.

1558 She married the heir to the French throne.

1559 Her husband became King Francis II of France.

1560 Francis II died. His sudden death left Mary a widow at the age of eighteen. Her mother died the same year. The situation in France was chaotic with the beginning of what is known as the French Wars of Religion between Catholics and Huguenots (French Protestants).

1561 Mary returned to Scotland to assume the role of Queen there. Since the Treaty of Edinburgh (see Chapter 6, page 161) peace had been restored between England and Scotland and the government was supportive of Protestantism. Rival groups of nobles threatened a situation of civil war. Mary was not allowed any power or even influence. At that point, as the obvious heir to the English throne (except that she was Catholic!), Mary probably saw more of a future for herself in England than in Scotland. After all, she had not even been raised in Scotland and spoke fluent French.

1565 Mary married Lord Darnley (a great grandson of Henry VII), prompting speculation that she intended to claim the English throne – either from Elizabeth as the Catholic heir or after Elizabeth's death. Mary and Lord Darnley were first cousins. He himself had a strong claim to the English throne as well as a more distant one to the Scottish throne. The marriage to Darnley was a disaster. Mary became pregnant, but it was rumoured that the man responsible was David Rizzio, her secretary and lover. Rizzio was murdered in 1566 in front of the pregnant Mary by henchmen under the direction of Lord Darnley. It was widely believed that the murder was the result of Darnley's jealousy. At any rate, Mary gave birth to a boy, James, later in the year – the heir to the Scottish throne and, after his mother, the heir to the throne of England.

In this section on Mary Queen of Scots you should make notes on:
- why Mary in France and Scotland was an issue for Elizabeth
- why Mary fled to England
- how and why Mary was an increasing problem as a prisoner in England
- why she was eventually executed.

1567 Darnley had been recovering from an illness (perhaps smallpox or syphilis). Mary had taken another lover, the Earl of Bothwell. In February 1567 at 2 a.m. the house at Kirk-o-field where Darnley and his valet were sleeping was rocked by an explosion. The evidence suggests that Darnley had actually been murdered by being strangled before the explosion. Bothwell was suspected of being implicated and Mary may well have known of the plot. Suspicions became stronger when Mary and Bothwell ran away together and were married. She later miscarried twins – but by then the marriage had already ended and Bothwell had fled to Denmark. Not surprisingly, few people in Scotland thought that Mary's actions in the 1560s made her a suitable ruler. She was forced to abdicate in favour of her baby son, James. The Earl of Murray, the leader of the Protestant lords, became Regent.

Mary as a prisoner in England

In 1568 Mary fled to England. Elizabeth was in a difficult position. On the one hand she ought to show support for her deposed cousin, but this would mean attacking the Queen's Protestant allies in Scotland. On the other hand not to act would suggest that she agreed that a monarch could be deposed – with obvious implications for the sanctity of hereditary rule for herself as well as other European monarchs.

Elizabeth kept Mary under close scrutiny and house arrest for the next nineteen years. She had become a focal point for Catholic and noble discontent and a potential pawn of Spain or France should they seek to undermine or to depose Elizabeth. One of Elizabeth's ministers summed up the problem of Mary by saying that,

'As long as life is in her, there is hope. As they live in hope, we live in fear.'

Mary Stuart became the focus of plots and intrigues, but Elizabeth was reluctant to take action against her cousin.

Source A An analysis of the problem Mary Queen of Scots caused for Elizabeth in 1568. From *Tudor England* by S. T. Bindoff, (Pelican), 1952.

Mary's arrival set Elizabeth a problem which was only to be solved nineteen years later by her execution. There were really two Mary Stuarts to be dealt with. One was the sister sovereign in exile, who merited honourable asylum and perhaps assistance to regain her throne. The other was the Catholic claimant to the English succession, if not to the English throne, the woman who would be under Elizabeth – only much more actively and dangerously – what Elizabeth had been under Mary Tudor, and Mary Tudor under Somerset and Northumberland, the magnet drawing together scattered elements of religious and political discontent.

How powerful a magnet Mary was her first eighteen months in England amply demonstrated. They saw the first of the reign's conspiracies and its only serious rebellion.

> Explain in your own words the complications caused by Mary Queen of Scots, according to Source A.

Grounds of Mary's deposition

In 1568–69 Mary's case was legally examined, with all three sides represented (Mary, Murray and Elizabeth), first at York and then at Westminster. Murray produced the famous 'Casket' letters, which were documents allegedly found after Mary's flight which proved her to have been Bothwell's mistress and involved in a plot against Darnley even before his death at Kirk-o-Field. The case (using Scottish law) was found not proven, but this was damning enough. Murray returned to Scotland confirmed as Regent. Mary was kept in prison in England – under observation. Elizabeth was playing for time, but the presence of Mary in England soon proved to be a major problem.

Rebellion of the northern earls, 1569

The Spanish ambassador, De Spes, was in touch with Mary Stuart and with disgruntled noblemen, and encouraged rebellion. Spanish troops were in the Netherlands (ruled by Spain) and could be ready to help, but the Duke of Alva refused to intervene until the English had carried out a revolt. The Duke of Norfolk hated Elizabeth's trusted Chief Secretary, William Cecil, regarding his family as upstarts, and resented his dominance at court. As described in Chapter 7 (page 185), the Duke of Norfolk used the situation to plot with others against Elizabeth. At the very least, Mary Stuart would be declared the heir to the throne – assuming that Elizabeth continued to be Queen. In fact, the Northern rebellion did not amount to much, with the Duke of Norfolk surrendering. Other northern earls, having taken Durham, marched south, but their troops melted away when faced with Elizabeth's forces. The government acted severely against the rebels – 800 people, almost all of them commoners, were hanged.

Although the rebellion was not as serious as it first seemed it did have important consequences. Elizabeth took the opportunity to take firmer control of the north of England, which had in many respects been semi-independent under feudal lords. Now the Council of the North was reconstituted under the leadership of the Puritan Earl of Huntingdon. The second consequence was that Elizabeth and her government had to take the threat posed by Mary extremely seriously, especially as events unfolded in the next few years. The first of these was the Papal Excommunication of 1570 (see Chapter 7, page 201 for the significance of this).

Ridolfi Plot, 1571

Roberto Ridolfi was a Florentine merchant who had settled in England and had been involved in the plotting in favour of Mary Stuart in 1569. Now he took a leading part in a plot to get rid of Elizabeth and put Mary, married to Norfolk, on the English throne. William Cecil (now Lord Burghley) soon gathered much intelligence through his network of informers and then gained more through the use of torture. The leaders and accomplices were arrested. Norfolk was found guilty of treason and sentenced to death. Elizabeth hesitated over signing the execution warrant but had her hand forced by Parliament when it met in 1572. Elizabeth gave way to the pressure for his execution, but not to demands for the execution of Mary Stuart. The Spanish ambassador, De Spes, was expelled from England.

Mary was kept in prison, a continual embarrassment to Elizabeth and a constant threat. However, if Elizabeth had agreed to Mary's death, war against Spain would have been virtually inevitable at a time when Elizabeth was still using marriage diplomacy around Europe to try to ensure continuing peace.

In the 1580s the situation changed. A papal pronouncement in 1580 stated that anyone who assassinated Elizabeth with the 'pious intention of doing God's service, not only does not sin, but gains merit'. In the 1580s Catholic priests were joined by Jesuit missionaries, and the activities of Elizabethan seamen against the Spanish Empire made war against Spain almost inevitable. Mary herself saw Spanish intervention as the best hope of ending her imprisonment and gaining the throne of England.

Source B Elizabeth's attitude towards Mary in 1572. From *The Elizabethan Epic* by L. B. Smith, (Panther), 1969, p.194.

There is no doubt that had Elizabeth listened to her Parliament, Mary of Scotland would have died in 1572. Loyal Englishmen were convinced that she was an immoral and dangerous female and were determined to 'cut off her head and make no more ado about her', but Elizabeth could not bring herself to execute a divinely appointed sovereign. To do so was impolitic (it set a dangerous precedent) and immoral (Mary was one of God's lieutenants on earth). So Mary Stuart lived another fifteen years, surrounded by English spies but still possessed of a queen's household and always confident that some new plot might yet succeed.

In what ways does the author of Source B suggest that the situation between Elizabeth and Mary Queen of Scots was complex?

Throckmorton Plot, 1583–84

Francis Throckmorton, an English Catholic, became involved in a plot to get rid of Elizabeth. He acted as an intermediary between Mary and the Spanish ambassador, Mendoza, but was tortured and revealed details of the plot. Mendoza was expelled, bringing war with Spain very close.

Until 1585, Mary Stuart had been imprisoned in various places, first near the Scottish border and then further south. For many years she was kept at Sheffield Castle, guarded by the Earl of Shrewsbury and his formidable wife, Bess of Hardwick. But then Mary was transferred to Tutbury Castle in Staffordshire in the custody of Sir Amyas Paulet, a stern Puritan.

Babington Plot, 1586

There were still more plots, the most significant being led by Anthony Babington. He wrote to Mary outlining the details, and Mary replied agreeing.

Source C From a letter sent by Mary to Babington, 17 July 1586.

Everything being prepared, and the forces as well within as without ... then you must set the six gentlemen to work and give order that, their design accomplished, I may be in some way got away from there and that all your forces shall be simultaneously in the field to receive me while we await foreign assistance ...

Now as no certain day can be appointed for the performance of the said gentlemen's enterprise, I desire them to have always near them ... four brave men well horsed to advertise speedily the success of their design, as soon as it is done, to those appointed to get me away from hence ...

According to Source C, explain the level of involvement that Mary had in the Babington Plot of 1586.

All this was easily uncovered by Walsingham's secret agents. The conspirators were arrested and executed in September 1586. A special commission found Mary guilty in October 1586.

Elizabeth was still reluctant to see Mary executed, even though there was ample evidence. The country was already at war with Spain, so an execution would only provide another reason for Spain to be the enemy. In fact, Spain was already planning an invasion.

For several months, Elizabeth prevaricated, hoping to avoid making a decision. She regarded Mary as a family member and felt some sympathy for the difficulties that she had endured. Moreover, Elizabeth was careful not to support harsh treatment of a fellow female monarch, especially one with a rightful claim to the Scottish throne. Politically, it was also unwise to dispose of Mary. She had close relations with the Guise family in France, so could be useful to blunt any French action against England, especially if the complex marriage negotiations with the Dukes of Anjou and Alençon failed. These were, at best, flimsy excuses, given the mounting evidence that Spain and disaffected English Catholics were plotting fairly continuously by the late 1570s to put Mary on the throne. Only when the evidence of Mary's involvement apparently became overwhelming did Elizabeth finally agree to sign the warrant for her cousin's execution.

Execution of Mary Stuart

In February 1587, Elizabeth signed the warrant, but would not let it be put into action. However, Elizabeth's second Secretary of State, William Davison, released the warrant and Mary was executed at Fotheringay Castle.

Elizabeth flew into a rage. The Privy Council was blamed for allowing this to happen and Davison was fined heavily and put in the Tower. However, Elizabeth's rage passed, the Council was restored to favour and Davison was released and his fine remitted. Elizabeth wrote to James VI in Scotland protesting her innocence over the murder of his mother. However, James had no intention of fighting against England. He had, in effect, become the likely heir to the throne of England.

Source D From an account sent to Lord Burghley giving details of the execution of Mary Stuart, February 1587.

Groping for the block, she laid down her head, putting her chin over the block with both her hands, which, holding there still, would have been cut off had they not been seen. Then she, lying very still upon the block, one of the executioners holding her slightly with one of his hands, she endured two strokes of the other executioner with an axe, she making a very small noise or none at all, and not stirring any part of her from where she lay. And so the executioner cut off her head, save for one little gristle. Once cut asunder, he held up her head to the view of all the assembly and said, 'God Save The Queen'. Her lips stirred up and down a quarter of an hour after her head was cut off. Then one of the executioners, pulling off her garters, espied her little dog which had crept under her clothes. It could not be gotten away from her except by force, but afterwards came back to lay between her head and her shoulders, until it was carried away and washed.

Source E The justification for Mary's execution. From *Tudor England*, by S. T. Bindoff, (Pelican), 1950, pp.245–46.

Elizabeth never acted solely out of sentiment, and if she had earlier judged Mary's death a necessity, she would not have shrunk from its cruelty. When at last she yielded – although even then she left the final responsibility to others – the argument for Mary's death was overwhelmingly strong ... Mary living would be infinitely more dangerous than Mary dead. Justice had long demanded that Mary should die, but it was expediency not justice that sent her to her death in 1587.

How much of a threat to Elizabeth had Mary Queen of Scots been?

Having followed the narrative through from Mary's disastrous actions in Scotland in the 1560s to the nearly two decades in captivity in England during which she was involved in various plots against Elizabeth, can we assess the extent of the threat that Mary posed?

On the one hand, Mary had repeatedly shown that she was the focus of potential rebellion against Elizabeth. Mary was seen by her supporters as the queen-in-waiting. Her Catholicism meant that she was always likely to be supported by Philip II and the Pope. Therefore, Mary, alive and imprisoned, was always a major threat to Elizabeth. On the other hand, it can be argued that events had moved on by early 1587. England was actively at war with Spain and a Spanish invasion of England was already planned (see page 224). Mary's execution gave Philip II an additional motive, but in reality the threat from abroad was no worse than it had been.

Of course, Mary's death did not end speculation about the succession, but Elizabeth had successfully negotiated that for nearly thirty years and would continue to do so for the next fifteen. It was increasingly accepted that Mary's son, James – a Protestant – would eventually succeed to the throne. In one sense Mary's execution had marked the last stage of the Reformation; England, after Elizabeth's death, would remain a Protestant country. You will be able to trace the consequences of Mary's execution in various places in this chapter.

1 Why do you think the author sent this account of the execution of Mary Queen of Scots to Lord Burghley (Source D)?

2 What does the author mean in the last sentence of Source E?

KEY DATES: MARY QUEEN OF SCOTS

1542 Birth of Mary, only child of James V of Scotland who died one week later

1548 Taken to France to be educated at court

1558 Married the heir to the French throne, Francis II (King in 1559)

1560 Death of Francis II

1561 Mary returned to Scotland

1565 Married Lord Darnley

1567 Murder of Darnley; Mary married Earl of Bothwell

1568 Mary forced to flee to England, becoming prisoner of Elizabeth

1569 Rebellion of northern earls

1570 Excommunication of Elizabeth – encouraged Catholics to support Mary

1571 Ridolfi Plot

1583–84 Throckmorton Plot

1586 Babington Plot

1587 Execution of Mary

2 Foreign policy in the reign of Elizabeth

NOTE-MAKING

In this section you need to make notes on why England and Spain drifted towards war, and then focus on the results of the war for England.

The early years of Elizabeth's reign saw potential dangers from Scotland, France and Spain. Philip II himself hoped for a continued alliance with England. Traditionally, France and Scotland had been the enemies. However, by the late 1560s it was becoming obvious to all that it was Spain that was the biggest threat. Scotland was Protestant, with a regent acting on behalf of a young James VI, while France was suffering wars of religion and a series of crises focused elsewhere.

Tensions between England and Spain, 1558–88

Why did tensions increase between England and Spain in the 1570s and 1580s?

The deterioration of Anglo-Spanish relations became the key theme of Elizabethan foreign policy. Ironically, neither Elizabeth nor Philip II wanted this, but it became inevitable because of the situation over Mary Queen of Scots, the Papal excommunication of Elizabeth in 1570 and the situation in the Netherlands.

Emperor Charles V had regarded the Netherlands as central to the Habsburg inheritance and had insisted that it should be passed to his son Philip in 1555. It was a poor decision: Spain and the Netherlands were not only hundreds of miles apart, but very different in other ways. Local nobles in the provinces which comprised the Netherlands were used to a degree of independence with which Philip II's overly bureaucratic style of government could not cope. Spain was Europe's foremost Catholic power and Philip one of the faith's staunchest defenders, but the Netherlands contained a growing number of Calvinist converts. After a decade of Spanish rule, tensions within the Netherlands were developing into civil war in 1566. Philip adopted an uncompromising tone, telling the Pope:

'Before suffering the slightest damage to religion and the service of God, I would rather lose all my states, and a hundred lives if I had them, because I do not propose to be the ruler of heretics',

He sent the Duke of Alba and 10,000 troops to restore order, which they did in a brutal manner.

Increasing English concern over Spanish domination of the Netherlands

For England, the Netherlands had enormous economic and strategic importance:

- Much of the export trade in English cloth was organised through ports in the Netherlands, such as Antwerp.

▲ *The Massacre of the Innocents*, by Pieter Breughel. Paintings and propaganda such as this, which depicted the brutality of Alba's military government in the Netherlands, helped to create the 'Black Legend' of Spain among Protestant countries. This legend associated Spanish power and the Catholic Church with violent intolerance and strict royal control at the expense of people's liberties. It created a powerful fear of Spain and a determination within Protestant nations such as England to check the spread of Counter-Reformation values.

- English national security was believed to depend on ensuring that no powerful countries controlled the coastline across the Channel. During the Tudor period this sense of security had been reduced as France and Spain gained more control. France had defeated Brittany in Henry VII's reign as part of the growing strength of the French monarchy. Philip II had inherited the Netherlands in 1555 and Calais had been lost to the French in 1558. All this made an invasion of England more possible.
- As a result, it seemed to be of overwhelming importance to ensure that when rebellion broke out in the Netherlands, Spain should not recover control. Elizabeth had little sympathy for the plight of the Dutch people – they were, after all, rebelling against a legitimate government – but she did recognise

that England's interests were best served by encouraging the rebellion while not openly antagonising Spain. It was another difficult balancing act and one which provoked the most argument among her councillors. Elizabeth was extremely cautious in maintaining her distance from the rebels (although she did nothing to discourage unofficial support, such as allowing rebel ships to stay in English ports or English pirates to disrupt supplies being transported to Alba's army). This policy was supported by the 'peace party' within the Privy Council, who felt that war against Spain was beyond England's capabilities. However, a second group of courtiers, led by the Earl of Leicester and Francis Walsingham, favoured military action. The debate between these opposing views dragged on for nearly 20 years until a true crisis was reached in 1584–85 and Elizabeth was forced to commit the country to war.

The collapse of Anglo-Spanish relations was gradual and not simply confined to their disagreements over the Netherlands, as Figure 1 reveals. Some of the reasons were over religion (see Chapter 7, page 200); some were over the activities of Elizabethan seamen who were seen as pirates.

WORKING TOGETHER

Work in pairs. Using Figure 1, one of you has access to the information in both columns; the other covers up the right-hand column and is asked questions about the significance of the events that are listed. Half-way through, swap roles.

Figure 1 Deterioration of Anglo-Spanish relations, 1559–85.

Date	Event	Significance
1559	Philip II offered to marry Elizabeth.	More a gesture than a genuine offer; designed to show support for Elizabeth.
1562	Philip protested to Elizabeth about her support for Huguenot rebels against a Catholic government in France.	Elizabeth responded to the complaint by keeping her troops from joining with the Huguenot army in Northern France.
1563	Philip's government in the Netherlands banned imports of English cloths.	Officially, this was to protect the Netherlands against infection by plague from England. However, the ban reflected annoyance that the balance of trade had turned in England's favour while Elizabeth turned a blind eye to piracy in the Channel and to the work of English merchants in spreading Protestant ideas in the Netherlands. Elizabeth responded by banning all imports from the Netherlands, but both sides backed down and normalised trade relations in 1564.
1566–67	Outbreak of the Revolt of the Netherlands. Spanish Duke of Alba sent to the Netherlands to crush rioting by Calvinists and to restore firm government.	Suddenly made the northern coast of the Channel insecure. Massive alarm in England that Alba's army might be turned against them once its work in the Netherlands was completed (possibly with the aid of Guise faction in France if they won the civil war).
1568	Spain expelled the English ambassador from Madrid and replaced its own ambassador in London with a more hard-line Catholic, De Spes.	Added to tensions of the previous year, although the changes were for apparently innocent reasons. De Spes made contact with Mary Queen of Scots.
1568	In the Caribbean, Spanish government ships attacked John Hawkins' fleet because it was trespassing on Spain's monopoly of the Atlantic slave trade.	First signs of an issue that was to become a major source of Spanish grievances.
1568	December: Elizabeth seized bullion being transported through the Channel for Alba's army.	Alba's army was already owed pay and this action created a real crisis. Alba retaliated by confiscating all English ships docked at ports in the Netherlands and Elizabeth responded by banning all trade with the Netherlands and Spain. Trade was not fully restored until 1573.

Date	Event	Significance
1569	De Spes negotiated with the northern earls, encouraging their rebellion to place Mary on the throne.	This showed that Philip II's official ambassador was plotting against Elizabeth.
1570	The Pope formally excommunicated Elizabeth and declared her deposed.	Repression of English Catholics began to prevent them from carrying out the Pope's wishes. Philip had not been involved in this decision and was genuinely angry that it had been taken – he refused to allow publication of the decision within his territories.
1570	Elizabeth began to consider marriage to the Duke of Anjou, one of the brothers of King Charles IX of France, as a way of preventing France and Spain from acting together against her.	Elizabeth, aged nearly 40, was still using her possible marriage as a diplomatic tool.
1571	Discovery of the Ridolfi Plot – uprising to overthrow Elizabeth in favour of Mary with Spanish military support – in which Philip and De Spes were implicated.	De Spes expelled, repression of Catholics in England intensified.
1572	Treaty of Blois – replaced idea of marriage to Duke of Anjou with a formal Anglo–French defensive alliance against Spain.	A 'diplomatic revolution', but it quickly foundered because Elizabeth was not prepared to go to war in the Netherlands to support French ambitions. England continued to give unofficial support to the Huguenots, especially after the Massacre of St Bartholomew in France in 1572 when thousands of Huguenots were killed.
1572	Intensification of civil war in the Netherlands when rebels seized the port of Brill.	Elizabeth was accused by Spain of encouraging the rebels by giving them safe harbour and allowing English volunteers to support the rebellion.
1576	Unpaid Spanish soldiers mutinied in the Netherlands in the 'Spanish Fury', ransacking towns across the country.	Elizabeth was urged by Leicester to send troops into the Netherlands, but she would only agree to financial help.
1579	A new Spanish commander, the Duke of Parma, began to recover lands lost in the Netherlands to the rebels.	This increased the danger to England of a possible Spanish invasion.
1580	Philip II inherited the Portuguese Crown and its overseas empire in Africa and Asia.	Spain controlled both of the huge overseas empires that had developed in the sixteenth century.
1581	Elizabeth began to fund resistance to Parma in the Netherlands.	Philip was aware of what Elizabeth was doing and began to think seriously of an attack on England.
1583–84	Spanish ambassador Mendoza expelled after being implicated in the Throckmorton Plot to overthrow Elizabeth and install Mary as queen.	War between England and Spain was becoming closer, especially with the activities of English privateers capturing Spanish treasure fleets.
1584	Treaty of Joinville signed between Spain and French Catholics.	Death of Henry III's last brother and heir put the Huguenot Henry of Navarre next in line to the French throne. Catholics were alarmed enough at this to approach Spain for assistance. This treaty was important because it gave Philip the impression that if he attacked England, France would not react.
1585	Elizabeth signed the Treaty of Nonsuch with the Dutch rebels.	Parma's success in recovering territory finally convinced Elizabeth that action was needed. She agreed to send 7,000 troops under the Earl of Leicester to maintain the rebellion. Unofficial start of the Anglo–Spanish war.

England at war, 1585–1604

English foreign policy shifted from maintaining independence from Spain to open warfare in 1584–85.

Move towards war

The change to open warfare occurred because at that point the possibility of a Spanish attack on England suddenly became a realistic prospect:

- In the Netherlands, the murder of William 'the Silent' in 1584 deprived the Protestant revolt against Spanish rule of its key leader. At the same time Philip II's military commander in the Netherlands, the Duke of Parma, was regaining control of much of the country from the Protestant rebels.
- In France, the death of the Duke of Alençon deprived Elizabeth of a useful ally who had been prepared to fight Spain in the Netherlands. It also pushed French Catholics into an alliance with Spain because the line of succession in France now led to a Huguenot King.

These changes suggested to Elizabeth that the revolt in the Netherlands was nearing collapse. If it ended, Spain would be in control of the northern part of the cross-Channel frontier and would have a large unused army stationed there. She also recognised that the alliance of French Catholics with Spain might mean a joint attack on England, or at the very least undo her efforts to use France as a shield against Spain.

The solution was to step up support for the Dutch rebels. In the Treaty of Nonsuch (1585), Elizabeth made an open agreement with the rebel government of the northern provinces of the Netherlands to provide military support of 5,000 troops and 1,000 cavalry. In return, the Dutch handed over Flushing and Brill and Elizabeth accepted the title of Protector of the Netherlands. By sending the Earl of Leicester and English troops into the Netherlands, Elizabeth was publicly defying Philip and inviting war with Spain. At the same time she sent out a fleet under Sir Francis Drake to raid Spanish shipping in the Caribbean.

Anglo-Spanish War

The most famous incident of the Anglo-Spanish War – and of Tudor foreign policy in general – was the defeat of the Spanish Armada, Spain's attempt to invade England in 1588. The year 1588 had, for many years, been predicted as a year of disasters and misfortunes. Elizabeth herself was always keen to learn from astrologers, who at this time were prophesying the collapse of empires and global catastrophe. Thus it was not surprising that many English people were terrified when news reached England that a Spanish armada had set sail in May, heading for the English Channel.

> **Armada** – The Spanish word for an armed fleet.

The Spanish plan was that troops would depart from Spain, to the Netherlands, where they would link up with additional soldiers, who would then be transported to England for the invasion. However, the plan was flawed from the outset:

- The distance involved ensured the English would hear about, and therefore prepare for, the invasion long before ships could reach the Channel.
- The venture would depend upon good communication between the two sets of troops which was well-nigh impossible once they had set sail.
- Philip's advisers had ignored two key geographical facts: that Dutch ports were in shallow water which would make boarding the Armada from the port impossible; and that the south-westerly winds which blow into the Channel would make sailing into it a very difficult task.

- The fleet itself was under-provisioned and poorly led by the Duke of Medina Sidonia.
- Philip had unfounded hopes that the mere presence of the Armada would force Elizabeth to see reason over the Netherlands and her Protestantism.

In the event, brilliant naval tactics played their part for the English, as the navy positioned itself to force the Armada to sail into the Channel's south-westerly winds, which then enabled the navy to use long-range guns to batter the fleet. When the Armada tried to seek refuge along the French coast, English fire-ships burned and scattered its ships. The Battle of Gravelines took place on 29 July off the coast of Flanders, which left the Duke of Medina Sidonia no alternative but to pull away from the English gunfire and take his fleet on a suicidal journey home around the west coast of Ireland and north coast of Scotland. Bad weather resulted in the wreckage of many ships along this coastline, and fewer than half the original fleet limped back to Spain.

The defeat of the Armada was hailed as a magnificent English victory against a larger and more powerful enemy. It seemed to indicate God's approval of Elizabeth's government and the Anglican Church it had created. Elizabeth was quick to see the propaganda value of the victory, as the 'Armada Portrait' on page 181 of Chapter 7 shows.

> **Fire-ships** – Ships deliberately set on fire and sent towards the enemy's ships to cause them to scatter.

▲ A nineteenth-century depiction of Sir Francis Drake's flagship *Revenge* capturing a Spanish galleon.

However, the long-term effects of the defeat of the Armada were negligible. The war just continued for the last fifteen years of Elizabeth's reign, without any decisive battles. The event, like some other episodes in English history, became surrounded by exaggeration and myths in the story of the emerging Protestant Empire on a small group of islands on the edge of Europe, fighting against the might of Catholic Europe. At the time it was not even immediately obvious that the events of 1588 marked a decisive turning point.

Source F From a report of the victory by Drake to Walsingham, July 1588.

God hath given us so good a day in forcing the enemy so far to leeward as I hope in God that the Prince of Parma and the Duke of Sidonia shall not shake hands these few days; and whensoever they shall meet, I believe neither of them will greatly rejoice of this day's service … From aboard her Majesty's good ship the Revenge, this 29th July 1588.

Foreign policy after the Armada

The war continued with Elizabeth sending Drake to Portugal in 1589 for a counter-attack. He landed with 15,000 men and 130 ships, with the aim of throwing out the Spaniards. But there was no Portuguese rising in their favour and they were forced to withdraw, having failed to capture Lisbon. Many men were lost, mostly through disease. This time Drake returned to England under a cloud.

There were continued attacks on Spanish bullion ships, though with decreasing success, as the Spanish had developed a convoy system. For example, in 1591 Sir Richard Grenville in *Revenge* was surrounded by a Spanish fleet and Grenville and most of his men were killed.

Increasingly, Elizabeth was more concerned with Northern Europe rather than Spain itself:

- In France in 1589, Henry IV, a Huguenot, came to the throne. Elizabeth saw him as a potentially valuable ally.
- In 1590 the Duke of Parma invaded France from the Spanish Netherlands. In 1592 Elizabeth sent an English force to Normandy to aid Henry – led by the twenty-six-year-old Robert Devereux, Earl of Essex. He achieved nothing and returned the following year. In any case, the situation in France changed the following year. Henry IV effectively stopped the civil war by declaring himself a Catholic.
- More expeditions set sail. In 1595 Drake and Hawkins led an expedition to the Caribbean, but it marked a sad end to their fine careers. Hawkins died at sea and Drake died in the Caribbean.
- In 1596, Lord Howard of Effingham, with Walter Raleigh and the Earl of Essex, led a raid on Spain. With 80,000 men they captured Cadiz and destroyed nearly 50 ships. Essex wanted to establish a permanent base there, but he was overruled.
- In October 1596, a second Armada, which intended to invade via Ireland, was battered by storms and the remnants returned to Spain. By this time Philip II was officially bankrupt.
- In 1597 Essex and Raleigh tried to repeat their escapades of the previous year, but it was a disaster with quarrels and bad weather. In the same year Philip's third attempt at an Armada failed because of the weather.
- In 1598 a peace treaty, The Treaty of Vervins, between Spain and France was signed – just before Philip II died. However, the war between England and Spain continued, especially as the Dutch were still in arms against Spanish rule.

1 What did Drake mean by 'shall not shake hands these few days'?

2 Bearing in mind the date of the letter, how reliable is Source F for explaining England's victory over the Armada?

In the very last years of Elizabeth's reign the preoccupation was Ireland (see page 233). Indeed, in the last Armada of 1601 the Spanish managed to land troops in Ireland, eventually being defeated by the English. The war dragged on, with a peace treaty being signed in 1604. The Dutch rebels gained their independence from Spain in 1609, with the Spanish retaining what became known as the Spanish Netherlands.

Assessment of Elizabeth's foreign policy

At first glance, Elizabeth was obviously successful – she had reigned for nearly half a century and the country had not been invaded. The foundations of the future English Empire had been laid in the form of the beginnings of trade with India and beyond (see page 232) and the country's economic interests were being served by building up networks for overseas trade.

However, the war cost England dearly. The economic depression of the 1590s was partly caused by the loss of legitimate trade with Spanish possessions as well as by the poor harvests of the 1590s. It has been estimated that Elizabeth was spending twice as much as her revenues normally yielded. To cover the shortfall, she sold valuable Crown lands and resorted to unpopular financial expedients such as the sale of monopolies (which provoked the opposition of the 1601 Parliament). In the short term, these raised enough money to avoid bankruptcy, but in the long run the loss of land deprived later monarchs of regular income, while the legacy of repeated demands on Parliament for money created a sense of grievance that was to have important repercussions for her Stuart successors.

Source G An assessment of Elizabeth's foreign policy success. From 'Elizabethan War Aims and Strategy' by R. B. Wernham, in *Elizabethan Government and Society* by S. T. Bindoff, J. Hurstfield and C. H. Williams, (Athlone Press), 1961, p.368.

She was not one of England's great war leaders and she only half achieved her aims. Yet to have helped the French monarchy to its feet, to have saved half of the Netherlands from Spanish 'tyranny', to have kept the other half out of Spanish possession, and England itself out of bankruptcy, was a fair achievement against the Spain of Philip II.

> **LOOK AGAIN**
>
> Divide a page into two columns, headed 'France' and 'Spain'. Trace Tudor foreign relations with both countries throughout the period.

> Many assessments of Elizabeth's foreign policy are not as glowing as that in Source G. Following your study of Elizabeth's foreign policy, does Source G give a fair assessment?

KEY DATES: ENGLAND AT WAR 1585–1604

1585 War with Spain, though not officially declared

1587 Drake's raid on Cadiz harbour

1588 Spanish Armada defeated

1589 Drake led a failed expedition to Portugal

1595 Drake and Hawkins led expedition to Caribbean

1596–97 Raids on Spain and attempted Spanish Armadas

1598 Death of Philip II

1601 Fourth Spanish Armada landed in Ireland

1604 Peace between England and Spain

3 Trade, exploration and colonisation

By the middle of the sixteenth century Spain and Portugal had well-established patterns of trade and colonisation in America and the East. England's discoveries so far were limited to Newfoundland and the cod fisheries. During the reign of Elizabeth this changed so that England started on the process of creating an empire centred on international trade. Flanders was still important, but it was always going to be limited and at risk when conflicts within Europe broke out.

Changing attitudes in Elizabeth's reign

How much was achieved, and why, in Elizabeth's reign in trade, exploration and colonisation?

Spanish and Portuguese achievements had partly depended on their countries' geographical position, but were also due to technical advances in ship design for ocean travel and to state encouragement in the form of loans and charters. Henry VIII had initially shown some interest in creating a Navy in the early years of his reign, but thereafter there was virtually no state investment and little encouragement either. For most of his reign Henry did not want to quarrel with Spain. He was still obsessed about gaining conquests in France rather than realising that England's prosperous future might depend on lands further away.

By 1600 this attitude had changed. Although there were few technical advances in shipping, England had gained the reputation of being a sea-faring nation that was developing its trade links in different parts of the world. England had also successfully challenged the claim by Spain and Portugal that all the newly discovered lands were automatically theirs, following the Treaty of Tordesillas in 1494. Spain, the most powerful nation, had suffered defeats at English hands, notably the Spanish Armada.

In particular, some English sailors were convinced that they could find a new route to the Far East by sailing north-east or north-west. We know that these missions were doomed to failure, but they did create various new opportunities and developments.

North-East Passage

In 1553 at the start of Mary I's reign, Willoughby and Chancellor had sailed north-east and found their route blocked by ice. However, a profitable trade with Russia was started with the creation of the Muscovy Company. On a second voyage in 1555, Willoughby died and Chancellor was drowned. However, in the 1560s Jenkinson explored south from Russia into Persia and tried to establish new trading links there. The Muscovy Company also helped to break the monopoly of the Hanseatic League in the Baltic (see Chapter 1, page 30).

North-West Passage

Frobisher sailed north of Canada in 1576, 1577 and 1578 and discovered what he named as the Frobisher Strait. However, his belief that he had found a route to China was, of course, wrong. Drake also was interested in the possibility of a route to China via the north of the American continent.

During his circumnavigation of the globe (1577–80) he sailed up the west coast of North America to try to find where such a route would emerge, but he too failed.

In 1585–87, John Davis, on three voyages, found nothing of commercial value, but he made a valuable contribution to the mapping of the Arctic. In particular, he established that Greenland is separate from America, and sailed into Baffin's Bay.

All this was a necessary prelude to the success in the early seventeenth century when Hudson explored what became known as Hudson's Bay. The Hudson Bay Company. was founded for trade which developed during the Stuart period.

Africa and the slave trade with the West Indies

Others attempted to break into the monopolies established by Portugal and Spain. In 1562 John Hawkins went to Africa, with brightly-coloured cloth and trinkets to sell, captured some locals and took them as slaves to West Indian islands. In return he was able to bring home money and sugar. Such profit meant that the idea was repeated. In 1564 a group of shareholders funded the second expedition, including William Cecil, Leicester and (secretly) the Queen herself.

The success of this second voyage prompted Philip II to warn England about privateering. However, in 1567 Hawkins sailed again, with Elizabeth supplying one of the ships herself, *The Jesus of Lubeck.* The expedition was nearly a total failure with Hawkins just escaping capture by the Spanish Viceroy of Mexico.

THE JESUS OF LUBECK

▲ *The Jesus of Lubeck*, an Elizabethan ship.

In 1572–73 Francis Drake took up the challenge and led an expedition which succeeded in capturing Spanish silver at Nombre de Dios. The dangers of such expeditions were shown, however, when John Oxenham tried to repeat the same escapade but was caught and hanged.

Drake's epic voyage round the world (1577–80) further dented Spain's reputation on the seas. He raided the west coast of Spanish America and captured the *Cacafuego* and her cargo of silver. He returned as leader of only the second expedition to circumnavigate the globe, and had made a profit of 4,000 per cent.

These beginnings stalled in the remainder of Elizabeth's reign, because she and her ministers were forced to concentrate on defence and on events in Europe. However, the pattern of confident English privateers had been established.

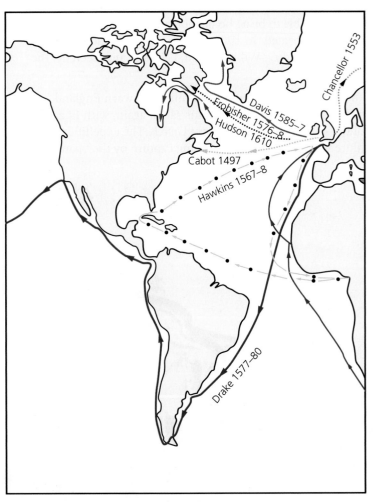

▲ Figure 2 Map showing English voyages of discovery and the origins of trade and slave routes from Africa to the West Indies

Colonisation

Having seen the huge success of the Spanish and Portuguese Empires, there was obvious interest in English colonisation. A 700,000-word book by Richard Hakluyt called *Principal Navigations, Voyages and Discoveries of the English Nation*, published in 1589, stirred interest in expansion. He meticulously sought out first-hand accounts from sailors when they returned from expeditions. John Dee did similarly for revising maps and charts when sailors returned with new information.

Source H The achievements of English sailors. From *Principal Navigations, Voyages and Discoveries of the English Nation* by Richard Hakluyt, published in 1589.

It cannot be denied they have been men full of activity, stirrers abroad, and searchers of remote parts of the world, so in this most famous and peerless government of her most excellent Majesty, her subjects, through the special assistance and blessing of God, in searching the most opposite corners and quarters of the world and, to speak plainly, in compassing the vast globe of the earth more than once, have excelled all the nations and people of the earth.

> In what ways is Hakluyt, Source H, suggesting that English people are special?

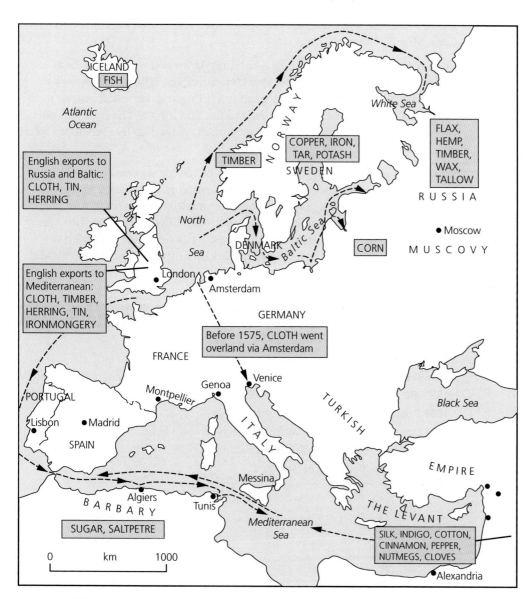

▲ Figure 3 Map showing trade in the Baltic and Mediterranean during Elizabeth's reign.

Humphrey Gilbert was interested in establishing colonies in the north-west of America for trading purposes. With a patent from the Queen, giving him rights over any land that was taken, and financed mostly by the Cathay Company, he himself sailed in 1578 to try to set up a colony. It was unsuccessful, as was another expedition to Newfoundland in 1583. His half-brother, Walter Raleigh, gained a patent for a colony which would be called Virginia, but two attempts in 1585 and 1587 failed.

With the focus firmly on Europe after the 1588 Armada, Raleigh's only other trip was in 1595 up the Orinoco in Guiana in search of El Dorado, a mythical Inca civilisation. It was not until the reign of James I that colonies were successfully established at Jamestown in 1607 and in New England in 1620.

Attempts to develop trade with India

Some sailors thought that success in the tantalising trades in India and beyond was the key to future trading wealth. The Portuguese Empire there was weakly defended and could be infiltrated, although early attempts did not achieve much. For example, in 1583 Newbery and Fitch made a famous overland journey to India. They reached Portuguese Goa and visited the court of the Great Mogul, Akbar.

In 1591 Lancaster successfully sailed around Africa and reached the East Indies, capturing two Portuguese ships. However, the return journey was a nightmare, with insufficient supplies to reach England. He sailed instead to the West Indies where the crew mutinied and put him ashore. The crew was not heard of any more, but Lancaster was eventually picked up by French privateers and returned home to tell his story in 1594.

All this was a prelude to what turned out to be the big success story of the Elizabethan period. In 1600 the East India Company was created by a group of merchants, and with its backing Lancaster made another trip. It was after Elizabeth's death in 1603 when he returned with fully-laden ships. This was the beginning of the development of the East India Company which led to India being the jewel in the crown of the British Empire in the eighteenth and nineteenth centuries.

KEY DATES: TRADE, EXPLORATION AND COLONISATION

1553 Muscovy Company established

1562 John Hawkins established trade with Africa

1576–78 Frobisher's expeditions to Canada looking for north-west route

1577–80 Drake's voyage round the world

1589 Publication by Richard Hakluyt

1591 Lancaster set up trade with East Indies

1595 Raleigh sailed up the Orinoco in Guiana

1600 East India Company established

4 Closing years of Elizabeth's reign

Elizabeth had come to the throne a cautious but intelligent 25 year old, but as she aged, she had become more difficult and bitter. There was a definite air of decline about her reign in its closing years. The 1590s were characterised by war, rebellion, disease and famine, presided over by a Queen who seemed to have lost the sureness of control that had characterised her early years.

Issues of the last years of Elizabeth's reign

To what extent were the problems of the last few years of her reign the fault of the Queen, and how much were due to other events and forces?

Queen Elizabeth could be said to be unlucky. After the highpoint of the victory over the Spanish Armada, various factors together contributed to the last years of her reign becoming more fractious and less happy.

Economic and social problems

The 1590s were difficult years for the people of England. Although the decade began with successful harvests, the years 1594–97 saw four successive serious crop failures. One effect was to push up agricultural prices even further; during the decade, it has been estimated that prices rose by over one-third. There were also outbreaks of plague, whose severity was worsened by the lack of food. Thousands died in the first visitation of 1592–93 and the effects continued to decimate urban and rural populations for the next ten years at least. Overall, the 1590s contained some of the most miserable years of the century. Many parish registers for the 1590s show many entries for burials and few for marriages and baptisms.

The Poor Laws passed in 1598 and 1601 reflected the scale of the problem for the poorest in society (see Chapter 6, pages 171–74). The Privy Council was afraid of a recurrence of the social unrest seen in 1549 at the time of Kett's rebellion. It is likely that the desperate poor migrated to nearby towns looking for food and work, the problem being exacerbated by the population growth that was taking place.

Yet what is noticeable is the lack of significant popular rebellion. There were local riots, especially when it was rumoured that foodstuffs were being hoarded by merchants hoping to drive up prices still further. There were food riots in London, the south-east and west in 1595 and in East Anglia in 1596–97. However, only one national revolt occurred (see below) and this was not caused by economic hardship.

Ireland

In theory, Ireland had been an official part of the English Crown since 1541 (see Chapter 4, page 104), but in reality English control extended little further than 'the Pale'. In the rest of the island clans exercised real power based on local tradition and custom rather than English law. There had been successive attempts by English governments to strengthen their control over the clans

NOTE-MAKING

In this section you need notes on each of the topics – but also consider how each affected the overall reputation of Elizabeth and her reign.

The Pale – The Pale was England's foothold in Ireland, a region on the eastern coast around Dublin. It was the centre of English government on the island during the fifteenth and sixteenth centuries, heavily manned and fortified against the Irish clans who lived 'beyond the Pale'.

Plantation – Plantations involved settling English colonists on lands formerly owned by Irish clans in order to extend the Pale and slowly establish control over the whole island. The policy began in Edward VI's reign, but was extended under Mary. During Elizabeth's reign further plantation was encouraged, especially in the northern county of Ulster and in the western county of Munster. Although the policy aimed to bring peace and stability by planting English settlers in Ireland, it often had precisely the opposite effect, provoking Irish clans whose lands had been seized into open rebellion.

because Ireland was regarded as strategically important to national security. Like Scotland, it offered foreign powers a tempting base from which to threaten the mainland. This potential threat grew worse under Elizabeth because Irish clans remained loyal to the Catholic Church while England moved towards Protestantism. Spain in particular saw the potential in this religious disagreement to make Ireland a distraction for the English Crown.

Under Edward VI, clumsy attempts to export the Reformation to Ireland had resulted in the collapse of earlier efforts to extend royal control beyond the Pale. During the 1550s relations deteriorated further when settlers began arriving from England to implement the policy of plantation. Elizabeth therefore came to the throne with Ireland in rebellion over religious and land changes and periodic outbursts kept the problem alive for the rest of her reign.

Hugh O'Neill's rebellion

The most serious challenge within Ireland was mounted by Hugh O'Neill, the Earl of Tyrone, between 1598 and 1603. Tyrone's army of about 6,000 men easily defeated the much smaller English force at the Battle of the Yellow Ford in August 1598, threatening then to move on to dismantle all the control built up by the plantation policy. Equally dangerous were the links that Tyrone had built with Spain, which promised to double the men at his disposal. Elizabeth quickly sent over a larger force commanded by the Earl of Essex, but it was a complete failure. He failed to follow specific instructions and failed to exploit the military advantages that existed on his arrival. Essex returned home in disgrace (losing his influence at court and driving him to rebellion, as we will see below). His replacement, Lord Mountjoy, managed to defeat Tyrone's forces by constantly harassing them in year-round campaigns. The turning point came when a Spanish relief force was defeated at Kinsale in 1602, depriving Tyrone of desperately needed assistance. From this moment, opposition to the English army rapidly crumbled and order was restored to the devastated country as the Crown passed from Elizabeth to James I.

Essex Rebellion, 1601

As we saw in Chapter 7 (pages 184–86), manipulating patronage effectively was central to Elizabeth's achievement. As she grew older, however, her skill at handling the different factions and interests swirling around her at court weakened. It seems to have deserted her almost completely in 1601 when the Earl of Essex rebelled.

Essex had come to the court as the stepson of the Earl of Leicester, and when Leicester died he became the leader of the group of courtiers who favoured stepping up military action against Spain. Elizabeth, however, did not favour such action and Essex found that he was unable to gain seats on the Privy Council or positions at court for his allies. Instead, the so-called 'peace party', led by Lord Burghley and his son, monopolised key posts. There is no doubt that Essex was infuriated by the Queen's obstinacy and his lack of progress. On one famous occasion, she hit him and he had to be forcibly restrained from drawing his sword.

◀ Elizabeth's rebellious courtier, the Earl of Essex. According to the French ambassador, 'He was a man who did not content himself with a small fortune and aspired to greatness'.

In 1599 Elizabeth finally gave Essex a chance to show his talents and to reward his supporters by appointing him to command her army in Ireland. He threw away this opportunity, however, and fell from royal favour once again and was banished from court. As a result, he lost valuable monopolies and a possible government position in the Court of Wards.

Nearly bankrupt by February 1601, Essex attempted to seize strategic places in London by force of arms, including the palace at Whitehall and the Tower. He and his supporters also detested the power of families such as the Cecils who he intended to remove from power and have James VI officially recognised as the heir to the throne. (These were unfulfilled aims, though the second one did happen in spite of this.)

The 'rebellion' was a miserable failure – few people actively joined it and Essex was quickly arrested and executed for treason. What concerned Elizabeth was the fact that it had happened in the capital, close to the centre of power, and that a number of noblemen had joined Essex in his abortive coup. None of these supporters was put on trial for fear of provoking further rebellion.

In her final years, therefore, Elizabeth seems to have failed to distribute patronage evenly enough to maintain the loyalty of some of her leading subjects. By favouring Lord Burghley's family and circle of supporters, Elizabeth alienated other families, but the Essex rebellion seems to have done no more than to reinforce her dependence on them. It is dangerous to read too much significance into the Essex rebellion, but it is tempting to see some degree of polarisation between courtiers who had the ear of the Queen and the Privy Councillors and those who felt excluded. This can be seen as one of the background reasons for the development of opposition in the reigns of James I and Charles I.

LOOK AGAIN

Compare the causes of the Essex Rebellion with other rebellions in the Tudor period.

The succession

Elizabeth steadfastly refused to name her successor. She knew that, had she done so, her courtiers would have drifted away and contacted James VI. Courtiers would have been jockeying for position under the new monarch.

In February 1603 Elizabeth was seriously ill. Robert Cecil acted by talking with leading nobles and the Lord Lieutenants. He was trying to ensure that the succession would occur peacefully with no opposition.

By 20 March Elizabeth was clearly dying. She refused food and advice from doctors. She refused to take to her bed and spent hours pacing around. She had lost her power of speech, but allegedly confirmed with a sign that James was her chosen successor. Eventually she collapsed on a pile of cushions on the floor, and died on 24 March.

James had already been sent a draft of the succession proclamation. This was announced in London, accompanied with bonfires to celebrate the accession of James Stuart. The news quickly spread around England and James was unanimously accepted as Elizabeth's heir.

The Tudor legacy

How good was the legacy that Elizabeth left for James Stuart to inherit?

The largely uncritical view of Elizabeth's reign which persisted among historians for so long has broken down in the last generation or so. Now a richer and more complex picture both of the Queen herself and of her achievements is emerging. One of the key areas of debate has been whether the Tudors left England politically stable and strengthened, or whether the seeds of the seventeenth-century struggle between Crown and Parliament had been planted during their reigns.

The real problem by 1603 was that rapid and profound religious, social, economic and cultural changes had taken place without a similar revolution in government. Although there were more professional administrators and fewer amateur nobles running government by 1603, the system remained in essence what it had been in 1485: a personal monarchy. Under Elizabeth the country had a capable monarch whose character and political skills were mostly sufficient to hold the political system together.

However, there was no guarantee that every monarch would possess such abilities or would even have the interest to be a strong ruler. The fragility of personal monarchy was evident throughout the 1540s and 1550s and became apparent once again in the 1590s. Elizabeth's achievement was to keep control for nearly half a century, rather than to create the conditions necessary for continued stability under her Stuart successors. She left James I a potentially strong monarchy, a stable society and the goodwill of most Englishmen. At the same time, she also provided him with an expensive war against Spain, financial problems and political and religious tensions.

Source I From the writer Thomas Dekker's description of the effect of Elizabeth's death on the nation, 1603.

The report of her death, like a thunderclap, was able to kill thousands. It took away the heart from millions. For having brought up, under her wing, a nation of people who were almost all born under her, that never saw the face of any prince but herself, never understood what the strange outlandish word 'change' signified – how was it possible but that her sickness should throw abroad a universal fear, and her death an astonishment?

> ## LOOK AGAIN
>
> Look at Key Questions 1 and 2 on page viii. How much had changed during the Tudor period, and how much reflected continuity?

Source J The achievement of the Tudors over the nobility. From *New Worlds, Lost Worlds: The Rule of the Tudors, 1485–1603* by Susan Brigden, (Penguin Books), 2000, pp.363–64.

The Tudors had succeeded in their ambition that loyalty to the Crown replace loyalty to the old nobility. The ancient nobility had yielded power – though very far from all their power – to a service nobility which owed its advancement to royal favour and employment at court. Essex was almost the last noble to dream of a throne...

The new world of the court had become the centre of power, patronage and stability, and everyone who mattered in the realm was drawn to it.

Figure 4 Tudor legacy – stability or instability?

Arguments for political stability	Arguments for political instability
The image and status of monarchy had been cultivated carefully by Elizabeth's propagandists. Victories over her Catholic enemies at home and abroad in the 1580s and 1590s strengthened her position considerably.	During the 1590s, social, economic and political crises came together to expose the fragility of Elizabeth's control. Her need to placate Parliament in 1601 over monopolies and the sudden rebellion by the Earl of Essex revealed that the elderly Elizabeth had lost some of her youthful charm.
Parliament met infrequently and was summoned and dismissed according to the monarch's wishes. Despite occasional criticism, Parliament was a loyal supporter of royal policy.	By involving Parliament in legislating major constitutional changes, such as the break with Rome and the establishment of a national Church and doctrine, Tudor monarchs raised the status of MPs and inadvertently created the impression that there was more of a partnership between Crown and Parliament than actually existed.
There were few serious rebellions after 1549, showing the extent of the nobility's support for a monarchy which offered them stability and patronage.	By assuming control over the English Church the monarchy became a focus for religious as well as political criticism, but unreconciled Catholics remained hostile to the nature of the Elizabethan settlement.

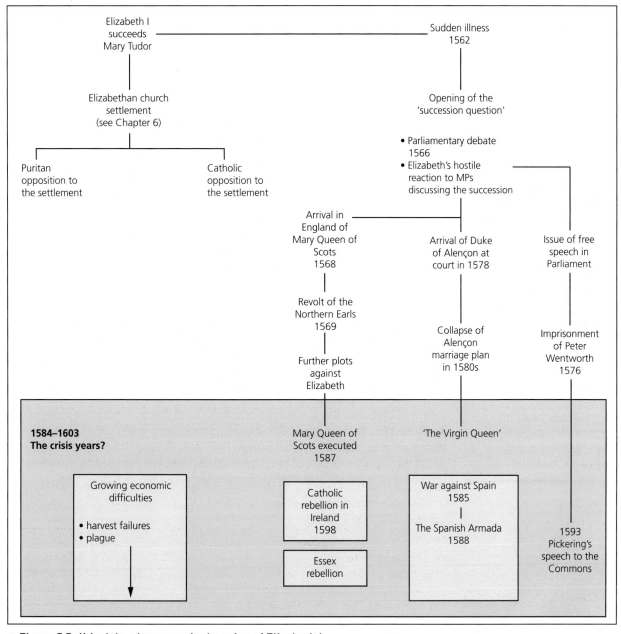

▲ Figure 5 Political developments in the reign of Elizabeth I.

WORKING TOGETHER

Organise a debate on how stable or unstable Tudor rule was near the end of Elizabeth's reign.

How historians have approached the topic

Elizabeth herself has, until recently, been treated generously by historians. Sir John Hayward wrote one of the first accounts of the entire reign in 1612 and was overawed by Elizabeth's personality and achievements:

'Excellent Queen! What do my words but wrong thy worth? What do I but gild gold? What but show the sun a candle in attempting to praise thee whose honour doth fly over the whole world upon the wings of Magnanimity and Justice, whose perfection shall much dim the lustre of all other that shall be of thy sex?'

Most historical writing about Elizabeth I had been full of congratulation for the Queen and her achievements. Since her reign included the establishment of the Anglican tradition in English religion, the defeat of the Spanish Armada and the development of cultural life at court as well as the writings of Shakespeare and others, it is easy to see why. It was not until the 1950s and 1960s that serious consideration was given to the role of Elizabeth's ministers (a trend which echoed the work of Geoffrey Elton and others in reappraising Henry VIII's style of government – see Chapter 3, page 87).

One of the key debates about Elizabethan politics has focused on the development of Parliament as an institution. According to Sir John Neale (who was writing in the 1930s and in the decade after the Second World War), Elizabethan Parliaments were centres of political dispute and division, especially on matters of religion. Looking forward to the 1640s, when civil war broke out between Crown and Parliament, partly over the future direction of the Church, some historians saw Elizabeth's reign as sowing the seeds of this dispute. More recently, writers have challenged this connection, particularly by showing that Parliaments were much more co-operative and less fragmented than was supposed.

It is only in the last 30 years, however, that a serious attempt to challenge the overall perception of Elizabeth's reign as a 'Golden Age' has emerged. Christopher Haigh in *The Reign of Elizabeth I* (1984) has led the way by playing up the problems and insecurities of the reign. Since the mid-1980s other historians, such as David Starkey, have begun to reveal more about Elizabeth's difficult personality and how it was shaped by her troubled early life.

Source K An assessment of Elizabeth after the first fourteen years of her reign in 1572. From *Elizabeth I: Queen of England* by Neville Williams, (Sphere Books), 1971, p.178.

She was still single and had deliberately left the problem of her succession still in the air. She was at odds with her Council, with both Houses of Parliament and with Convocation (the Church of England's ruling body), and the unity she had striven for in religion had been shattered. England was still isolated, without an ally in Christendom, a negligible country, weak, poor and divided against itself. Had Elizabeth died in 1572 she would have gone down in history as an unremarkable failure, who had broken faith with all who had put their trust in her at the joyous moment of her accession and had been proved by events to be incapable of living up to the promise expected of her father's daughter.

1 To what extent do you agree with the assessment of Elizabeth's first fourteen years as queen, given in Source K?

2 To what extent is your assessment of Elizabeth's reign different when looking at the reign as a whole?

Chapter summary

- Mary Queen of Scots as Elizabeth's cousin was at the centre of Catholic plots (Ridolfi, Throckmorton, Babington, etc.).
- Elizabeth was reluctant to execute Mary; it was only done when war with Spain had started.
- Elizabeth tried to avoid war with Spain for as long as possible.
- War was seen as necessary over the Netherlands and because of the Catholic threats in England.
- English success over the Spanish Armada in 1588 was achieved by a mixture of good tactics and luck with the weather.
- English sailors were adventurous in seeking new routes, for example seeking a north-west passage.
- Privateers, such as Drake and Hawkins, attacked Spanish treasure ships.
- English overseas trade expanded, and this was confirmed with the founding of the East India Company in 1600.
- Back at home, people in 1590s suffered a series of bad harvests, outbreaks of plague and social unrest, with Ireland and a revolt led by the Earl of Essex creating political problems as well.
- The legacy of Elizabeth: the extent of her success and her greatness are still debated.

KEY DATES: THE CLOSING YEARS OF ELIZABETH'S RULE

1594 First of series of bad harvests

1595–97 Food riots in various parts of the country

1598 Rebellion in Ireland led by Hugh O'Neill; Poor Law in response to problems of wandering vagrants

1601 Elizabethan Poor Law (main details in force until 1834); rebellion led by Earl of Essex defeated

1603 Death of Elizabeth

Chapter summary diagram

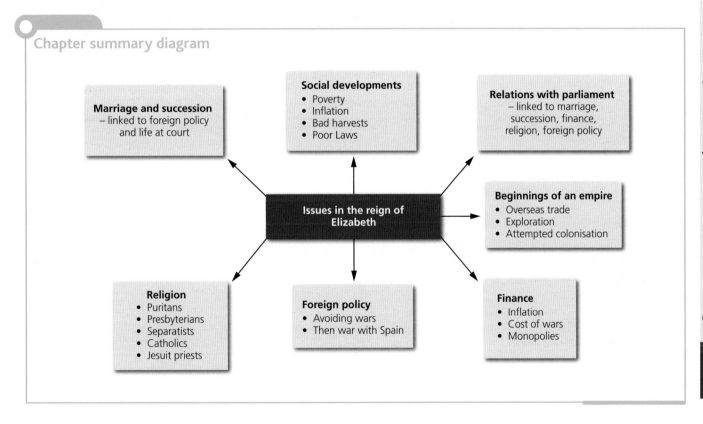

8 Conflict and exploration in Elizabeth's reign

Working on essay technique

In previous chapters, you have built up skills in planning and writing essays. In particular, in the second part of this book you should have become more confident in producing answers at a higher level.

ACTIVITY

Here is another A-level practice question:

'Elizabeth's foreign policy was mostly a series of disasters.' Assess the validity of this view. (25 marks)

As in previous chapters, you can plan an answer by looking at Elizabeth's foreign policy, episode by episode. It is perhaps easiest to divide the reign into mini-periods, e.g. up to 1570; 1570–84; and the rest of the reign. Then look at aspects or themes in each period, e.g. Scotland, France, Spain, marriage diplomacy, overseas trade.

Before you start writing, think how you can write an effective plan that:

- balances disasters with successes
- has precise dates and events
- ranges across the reign without becoming a chronological description
- reaches a substantiated judgement.

After writing the essay, look at the generic mark scheme for essays. Start at Level 4 and consider whether you have shown those skills. Then look at Level 5 to see if you think you deserve this top level. You may wish to compare answers with a friend and mark each other's work.

Working on interpretation skills: extended reading

Was there a general crisis of government in the last years of Elizabeth I's reign, 1589–1603?

Historian Stuart Minson provides an interpretation of the last years of Elizabeth's reign.

During the final decade of Elizabeth's reign, back-to-back harvest failures and a period of price inflation across Europe saw the wages of workers reach their lowest value relative to the price of goods at any time between the Black Death and the present day. Yet weather conditions and the course of the European economy were not really in the government's control. It 5
was perhaps the structural inequalities of early modern English society which actually made harvest failures and price increases problematic, but it is neither a surprise nor an aspect of crisis that Elizabethan governors should have failed to address this. In fact, the government's responses to these problems were better co-ordinated and more effective than 10
elsewhere in Europe. If the severity of the dearth is measured in terms of actual mortality, it appears that northern France and the Rhineland fared worse than England, while for the English themselves the 1590s were not as bad as the 1550s or 1630s. Moreover, deaths far above the norm were limited to the terrible year of 1597–98, and only in particular areas, such 15
as Cumberland or Newcastle, did many people actually perish. In some regions like Kent people rioted repeatedly over grain supplies, but these episodes were small in scale and limited in aim. London experienced only one serious riot, in 1595, and the city's government did much to alleviate famine and build solidarity. The Poor Laws of 1598 and 1601 were not new 20
ideas, but they turned the strategies of poor relief, pioneered in towns and national legislation since the early 1500s, into a form that could be systematically implemented. In themselves they had little effect in the 1590s, but they reflect the extensive apparatus of poor relief which was already in operation at this time. 25

Certainly there was an acute 'sense' of crisis among the elite, as seen in the terrified reports of the Somerset JP Edward Hext on the breakdown of law and order or the dangerous over-reaction by the Privy Council to a failed attempt at a popular march in Oxfordshire in 1596. There was also a sense of desperation among the wider population. Analysis has shown that peaks 30
in prosecution for theft coincided with times of greatest dearth. However, it must be noted that capital convictions, while significantly increasing in 1598, only did so after a third harvest failure followed the previous two. Indeed, the fear and desperation which people experienced was not just a product of conditions during Elizabeth's final years. They were also part of 35
a longer-term process of social polarisation which was dividing families of middling wealth and status down the centre, some being pushed into poverty while others enlarged their property and began to identify with the values of the social elite. Importantly, while the latter were terrified of the possibility of popular rebellion, this also spurred action. A combination of 40
preventative measures, attempts to mitigate the worst suffering and severe repression of those caught in agitation served to contain unrest.

For instance, in London, the provision of subsidised grain stocks and the central organisation of poor relief was combined with the execution of
45 rioters and the appointment of new officials like the Provost Marshal to co-ordinate policing across the wider metropolitan area.

It must be understood that an actual crisis involves either a breakdown or transformation as a result of problems. In some respects, the harvest failures and unrest of the 1590s did contribute to change. The management
50 of the agricultural economy became more co-ordinated and strategies for insulating communities against problems like famine, plague and disorder were improved. But again, these were part of a longer process, and if the stresses of the 1590s affected this, they were neither a necessary or sufficient cause. Ultimately, the government continued to function, the
55 strategies employed were traditional in themselves and the structures of government were not drastically transformed. The poor faced crisis on a daily basis and many lost their lives, but society as a whole did not; the broadening of the elite turned those who might previously have led a popular uprising into loyal supporters of the status quo. The government
60 saw itself as facing crisis conditions, but that is not the same as a 'crisis of government'. Of course, that is not to say that Elizabethan government was just or successful. As J.A. Sharpe has pointed out, although Elizabethan England survived, it did so at the unjustifiable expense of society's most vulnerable and disadvantaged.

65 **Dr Stuart Minson is a guest teacher at the London School of Economics and Political Science**

ACTIVITY

Having read the essay, answer the following questions. You might also find it useful to look back at the section on Mid-Tudor society in Chapter 6, pages 167–69.

Evidence

1 Using lines 1–46, list, according to the author:
   a) the evidence for problems facing Elizabeth's government, 1589–1603
   b) the evidence to suggest that these should not be magnified.

Interpretation

2 Using your knowledge, with which of the two viewpoints above do you find more in agreement?

3 Does your knowledge support the interpretation of the last paragraph that there was no breakdown in government?

Evaluation

4 Using your understanding of the historical context, assess how convincing you find the arguments in relation to a possible crisis in Elizabeth's government, 1589–1603.

Key questions: England, 1485–1603

The specification you have been studying on the Tudors highlights six key issues. We reviewed these at the end of Part One (page 122), providing opportunities for you to think about themes that run through your study of the period. Now there is an opportunity for you to review the themes of the whole period.

In the examination the essays will be focused on broad areas of the content and will reflect one or more of the six key questions. Therefore, this section should be of great help to you in your revision, both looking at themes and also revisiting the detailed content you have studied.

KEY QUESTION 1
How effectively did the Tudors restore and develop the powers of the monarchy?

Questions to consider:

- At the end of Chapter 4, you were asked to consider how monarchical powers developed under Henry VII and Henry VIII. Think what these were – considering the Church as well as the machinery of State government.
- The reigns of Edward VI and Mary – did the powers of the monarchy change at all in theory? Was there any change in practice?
- Did Elizabeth restore and develop the powers of the monarchy? Think of the Church and how the government was run under William Cecil, Lord Burghley.

Working in groups

Taking the Tudor monarchs as a whole:
1 Discuss the effects of having a boy king and two women as monarchs on the power of the Tudors.
2 Discuss what other factors limited the power of the monarchy in Tudor England.
3 Where the Tudors were able to increase the powers of the monarchy, how much of it was theoretical, and how much was through personality? How much was skill and how much was luck?
4 Discuss how historians have, over time, assessed and re-assessed how powerful the Tudors were.
5 Imagine you were living in March 1603. Discuss the strengths and the weaknesses of the monarchy as inherited by Elizabeth's successor, James Stuart.

• •

KEY QUESTION 2
In what ways and how effectively was England governed during this period?

Questions to consider:

- Revise the ways in which the government of England was improved in the reigns of Henry VII and Henry VIII.
- Discuss the ways in which the reigns of Edward VI and Mary suggested less effective government.
- Discuss the ways in which Elizabeth and her ministers made government more effective.

Working in groups

Taking the reigns as a whole:
1 Discuss how effective central government was in the Tudor period. To what extent and why did it become more effective over the period as a whole?
2 Discuss how much was changed in the so-called Tudor Revolution in government in the 1530s.
3 Local government developed in the Tudor period. In what ways and to what extent did it become more effective?
4 Rebellions and revolts in the Tudor period were all relatively easily defeated. Does this mean that most people were happy to accept the rule of the Tudors, or are there other reasons for the stability of the Tudors?

How did relations with foreign powers change and how was the succession secured?

Questions to consider:

- Discuss the reasons why England found it difficult to have a consistent foreign policy in the reigns of Henry VII and Henry VIII.
- Discuss how important, and why, Scotland was in foreign policy considerations in the mid- and later sixteenth century.
- Discuss the reasons why England's foreign policy became focused on seeing Spain as the enemy in the later sixteenth century.
- Discuss how the succession was secured each time a Tudor monarch died.

Working in groups

Taking the reigns as a whole:

1 Discuss relations between England and Spain between 1485 and 1603. On what occasions did they change and why?
2 Discuss relations with France, 1485–1603. When was France an enemy and when was she an ally? Why?
3 Why was Scotland frequently seen as an enemy? On what occasions and why did this cease to be the case?
4 Why was there so much concern over the succession in the Tudor period?
5 Why was a peaceful succession achieved in 1558 and in 1603?

● ●

KEY QUESTION 4
How did English society and economy change and with what effects?

Questions to consider:

- Think of the ways society changed during the Tudor period, e.g. land ownership.
- Think of how the poor were affected by population increases, price rises, poor harvests and other factors at different times during the Tudor period. Were the effects consistent during the period?
- Think of the ways in which trade and industry developed in the Tudor period. Who gained and who did not?
- Think how increasing involvement overseas, especially in Elizabeth's reign, affected society and the economy.

Working in groups

Taking the reigns as a whole:

1 Discuss the extent of the changes within society and the reasons for them happening, e.g. affecting nobility, gentry, clergy, the poor.
2 In spite of changes, the social structure of England remained fundamentally the same. How was this possible?
3 Who benefited from changes in agriculture, industry and trade?
4 Were the poor in 1603 worse off than they had been in 1485?

How far did intellectual and religious ideas change and develop and with what effects?

Questions to consider:

- In the first half of the century intellectual thought was developing through humanism, the spread of the printing press and criticisms of the Catholic Church. Did intellectual thought continue along the same lines in the second half of the century, or were there new developments?
- How did Protestant religious ideas develop after 1547?
- How did Catholics manage to re-group and maintain their identity in the Protestant England of Elizabeth?
- What were the effects on society and on government of developments in religious beliefs?

Working in groups

Taking the reigns as a whole:

1 Discuss the changes in intellectual ideas and the extent to which they changed people's attitude to life.
2 Discuss the ways in which Protestants were divided in their religious beliefs by the end of the Tudor period.
3 Discuss the ways in which Catholics reaffirmed their religious beliefs after the Reformation and how they maintained these in a Protestant country.
4 Did changes in intellectual and religious beliefs over the century affect the poor or were the effects only on those in the upper classes of society? What factors determined who was affected the most?

KEY QUESTION 6
How important was the role of key individuals and how were they affected by developments?

Questions to consider:

- Why was William Cecil able to make a key contribution in the reign of Elizabeth?
- Why were Leicester and Essex more limited in what they achieved?
- Were there any groups that made a key contribution in the later sixteenth century? Think of politics, religion, overseas activities, etc.
- Think of examples of how individuals and groups were affected by developments, e.g. Mary Queen of Scots in her years in England; how the attitudes of English Protestants and Catholics were affected by the Spanish Armada. Try to think of your own examples as well.

Working in groups

Taking the reigns as a whole:

1 Compare the contributions of leading politicians in the Tudor period. Who made the most important contributions in government reforms? Who made the most important contributions in maintaining stability? What other types of contribution can you evaluate?
2 'Groups' that had influence could include the nobility, the Church, Parliament, etc. Were there specific occasions during the Tudor period when they had a particular influence or importance?
3 Discuss why the lives of some key individuals ended in execution whereas others survived to a natural death.
4 Discuss which groups in society were most affected by changes in the Tudor period. These changes could be religious (e.g. monks), social (e.g. nobility affected by government reforms), economic (e.g. the poor and price rises).

Further research

General books on the Tudors

There are many excellent books on the Tudors, some more detailed than others. Some are written specifically with A-level students in mind. Other academic books are written for more specialist audiences, but many are very accessible to students who already possess the necessary background knowledge.

Also listed at the end of Further research are novels, films and places to visit which are recommendations intended to extend your overall sense of the period.

Duffy, E. (1992) *The Stripping of the Altars: Traditional Religion in England, 1400–1580*. Oxford: Oxford University Press.

A pioneering book that looked at religion from the local perspective rather than just concentrating on official Church policies and beliefs.

Elton, G. R. (1991) *England under the Tudors* (3rd edn.) London: Routledge.

The classic account of Tudor England, but with emphasis on the 1530s.

Fletcher, A. and MacCulloch, D. (2008) *Tudor Rebellions: Revised 5th Edition*. London: Longman.

The most up-to-date edition reflecting recent research on rebellions in the Tudor period.

Guy, J. (1990) *Tudor England*. Oxford: Oxford University Press.

Contains a complete narrative of political and religious developments, as well as the social and economic background.

Haigh, C. (1987) *English Reformation Revised*. Cambridge: Cambridge University Press.

A series of specialist essays on particular aspects of the English Reformation, as well as an overview of recent research by the editor.

Hoskins, W. (1988) *The Age of Plunder, England of Henry VIII, 1500–1547* (Social and Economic History of England) London: Longman.

Excellent survey of economic and social aspects.

Palliser, D. (1992) *The Age of Elizabeth: England under the Later Tudors* (Social and Economic History of England) (2nd edn.) London: Routledge.

The companion volume to the book by Hoskins, this is excellent on social and economic aspects of the later Tudor period.

Russell, C. (1971) *The Crisis of Parliaments: English History 1509–1660*. Oxford: Oxford University Press.

A general textbook that is very comprehensive in its coverage and views.

Books relevant to particular chapters

Some of the books listed are relevant to more than one chapter. In general, they are listed for the first chapter in which the book is particularly relevant.

Chapter 1

There are several excellent books published on the reign of Henry VII in recent years. Some of these are listed below

Brigdon, S. (2001) *New Worlds, Lost Worlds: The Rule of the Tudors 1485–1603* (Penguin History of Britain). London: Penguin Books.

This book starts with the year 1485 and paints a vivid picture of what England would have seemed like to Henry when he arrived in Wales and marched to Bosworth. Excellent descriptive writing.

Chrimes, B. (1999) *Henry VII*. London: Yale University Press.

A book which has detailed analysis, but not necessarily the basic narrative. An excellent book to read when you have studied the outline of the reign.

Lockyer, R. and Thrush, A. (1997) *Henry VII*. London: Routledge.

The classic account aimed at A-level students.

Pendrill, C. (2004) *The Wars of the Roses and Henry VII, 1459–c.1513*. London: Heinemann.

This clearly argued book takes a less positive view of Henry's achievements.

Penn, T. (2012) *Winter King: The Dawn of Tudor England*. London: Penguin Books.

This is based on extensive research and provides a very detailed and brilliant description of life at the time. Eminently readable.

Towle, C. and Hunt, J. (1998) *History in Depth: Henry VII*. London: Longman.

This again provides a detailed readable depiction of the reign.

Turvey, R. and Roger, C. (2005) *Henry VII*. London: Hodder Education.

This is a title in the popular Hodder *Access* series, and it covers all the aspects of the reign very clearly, with substantial factual depth.

Williams, N. (1973) *The Life and Times of Henry VII*. London: Weidenfeld and Nicolson.

This is lavishly illustrated and, as the title implies, paints a picture in illustrations and words of the reign.

Chapter 2

There are many books on Henry VIII, as well as some that focus on the first part of the reign.

Guy, J. 'Henry VIII and his Ministers'. In: *History Today* No. 23, December 1995.

An article that contrasts Wolsey with Thomas Cromwell, and compares Henry's relationship with each of them.

Gwyn, P. (1992) *The King's Cardinal: The Rise and Fall of Thomas Wolsey*. London: Pimlico.

The first major study of Wolsey since Pollard's ground-breaking book published in 1929.

Marshall, P. 'Cardinal Wolsey and the English Church'. In: *History Review* No. 60, March 2008.

This article sets out what Wolsey achieved as head of the English Church – and also his shortcomings.

Pollard, A.F. (1965) *Wolsey* (Fontana Library). *Elton*. London: Collins.

This edition has an excellent essay by Professor Elton which explains developments in historical research since 1929 when Pollard's book was first published.

Randell, K. and Turvey, R. (2008) *Henry VIII to Mary I: Government and Religion, 1509–1558*. London: Hodder Education.

This is useful because it provides a clear overview of the period, putting Wolsey into context and providing sections that feature interpretations.

Scarisbrick, J.J. (1997) *Henry VIII*. London: Yale University Press.

A very detailed study of the reign, with an emphasis on the divorce, but with useful sections on Wolsey's period in office.

Starkey, D. (1985) *The Reign of Henry VIII: Personalities and Politics*. London: George Philip and Son.

A very interesting description of personalities and how they influenced the reign of Henry VIII. Also very relevant to Chapters 3 and 4.

Chapter 3

There are many excellent books on the 1530s, as the decade has been the subject of much detailed research in the last 60 or so years.

Borman, T. (2014) *Thomas Cromwell – the Untold Story*. London: Hodder & Stoughton.

A new biography which is excellent on the politics of the period and detailed on the architecture and lives of the people.

Elton, G.R. (1967) *The Tudor Revolution in Government*. Cambridge: Cambridge University Press.

This is extremely detailed and Professor Elton sets out to convince his readers that there really was a revolution in government in the 1530s.

Guy, J. 'Henry VIII and his Ministers'. In: *History Today* No. 23, December 1995.

An article which compares the roles and achievements of Wolsey and Cromwell.

Ives, E.W. (1986) *Anne Boleyn*. London: Wiley-Blackwell.

Very readable on Anne Boleyn's personal ambitions and character.

MacCulloch, D. (ed.) (1995) *The Reign of Henry VIII: Politics, Policy and Piety*. London: Palgrave Macmillan.

Contains interesting essays on specialist topics, some of which are centred on the 1530s.

MacCulloch, D. (1996) *Thomas Cranmer*. London: Yale University Press.

A detailed study of the first Archbishop of Canterbury for the Church of England who was responsible for so much of the liturgy of the Church, much of it surviving into the twenty-first century.

Matusiak, J. (2014) *Henry VIII: The Life and Rule of England's Nero*. Stroud: The History Press.

As the title suggests, a biography of Henry VIII that is heavily critical and reaches different conclusions from those of other works of recent scholarship.

Starkey, D. (1991) *The Reign of Henry VIII*. London: Collins and Brown.

This title emphasises the factionalism of the period as well as reassessing the debate about the Tudor revolution in government.

Turvey, R. and Randell, K. (2008) *Henry VIII to Mary I: Government and Religion, 1509–1558*. London: Hodder Education.

This volume in the 'Access to History' series is clearly written and summarises recent historiography very well.

Youings, J. (1972) *The Dissolution of the Monasteries*. Sydney: Allen and Unwin.

A detailed study of the monasteries and their dissolution.

Novels by Hilary Mantel on Cromwell (transferred to stage and television) provide a reassessment of the character and achievements of Thomas Cromwell – *Wolf Hall* (2009), *Bring up the Bodies* (2012) and *The Mirror and the Light* (due 2016).

Chapter 4

The essential books are mostly listed at the end of Chapter 3.

Loades, D. (1992) *The Mid-Tudor Crisis, 1545–1565*. London: Palgrave Macmillan.

Has an excellent first section outlining the economic and social upheavals that faced England in the last years of Henry VIII's reign.

Scarisbrick, J.J. (1984) *The Reformation and the English People*. London: Wiley-Blackwell.

Consists of a series of lectures given in 1982 at Oxford. They highlight detailed research into the religious beliefs of ordinary people and their attitude to the Reformation.

Chapter 5

Various books are available, some aimed at Advanced level work and some at university studies.

Fletcher, A. and Stevenson, J. (1987) *Order and Disorder in Early Modern England*. Cambridge: Cambridge University Press.

Sets the mid-Tudor period in a wider context.

Hoak, D. (1998) *Edward VI*. London: Addison-Wesley.

One of the very reliable series of books in the Longman Seminar Series.

Jones, W.R.D. (1973) *The Mid-Tudor Crisis, 1539–1563*. London: Macmillan.

This book was the one that popularised the view of a mid-century crisis.

Loach, J. (1992) *A Mid-Tudor Crisis?* London: The Historical Association.

This pamphlet reviews the historiography of the subject.

Loades, D. (1992) *The Mid-Tudor Crisis, 1545–1565*. London: Palgrave-Macmillan.

One of several books by this author that analyse the period in depth, and which largely rejects the idea of a mid-century crisis.

Tittler, R. and Richards, J. (2013) *The Reign of Mary I*. London: Routledge.

Highlights Mary's achievements and dismisses the idea that she was a weak ruler.

Turvey, R. and Heard, N. (2006) *Edward VI and Mary: A Mid-Tudor Crisis? 1540–1558* (3rd edn.) London: Hodder Education.

This title provides a clear outline of events and an analysis of the supposed crisis.

Chapter 6

This chapter covers the start of the reign of Elizabeth I, on whom, there are of course many books, some extremely favourable to the Queen, others more critical.

Adams, S. (1991) *Elizabeth I*. London: Longman.

Another book in the reliable Longman Seminar Series.

Alexander, H.G. (1968) *Religion in England, 1558–1662*. London: Hodder and Stoughton.

The opening sections are particularly useful for understanding Elizabeth's religious settlement.

Beier, A.L. (1983) *The Problem of the Poor in Tudor and Early Stuart England*. London: Routledge.

One of several good studies on society and the poor in Tudor England.

Doran, S. (1996) *Monarchy and Matrimony: The Courtships of Elizabeth I*. London: Routledge.

A study in Elizabeth's non-marriage – worth reading.

Haigh, C. (2001) *Elizabeth I*. London: Longman.

A fairly critical account of Elizabeth's reign.

Warren, J. (2008) *Elizabeth I: Meeting the Challenge, England 1541–1603*. London: Hodder Education.

An Access to History title which is partly relevant to this chapter.

Williams, N. (1971) *Elizabeth I: Queen of England*. London: Sphere Books.

Full of fascinating descriptions of events such as the coronation of Elizabeth.

Chapters 7 and 8

There are many books on the reign of Elizabeth I in general, as well as more detailed studies on aspects of the reign.

Collinson, P. (1983) *English Puritanism*. The Historical Association.

This pamphlet provides a clear concise enquiry into aspects of Puritanism in Elizabeth's reign.

Dures, A. (1983) *English Catholicism, 1558–1642*. London: Longman.

Traces the shadowy existence of Catholic followers in Elizabeth's reign.

Graves, M.R. and Lockyer, R. (1996) *Elizabethan Parliaments*. London: Longman.

Another book in the useful Longman series.

Haigh, C. (2001) *Elizabeth I*. London: Longman

Has a well-argued account of religious affairs in the reign.

Randell, K. (1994) *Elizabeth I and the Government of England*. London: Hodder Education.

Provides a clear account of how England was governed and biographies of Elizabeth's chief ministers.

Warren, J. (2008) *Elizabeth I: Meeting the challenge, England*, 1541–1603. London: Hodder Education.

Provides an interesting account that focuses on religion and foreign policy.

Williams, P. (1981) *The Tudor Regime*. Oxford: Oxford University Press.

Particularly useful in helping to explain the nature of Tudor authority and government.

Other areas of research

Novels

There are many novels set in the Tudor period. Many of the most famous ones faithfully follow accepted historical facts but then obviously invent scenarios that fill in the gaps and develop historical characters according to the viewpoint of the author. The selection of certain authors and titles is not meant to imply that others are not useful, though some move further away from the historical record.

P. Gregory (2001) *The Other Boleyn Girl*. London: HarperCollins.

Mary Boleyn comes to court and catches the eye of Henry VIII. She falls in love with him and becomes his mistress. She comes to realise that she is just a pawn in her family's ambitious plans at court, and then Henry transfers his affections to her younger sister, Anne.

P. Gregory (2006) *The Boleyn Inheritance*. London: HarperCollins.

The story of three women, Anne of Cleves, Katherine Howard and Jane Rochford, whose positions at court brought them wealth, admiration and power as well as deceit, betrayal and terror.

H. Mantel (2009) **Wolf Hall**.

After Wolsey fails to obtain a divorce for Henry VIII, Thomas Cromwell enters the atmosphere of distrust and intrigue. He gains the ear of Henry, is able to carry out his reforming programme, but has to accept his responsibilities when Henry requires another change of wife.

H. Mantel (2012) *Bring up the Bodies*.

The second part of the Thomas Cromwell trilogy.

A. Weir (2006) *Innocent Traitor*.

The story of Lady Jane Grey – the 'Nine-Day Queen' – a fifteen-year-old girl who unwillingly finds herself at the centre of the religious and civil unrest that nearly toppled the Tudor monarchy.

A. Weir (2008) *The Lady Elizabeth*.

This tells the story of the young Elizabeth Tudor who grew up to be Elizabeth I.

J. Plaidy (1963) *The Thistle and the Rose*.

The story of Princess Margaret Tudor whose life of tragedy, bloodshed and scandal rivalled that of her younger brother, Henry VIII.

J. Plaidy (1985) *Queen of this Realm*.

Story of the life of Elizabeth I.

J. Plaidy (1989) *In the Shadow of the Crown*.

The story of Princess Mary, daughter of Katherine of Aragon, whose life would be shattered by her father's ill-fated love for Anne Boleyn.

J. Fox (2007) *Jane Boleyn – the True Story of the Infamous Lady Rochford*.

The story of Jane, devoted spy for her uncle, Duke of Norfolk. It was her evidence that helped to send her sister-in-law, Anne, to the block.

Films and TV series

The Tudors have featured in several TV series and in many films. Almost all of these should be easily available on DVD or other formats. Remember that in all cases the history will have been simplified and that each director decides on the focus of the content. This is especially true of biographical films in which the audience is expected to empathise with the hero/heroine or hate the 'bad guy'. The ones listed below are just a selection of some of those that do make an attempt to use rather than reinvent the history.

Films

Drake of England Arthur B. Woods (dir.), 1935.

The story of the famous seaman from the reign of Elizabeth.

A Man for all Seasons Fred Zinnemann (dir.), 1966.

Paul Schofield as Thomas More – a sympathetic portrait.

Anne of a Thousand Days Charles Jarrott, 1969.

The story of Anne Boleyn's marriage to Henry VIII.

Lady Jane Trevor Nunn (dir.), 1986, (PG).

Helena Bonham Carter as the tragic 'Nine-Day Queen'.

Shakespeare in Love John Madden (dir.), 1998.

Joseph Fiennes as the Bard and Dame Judy Dench has a small cameo as an older Elizabeth I.

The Other Boleyn Girl Justin Chadwick (dir.), 2008, (PG).

Big screen adaptation of Philippa Gregory's novel with Scarlett Johannson as Mary Boleyn, mistress of Henry VIII.

TV series

Elizabeth R, 1971.

TV series starring Glenda Jackson.

Henry VIII and his Six Wives Warris Hussein (dir.), 1972.

TV series of six episodes starring Keith Michell as Henry.

Elizabeth I Tom Hooper (dir.), 2005.

TV mini-series starring Helen Mirren as Elizabeth and Jeremy Irons as Leicester.

Wolf Hall Peter Kosminsky (dir.), 2015.

TV adaptation of the book by Hilary Mantel, with Damian Lewis as Henry VIII and Mark Rylance as Cromwell.

Places to visit

There are many places to visit that either date from Tudor times or have strong associations with the period. There may well be examples near you. The following provides just an introductory list.

Hampton Court Palace, London

Exhibition of the young Henry. Access to the Formal Gardens and Henry's kitchen and apartments.

Greenwich: National Maritime Museum and Royal Observatory, London

A favourite residence of Henry VII, Henry VIII and Elizabeth I, though little remains of the Tudor palace.

Tower of London, London

The Tower was a palace and a set of government – not just a prison – for many centuries.

Shakespeare's Globe Theatre, London

An accurate reconstruction of the famous Elizabethan theatre only 200 yards from the site of the original on London's South Bank. Many productions are designed and costumed authentically for a real taste of the original Tudor stage experience.

The Museum of London, London

Fascinating displays of Tudor and Elizabethan artefacts. Excellent website.

Hatfield Old Palace, Hatfield

The nursery place of the children of Henry VIII and Elizabeth's refuge during the reign of her sister Mary. The palace remains largely intact and the gardens have been restored.

Hardwick Hall, Chesterfield

Home of the ambitious and strong-willed Countess of Shrewsbury – better known as Bess of Hardwick. Thanks to her, many of the Elizabethan textiles have survived.

The Mary Rose, Portsmouth

Henry VIII's famous warship that sank in 1545. Painstakingly being conserved, it is now the only original sixteenth-century warship on display in the world. The website is excellent.

Tudor music

The following website has fascinating details about Tudor music and you can hear examples.

www.sixwives.info/tudor-music.htm

Glossary of terms

America America was named in 1500 on an early sketch map of the newly-discovered continent after the explorer Amerigo Vespucci.

Annates A special tax paid by members of the higher clergy to Rome during their first year in office.

Arable farming Labour intensive farming which produced crops using basic tools including ploughs.

Armada The Spanish word for an armed fleet.

Book of Rates All goods leaving the country were taxed and the income passed to the Crown as part of ordinary revenues. The Book of Rates (1558) set out the level of tax on a wide range of products but had not been updated since the beginning of Henry VIII's reign and therefore took no account of mid-Tudor inflation. The effect of updating rates was to treble Crown income from customs duties, but provoked hostility from the merchant community since the new rates coincided with the collapse of the cloth market.

Cardinal One of the senior officials of the Catholic Church, having the right to vote in the election of a Pope. Cardinals were appointed by the Pope, usually with the approval of the monarch. In return for wealth, status and the protection of its privileges, the Church provided monarchs with an educated force of trained administrators and a cheap way of rewarding those who served them well.

Chantries Small religious houses endowed with lands to support priests who sang masses for the souls of the deceased – usually for the founder or other important people who paid in money or in kind.

The Council Learned in Law An offshoot from the main Royal Council which dealt initially with managing and pursuing the King's feudal rights, but soon assumed control of all financial matters relating to Crown lands. All the members of the Council had legal training (hence the name) and acted both as investigators and judges in cases where there was suspicion that a nobleman was not paying his proper dues to the King. As a result, the Council and its leading figures – Sir Reginald Bray to 1503, then Edmund Dudley and Richard Empson – were universally hated and feared.

Counter-Reformation An offensive against Protestantism, taken by the Catholic Church centred on Rome. It started with the Council of Trent which first met in 1545. Catholic doctrines were re-stated in order to provide clear arguments against Protestant doctrines. Jesuits and the Inquisition were trained to go abroad and convert people back to Catholicism.

Customs duties Money paid on goods entering or leaving the country. Money came from tunnage (taxes on exports) and poundage (taxes on imports).

Debasement of the coinage A process whereby silver coins had their silver content reduced by substituting cheaper metals such as copper. By March 1545 the silver content was only 50 per cent of what it had been, and by March 1546 only 33 per cent. The process continued in the reign of Edward VI when it was only 25 per cent. The process allowed more coins to be circulated by the government.

Divine Right of Kings The belief that monarchs were ruling on behalf of God. They were therefore answerable to God, and the monarch's subjects were expected to obey the monarch, otherwise they were disobeying God.

Enclosure The fencing off of land from open fields with the ending of all common rights over it.

Excommunicate The Pope had the power to cut off anyone from receiving the sacraments of the Church. This meant, in effect, cutting them off from God and salvation.

Factionalism The royal court, not Parliament, was the centre of political power and influence during the Tudor period. Courtiers advanced by attracting the King's attention, often with the help of someone who was one of his friends or supporters. In this way, groups of ambitious courtiers clustered around powerful nobles and ministers. Rivalry developed between these groups – or factions – as all were keen to win what limited royal patronage there was.

Finishing The final stages of woollen production when spun yarn is converted into cloth by weaving, which includes fulling (cleansing the wool to eliminate oils, dirt and other impurities) and dyeing.

Fire-ships Ships deliberately set on fire and sent towards the enemy's ships to cause them to scatter.

Hanseatic League A league of German towns which dominated trade in the Baltic. They aimed to maintain a monopoly of trade there.

Huguenot The name given to Protestants in France who were followers of John Calvin.

Indulgences The indulgence was a document, issued with the Pope's authority, setting out the cancellation of punishment in purgatory – a place where it was believed souls of the dead went to while waiting to be sent to heaven.

Inflation An increase, usually over a long period, of a wide range of prices and services.

Inns of Court Residences in London where barristers received training and where they could lodge while studying.

John Calvin – Protestant reformer who developed more extreme ideas than Luther, in particular about some being pre-chosen (predestined) by God to be saved. Calvin also moved further away from the Catholic view of the Eucharist than Luther had done. For Calvin the remembrance of the Last Supper of Jesus with his disciples was really just that. The bread and wine were symbols, but Christ was spiritually present. Calvin gained many followers in Scotland where they became known as Presbyterians.

King-in-Parliament King-in-Parliament refers to government by the King, but implies that some of his functions, in particular the making of law, are carried out in Parliament rather than by the King alone. Through Parliament, the King could make statute law, the highest form of law: a statute (Act of Parliament) that had been agreed by both houses and signed by the King took precedence over any earlier law or custom, and could only be changed by another statute.

Laity/Laymen A general term referring to people who had not been trained and accepted as priests.

Magnate A term describing a member of the greater nobility – the barons – who owned large estates. The greater families had consolidated their holdings through marriage and family links, building up a significant territorial base where they effectively governed in the king's name.

Marks Two-thirds of a pound (in pre-decimal currency, 13s 4d).

Martin Luther Luther led the protest movement in Germany that started what we know as the Reformation. He criticised the practices of the Catholic Church and argued for some changes in religious belief.

Metrical psalms Psalms translated into English poetry and set to hymn tunes.

Monopolies Such rights were granted by royal charter, declaring that a particular group of merchants had the sole legal right to make or to import a commodity such as soap or sugar. Monopolies were unpopular because they were often granted in everyday products, allowing the group of merchants who controlled the monopoly to fix prices at artificially high levels to make a profit.

New World This was the term being used to describe the continent of America that was being discovered by Spanish sailors during the reign of Henry VII.

Norman Conquest The events in which William came from Normandy and defeated the English King, Harold. William and his successors imposed their own laws and system of government.

Ottoman power The Ottoman Turks had become powerful in Persia (now Iran) by the fifteenth century and had begun to expand around the east end of the Mediterranean. They were Muslim and keen to spread their religion and build up an empire. Constantinople had been conquered in 1453. By the early 1500s they were expanding their control around the Mediterranean.

Pale, the The Pale was England's foothold in Ireland, a region on the eastern coast around Dublin. It was the centre of English government on the island during the fifteenth and sixteenth centuries, heavily manned and fortified against the Irish clans who lived 'beyond the Pale'.

Papal Legate Someone appointed by the Pope to act on his behalf in a particular country, usually for a specified purpose on a limited timescale.

Patronage The monarch giving special favours, such as land or positions at court, to groups of people, in order to retain their support. The term can also be used for the actions of local nobles who showed favours to people in their locality.

Pension money An agreement dating from 1475 when Louis XI promised to pay Edward IV £10,000 per year. By this time the pension arrears totalled over £200,000.

Plantation Plantations involved settling English colonists on lands formerly owned by Irish clans in order to extend the Pale and slowly establish control over the whole island. The policy began in Edward VI's reign, but was extended under Mary. During Elizabeth's reign further plantation was encouraged, especially in the northern county of Ulster and in the western county of Munster. Although the policy aimed to bring peace and stability by planting English settlers in Ireland, it often had precisely the opposite effect, provoking Irish clans whose lands had been seized into open rebellion.

Praemunire A Latin term used in medieval laws which made it a crime to use powers derived from the Pope to the disadvantage of the King or his subjects.

Primogeniture The eldest son or nearest male relative inherited everything.

Proclamations Decrees by the King on policy matters either falling outside the scope of parliamentary authority or made when Parliament was not in session to cope with an unusual circumstance or emergency. In 1539 the Proclamations Act gave these royal decrees equal force with parliamentary statutes, but also said that proclamations could not contravene existing statutes.

Recusant The term recusant applies to those who refused to attend their parish church on a regular basis. Attendance was made compulsory by Parliament and anyone who failed to go was fined, initially 1 shilling (5 pence) for each failure. This was a significant amount of money for anyone below the gentry and may be one reason why Catholicism lasted longer within the gentry and nobility.

Secular The opposite of 'sacred', i.e. worldly things, not spiritual.

Statute law Laws made by Parliament with royal consent. By the sixteenth century statute law was generally regarded as the highest form of law in England.

Stipend The term used for the payment received by a priest for his appointment to a parish.

Index